D1236633

HISTORY OF THE HIGHLAND CLEARANCES.

THE
HISTORY

OF THE

HIGHLAND CLEARANCES

CONTAINING A REPRINT OF DONALD MACLEOD'S "GLOOMY
MEMORIES OF THE HIGHLANDS"; ISLE OF SKYE
IN 1882; AND A VERBATIM REPORT OF THE
TRIAL OF THE BRAES CROFTERS,

BY

ALEXANDER MACKENZIE, F.S.A. Scot.,

EDITOR OF THE *Celtic Magazine*; AUTHOR OF *The History of the Mackenzies*;
The History of the Macdonalds and Lords of the Isles; *The Macdonalds of
Glengarry*; *The Macdonalds of Clanranald*; *The History of the
Mathesons*; *The Prophecies of the Brahan Seer*; *Historical
Tales and Legends of the Highlands*, ETC.

FOREWORD BY JOHN PREBBLE

MERCAT PRESS
EDINBURGH

First published by A & W MacKenzie, Inverness, 1883
© Introduction, John Prebble, 1979
Reprinted 1986 by Melven Press, Perth
Reprinted 1991, 1994, 1997, 1999 by Mercat Press at James Thin
53 South Bridge, Edinburgh

ISBN 0901824 968

Acknowledgements are due to Rory MacKay of Inverness for
permission to print from his copy

Printed and bound in Finland by WSOY

PREFACE.

—————

THE late Robert Carruthers, LL.D., reviewing in
1878 in the *Inverness Courier*, a paper on the
Strathglass evictions, by Mr. Colin Chisholm, published
in the Transactions of the Gaelic Society of Inverness,
wrote :—"A good history of the changes in the Highlands, . . . and the 'Clearances,' since the great
Glengarry emigration, for the last century and a half,
would form a most interesting volume, and sufficient
materials exist for a diligent and honest enquirer.
We recommend the task to the editor of the *Celtic
Magazine*."

We had an idea long before this, that we might
possibly some day attempt a work such as our venerable friend here suggested, and the high compliment,
from such a quarter, implied in the terms of the
proposal, induced us to pay more attention to the
subject and keep a sharper eye than ever on anything which could throw light on the history of
the Highland Clearances. The result will be found
in the following pages. There is little attempt to

do more than place the facts before the reader, so far as they can be ascertained, accompanied by the views of contemporary writers, and others, whose opinions are sure to command respect. This we hold to be infinitely more valuable than anything original which we could have written on the subject.

Some people may ask "Why rake up all this iniquity just now?" We answer that the same laws which permitted the cruelties, the inhuman atrocities, described in this book, are still the laws of the country, and any tyrant who may be indifferent to the healthier public opinion which now prevails, may *legally* repeat the same proceedings whenever he may take it into his head to do so.

It is not in our power to alter the Laws of the Land so that a repetition of these evictions cannot take place, but the fear of getting pilloried, in a work like this, may possibly induce the tyrant to hold his hand, for very shame, until a more just and humane law shall make such mean and cruel work as the Highland Clearances for ever impossible ; and there is hope for such a result in the fact that the descendants of the oppressors of a past generation are so much ashamed of what was done by their predecessors that they would give much of what they at present possess if they could but recal the mean, indefensible, and harsh evictions of the past.

There is nothing in History so absolutely *mean* as the Eviction of the Highlanders by chiefs solely indebted for every inch of land they ever held to the strong arms and trusty blades of the progenitors of those whom the effeminate and ungrateful chiefs of the nineteenth century have so ruthlessly oppressed, evicted, and despoiled.

The interest in the subject of the Highland Evictions may be gathered from the fact, that of a pamphlet published by the present writer, in 1881, an edition of fifteen hundred copies went out of print in a few months, and that it has supplied the material for most of the speeches made, and many of the newspaper articles written, on the subject ever since, though seldom or ever acknowledged by those who had found it so useful and convenient !

It is hoped that the portion of this work relating to the Social state of the Isle of Skye in 1882, illustrated by the Trial of the Braes Crofters, and other proceedings connected with the Island, will be found both instructive and interesting.

The statistics of the population of the Highland Counties and Parishes, given in the Appendix, will be found in a convenient form for reference, and they may possibly prove useful, and perhaps interesting to those who concern themselves about the steady and rapid decrease of the rural population in the Highlands during the last fifty years.

For many items which we could not otherwise obtain (most of the Census Returns having gone out of print), we are indebted to the prompt and obliging courtesy of the Registrar-General for England ; for there are no copies prior to 1841 kept in the Scotch Office! All others to whom we are indebted—and to many of them we are under deep obligations—are mentioned in the body of the work, except Mr. Dugald Cowan, who, after considerable trouble and difficulty, succeeded in procuring for us some valuable information in the Library of the Royal College of Physicians, Edinburgh.

A. M.

Inverness, *January*, *1883.*

An Introduction by
John Prebble

"How we enjoyed ourselves in those far away
days! Those were the happy days and there was
neither sin nor sorrow in the world for us. But
the clearances came upon us, destroying all . . .
turning our joy into misery, our gladness into
bitterness, our blessing into blasphemy . . . Oh,
dear man, the tears come on my eyes when I think
of all we suffered, and of the sorrows, hardships,
and oppressions we came through"
—Peigidh nic Cormaig

The words are an English translation. They are
more moving in the Gaelic which Peggy MacCormack used. She had been born a MacDonald and she
lived at Aird Bhuidhe, the yellow hill above Loch
Boisdale. In her old age, many years after the Clearances came upon her, she would still weep if reminded
of the time when her chief sold Uist and Benbecula
for £96,000, when his evicted and unwanted people
were driven to the loch shore and the waiting boats
of the emigrant ship *Admiral*. "Were you to see,"
said another witness of those days, "were you to see

the racing and chasing of policemen, you would think that you had been transported to the banks of the Gambia on the slave coast of Africa." It was the last great sale of the wide lands which the chiefs of Clanranald had once held in Arisaig and Moidart, in the westering islands of the Hebrides. By 1838, when Ranald George MacDonald, twentieth chief of Clanranald, sold South Uist and Benbecula to that great evictor John Gordon of Cluny, he had received more than £200,000 for the surrender of his inheritance. He was improvident, crippled by self-indulgent debts and the failure of the kelp industry, and it does not appear to have distressed him that the abandoned people of his clan might not be wanted by the new proprietors, that indeed they would be removed to make room for sheep. He had little recognisable feeling for them, being inclined to remove them himself if he thought their black stone cabins spoiled the view from his windows.

He lies now in a mouldering tomb in Brompton Cemetery, in London where he always preferred to reside, but the descendants of his clan are scattered across the world.

When Peggy MacCormack's sad lament first appeared in print at the turn of this century, the great waves of the Highland Clearances had subsided into the small tidal movements which still continue to-day. In 1881 the people of Glendale and other valleys on Skye had begun their long and ultimately victorious struggle against intransigent landlordism. In 1884 the

Crofters Commission had produced its monumental and influential report on the state of the Highlands, recording the evidence of old Highlanders who spoke with anguish of the days of eviction five, six, and seven decades before, their eloquent Gaelic literally translated into poetic English. In 1883, between the Battle of the Braes on Skye and the report of the Commission, the indefatigable editor of the *Celtic Magazine* had published this book, an indignant, impassioned and uncompromising indictment of Highland landlords and the diaspora of a people. It might be thought that these three events would have been strong and prevailing winds, blowing away the persuasive romance in which most men prefer their history to be cocooned. That they were not, that it was not until the second half of this century that a proper study of the Clearances was thought important, indeed imperative for a deeper understanding of the present state of Scotland, may also be an indictment—of our persistent and perilous indifference to the lessons of the past.

Alexander Mackenzie was forty-five when he published this account of the Clearances. Since 1875 he had edited the *Celtic Magazine*, "written almost entirely in English" and harmlessly devoted to Gaelic history, folk-lore and antiquities, "the Moral and Material interests of Celts at Home and Abroad." He had written or published several clan histories of a customary nature, and three editions of the Prophecies of the Brahan Seer. It may be—the thought is compelling if conjectural—that his first-hand experience as a journalist of the Glendale revolt, the trial of the Braes Crofters, turned his mind more actively to an obligatory work on the Clearances from the beginning. He was not the first polemicist to attack them. There had been others over the preceding seventy years upon whose work he greatly relied— men like Donald Macleod the stonemason of Strathnaver, Thomas Mulock the wayward father of the author of *John Halifax, Gentleman*, Donald Ross who got his information on the Strathcarron evictions from the bloodstained women who resisted them, and lastly an anonymous correspondent of the *Times*, who was sent to the Highlands after the Glencalvie removals of 1845.

The great strength of Mackenzie's narrative is its readable simplicity. However amateurish, even disjointed, it sometimes is, it is also a threnody for the abused and abandoned race to which he belonged. It is of no great consequence now that much of it is second or third-hand information, that a lack of referential dates produces occasional confusion, that truth is sometimes clouded by factual contradictions. Subsequent research has justified what Mackenzie was trying to tell his contemporaries, and his voice is still more powerful, more moving than the cautious confirmation of later scholars.

The wall of prejudice and ignorance he hoped to break was strong. He was attacking the sacred rights of wealth and property upon which Victorian Britain prospered, the belief that greater profit to the few must ease the deprivation of the many. This was probably not his intention in a general sense, and he did not condemn the Clearances as the Swiss social scientist, Simonde de Sismondi, had done forty years before, as an "absurd and revolting" contradiction of the arguments advanced in their defence. Mackenzie's sense of outrage was perhaps closer to the truth. He knew that they were a crime of betrayal, a deep and killing breach of faith. Whatever the gentry now thought their role in society to be, the common people of the Highlands still responded to older compulsions. The chief was the father of the clan, *ceann-cinnidh*, responsible for his children, obliged to protect them as they were to obey and defend him. This already obsolescent relationship had been blown away by cannon at Culloden, destroyed by punitive laws and reforming statutes, but the people still clung to their belief in it. When the Chief abandoned his obligations in favour of profit, they still responded to their own, and often walked to the emigrant ships with the meekness of the sheep that replaced them. Even their resistance, when it occurred, was despairingly brief, as if halted by guilt. That was the betrayal.

Mackenzie's book was a harsh intrusion upon the view of the Highlands enjoyed by southern Britain. Scotland was the land of romance, of Gothic tragedy, superb landscapes and stimulating climate. Its History, as it was understood, conspired to make it favoured by the English. The incredible expenditure of Highland lives in the Napoleonic wars, the publication of *Waverley*, the Balmorality of the monarchy and society, had replaced a bitter past with a romantic present. The clan system, once an omnipresent threat to the Lowlands and to the security of the realm, was thought to have survived the last Jacobite rebellion and was now, decently disinfected and respectfully loyal, the model of a quaintly archaic society. The thought of the Highland squares at Waterloo, of Sutherland men standing firm against Russian cavalry on Balaclava heights, staunch gillies on splendid moors, justified the English belief that the best had come from the worst of worlds and that it was the qualities of the English that had made it possible. So oppressive was this view that many Scots accepted their junior partnership in the Union to such a self-effacing degree that a Highland soldier in the Indian Mutiny could speak of the bravery of his regiment as being in the finest traditions of English valour.

Behind this gloss, which they enjoyed as much as others, Highland chiefs and proprietors in the early 19th century were greedy for the privileges and wealth of their southern peers. Land-rich and purse-poor, they had not shared in the increasing wealth of their class. Their glens were over-populated, and emigration had begun its drain as some small tacksmen escaped from the rack-renting of their chiefly cousins. Their tenants and sub-tenants, as their onetime clansmen now were, had no security of tenure, were annually dependent upon the will of the proprietor (to whom that fact would soon become most beneficial). Their mountain acres, thin soil on skeleton rock, scarcely supported a blackcattle economy and a run-rig husbandry. Their debts were becoming astronomical, their wives more eager for Edinburgh town-houses, their sons for expensive commission in English regiments, their daughters for marriages for which no dowries were available. Their problems seemed insoluble, and their wounded pride was only partly soothed by the elaborate Highland dress they some-times wore, monstrous caricatures of what had once been the simple dress of their people.

Providentially, if that is not an inapposite word, they were saved by an inoffensive, tractable, bleating animal which the people would soon call "the four-footed clansmen". The Great Cheviot Sheep, "finely-shaped, with countenance mild and pleasant", was man-made, the strain of its Border progenitors im-proved by Lincoln ewes, by Ryeland and Spanish rams, until it would not only survive in the Highlands but would actually flourish there. It was an answer to the dying black cattle economy, to recurring debt and eager ambition. By the end of the 18th century the Great Cheviot had reached the hills of Ross, and by the beginning of the next it had moved into Sutherland.

Few if any Highland landowners wished to become sheep-farmers. In the beginning they leased their lands to graziers from the Borders and Northumbria, only later would their improvidence or incompetence force them to sell the land itself. To free the required pastures, tenant and sub-tenant were evicted. Bred for centuries to accept the authority of the chief, in the customary belief that it was by definition benevolent, the people were willing victims of the great change. In 1792, *Bliadhna nan Caorach* the Year of the Sheep, there was indeed a spirited attempt to stop the northward flow of the Great Cheviot. The men of Ross drove the alien flocks from their glens, but they were quickly suppressed by armed gentry and men of the Black Watch, many of whom were their young kinsmen. Thenceforward, all resistance was brief and sporadic, and in the savage little encounters which did occur between the evicted and the sheriff's officers, it was the women of the glens who fought.

Sir John Sinclair of Ulbster, who had brought the Great Cheviot to Caithness, had warned Highland proprietors against any rash brutal change, any harsh removal of their tenantry before they considered how the people might share in a new prosperity. But his reasoned advocacy of sheep-farming also gave them good cause for greedy haste. Pasture which had once produced twopence an acre under lean cattle, he said, might now give two shillings under sheep. At its best, the annual yield of beef on the Highlands had never been more than £200,000, whereas the proprietors might now expect £900,000 from the sale of fine wool alone.

Although the majority of the Clearances were moti-
vated by greed, some landlords in the beginning
were genuinely moved by an obligation to improve
the economy and society of the Highlands, believing
that a duty to their conscience as much as to the
fashionable theory that the richer a rich man grew,
so must the poor become less poor. Without exception
however, these men and their factors failed to understand the nature of a people who, they believed,
should accept their eviction in the grand spirit of
that improvement. The most dramatic Clearances
recorded by Mackenzie are perhaps those which were
the earliest, and which took place upon the Sutherland estates which the Marquess of Stafford, already
one of the richest men in Britain, had acquired by
marriage to Elizabeth Gordon, Countess of Sutherland. His Commissioner James Loch, who first used
the word Improvement in this context, was a man of
dangerous rectitude and consuming dedication, convinced that his work for his noble master would bring
nothing but good to an ignorant, credulous, lazy and
slothful people, as he believed the Highlanders to be.

The exercise of good intentions, where profit on
private property is both cause and incentive, becomes
more ruthless when it is resisted, and humane concern
for those who suffer as a result decreases in inverse
proportion to the self-righteousness of the executors.
Thus brutality became a feature of all Clearances,
whether modelled on Loch's Policy of Improvement
or the result of a landlord's hunger for riches. To

force a man from his cottage, to burn his roof-tree before him, is brutal enough, without the clubbing, the use of truncheon and bayonet which often became necessary before an estate could be cleared. To take a man from his mountain, to place him on a barren sea-coast as Loch did, to tell him that he must now be a fishermen, to tell his sons that they may not marry without permission, is also a brutal assault on the self-respect of inoffensive men. When the Policy failed, or when stubborn and bewildered men failed to do as it required, there was no return to their old life. Their townships were gone, and in their glens, said their bards, "nothing was heard but the bleating of sheep and the voices of English-speakers." For most of the evicted, on the mainland or the Isles, there were not even the alternative industries which Loch's Policy hopefully proposed. There were only the destitution roads south, the slums in Glasgow, the emigrant ships at Wick, at Thurso, Fort William, Loch Boisdale and Loch Broom.

The great Clearances came in three distinguishable waves, first rising in Sutherland, subsiding to rise again in the West and in the Isles, falling once more to rise again in Ross, Knoydart, Kintail and the Isles. By the sixth decade new dimensions had been added. Emigration, which had at first been resisted by Government and gentry because it robbed the nation of its "nursery of soldiers" and the landowners of a necessary tenantry, was now actively encouraged. Incoming proprietors wanted no estate encumbered by a pauper population for which they might be responsible under the Poor Laws; and famine, cholera and neglect had greatly increased poverty among the Highlanders. When a national Society was established, under Royal patronage, to facilitate emigration it was natural for the Victorians to see it as a humane and philanthropic venture. Although James Loch had once said that "the idle alone think of emigration", and others had protested against the departure of young men who should have been serving in the Army, it was now said that the colonies needed and would profit from the sturdy virtues of the Highland people. Vestigial Highland chiefs, like the MacDonell masters of Glengarry, wasted no time on such notions. They saw the Society for what it truly was, and asked it to send its emigrant ships to their sea-lochs even before they served writs of eviction upon their remaining people. And as before, men were chained and bound before they could be carried to the boats. "I see the bands departing," sang a Gaelic bard, "on the white-sailed ships. I see the Gael rising from his door, I see the people going . . ."

The Highlander had one blow he could strike against his chief, against Government and establishment. When the Crimean War began in 1854 it was confidently believed in Whitehall that the Highlands would again be the military nursery they had been in the past. But recruiters who went to the West and the Isles were met by angry men who baa-ed like sheep as the drums beat and the fifes played. On his own ground the Duke of Sutherland was bluntly told "Since you have preferred sheep to men, let sheep defend you." There were no replacements for the depleted Highland battalions of Alma and Balaclava.

Alexander Mackenzie was born too late to be a witness of the earlier Clearances, and he was only sixteen when the last great wave subsided on Glengarry's land. Yet he knew and talked with many of the victims, and this book is his response to the obligations they placed upon his professional conscience. He had the courage to defend himself defiantly when it was attacked. It makes great use of Donald Macleod's *Gloomy Memories*, a bitter personal account of the Sutherland evictions and an attack on Patrick Sellar, the Marquess's factor who was tried and acquitted of culpable homicide for his part in the Strathnaver evictions. Mackenzie believed, as many still do, that the trial and the verdict were an offence to justice. In March, 1883, shortly after his book was published, he received a letter from Sellar's son, complaining of his "disproved calumnies on a dead man", demanding a retraction and reserving the right to take action if it were not made. Mackenzie's response was spirited and unrepentant, he would not retract what he had written, he would not apologise.

> The great fact of the Sutherland Clearances, as described in McLeod's book, and fully corroborated by other writers, are as true historically as those of the massacre of Cawnpore, and I cannot understand how anyone, however closely interested,

can expect that such a chapter in the history of the Highlands, with its various lessons, can be permitted to fall into oblivion. Your father was acquitted of the specific charges brought against him in Court, but the object of my book is to make it impossible that a law should be allowed to remain on the Statute Book which still permits the same cruelties to be carried out in the Highlands as were carried out in Sutherland during the first half of the present century. I am of the opinion that I have, in all the circumstances, simply done my duty in republishing so much of McLeod's book.

The laws which had given the Highlander no security of tenure, which had made him the helpless victim of Clearance and eviction, were changed as a result of the Crofters Commission Report. This did not stop the draining of the Highlands of their ancient people, it did not stop the transformation of that once populous area into a beautiful desert of sheep-walks, deer-forests and timber plantations.

This book is perhaps as much a valediction as it was meant to be a protest. Despite its faults—and they are pardonable errors of judgement and emotion—it has been and will remain a book to be read, an essential part of any study of the Clearances. There was a great need for it when it was first published, and in human terms that need remains. It does not contain the words of Peggy MacCormack quoted at the beginning of this Introduction. They were printed in 1900, two years after Mackenzie's death, and in Alexander Carmichael's *Carmina Gad-*

elica, but they echo much of the sorrow and despair that is to be found in this work. As do the words of Catherine MacPhee, another cottar of Uist whom Carmichael recorded:

> Many a thing I have seen in my own day and generation. Many a thing, O Mary Mother of the Black Sorrows. I have seen the townships swept and the big holdings being made of them, the people driven out of the countryside to the streets of Glasgow and to the wilds of Canada, such of them as did not die of hunger and plague and smallpox going across the ocean . . . I have seen the big strong men, the champions of the country-side, being bound on Loch Boisdale quay and cast into the ship as would be done to a batch of horses and cattle, the bailiffs and the ground-officers and the constables and the policemen behind them in pursuit of them. The God of Life, and He only, knows all the loathesome work of men on that day.

John P. Rule

1979.

CONTENTS.

THE HIGHLAND CLEARANCES.

SUTHERLAND.

DONALD MACLEOD'S " Gloomy Memories,"
originally appeared as a series of Letters in
the Edinburgh *Weekly Chronicle.* These letters were
afterwards published separately in a thick pamphlet ;
which has long become so rare in this country that no
money will procure it. After a search of more than
twenty years, we' were fortunate enough to pick up a
copy of the enlarged Canadian edition in Nova Scotia,
during a visit there, in 1879. The Letters originally
published in this country, are given in the following
pages in the form in which they first appeared, with
the exception of a slight toning down in two or three
instances.

LETTER I.

I AM a native of Sutherlandshire, and remember when
the inhabitants of that country lived comfortably and
happily, when the mansions of proprietors and the abodes
of factors, magistrates, and ministers, were the seats of honour,
truth, and good example—when people of quality were
indeed what they were styled, the friends and benefactors of

all who lived upon their domains.   But all this is changed.
Alas, alas !   I have lived to see calamity upon calamity
overtake the Sutherlanders.   For five successive years, on
or about the term day, has scarcely anything been seen but
removing the inhabitants in the most cruel and unfeeling
manner, and burning the houses which they and their forefathers had occupied from time immemorial.   The country
was darkened by the smoke of the burnings, and the descendants of those who drew their swords at Bannockburn,
Sheriffmuir, and Killicrankie—the children and nearest relations of those who sustained the honour of the British name in
many a bloody field—the heroes of Egypt, Corunna, Toulouse,
Salamanca, and Waterloo—were ruined, trampled upon,
dispersed, and compelled to seek an asylum across the
Atlantic ; while those who remained from inability to emigrate, deprived of all the comforts of life, became paupers—
beggars—a disgrace to the nation whose freedom and honour
many of them had maintained by their valour and cemented
with their blood.

   To these causes the destitution and misery that exists in
Sutherlandshire are to be ascribed ; misery as great, if not
the greatest to be found in any part of the Highlands, and
that not the fruit of indolence or improvidence, as some
would allege, but the inevitable result of the avarice and
tyranny of the landlords and factors for the last thirty or
forty years ; of treatment, I presume to say, without a
parallel in the history of this nation.   I know that a great
deal has been done to mitigate the sufferings of the Highlanders some years back, both by Government aid and public
subscriptions, but the unhappy county of Sutherland was
excluded from the benefits derived from these sources, by
means of false statements and public speeches, made by
hired agents, or by those whose interest it was to conceal

the misery and destitution in the country of which themselves were the authors. Thus the Sutherlandshire sufferers have been shut out from receiving the assistance afforded by Government or by private individuals ; and owing to the thraldom and subjugation in which this once brave and happy people are to factors, magistrates, and ministers, they durst scarce whimper a complaint, much less say plainly, " Thus and thus have you done ".

On the 20th of last April, a meeting of noblemen and gentlemen, connected with different districts of Scotland, was held in the British Hotel, Edinburgh, for the purpose of making inquiry into the misery and destitution prevailing in Scotland, and particularly in the Highlands, with a view to discover the causes and discuss means for meeting the prevailing evil. Gentlemen were appointed to make the necessary inquiry, and a committee named, with which these gentlemen were to communicate. At this meeting a Sutherlandshire proprietor made such representations re- garding the inhabitants of that county, that, relying, I suppose, on his mere assertions, the proposed inquiry has never been carried into that district. Under these circumstances, I, who have been largely a sufferer, and a spectator of the sufferings of multitudes of my countrymen, would have felt myself deeply culpable if I kept silence, and did not take means to lay before the committee and the public the information of which I am possessed, to put the benevolent on their guard respecting the men who undertake to pervert, if they cannot stifle, the inquiry as to the causes and extent of distress in the shire of Sutherland. With a view to dis- charging this incumbent duty, I published a few remarks, signed " A Highlander," in the *Edinburgh Weekly Journal* of 29th May last, on the aforesaid proprietor's speech ; to which he made a reply, accusing me of singular ignorance and misrepresentation, and endeavouring to exonerate himself. Another letter has since appeared in the same paper, signed, " A Sutherlandshire Tenant," denying my assertions and challenging me to prove them by stating facts. To meet this challenge, aud to let these parties know that I am not so ignorant as they would represent ; and also to afford information to the before-mentioned committee, it being impossible for those gentlemen to apply an adequate remedy till they know the real cause and nature of the disease, I addressed a second letter to the editor of the *Weekly Journal;* but, to my astonishment, it was refused insertion ; through what influence I am not prepared to say. I have, in consequence, been subjected to much reflection and obloquy for deserting a cause which would be so much benefited by public discussion ; and for failing to substantiate charges so publicly made. I have, therefore, now to request, that, through the medium of your valuable and impartial paper, the public may be made acquainted with the real state of the case ; and I pledge myself not only to meet the two opponents mentioned, but to produce and substantiate such a series of appalling facts, as will sufficiently account for the distress prevailing in Sutherlandshire ; and, I trust, have a tendency towards its mitigation.

LETTER II.

PREVIOUS to redeeming my pledge to bring before the Public a series of facts relating to the more recent oppressions and expatriation of the unfortunate inhabitants of Sutherlandshire, it is necessary to take a brief retrospective glance at the original causes.

Down from the feudal times, the inhabitants of the hills

and straths of Sutherlandshire, in a state of transition from vassalage to tenancy, looked upon the farms they occupied from their ancestors as their own, though subject to the arrangements as to rent, duties and services imposed by the chief in possession, to whom, though his own title might be equivocal, they habitually looked up with a degree of clannish veneration. Every thing was done "to please the Laird". In this kind of patriarchial dominion on the one side, and obedience and confidence on the other, did the late tenantry and their progenitors experience much happiness, and a degree of congenial comfort and simple pastoral enjoyment. But the late war and its consequences interfered with this happy state of things, and hence a foundation was laid for all the suffering and depopulation which has followed. This has not been peculiar to Sutherlandshire; the general plan of almost all the Highland proprietors of that period being to get rid of the original inhabitants, and turn the land into sheep farms, though from peculiar circumstances this plan was there carried into effect with more revolting and wholesale severity than in any of the surrounding counties.

The first attempt at a general *Clearing* was partially made in Ross-shire, about the beginning of the present century; but from the resistance of the tenantry and other causes, it has never been carried into general operation. The same was more or less the case in other counties. Effects do not occur without cause, nor do men become tyrants and monsters of cruelty all at once. Self-interest, real or imaginary, first prompts; the moral boundary is overstepped, the oppressed offer either passive or active resistance, and, in the arrogance of power, the strong resort to such means as will effect their purpose, reckless of consequences, and enforcing what they call the rights of property, utterly

neglect its duties. I do not pretend to represent the late
Duchess or Duke of Sutherlandshire in particular, as
destitute of the common attributes of humanity, however
atrocious may have been the acts perpetrated in their name,
or by their authority. They were generally absentees, and
while they gave-in to the general clearing scheme, I have no
doubt they wished it to be carried into effect with as little
hardship as possible. But their prompters and underlings
pursued a more reckless course, and, intent only on their
own selfish ends, deceived these high personages, representing the people as slothful and rebellious, while, as they
pretended, everything necessary was done for their accommodation.

I have mentioned above that the late war and its
consequences laid the foundation of the evil complained of.
Great Britain with her immense naval and military establishments, being in a great measure shut out from foreign
supplies, and in a state of hostility or non-intercourse with
all Europe and North America, almost all the necessaries of
life had to be drawn from our own soil.   Hence, its whole
powers of production were required to supply the immense
and daily increasing demand ; and while the agricultural
portions of the country were strained to yield an increase of
grain, the more northern and mountainous districts were
looked to for additional supplies of animal food.   Hence,
also, all the speculations to get rid of the human inhabitants
of the Highlands, and replace them with cattle and sheep
for the English market.   At the conclusion of the war, these
effects were about to cease with their cause, but the corn
laws, and other food taxes then interfered, and the excluding
of foreign animal food altogether, and grain till it was at
a famine price, caused the increasing population to press
against home produce, so as still to make it the interest of

the Highland lairds to prefer cattle to human beings, and to encourage speculators with capital from England and the south of Scotland to take the lands over the heads of the original tenantry. Thus Highland wrongs were continued, and annually augmented, till the mass of guilt on the one hand, and of suffering on the other, became so great as almost to exceed description or belief. Hence the difficulty of bringing it fully before the public, especially as those interested in suppressing inquiry are numerous, powerful, and unsparing in the use of every influence to stop the mouths of the sufferers. Almost all the new tenants in Sutherlandshire have been made justices of the peace, or otherwise armed with authority, and can thus, under colour of law, commit violence and oppression whenever they find it convenient—the poor people having no redress and scarce daring even to complain. The clergy also, whose duty it is to denounce the oppressors, and aid the oppressed, have all, the whole seventeen parish ministers in Sutherlandshire, with one exception, found their account in abetting the wrong-doers, exhorting the people to quiet submission, helping to stifle their cries, telling them that all their sufferings came from the hand of God, and was a just punishment for their sins ! In what manner these reverend gentlemen were benefited by the change, and bribed thus to desert the cause of the people, I shall explain as I proceed.

The whole county, with the exception of a comparatively small part of one parish, held by Mr. Dempster of Skibo, and similar portions on the outskirts of the county held by two or three other proprietors, is now in the hands of the Sutherland family, who, very rarely, perhaps only once in four or five years, visit their Highland estates. Hence the impunity afforded to the actors in the scenes of devastation and cruelty—the wholesale expulsion of the people, and pulling down and burning their habitations, which latter proceeding was peculiar to Sutherlandshire. In my subsequent communications I shall produce a selection of such facts and incidents, as can be supported by sufficient testimony, to many of which I was an eye-witness, or was otherwise cognizant of them. I have been, with my family, for many years, removed, and at a distance from those scenes, and have no personal malice to gratify, my only motive being a desire to vindicate my ill-used countrymen from the aspersions cast upon them, to draw public attention to their wrongs, and, if possible, to bring about a fair inquiry, to be conducted by disinterested men, as to the real causes, of their long-protracted misery and destitution, in order that the public sympathies may be awakened in their behalf, and something effected for their relief. With these observations I now conclude, and in my next letter I will enter upon my narration of a few of such facts as can be fully authenticated by living testimony.

LETTER III.

In my last letter, I endeavoured to trace the causes that led to the general clearing and consequent distress in Sutherlandshire, which dates its commencement from the year 1807. Previous to that period, partial removals had taken place, on the estates of Lord Reay, Mr. Honeyman of Armidale, and others: but these removals were under ordinary and comparatively favourable circumstances. Those who were ejected from their farms, were accommodated with smaller portions of land, and those who chose to emigrate had means in their power to do so, by the sale of their cattle, which then fetched an extraordinary high price. But in the year above mentioned, the system commenced on the Duchess of Sutherland's property; about 90 families were removed from the parishes of Farr and Larg. These people were, however, in some degree provided for, by giving them smaller lots of land, but many of these lots were at a distance of from 10 to 17 miles, so that the people had to remove their cattle and furniture thither, leaving the crops on the ground behind. Watching this crop from trespass of the cattle of the incoming tenants, and removing it in the autumn, was attended with great difficulty and loss. Besides, there was also much personal suffering, from their having to pull down their houses and carry away the timber of them, to erect houses on their new possessions, which houses they had to inhabit immediately on being covered in, and in the meantime, to live and sleep in the open air, except a few, who might be fortunate enough to get an unoccupied barn, or shed, from some of their charitable new-come neighbours.

The effects of these circumstances on the health of the aged and infirm, and on the women and children, may be readily conceived—some lost their lives, and others contracted diseases that stuck to them for life.

During the year 1809, in the parishes of Dornoch, Rogart, Loth, Clyne, and Golspie, an extensive removal took place; several hundred families were turned out, but under circumstances of greater severity than the preceding. Every means were resorted to, to discourage the people, and to persuade them to give up their holdings quietly, and quit the country; and to those who could not be induced to do so, scraps of moor, and bog lands, were offered in Dornoch moor, and Brora links, on which it was next to impossible to exist, in order that they may be scared into going entirely away. At this time, the estate was under the management of Mr. Young, a corn-dealer, as chief, and Mr. Patrick Sellar, a writer, as under-Factor, the latter of whom will make a conspicuous figure in my future communications. These gentlemen were both from Morayshire; and, in order to favour their own country people, and get rid of the natives, the former were constantly employed in all the improvements and public works under their direction, while the latter were taken at inferior wages, and only when strangers could not be had.

Thus, a large portion of the people of these five parishes were, in the course of two or three years, almost entirely rooted out, and those few who took the miserable allotments above mentioned, and some of their descendants, continue to exist on them in great poverty. Among these were the widows and orphans of those heads of families who had been drowned in the same year, in going to attend a fair, when upwards of one hundred individuals lost their lives, while crossing the ferry between Sutherland and Tain. These destitute creatures were obliged to accept of any spot which afforded them a residence, from inability to go elsewhere.

From this time till 1812 the process of ejection was carried on annually, in a greater or less degree, and during this period the estates of Gordonbush and Uppet were added, by purchase, to the ducal property, and in the subsequent years, till 1829, the whole of the county, with the small exceptions before mentioned, had passed into the hands of this great family.

In the year 1811 a new era of depopulation commenced; summonses of removal were served on large portions of the inhabitants. The lands were divided into extensive lots, and advertised to be let for sheep farms.

Strangers were seen daily traversing the country, viewing these lots, previous to bidding for them. They appeared to be in great fear of rough treatment from the inhabitants whom they were about to supersede; but the event proved they had no cause; they were uniformly treated with civility, and even hospitality, thus affording no excuse for the measures of severity to which the factors and their adherents afterwards had recourse. However, the pretext desired was soon found in an apparently concerted plan. A person from the south, of the name of Reid, a manager on one of the sheep farms, raised an alarm that he had been pursued by some of the natives of Kildonan, and put in bodily fear. The factors eagerly jumped as this trumped-up story; they immediately swore-in from sixty to one hundred retainers, and the new inhabitants, as special constables; trimmed and charged the cannon at Dunrobin Castle, which had reposed in silence since the last defeat of the unfortunate Stuarts. Messengers were then dispatched, warning the people to attend at the castle at a certain hour, under the pretence of making amicable arrangements. Accordingly, large numbers prepared to obey the summons, ignorant of their enemies' intentions, till, when about six miles from the castle, a large body of them got a hint of their danger from some one in the secret, on which they called a halt and held a consultation, when it was resolved to pass on to the Inn at Golspie, and there await the recontre with the factors. The latter were much disappointed at this derangement of their plans; but on their arrival with the sheriff, constables, and others, they told the people, to their astonishment, that a number of them were to be apprehended, and sent to Dornoch Jail, on *suspicion* of an attempt to take Mr. Reid's life! The people, with one voice, declared their innocence, and that they would not suffer any of their number to be imprisoned on such a pretence. Without further provocation, the sheriff proceeded to read the riot act, a thing quite new and unintelligible to the poor Sutherlanders so long accustomed to bear their wrongs patiently; however, they immediately

dispersed and returned to their homes in peace. The
factors, having now found the pretext desired, mounted their
horses and galloped to the castle in pretended alarm, sought
protection under the guns of their fortress, and sent an
express to Fort George for a military force to suppress the
rebellion in Sutherlandshire ! The 21st Regiment of foot
(Irish) was accordingly ordered to proceed by forced marches,
night and day, a distance of fifty miles, with artillery, and
cart-loads of ammunition. On their arrival, some of them
were heard to declare they would now have revenge on the
Sutherlanders for the carnage of their countrymen at Tara-
hill and Ballynamuck ; but they were disappointed, for they
found no rebels to cope with ; so that, after having made a
few prisoners, who were all liberated on a precognition being
taken, they were ordered away to their barracks. The
people, meantime, dismayed and spirit-broken at the array
of power brought against them, and seeing nothing but
enemies on every side, even in those from whom they should
have had comfort and succour, quietly submitted to their
fate. The clergy, too, were continually preaching submission, declaring these proceedings were fore-ordained of
God, and denouncing the vengeance of Heaven and eternal
damnation on those who should presume to make the least
resistance. No wonder the poor Highlanders quailed under
such influences ; and the result was, that large districts of
the parishes before mentioned were dispossessed at the May
term, 1812.

The Earl of Selkirk hearing of these proceedings, came
personally into Sutherlandshire, and by fair promises of
encouragement, and other allurements, induced a number of
the distressed outcasts to enter into an arrangement with him,
to emigrate to his estates on the Red River, North America.
Accordingly, a whole shipful of them went thither ; but on

their arrival, after a tedious and disastrous passage, they found themselves deceived and deserted by his lordship, and left to their fate in an inclement wilderness, without protection against the savages, who plundered them on their arrival, and, finally massacred them all, with the exception of a few who escaped with their lives, and travelled across trackless wilds till they at last arrived in Canada.

This is a brief recital of the proceedings up to 1813; and these were the only acts of riot and resistance that ever took place in Sutherlandshire.

LETTER IV.

IN the month of March, 1814, a great number of the inhabitants of the parishes of Farr and Kildonan were summoned to give up their farms at the May term following, and, in order to ensure and hasten their removal with their cattle, in a few days after, the greatest part of the heath pasture was set fire to and burnt, by order of Mr. Sellar, the factor, who had taken these lands for himself. It is necessary to explain the effects of this proceeding. In the spring, especially when fodder is scarce, as was the case in the above year, the Highland cattle depend almost solely on the heather. As soon, too, as the grass begins to sprout about the roots of the bushes, the animals get a good bite, and are thus kept in tolerable condition. Deprived of this resource by the burning, the cattle were generally left without food, and this being the period of temporary peace, during Buonaparte's residence in Elba, there was little demand for good cattle, much less for these poor starving animals, who roamed about over their burnt pasture till a great part of them were lost, or sold for a mere trifle. The arable parts of the land were cropped by the outgoing tenants, as is customary, but the fences being mostly destroyed by the burning, the cattle of the incoming tenant were continually trespassing throughout the summer and harvest, and those who remained to look after the crop had no shelter; even watching being disallowed, and the people were hunted by the new herdsmen and their dogs from watching their own corn! As the spring had been severe, so the harvest was wet, cold, and disastrous for the poor people, who, under every difficulty, were endeavouring to secure the residue of their crops. The barns, kilns, and mills, except a few necessary to the new tenant, had, as well as the houses, been burnt or otherwise destroyed and no shelter left, except on the other side of the river, now overflowing its banks from the continual rains; so that, after all their labour and privations, the people lost nearly the whole of their crops, as they had already lost their cattle, and were thus entirely ruined.

But I must now go back to the May term and attempt to give some account of the ejection of the inhabitants; for to give anything like an adequate description I am not capable. If I were, its horrors would exceed belief.

The houses had been all built, not by the landlord as in the low country, but by the tenants or by their ancestors, and, consequently, were their property by right, if not by law. They were timbered chiefly with bog fir, which makes excellent roofing but is very inflammable: by immemorial usage this species of timber was considered the property of the tenant on whose lands it was found. To the upland timber, for which the laird or the factor had to be asked, the laird might lay some claim, but not so to the other sort, and in every house there was generally a part of both.

In former removals the tenants had been allowed to carry

away this timber to erect houses on their new allotments but now a more summary mode was adopted, by setting fire to the houses! The able-bodied men were by this time away after their cattle or otherwise engaged at a distance, so that the immediate sufferers by the general house-burning that now commenced were the aged and infirm, the women and children. As the lands were now in the hands of the factor himself, and were to be occupied as sheep-farms, and as the people made no resistance, they expected at least some indulgence, in the way of permission to occupy their houses and other buildings till they could gradually remove, and meanwhile look after their growing crops. Their consternation, was, therefore, the greater when, immediately after the May term day, and about two months after they had received summonses of removal, a commencement was made to pull down and set fire to the houses over their heads! The old people, women, and others, then began to try to preserve the timber which they were entitled to consider as their own. But the devastators proceeded with the greatest celerity, demolishing all before them, and when they had overthrown the houses in a large tract of country, they ultimately set fire to the wreck. So that timber, furniture, and every other article that could not be instantly removed, was consumed by fire, or otherwise utterly destroyed.

These proceedings were carried on with the greatest rapidity as well as with most reckless cruelty. The cries of the victims, the confusion, the despair and horror painted on the countenances of the one party, and the exulting ferocity of the other, beggar all description. In these scenes Mr. Sellar was present, and apparently, (as was sworn by several witnesses at his subsequent trial,) ordering and directing the whole. Many deaths ensued from alarm, from fatigue, and cold; the people being instantly deprived of shelter, and left

to the mercy of the elements.   Some old men took to the
woods and precipices, wandering about in a state approaching
to, or of absolute insanity, and several of them, in this situation, lived only a few days.   Pregnant women were taken
with premature labour, and several children did not long
survive their sufferings.   To these scenes I was an eye-
witness, and am ready to substantiate the truth of my statements, not only by my own testimony, but by that of many
others who were present at the time.

   In such a scene of general devastation it is almost useless
to particularize the cases of individuals—the suffering was
great and universal.   I shall, however, just notice a very few
of the extreme cases which occur to my recollection, to most
of which I was an eye-witness.   John MacKay's wife,
Ravigill, in attempting to pull down her house, in the absence
of her husband, to preserve the timber, fell through the roof.
She was, in consequence, taken with premature labour, and
in that state, was exposed to the open air and the view of
the by-standers.   Donald Munro, Garvott, lying in a fever,
was turned out of his house and exposed to the elements.
Donald Macbeath, an infirm and bed-ridden old man, had
the house unroofed over him, and was, in that state, exposed
to wind and rain till death put a period to his sufferings.   I
was present at the pulling down and burning of the house of
William Chisholm, Badinloskin, in which was lying his wife's
mother, an old bed-ridden woman of near 100 years of age,
none of the family being present.   I informed the persons
about to set fire to the house of this circumstance, and
prevailed on them to wait till Mr. Sellar came.   On his
arrival I told him of the poor old woman being in a condition
unfit for removal.   He replied, "Damn her, the old witch,
she has lived too long; let her burn".   Fire was immediately
set to the house, and the blankets in which she was carried

were in flames before she could be got out. She was placed
in a little shed, and it was with great difficulty they were
prevented from firing it also. The old woman's daughter
arrived while the house was on fire, and assisted the neighbours in removing her mother out of the flames and smoke,
presenting a picture of horror which I shall never forget, but
cannot attempt to describe. She died within five days.

I could multiply instances to a great extent, but must
leave to the reader to conceive the state of the inhabitants
during this scene of general devastation, to which few
parallels occur in the history of this or any other civilized
country. Many a life was lost or shortened, and many a
strong constitution ruined ;—the comfort and social happiness of all destroyed ; and their prospects in life, then of the
most dismal kind, have, generally speaking, been unhappily
realized.

LETTER V.

At the spring assizes of Inverness, in 1816, Mr. Sellar was
brought to trial, before Lord Pitmilly, for his proceedings, as
partly detailed in my last letter. The indictment, charging
him with culpable homicide, fire-raising, &c., was prosecuted
by his Majesty's advocate. In the report of the trial, published by Mr. Sellar's counsel, it is said, " To this measure
his lordship seems to have been induced, chiefly for the
purpose of satisfying the public mind and putting an end to
the clamours of the country ". If this, and not the ends of
justice, was the intention, it was completely successful, for
the gentleman was acquitted, to the astonishment of the
natives, and the oppressors were thereby emboldened to
proceed in their subsequent operations with a higher hand,
and with perfect impunity, as will be seen in the sequel.

It is a difficult and hazardous attempt to impugn proceedings carried on by his Majesty's advocate, presided over by an honourable judge, and decided by a jury of respectable men; but I may mention a few circumstances which might have a tendency to disappoint the people. Out of forty witnesses examined at a precognition before the sheriff, there were only eleven, and those not the most competent, brought forward for the crown; and the rest, some of whom might have supported material parts of the indictment—as, for instance, in the case of Donald Monro—were never called at all. Besides, the witnesses for the prosecution, being simple, illiterate persons, gave their testimony in Gaelic, which was interpreted to the court; and, it is well known, much depends upon the translator, whether evidence so taken, retains its weight and strength or not. The jury, with very few exceptions, was composed of persons just similiarly circumstanced with the *new* tenants in Sutherlandshire, and consequently, might very naturally have a leaning to that side, and all the exculpatory witnesses were those who had been art and part, or otherwise interested, in the outrageous proceedings. Mr. Sellar was a man of talent, an expert lawyer, and a justice of the peace, invested with full powers, as factor and law agent to a great absentee proprietor, and strongly supported by the clergy and gentry in the neighbourhood : he was also the incoming tenant to the lands which were the scene of his proceedings—too great odds against a few poor simple Highlanders, who had only their wrongs to plead, whose minds were comparatively uncultivated, and whose pecuniary means were small.

The immediate cause which led to these legal proceedings was, that several petitions from the expelled tenants had been sent to the noble proprietors, representing the illegal and cruel treatment they had received ; and, in consequence of the answers received expressing a wish that justice might be done, the case was laid before the sheriff-depute, Mr. Cranstoun, who sent an express injunction to Mr. Robert MacKid, sheriff-substitute for the county, to take a precognition of the case, and if there appeared sufficient cause, to take Mr. Sellar into custody. The sheriff-substitute was a man of acknowledged probity, but from the representations he had previously received, was considered unfavourable to the cause of the people. On examining the witnesses, however, a case of such enormity was made out as induced him to use some strong expressions contained in a letter to Lord Stafford, which I here subjoin, and which, with some false allegations, were urged against him on the trial, so that, under the direction of the court, the advocate-depute passed from his evidence on the grounds of malice and unduly expressed opinion, and thus Mr. MacKid's important testimony was lost. On the whole, this case furnishes an instance of "the glorious uncertainty of LAW".

TO LORD STAFFORD.

KIRKTOWN P. GOLSPIE, 30th May, 1815.

MY LORD,—I conceive it a duty I owe to your Lordship, to address you upon the present occasion, and a more distressing task I have seldom had to perform.

Your Lordship knows, that in summer last, a humble petition, subscribed by a number of tenants on Mr. Sellar's sheep farm in Farr and Kildonan, was presented to Lady Stafford, complaining of various acts of injury, cruelty and oppression, alleged to have been committed upon their persons and property, by Mr. Sellar, in the spring and summer of that year.

To this complaint, her ladyship, upon the 22nd of July last, was graciously pleased to return an answer in writing. In it, her Ladyship, with her usual candour and justice, with much propriety observes, "That if any person on the estate shall receive any illegal treatment, she will never consider it as hostile to her if they have recourse to legal redress, as a most secure way to receive the justice which she always desires they should have on every occasion". Her Ladyship also intimates, "That she had communicated the complaint to Mr. Sellar, that he may make proper inquiry and answer to her".

It would appear, however, that Mr. Sellar still refused, or delayed, to afford that redress to the removed tenants to which they conceived themselves entitled, which emboldened them to approach Earl Gower with a complaint, similar to the one they had presented to Lady Stafford.

To this complaint his Lordship graciously condescended, under date 8th February last, to return such an answer as might have been expected from his Lordship. His Lordship says that he has communicated the contents to your Lordship and Lady Stafford, who, as his Lordship nobly expresses himself, "Are desirous, that the tenants should know, that it is always their wish that justice should be impartially administered". His lordship then adds, that he has sent the petition, with directions to Mr. Young, that proper steps should be taken for laying the business before the sheriff-depute; and that the petitioners would therefore be assisted by Mr. Young, if they desired it, in having the precognition taken before the sheriff-depute, according to their petition.

Soon after receipt of Earl Gower's letter, it would appear that a copy of the petition, with his Lordship's answer, had been transmitted to the sheriff-depute by the tenants. Mr. Cranstoun, in answer, upon 30th March last, says, "that if the tenants mean to take a precognition immediately, it will proceed before the sheriff-substitute, as my engagement will not permit me to be in Sutherland until the month of July ".

In consequence of these proceedings, on an express injunction from his Majesty's advocate-depute, and a similar one from the sheriff-depute, I was compelled to enter upon an investigation of the complaints.

With this view I was induced to go into Strathnaver, where, at considerable personal inconvenience and expense, and with much patient perseverance, I examined about forty evidences upon the allegations stated in the tenants' petition ; and it is with the deepest regret I have to inform your lordship, that a more numerous catalogue of crimes, perpetrated by an individual, has seldom disgraced any country, or sullied the pages of a precognition in Scotland.

This being the case, the laws of the country imperiously call upon me to order Mr. Sellar to be arrested and incarcerated, in order for trial, and before this reaches your Lordship this preparatory legal step must be put in execution.

No person can more sincerely regret the cause, nor more feelingly lament the effect, than I do; but your Lordship knows well, and as Earl Gower very properly observed, "Justice should be impartially administered ".

I have, in confidence, stated verbally to Mr. Young my fears upon this distressing subject, and I now take the liberty of stating my sentiments also to your lordship, in confidence.

The crimes of which Mr. Sellar stands accused are,—

1. Wilful fire-raising; by having set on fire, and reduced to ashes, a poor man's whole premises, including dwelling-house, barn, kiln, and sheep-cot, attended with most aggravated circumstances of cruelty, if not murder.

2. Throwing down and demolishing a mill, also a capital crime.

3. Setting fire to and burning the tenants' heath pasture, before the legal term of removal.

4. Throwing down and demolishing houses, whereby the lives of sundry aged and bed-ridden persons were endangered, if not actually lost.

5. Throwing down and demolishing barns, kilns, sheep-cots, &c., to the great hurt and prejudice of the owners.

6. Innumerable other charges of lesser importance swell the list.

I subjoin a copy of Mr. Cranstoun's letter to me upon this subject, for your lordship's information, and have the honour to be, &c.,

(Signed)   ROBT. MACKID.

Here I must part with Messrs. Young and Sellar as agents for the noble family of Sutherland, for about this time they ceased to act as such. I shall in my next, proceed to describe the devastating removals of 1819 and '20—those which happened in the intermediate years between these and the year 1815, being similar in character to the removals I have already described. Mr. Sellar shall hereafter only figure in my narrative as a leviathan tenant, who individually supplanted scores of the worthy small farmers of the parish of Farr.

LETTER VI.

THE integrity manifested by the sheriffs, Cranstoun and MacKid, led to their dismissal from office, immediately after the trial. This dismissal operated as a sentence of banishment and ruin to Mr. MacKid—his business in Sutherlandshire was at an end; he retired to Caithness with a large family, and commenced business as a writer, where every malignant influence followed him from the ruling powers in the former county. It is to be hoped that this upright gentleman has since surmounted his difficulties; he must at all events have enjoyed a high reward in the testimony of a good conscience.

I have hitherto given the noble proprietors the title they bore at the time of the occurrences mentioned, but in order to avoid ambiguity, it may be necessary to give a very brief historical sketch of the family. The late Duchess of Sutherland, premier peeress of Scotland, in her own right, succeeded to the estates of her father, William, 21st Earl of Sutherland, with the title of Countess, in the year 1766, being then only one year old. In 1785 she married the Marquis of Stafford and took his title in addition.

In the year 1833, the Marquis was created a Duke, and his lady was subsequently styled Duchess-Countess of Sutherland. She was a lady of superior mind and attainments, but her great and good qualities were lost to her Highland tenantry, from her being non-resident, and having adopted the plan of removing the natives, and letting the lands to strangers. Their eldest surviving son, Lord Leveson Gower, also an eminent person, succeeded to the titles and estates of both parents on their decease, and is now the Duke of Sutherland.

The family mansion, Dunrobin Castle, is situated on the southern border of the county, and in the rare case of any of the noble family coming to the Highlands during the period of the removals, they only came to the castle and stopped there, where the old tenants were strictly denied access, while the new occupiers had free personal communication with the proprietors. When any memorial or petition from the former could be got introduced, there was no attention paid to them if not signed by a minister ; and this was next to impossible, as the clergy, with one honourable exception, had taken the other side. In every case it appeared that the factors and ministers were consulted, and the decision given according to their suggestions and advice.

On the resignation or dismissal of Messrs. Young and Sellar, Mr. Loch, now M.P. for the Northern Burghs, came into full power as chief, and a Mr. Suther as under factor. Mr. Loch is a Scotsman, but not a Highlander. He had previously been chief agent on the English estates, general adviser in the proceedings relative to the Sutherland tenantry, and cognizant of all the severities towards them. This gentleman has written a work entitled, " An Account of the Improvements on the estates of the Marquis of Stafford, in the counties of Stafford and Salop, and on the estate of Sutherland," in which he has attempted to justify or palliate the proceedings in which he bore a most important part. His book is, therefore, scarce ever to be relied on for a single fact, when the main object interfered; he vilifies the High-landers, and misrepresents every thing to answer his purpose. He has been fully answered, his arguments refuted, and his sophistries exposed by Major-General Stewart, in his " Sketches of the Character and Manners of the Highlanders of Scotland," to which excellent work I beg to call the attention of every friend to truth and justice, and especially those who take an interest in the fate of the expatriated tenantry. The General has completely vindicated the character of the Highland tenantry, and shown the impolicy, as well as cruelty, of the means used for their ejection. The removal of Messrs. Young and Sellar, particularly the latter, from the power they had exercised so despotically, was hailed with the greatest joy by the people, to whom their very names were a terror. Their appearance in any neighbour-hood had been such a cause of alarm, as to make women fall into fits, and in one instance caused a woman to lose her reason, which, as far as I know, she has not yet recovered ; whenever she saw a stranger she cried out, with a terrific tone and manner, *Oh! sin Sellar!*—" Oh! there's Sellar!"

Bitter, however, was the people's disappointment when they found the way in which the new factors began to exercise their powers. The measures of their predecessors were continued and aggravated, though, on account of unexpired leases, the removals were but partial till the years 1819 and 1820. However, I must not pass over the expulsion and sufferings of forty families who were removed by Mr. Sellar, almost immediately after his trial. This person, not finding it convenient to occupy the whole of the 6,000 or 7,000 acres, which he had obtained possession of, and partially cleared in 1814, had agreed to let these forty families remain as tenants at will; but he now proceeded to remove them in the same unfeeling manner as he had ejected the others, only he contented himself with utterly demolishing their houses, barns, &c., but did not, as before, set fire to them till the inmates were removed; they leaving their crops in the ground as before described. This year (1816) will be remembered for its severity by many in Scotland. The winter commenced by the snow falling in large quantities in the month of October, and continued with increasing rigour, so that the difficulty—almost impossibility—of the people, without barns or shelter of any kind, securing their crops, may be easily conceived. I have seen scores of these poor outcasts employed for weeks together, with the snow from two to four feet deep, watching their corn from being devoured by the hungry sheep of the incoming tenants; carrying *on their backs*—horses being unavailable in such a case, across a country, without roads—on an average of twenty miles, to their new allotments on the sea-coast, any portion of their grain and potatoes they could secure under such dreadful circumstances. During labour and sufferings, which none but a Highlander could sustain, they had to subsist entirely on potatoes dug out of the snow; cooking them as they could, in the open air, among the ruins of their once comfortable dwellings! While alternate frosts and thaws, snow-storms and rain were succeeding each other in all the severity of mid-winter, the people might be seen carrying on their labours, and bearing their burdens of damp produce, under which many, especially the females, were occasionally sinking in a fainting state, till assisted by others little better off than themselves. In some very rare instances only, a little humane assistance was afforded by the shepherds; in general, their tender mercies, like those of their unfeeling masters, were only cruelties.

The filling up of this feeble outline must be left to the imagination of the reader, but I may mention that attendant on all previous and subsequent removals, and especially this one, many severe diseases made their appearance; such as had been hitherto almost unknown among the Highland population; viz., typhus fever, consumption, and pulmonary complaints in all their varieties, bloody flux, bowel complaints, eruptions, rheumatisms, piles, and maladies peculiar to females. So that the new and uncomfortable dwellings of this lately robust and healthy peasantry, " their country's pride," were now become family hospitals and lazar-houses of the sick and the dying! Famine and utter destitution inevitably followed, till the misery of my once happy country-men reached an alarming height, and began to attract attention as an almost national calamity.

Even Mr. Loch in his before-mentioned work, has been constrained to admit the extreme distress of the people. He says, (page 76,) " Their wretchedness was so great, that after pawning everything they possessed, to the fishermen on the coast, such as had no cattle were reduced to come down from the hills in hundreds, for the purpose of gathering cockles on the shore. Those who lived in the more remote situations

of the country were obliged to subsist upon broth made of
nettles, thickened with a little oatmeal.   Those who had
cattle had recourse to the still more wretched expedient of
bleeding them, and mixing the blood with oatmeal, which
they afterwards cut into slices and fried.   Those who had a
little money, came down and slept all night upon the beach,
in order to watch the boats returning from the fishing, that
they might be in time to obtain a part of what had been
caught."   This gentleman, however, omits to mention, the
share he had in bringing things to such a pass, and also that,
at the same time, he had armed constables stationed at
Little-ferry, the only place where shell-fish were to be found,
to prevent the people from gathering them.   In his next page
he gives an exaggerated account of the relief afforded by the
proprietors.   I shall not copy his mis-statements, but proceed
to say what that relief, so ostentatiously put forth, really consisted of.   As to his assertion that "£3,000 had been given
by way of loan to those who had cattle," I look upon it as
a fabrication, or, if the money really was sent by the noble
proprietors, it must have been retained by those intrusted
with its distribution ; for, to my knowledge, it never came to
the hands of any of the small tenants.   There was, indeed, a
considerable quantity of meal sent, though far from enough
to afford effectual relief, but this meal represented to be given
in charity, was charged at the following Martinmas term, at
the rate of 50s. per boll.   Payment was rigorously exacted,
and those who had cattle were obliged to give them up for
that purpose, but this latter part of the story was never sent
to the newspapers, and Mr. Loch has also forgotten to
mention it !   There was a considerable quantity of medicine
given to the ministers for distribution, for which no charge
was made, and this was the whole amount of relief afforded.

LETTER VII.

THE honourable acquittal of Mr. Sellar, and the compliments he received, in consequence, from the presiding judge, with the dismissal of the sheriffs, had the desired effect upon the minds of the poor Sutherlanders, and those who took an interest in their case. Every voice in their behalf was silenced and every pen laid down—in short, every channel for redress or protection from future violence was closed; the people were prostrated under the feet of their oppressors, who well knew how to take advantage of their position. It appeared, that, for a considerable interval, there were no regular sheriffs in the county, and that the authority usually exercised by them was vested in Captain Kenneth MacKay, a native of the county, and now one of its extensive sheep farmers. It was by virtue of warrants granted by this gentleman that the proceedings I am about to describe took place, and, if the sheriff-officers, constables, and assistants, exceeded their authority, they did so under his immediate eye and cognizance, as he was all the time residing in his house, situated so that he must have witnessed a great part of the scene from his own front windows. Therefore, if he did not immediately authorize the atrocities to the extent committed (which I will not assert), he at least used no means to restrain them.

At this period a great majority of the inhabitants were tenants-at-will, and therefore liable to ejectment on getting regular notice; there were, however, a few who had still existing tacks (although some had been wheedled or frightened into surrendering them), and these were, of course, unmolested till the expiration of their tacks; they were then turned out like the rest; but the great body of the tenantry were in the former condition. Meantime, the factors, taking advantage of the broken spirit and prostrate state of the people—trembling at their words or even looks—betook themselves to a new scheme to facilitate their intended proceedings, and this was to induce every householder to sign a bond or paper containing a promise of removal; and alternate threats and promises were used to induce them to do so.   The promises were never realised, but, notwithstanding the people's compliance, the threats were put in execution.   In about a month after the factors had obtained this promise of removal, and thirteen days before the May term, the work of devastation was begun.   They commenced by setting fire to the houses of the small tenants in extensive districts—part of the parishes of Farr, Rogart, Golspie, and the whole parish of Kildonan.   I was an eye-witness of the scene.   This calamity came on the people quite unexpectedly. Strong parties, for each district, furnished with faggots and other combustibles, rushed on the dwellings of this devoted people, and immediately commenced setting fire to them, proceeding in their work with the greatest rapidity till about three hundred houses were in flames !   The consternation and confusion were extreme; little or no time was given for removal of persons or property—the people striving to remove the sick and the helpless before the fire should reach them—next, struggling to save the most valuable of their effects.   The cries of the women and children—the roaring of the affrighted cattle, hunted at the same time by the yelling dogs of the shepherds amid the smoke and fire— altogether presented a scene that completely baffles description : it required to be seen to be believed.   A dense cloud of smoke enveloped the whole country by day, and even extended far on the sea ; at night an awfully grand, but terrific scene presented itself—all the houses in an extensive district in flames at once !   I myself ascended a height about eleven o'clock in the evening, and counted two hundred and fifty blazing houses, many of the owners of which were my relations, and all of whom I personally knew; but whose present condition, whether in or out of the flames, I could not tell. The conflagration lasted six days, till the whole of the dwellings were reduced to ashes or smoking ruins. During one of these days a boat lost her way in the dense smoke as she approached the shore; but at night she was enabled to reach a landing place by the light of the flames!

It would be an endless task to give a detail of the sufferings of families and individuals during this calamitous period; or to describe its dreadful consequences on the health and lives of the victims. I will, however, attempt a very few cases. While the burning was going on, a small sloop arrived, laden with quick-lime, and while discharging her cargo, the skipper agreed to take as many of the people to Caithness as he could carry, on his return. Accordingly, about twenty families went on board, filling deck, hold, and every part of the vessel. There were childhood and age, male and female, sick and well, with a small portion of their effects, saved from the flames, all huddled together in heaps. Many of these persons had never been on sea before, and when they began to sicken a scene indescribable ensued. To add to their miseries, a storm and contrary winds prevailed, so that instead of a day or two, the usual time of passage, it was *nine days* before they reached Caithness. All this time, the poor creatures, almost without necessaries, most of them dying with sickness, were either wallowing among the lime, and various excrements in the hold, or lying on the deck, exposed to the raging elements! This voyage soon proved fatal to many, and some of the survivors feel its effects to this day. During this time, also, typhus fever was

raging in the country, and many in a critical state had to fly,
or were carried by their friends out of the burning houses.
Among the rest, a young man, Donald MacKay of Grumb-
mor, was ordered out of his parents' house; he obeyed, in
a state of delirium, and (nearly naked) ran into some bushes
adjoining, where he lay for a considerable time deprived of
reason; the house was immediately in flames, and his
effects burned. Robert MacKay, whose whole family were
in the fever, or otherwise ailing, had to carry his two
daughters on his back a distance of about twenty-five miles.
He accomplished this by first carrying one, and laying her
down in the open air, and returning, did the same with the
other, till he reached the sea-shore, and then went with them
on board the lime vessel before mentioned. An old man of
the same name, betook himself to a deserted mill, and lay
there unable to move; and to the best of my recollection,
he died there. He had no sustenance but what he obtained
by licking the dust and refuse of the meal strewed about,
and was defended from the rats and other vermin, by his
faithful *collie*, his companion and protector. A number of
the sick, who could not be carried away instantly, on account
of their dangerous situation, were collected by their friends
and placed in an obscure, uncomfortable hut, and there, for
a time, left to their fate. The cries of these victims were
heart-rending—exclaiming in their anguish, " Are you going
to leave us to perish in the flames?" However, the
destroyers passed near the hut, apparently without noticing
it, and consequently they remained unmolested, till they
could be conveyed to the shore, and put on board the
before-mentioned sloop. George Munro, miller at Farr,
residing within 400 yards of the minister's house, had his
whole family, consisting of six or seven persons, lying in a
fever; and being ordered instantly to remove, was enabled,

with the assistance of his neighbours to carry them to a damp kiln, where they remained till the fire abated, so that they could be removed. Meantime the house was burnt. It may not be out of place here to mention generally, that the clergy, factors, and magistrates, were cool and apparently unconcerned spectators of the scenes I have been describing, which were indeed perpetrated under their immediate authority. The splendid and comfortable mansions of these gentlemen, were reddened with the glare of their neighbours' flaming houses, without exciting any compassion for the sufferers ; no spiritual, temporal, or medical aid was afforded them ; and this time they were all driven away without being allowed the benefit of their outgoing crop ! Nothing but the sword was wanting to make the scene one of as great barbarity as the earth ever witnessed ; and in my opinion, this would, in a majority of cases, have been mercy, by saving them from what they were afterwards doomed to endure. The clergy, indeed, in their sermons, maintained that the whole was a merciful interposition of Providence to bring them to repentance, rather than to send them all to hell, as they so richly deserved ! And here I beg leave to ask those rev. gentlemen, or the survivors of them, and especially my late minister, Mr. MacKenzie of Farr, if it be true, as was generally reported, that during these horrors I have been feebly endeavouring to describe—there was a letter sent from the proprietors, addressed to him, or to the general body, requesting to know if the removed tenants were well provided for, and comfortable, or words to that effect, and that the answer returned was, that the people were quite comfortable in their new allotments, and that the change was greatly for their benefit. This is the report that was circulated and believed ; and the subsequent conduct of the clergy affords too much reason for giving it credence, as I shall soon have occasion to show.

LETTER VIII.

THE depopulation I have been treating of, with its attendant horrors and miseries, as well as its impolicy, is so justly
reasoned upon by General Stewart, in the work formerly
alluded to, that I beg to transcribe a paragraph or two.
At page 168 he says:—" The system of overlooking the
original occupiers, and of giving every support to strangers,
has been much practised in the highland counties; and on
one great estate (the Sutherland) the support which was
given to farmers of capital, as well in the amount of sums
expended on improvements, as in the liberal abatement of
rents, is, I believe, unparalleled in the United Kingdom,
and affords additional matter of regret, that the delusions
practised on a generous and public-spirited landholder,
have been so perseveringly and successfully applied, that it
would appear as if all feeling of former kindness towards
the native tenantry had ceased to exist. To them any
uncultivated spot of moorland, however small, was considered sufficient for the support of a family; while the
most lavish encouragement has been given to the new
tenants, on whom, and with the erection of buildings, the
improvement of lands, roads, bridges, etc., upwards of
£210,000 has been expended since the year 1808. With
this proof of unprecedented liberality, it cannot be sufficiently lamented, that an estimate of the character of these
poor people was taken from the misrepresentations of interested persons, instead of judging from the conduct of
the same men when brought into the world, where they obtained a name and character which have secured the esteem
and approbation of men high in honour and rank, and,
from their talents and experience, perfectly capable of judging with correctness. With such proofs of capability, and

with such materials for carrying on the improvements, and maintaining the permanent prosperity of the county, when occupied by a hardy, abstemious race, easily led on to a full exertion of their faculties, by a proper management, there cannot be a question but that if, instead of placing them, as has been done, in situations bearing too near a resemblance to the potato-gardens of Ireland, they had been permitted to remain as cultivators of the soil, receiving a moderate share of the vast sums lavished on their richer successors, such a humane and considerate regard to the prosperity of a whole people, would undoubtedly have answered every good purpose." In reference to the new allotments, he says : " when the valleys and higher grounds were let to the shepherds, the whole population was driven to the sea shore, where they were crowded on small lots of land, to earn their subsistence by labour and by sea fishing, the latter so little congenial to their former habits." He goes on to remark, in a note, that these *one or two acre lots*, are represented as an *improved* system. " In a country without regular employment and without manufactures, a family is to be supported on one or two acres ! ! " The consequence was and continues to be, that, " over the whole of this district, where the sea shore is accessible, the coast is thickly studded with wretched cottages, crowded with starving inhabitants." Strangers "with capital " usurp the land and dispossess the swain. " Ancient respectable tenants, who passed the greater part of life in the enjoyment of abundance, and in the exercises of hospitality and charity, possessing stocks of ten, twenty, and thirty breeding cows, with the usual proportion of other stock, are now pining on one or two acres of bad land, with one or two starved cows ; and for this accommodation, a calculation is made, that they must support their families and pay the rent of their lots, not from the produce but from the sea. When the herring fishery succeeds they generally satisfy the landlords, whatever privations they may suffer; but when the fishing fails, they fall in arrears and are sequestrated, and their stock sold to pay the rents, their lots given to others, and they and their families turned adrift on the world. There are still a few small tenants on the old system; but they are fast falling into decay, and sinking into the class just described." Again, "we cannot sufficiently admire their meek and patient spirit, supported by the powerful influence of moral and religious principle." I need not go further, but again beg the reader's attention to this most valuable work, especially the article "Change of Tenancy," as illustrative of the condition and exponent of the character and feelings of my poor countrymen, as well as corroborative of the facts to which I am endeavouring to call public attention, as causes of the distress and destitution still prevailing in Sutherland-shire.

By the means described, large tracts of country were depopulated, and converted into solitary wastes. The whole inhabitants of Kildonan parish (with the exception of three families), amounting to near 2,000 souls, were utterly rooted and burned out. Many, especially the young and robust, left the country; but the aged, the females and children, were obliged to stay and accept the wretched allotments allowed them on the sea shore, and endeavour to learn fishing, for which all their former habits rendered them unfit; hence their time was spent in unproductive toil and misery, and many lives were lost. Mr. Sage, of evergreen memory, was the parish minister—

Among the faithless, faithful only he !

This gentleman had dissented from his brethren, and, to

the best of his power, opposed their proceedings ; hence he was persecuted and despised by them and the factors, and treated with marked disrespect. After the burning out, having lost his pious elders and attached congregation, he went about mourning till his demise, which happened not long after. His son had been appointed by the people minister of a chapel of ease, parish of Farr, and paid by them; but, when the expulsion took place, he removed to Aberdeen, and afterwards to a parish in Ross-shire. On account of his father's integrity he could not expect a kirk in Sutherlandshire.

After a considerable interval of absence, I revisited my native place in the year 1828, and attended divine worship in the parish church, now reduced to the size and appearance of a dove-cot. The whole congregation consisted of eight shepherds, with their *dogs*, to the number of between 20 and 30, the minister, three of his family, and myself ! I came in after the first singing, but, at the conclusion, the 120th psalm was given us, and we struck up to the famous tune Bangor ; when the four-footed hearers, became excited, got up on the seats and raised a most infernal chorus of howling. Their masters then attacked them with their crooks, which only made matters worse; the yelping and howling continued to the end of the service. I retired, to contemplate the shameful scene, and compare it with what I had previously witnessed in the large and devout congregations formerly attending in that kirk. What must the worthy Mr. Campbell have felt while endeavouring to edify such a congregation !

The Barony of Strathnaver, in the parish of Farr, 25 miles in length, containing a population as numerous as Kildonan, who had been all rooted out at the general conflagration, presented a similar aspect. Here, the church no longer found necessary, was razed to the ground, and the timber of it conveyed to Altnaharrow, to be used in erecting an Inn (one of the new *improvements*) there, and the minister's house converted into the dwelling of a fox-hunter. A woman, well known in that parish, happening to traverse the Strath the year after the burning, was asked, on her return, what news? "Oh," said she, "Sgeul bronach, sgeul bronach? sad news, sad news! I have seen the timber of our well-attended kirk, covering the Inn at Altnaharrow; I have seen the kirk-yard, where our friends are mouldering, filled with tarry sheep, and Mr. Sage's study room, a kennel for Robert Gunn's dogs; and I have seen a crow's nest in James Gordon's chimney head!" On this she fell into a paroxysm of grief, and it was several days before she could utter a word to be understood. During the late devastations, a Captain John MacKay was appointed sub-factor, under Mr. Loch, for the district of Strathnaver. This gentleman, had he been allowed his own way, would have exercised his power beneficially; but he was subject to persons cast in another mould, and had to sanction what he could not approve. He did all he could to mitigate the condition of the natives by giving them employment, in preference to strangers, at the public works and improvements, as they were called; but finding their enemies too powerful and malignant, and the misery and destitution too great to be even partially removed, he shrunk from his ungracious task and went to America, where he breathed his last, much regretted by all who knew him on both sides of the Atlantic.

LETTER IX.

I have already mentioned that the clergy of the Established Church (none other were tolerated in Sutherland), all but Mr. Sage, were consenting parties to the expulsion of the inhabitants, and had substantial reasons for their readiness to accept woolly and hairy animals—sheeps and dogs—in place of their human flocks. The kirks and manses were mostly situated in the low grounds, and the clergy hitherto held their pasturage in common with the tenantry; and this state of things, established by law and usage, no factor or proprietor had power to alter without mutual consent. Had the ministers maintained those rights, they would have placed in many cases, an effectual bar to the oppressive proceedings of the factors; for the strange sheep-farmers would not bid for, or take the lands where the minister's sheep and cattle would be allowed to co-mingle with theirs. But no! Anxious to please the "powers that be," and no less anxious to drive advantageous bargains with them, these reverend gentlemen found means to get their lines laid "in pleasant places," and to secure good and convenient portions of the pasture lands enclosed for themselves : many of the small tenants were removed purely to satisfy them in these arrangements. Their subserviency to the factors, in all things, was not for nought. Besides getting their hill pasturage enclosed, their tillage lands were extended, new manses and offices were built for them, and roads made specially for their accommodation, and every arrangement made for their advantage. They basked in the sunshine of favour : they were the bosom friends of the factors and new tenants (many of whom were soon made magistrates), and had the honour of occasional visits, at their manses, from the proprietors themselves. They were always employed to explain and interpret to the assembled people the orders and designs of the factors; and they did not spare their college paint on these occasions. Black was

made white, or white black, as it answered their purpose, in
discharging what they called their duty! They did not
scruple to introduce the name of the Deity; representing
Him as the author and abetter of all the foul and cruel proceedings carried on; and they had at hand another useful
being ready to seize every soul who might feel any inclination
to revolt. Indeed, the manifest works of the latter in their
own hands, were sufficient to prove his existence; while the
whole appearance of the country, and the state of its inhabitants at this period, afforded ample proof that the principle
of evil was in the ascendant. The tyranny of one class,
and the wrongs and sufferings of the other, had demoralising
effects on both; the national character and manners were
changed and deteriorated; and a comparatively degenerate
race is the consequence. This was already manifest in the
year 1822, when George IV. made his famous visit to Edinburgh. The brave, athletic and gallant men, who, in 1745,
and again more recently, in 1800, rose in thousands at the call
of their chief, were no longer to be traced in their descendants. When the clans gathered to honour His Majesty on the
latter occasion, the Sutherland turn-out was contemptible.
Some two or three dozen of squalid-looking, ill-dressed, and
ill-appointed men, were all that Sutherland produced. So
inferior, indeed, was their appearance to the other Highlanders, that those who had the management refused to
allow them to walk in the procession, and employed them
in some duty out of public view. If their appearance was
so bad, so also were their accommodations. They were
huddled together, in an old empty house, sleeping on straw,
and fed with the coarsest fare, while the other clans were
living in comparative luxury. Lord Francis Leveson Gower,
and Mr. Loch, who were present, reaped little honour by the
exhibition of their Sutherland retainers on that great occa-

sion. Moral degradation also, to some extent, followed that of physical. Many vices, hitherto almost unknown, began to make their appearance; and though the people never resorted to "wild savage justice," like those of Ireland in similar circumstances, the minor transgressions of squabbling, drunkeness, and incontinency became less rare—the natural consequence of their altered condition. Religion also, from the conduct of the clergy, began to lose its hold on their minds—and who can wonder at it?—when they saw these holy men closely leagued with their oppressors. "Ichabod," the glory of Sutherland had departed—perhaps never to return!

LETTER X.

I NOW proceed to describe the "allotments" on which the expelled and burnt-out inhabitants were allowed to locate during the pleasure of the factors. These allotments were generally situated on the sea-coast, the intention being to force those who could not or would not leave the country, to draw their subsistence from the sea by fishing; and in order to deprive them of any other means, the lots were not only made small, (varying from one to three acres) but their nature and situation rendered them unfit for any useful purpose. If the reader will take the trouble to examine the map of Sutherlandshire by Mr. Loch, he will perceive that the county is bounded on the north by the Northern Ocean, on the south by the county of Ross, on the west by the Mynch, on the north-east by Caithness, and on the south-east by the Moray Firth. To the sea-coasts, then, which surround the greatest part of the country were the whole mass of the inhabitants, to the amount of several thousand families, driven by unrelenting tyrants, in the manner I have described, to subsist as they could, on the sea or the air; for the spots allowed them could not be called land, being composed of narrow stripes, promontories, cliffs and preci-pices, rocks, and deep crevices, interspersed with bogs and deep morasses. The whole was quite useless to their superiors, and evidently never designed by nature for the habitation of man or beast. This was, with a few excep-tions, the character of the allotments. The patches of soil where anything could be grown, were so few and scanty that when any dispute arose about the property of them, the owner could almost carry them in a creel on his back and deposit them in another place. In many places, the spots the poor people endeavoured to cultivate were so steep that while one was delving, another had to hold up the soil with his hands, lest it should roll into the sea, and from its constant tendency to slide downwards, they had frequently to carry it up again every spring and spread it upon the higher parts. These patches were so small that few of them would afford room for more than a few handfuls of seeds, and in harvest, if there happened to be any crop, it was in con-tinual danger of being blown into the sea, in that bleak inclement region, where neither tree nor shrub could exist to arrest its progress. In most years, indeed, when any mentionable crop was realised, it was generally destroyed before it could come to maturity, by sea-blasts and mildew. In some places, on the north coast, the sea is forced up through crevices, rising in columns to a prodigious height and scattering its spray upon the adjoining spots of land, to the utter destruction of any thing that may be growing on them. These were the circumstances to which this devoted people were reduced, and to which none but a hardy, patient and moral race, with an ardent attachment to their country, would have quietly submitted; here they, with their cattle, had to remain for the present, expecting the southern dealers to come at the usual time (the months of June and July) to purchase their stocks; but the time came and passed, and no dealers made their appearance; none would venture into the country! The poor animals in a starving state, were continually running to and fro, and frequently could not be prevented from straying towards their former pasture grounds, especially in the night, notwithstanding all the care taken to prevent it. When this occurred, they were immediately seized by the shepherds and impounded without food or water, till trespass was paid! this was repeated till a great many of the cattle were rendered useless. It was nothing strange to see the pinfolds, of twenty or thirty yards square, filled to the entrance with horses, cows, sheep and goats, promiscuously for nights and days together, in that starving state, trampling on and goring each other. The lamentable neighing, lowing, and bleating of these creatures, and the pitiful looks they cast on their owners when they could recognise them, were distressing to witness; and formed an addition to the mass of suffering then prevailing. But this was not all that beset the poor beasts. In some instances when they had been trespassing, they were hurried back by the pursuing shepherds or by their owners, and in running near the precipices many of them had their bones broken or dislocated, and a great number fell over the rocks into the sea, and were never seen after. Vast numbers of sheep and many horses and other cattle which escaped their keepers and strayed to a distance to their former pastures, were baited by men and dogs till they were either partially or totally destroyed, or become meat for their hunters. I have myself seen instances of the kind, where the animals were lying partly consumed by the

dogs, though still alive, and their eyes picked out by birds
of prey.   When the cattle were detained by the shepherds
in the folds before mentioned, for trespass, to any amount
the latter thought proper to exact, those of their owners who
had not money—and they were the majority—were obliged
to relieve them by depositing their bed and body-clothes,
watches, rings, pins, brooches, etc., though many of these were
the relics of dear and valued relatives, now no more, not a
few of whom had shed their blood in defence of that country
from which their friends were now ignominiously driven, or
treated as useless lumber, to be got rid of at any price.   The
situation of the people with their families and cattle, driven
to these inhospitable coasts, harassed and oppressed in
every possible way, presented a lamentable contrast to their
former way of life.   While they were grudged those barren
and useless spots—and at high rents too—the new tenants
were accommodated with leases of as much land as they
choose to occupy, and *at reduced rents;* many of them holding
farms containing many thousand acres.   One farm held by
Messrs. Atkinson and Marshall, two gentlemen from Nor-
thumberland, contained a hundred thousand acres of good
pasture-land ! Mr. Sellar had three large farms, one of which
was twenty-five miles long ; and, in some places, nine or ten
miles broad, situated in the barony of Strathnaver.   This
gentleman was said to have lost, annually, large quantities
of sheep ; and others of the new tenants were frequently
making complaints of the same kind; all these depredations,
as well as every other, were laid to the charge of the small
tenants.   An association was formed for the suppression of
sheep-stealing in Sutherlandshire, and large rewards were
laid out—Lord Stafford himself offering £30 for the conviction of any of the offenders.   But though every effort
was used to bring the crime home to the natives (one gentle-

man, whom, for obvious reasons I will not name, said in my hearing, he would rather than £1000 get one conviction from among them) : yet, I am proud to say, all these endeavours were ineffectual. Not one conviction could they obtain ! In time, however, the saddle came to be laid on the right horse ; the shepherds could rob their masters' flocks in safety, while the natives got the blame of all, and they were evidently no way sparing ; but at last they were found out, and I have reason to know that several of them were dismissed, and some had their own private stocks confiscated to their masters to make good the damage of their depredations. This was, however, all done privately, so that the odium might still attach to the natives. In concluding this part of the subject, I may observe that such of the cattle as strayed on the ministers' grounds, fared no better than others ; only that, as far as I know, these gentlemen did not follow the practice of the shepherds in working the horses all day and returning them to the pinfold at night: and I am very happy in being able to give this testimony in favour of these reverend gentlemen.

I must not omit to mention here an anecdote illustrative of the state of things prevailing at that time. One of the shepherds on returning home one Sabbath evening, after partaking of the Lord's Supper, in the church of Farr, observed a number of the poor people's sheep and goats trespassing at the outskirts of his master's hill-pasturage, and, with the assistance of his dogs, which had also been at the kirk, drove them home and impounded them. On Monday morning he took as many of the lambs and kids as he thought proper, and had them killed for the use of his own family ! The owners complained to his master, who was a magistrate ; but the answer was, that they should keep them off his property, or eat them themselves, and then his servants could not do it for them, or words to that effect. One way or other, by starvation, accidents, and the depredations of the shepherds and their dogs, the people's cattle to the amount of many hundred head, were utterly lost and destroyed.

LETTER XI.

I HAVE now endeavoured to shadow forth the cruel expulsion of my " co-mates and brothers in exile" from their native hearths, and to give a faint sketch of their extreme sufferings and privations in consequence. Few instances are to be found in modern European history, and scarce any in Britain, of such a wholesale extirpation, and with such revolting circumstances. It is impossible for me to give more than an outline; the filling up would take a large volume, and the sufferings, insult, and misery, to which this simple, pastoral race were exposed, would exceed belief. But if I can draw public attention to their case, so as to promote that authorised inquiry, so much deprecated by Highland proprietors, my end will be attained. If the original inhabitants could have been got rid of totally, and their language and memory eradicated, the oppressors were not disposed to be scrupulous about the means. Justice, humanity, and even the laws of the land, were violated with impunity, when they stood in the way of the new plans on " Change of Tenancy"; and these plans, with more or less severity, continue to be acted upon in several of the Highland counties, but more especially in Sutherland, to this day. But there is still a number left, abject, '· scattered and peeled " as they are, in whose behalf I would plead, and to those wrongs I would wish to give a tongue, in hopes that the feeble remnant of a once happy and estimable people, may yet find some redress, or at least the comfort of public sympathy. I now proceed to give some account of the state of the Sutherlanders, on their maritime "allot-ments," and how they got on in their new trade of fishing.

People accustomed to witness only the quiet friths and petty heavings of the sea, from lowland shores, can form little conception of the gigantic workings of the Northern sea, which, from a comparatively placid state, often rises sud-denly without apparent cause, into mountainous billows; and, when north winds prevail, its appearance becomes terrific beyond description. To this raging element, however, the poor people were now compelled to look for their subsistence, or starve, which was the only other alternative. It is hard to extinguish the love of life, and it was almost as hard to extinguish the love of country in a Highlandman in past times; so that, though many of the vigorous and enter-prising pursued their fortunes in other climes, and in various parts of Scotland and England, yet many remained, and struggled to accommodate themselves to their new and appal-ling circumstances. The regular fishermen, who had hitherto pursued the finny race in the northern sea, were, from the extreme hazard of the trade, extremely few, and nothing could exceed the contempt and derision—mingled some-times with pity, even in their rugged breasts—with which they viewed the awkward attempts and sad disasters of their new landward competitors. Nothing, indeed, could seem more helpless, than the attempt to draw subsistence from such a boisterous sea with such means as they possessed, and in the most complete ignorance of all sea-faring matters ; but the attempt had to be made, and the success was such as might be expected in their circumstances ; while many—very many —lost their lives, some became in time expert fishermen.

Numerous as were the casualties, and of almost daily occurrence, yet the escapes, many of them extraordinary, were
happily still more frequent; their disasters, on the whole,
arose to a frightful aggregate of human misery.   I shall
proceed to notice a very few cases, to which I was a witness,
or which occur to my recollection.

William MacKay, a respectable man, shortly after settling
in his allotment on the coast, went one day to explore his
new possession, and in venturing to examine more nearly
the ware growing within the flood mark, was suddenly swept
away by a splash of the sea, from one of the adjoining
creeks, and lost his life, before the eyes of his miserable
wife, in the last month of her pregnancy, and three helpless
children who were left to deplore his fate.   James Campbell,
a man also with a family, on attempting to catch a peculiar
kind of small fish among the rocks, was carried away by the
sea, and never seen afterwards.   Bell MacKay, a married
woman, and mother of a family, while in the act of taking
up salt water to make salt of, was carried away in a similar
manner, and nothing more seen of her.   Robert MacKay,
who with his family was suffering extreme want, in endeavouring to procure some sea-fowls' eggs among the rocks,
lost his hold, and falling from a prodigious height was dashed
to pieces, and leaving a wife and five destitute children behind him.   John MacDonald, while fishing, was swept off
the rocks, and never seen again.

It is not my intention to swell my narrative, by reciting
the " moving accidents " that befel individuals and boats'
crews, in their new and hazardous occupation; suffice it to
say, they were many and deplorable.   Most of the boats were
such as the regular fishermen had cast off as unserviceable
or unsafe, but which those poor creatures were obliged to
purchase and go to sea with, at the hourly peril of their

lives; yet they often not only escaped the death to which others became a prey, but were very successful. One instance of this kind, in which I bore a part myself, I will here relate. Five venturous young men, of whom I was one, having bought an old crazy boat, that had long been laid up as useless, and having procured lines of an inferior description for haddock fishing, put to sea, without sail, helm, or compass, with three patched oars; only one of the party ever having been at sea before. This apparently insane attempt gathered a crowd of spectators, some in derision cheering us on, and our friends imploring us to come back. However, Neptune being then in one of his placid moods, we boldly ventured on, human life having become reduced in value; and, after a night spent on the sea, in which we freshmen suffered severely from sea-sickness, to the great astonishment of the people on shore, the *Heather-boat*, as she was called, reached land in the morning—all hands safe, with a very good take of fish. In these and similar ways, did the young men serve a dangerous and painful apprenticeship to the sea, " urged on by fearless want," in time became good fishermen, and were thereby enabled in some measure to support their families, and those dependent on them : but owing to peculiar circumstances, their utmost efforts were, in a great degree, abortive. The coast was, as I have said, extremely boisterous and destructive to their boats, tackle, etc. They had no harbours where they could land and secure their boats in safety, and little or no capital to procure sound boats, or to replace those which were lost. In one year, on the coast, between Portskerra and Rabbit Island (about 30 miles), upwards of one hundred boats had either been totally destroyed or so materially injured as to render them unserviceable ; and many of their crews had found a watery grave! It is lamentable to think, that while £210,000 were expended on the so-called improvements, besides £500 subscribed by the proprietors, for making a harbour, the most needful of all; not a shilling of the vast sum was ever expended for behoof of the small tenantry, nor the least pains taken to mitigate their lot! Roads, bridges, inns, and manses, to be sure, were provided for the accommodation of the new gentlemen tenantry and clergy, but those who spoke the Gaelic tongue were a proscribed race, and everything was done to get rid of them, by driving them into the forlorn hope of drawing subsistence from the sea, while squatting on their miserable allotments, where, in their wretched hovels, they lingered out an almost hopeless existence, and where none but such hardy " sons of the mountain and the flood " could have existed at all. Add to this, though at some seasons they procured abundance of fish, that they had no market for the surplus; the few shepherds were soon supplied, and they had no means of conveying them to distant towns, so that very little money could be realized to pay rent, or procure other necessaries, fishing tackle, etc., and when the finny race thought proper to desert their shores (as, in their caprice, they often did), their misery was complete! Besides those located on the sea-shore, there was a portion of the people sent to the moors, and these were no better off. Here they could neither get fish nor fowl, and the scraps of land given them were good for nothing—white or reddish gravel, covered with a thin layer of moss, and for this they were to pay rent, and raise food from it to maintain their families! By immense labour they did improve some spots in these moors, and raise a little very inferior produce, but not unfrequently, after all their toil, if they displeased the factors, or the shepherds, in the least, even by a word, or failed in paying the rent, they were unceremoniously turned out; hence, their state of bondage may be understood; they dare not even complain !* The people on the property of Mr. Dempster, of Skibo, were little, if anything, better off. They were driven out, though not by burning, and located on patches of moors, in a similiar way to those on the Sutherland property, with the only difference that they had to pay higher than the latter for their wretched allotments. Mr. Dempster says " he has kept his tenantry "; but how has he treated them ? This question will be solved, I hope, when the authorised inquiry into the state of the poor Highlands takes place.

LETTER XII.

WERE it not that I am unwilling to occupy your valuable columns to a much greater extent, I could bring forward, in the history of many families, several interesting episodes to illustrate this narrative of my country's misfortunes. Numerous are the instances (some of the subjects of them could be produced even in this city) of persons, especially females, whose mental and bodily sufferings, during the scenes I have described, have entailed on them diseases which baffle medical skill, and which death only can put an end to; but I forbear to dwell on these at present, and pass on to the year 1827.

The depopulation of the county (with the exceptions I have described) was now complete. The land had passed into the hands of a few capitalists, and everything was done to promote their prosperity and convenience, while everything that had been promised to the small tenants, was, as

* For corroboration of these statements see quotations from Hugh Miller, and other high authorities, in the sequel.—A. M.

regularly, left undone. But yet the latter were so stubborn
that they could not be brought to rob or steal, to afford
cause for hanging or transporting them ; nor were they even
willing to beg, though many of them were gradually forced
to submit to this last degradation to the feelings of the
high-minded Gael. It was in this year that her ladyship, the
proprietrix, and suite, made a visit to Dunrobin Castle.
Previous to her arrival, the clergy and factors, and the new
tenants, set about raising a subscription throughout the
county, to provide a costly set of ornaments, with complimentary inscriptions, to be presented to her ladyship in
name of her tenantry. Emissaries were despatched for this
purpose even to the small tenantry, located on the moors
and barren cliffs, and every means used to wheedle or scare
them into contributing. They were told that those who
would subscribe would thereby secure her ladyship's and the
factor's favour, and those who could not or would not, were
given to understand, very significantly, what they had to
expect, by plenty of menacing looks and ominous shakings
of the head. This caused many of the poor creatures to
part with their last shilling, to supply complimentary ornaments to honour this illustrious family, and which went to
purchase additional favour for those who were enjoying the
lands from which they had been so cruelly expelled.

These testimonials were presented at a splendid entertain-
ment, and many high-flown compliments passed between
the givers and receiver ; but, of course, none of the
poor victims were present ; no compliments were paid to
them ; and it is questionable if her ladyship ever knew that
one of them subscribed—indeed, I am almost certain that
she never did. Three years after, she made a more length-
ened visit, and this time she took a tour round the northern
districts on the sea-shore, where the poor people were lo-

cated, accompanied by a number of the clergy, the factors, etc. She was astonished and distressed at the destitution, nakedness, and extreme misery, which met her eye in every direction, made inquiries into their condition, and ordered a general distribution of clothing to be made among the most destitute; but unfortunately she confined her inquiries to those who surrounded her, and made them the medium for distributing her bounty—the very parties who had been the main cause of this deplorable destitution, and whose interest it was to conceal the real state of the people, as it continues to be to this day.

At one place she stood upon an eminence, where she had about a hundred of those wretched dwellings in view ; at least she could see the smoke of them ascending from the horrid places in which they were situated. She turned to the parish minister in the utmost astonishment, and asked, " Is it possible that there are people living in yonder places ? "—" O yes, my lady," was the reply. " And can you tell me if they are in any way comfortable ? " " Quite comfortable, my lady." Now, sir, I can declare that at the very moment this reverend gentlemen uttered these words, he was fully aware of the horrors of their situation ; and, besides that, some of the outcasts were then begging in the neighbouring county of Caithness, many of them carrying certificates from this very gentleman attesting that they were objects of charity !

Her ladyship, however, was not quite satisfied with these answers. She caused a general warning to be issued, directing the people to meet her, at stated places as she proceeded, and wherever a body of them met her, she alighted from her carriage, and questioned them if they were comfortable, and how the factors were behaving to them ? [N.B. The factors were always present on these occasions.]

But they durst make little or no complaints. What they did say was in Gaelic, and of course, as in other cases, left to the minister's interpretation ; but their forlorn, haggard, and destitute appearance, sufficiently testified their real condition. I am quite certain, that had this great, and (I am willing to admit, when not misled) good woman remained on her estates, their situation would have been materially bettered, but as all her charity was left to be dispensed by those who were anxious to get rid of the people, root and branch, little benefit resulted from it, at least to those she meant to relieve. As I mentioned above, she ordered bed and body clothes to all who were in need of them, but, as usual, all was entrusted to the ministers and factors, and they managed this business with the same selfishness, injustice, and partiality, that had marked their conduct on former occasions. Many of the most needy got nothing, and others next to nothing. For an instance of the latter, several families, consisting of seven or eight, and in great distress, got only a yard and a half of coarse blue flannel, each family. Those, however, who were the favourites and toadies of the distributors, and their servants, got an ample supply of both bed and body clothes, but this was the exception; generally speaking, the poor people were nothing benefited by her ladyship's charitable intentions ; though they afforded hay-making seasons to those who had enough already, and also furnished matter for glowing accounts in the newspapers, of her ladyship's extraordinary munificence. To a decent highland woman, who had interested her ladyship, she ordered a present of a gown-piece, and the gentleman factor who was entrusted to procure it, some time after sent six yards of cotton stuff not worth 2s. in the whole. The woman laid it aside, intending to show it to her ladyship on her next visit, but her own death occurred in the meantime. Thus, in every way, were her ladyship's benevolent intentions frustrated or misapplied, and that ardent attachment to her family which had subsisted through so many generations, materially weakened, if not totally destroyed, by a mistaken policy towards her people, and an undue confidence in those to whose management she committed them, and who, in almost every instance, betrayed that confidence, and cruelly abused that delegated power. Hence, and hence only, the fearful misery and destitution in Sutherlandshire.

LETTER XIII.

In the year 1832, and soon after the events I have been describing, an order was issued by Mr. Loch, in the name of the Duke and Duchess of Sutherland, that all the small tenants, on both sides of the road from Bighouse to Melness (about thirty miles), where their cottages were thickly studded, must build new houses, with stone and mortar, according to a prescribed plan and specification. The poor people, finding their utter inability, in their present condition, to erect such houses (which, when finished, would cost £30 to £40 each), got up petitions to the proprietors, setting forth their distressed condition, and the impossibility of complying with the requisition at present. These petitions they supplicated and implored the ministers to sign, well knowing that otherwise they had little chance of being attended to ; but these gentlemen could be moved by no entreaties, and answered all their applications by a contemptuous refusal. The petitions had, therefore, to be forwarded to London without ecclesiastical sanction, and, of course, effected nothing. The answer returned was, that if they did not immediately begin to build, they would be removed next term.   The very word *removed* was enough; it brought back to their minds the recollection of former scenes, with all their attendant horrors.   To escape was impossible, they had nowhere to go; and in such circumstances they would have consented to do anything, even to the making "bricks without straw," like their oppressed prototypes of old.

In the midst of hopeless misery, then, and many of them without a shilling in their pockets, did they commence the task of building houses, such as I have mentioned, on the barren spots, and without any security of retaining them, even when they were built.   The edict was law; supplication or remonstrance was in vain; so to it they went, under circumstances such as perhaps building was never carried on before, in a country called Christian and civilized.   Plans and specifications were published, and estimates required by the factors, directing the whole proceedings, and, as usual, without consulting the feelings of the poor people, or inquiring into the means they had for carrying them into effect.   All was bustle and competition among masons and mechanics, of whom few resided in the county; most of them were strangers; and when they commenced work, the people were obliged to feed them, whether they had anything themselves to eat or not, and to pay them, even if they had to sell the last movable for that purpose.   Some of the masons, however, showed great lenity, and are still unpaid.   Previous to this, in the year 1829, I and my family had been forced away like others, being particularly obnoxious to those in authority for sometimes showing an inclination to oppose their tyranny; and therefore we had to be made examples of, to frighten the rest, but in 1833 I made a tour to the districts, when the building was going on, and shall endeavour to describe a small part of what met my eye on that occasion. In one district (and this was a fair specimen of all the rest), when the building was going on, I saw fourteen different squads of masons at work, the natives attending them. Old grey-headed men, worn down by previous hardship and present want, were to be seen carrying stones, and wheeling them and other materials on barrows, or carrying them on their backs to the buildings, and, with their tottering limbs and trembling hands straining to raise the stones, etc., to the walls. The young men also, after toiling all night at sea endeavouring to obtain subsistence, instead of rest, were obliged to yield their exhausted frames to the labours of the day. Even female labour could not be dispensed with; the strong as well as the weak, the delicate and sickly, and (shame to the nature of their oppressors !) even the pregnant, bare-footed, and scantily clothed and fed, were obliged to join in these rugged, unfeminine labours, carrying stones, clay, lime, wood, etc., on their backs or on barrows, their tracks often reddened with the blood from their hands and feet, and from hurts received by their awkwardness in handling the rude materials. In one instance I saw the husband quarrying stones, and the wife and children dragging them along in an old cart to the building. Such were the building scenes of that period. The poor people had often to give the last morsel of food they possessed to feed the masons, and subsist on shell-fish themselves when they could get them. The timber for their houses was furnished by the factors, and charged them about a third higher than it could be purchased at in any of the neighbouring sea-ports. I spent two melancholy days witnessing these scenes, which are now present to my mind, and which I can never forget. This went on for several years, in the course of which, many hundreds of houses were erected on inhospitable spots, unfit for human residence. It might be thought that the design of forcing the people to build such houses, was to provide for their comfort and accommodation; but there was another object, which I believe was the only true motive, and that was, to hide the misery that prevailed. There had been a great sensation created in the public mind, by the cruelties exercised in these districts; and it was thought that a number of neat white houses, ranged on each side of the road, would take the eyes of strangers and visitors, and give a practical contradiction to the rumours afloat; hence, the poor creatures were forced to resort to such means, and to endure such hardships and privations as I have described, to carry the scheme into effect. And after they had spent their all, and much more than their all, on the erection of these houses, and involved themselves in debt, for which they have been harassed and pursued ever since, they are still but whitened tombs; many of them now ten years in existence, and still without proper doors or windows, destitute of furniture, and of comfort; merely providing a lair for a heart-broken, squalid, and degenerated race.

LETTER XIV.

DURING the period in which the building was going on, I think in the year 1833, Lord Leveson Gower, the present Duke of Sutherland, visited the country, and remained a few weeks, during which he had an opportunity of witnessing the scenes I have described in my last; and such was the impression made on his mind, that he gave public orders that the people should not be forced to build according to the specific plan, but be allowed to erect such houses as suited themselves. These were glad tidings of mercy to the poor people, but they were soon turned to bitter disappointment ; for no sooner had his lordship left the country, than Mr. Loch or his underlings issued fresh orders for the building to go on as before.

Shortly after this, in July, 1833, his Grace created first Duke of Sutherland, who had been some time in bad health, breathed his last in Dunrobin Castle, and was interred with great pomp in the family burying-place in the cathedral of Dornoch.   The day of his funeral was ordered to be kept as a fast-day by all the tenantry, under penalty of the highest displeasure of those in authority, though it was just then herring-fishing season, when much depended on a day.   Still this was a minor hardship.   The next year a project was set on foot, by the same parties who formerly got up the expensive family ornaments presented to her Grace, to raise a monument to the Duke.   Exactly similiar measures were resorted to, to make the small tenantry subscribe, in the midst of all their distresses, and with similiar results.   All who could raise a shilling gave it, and those who could not, awaited in terror the consequences of their default.   No doubt, the Duke deserved the highest posthumous honours from a portion of his tenantry—those who had benefited by the large sums he and the Duchess had lavished for their accommodation ; but the poor small tenantry, what had been done for them ?   While the ministers, factors, and new tenantry, were rich and luxurious, basking in the sunshine of favour and prosperity, the miseries and oppressions of the natives remain unabated ; *they* were emphatically in the shade, and certainly had little for which to be grateful to those whose abuse of power had brought them to such a pass—who had drained their cup of every thing that could sweeten life, and left only

A mass of sordid lees behind !

Passing the next two years, I now proceed to describe the failure of the harvest in 1836, and the consequences to the Highlands generally, and to Sutherland in particular. In this year the crops all over Britain were deficient, having had bad weather for growing and ripening, and still worse for gathering in. But in the Highlands they were an entire failure, and on the untoward spots occupied by the Sutherland small tenants there was literally nothing—at least nothing fit for human subsistence ; and to add to the calamity, the weather had prevented them from securing the peats, their only fuel ; so that, to their exhausted state from their disproportionate exertions in building, cold and hunger were now to be superadded. The sufferings of the succeeding winter, endured by the poor Highlanders, truly beggar description. Even the herring-fishing had failed, and consequently their credit in Caithness, which depended on its success, was at an end. Any little provision they might be able to procure was of the most inferior and unwholesome description. It was no uncommon thing to see people searching among the snow for the frosted potatoes to eat, in order to preserve life. As the harvest had been disastrous, so the winter was uncommonly boisterous and severe, and consequently little could be obtained from the sea to mitigate the calamity. The distress rose to such a height as to cause a universal sensation all over the island, and a general cry for government interference to save the people from death by famine ; and the appeal, backed by the clergy of all denominations throughout the Highlands (with the exception of Sutherland), was not made in vain.

Dr. MacLeod of Glasgow was particularly zealous on this occasion. He took reports from all the parish ministers in the destitute districts, and went personally to London to represent the case to government and implore aid, and the case was even laid before both houses of parliament. In consequence of these applications and proceedings, money and provisions to a great amount were sent down, and the magistrates and ministers entrusted with the distribution of them : and in the ensuing summer, vessels were sent to take on board a number of those who were willing to emigrate to Australia. Besides this, private subscriptions were entered into, and money obtained to a very great amount. Public meetings were got up in all the principal cities and towns in Great Britain and Ireland, and large funds collected; so that effectual relief was afforded to every place that required it, with the single exception of that county which, of all others, was in the most deplorable state—the county of Sutherland! The reason of this I will explain presently; but first let me draw the reader's attention for a moment to the new circumstances in which the Highlands were placed. Failure in the crops in those northern and north-western parts of Scotland was a case of frequent and common occurrence; but famine, and solicitations for national aid and charitable relief, were something quite new. I will endeavour to account for the change. Previous to the "change of tenancy," as the cruel spoliation and expatriation of the native inhabitants was denominated, when a failure occurred in the grain and potato crops, they had recourse to their cattle. Selling a few additional head, or an extra score of sheep, enabled them to purchase at the sea-ports what grain was wanted. But now they had no cattle to sell ; and when the crops totally failed on their spots of barren ground, and when, at the same time, the fishing proved unprosperous, they were immediately reduced to a state of famine ; and hence the cry for relief, which, as I have mentioned, was so generously responded to. But, I would ask, who were the authors of all this mass of distress ? Surely, the proprietors, who, unmindful that

" property has its duties as well as its rights," brought about this state of things.   They, in common with other landed legislators, enacted the food taxes, causing a competition for land, and then encouraged strange adventurers to supersede the natives, and drive them out, in order that the whole of the Highlands should be turned into a manufactory, to make beef and mutton for the English market.   And when, by these means, they had reduced the natives to destitution and famine, they left it to the government and to charitable individuals to provide relief!   Language is scarcely adequate to characterize such conduct ; yet these are the great, the noble, and right honourable of the land !   However, with the exception of my unfortunate native county, relief was afforded, though not by those whose right it was to afford it. Large quantities of oatmeal, seed oats, and barley, potatoes, etc., were brought up and forwarded to the North and West Highlands, and distributed among all who were in need; but nothing of all this for the Sutherlanders.   Even Dr. Mac-Leod, in all the zeal of his charitable mission, passed from Stornoway to the Shetland Islands without vouchsafing a glance at Sutherland on his way.   The reason of all this I will now explain.   It was constantly asserted and reiterated in all places, that there was no occasion for government or other charitable aid to Sutherland, as the noble proprietors would themselves take in hand to afford their tenantry ample relief.   This story was circulated through the newspapers, and repeated by the clergy and factors at all public meetings, till the public was quite satisfied on the subject.   Meantime the wretched people were suffering the most unparalleled distress ; famine had brought their misery to a frightful climax, and disease and death had commenced their work ! In their agony they had recourse to the ministers, imploring them to represent their case to government, that they might partake of the relief afforded to other counties; but all in vain! I am aware that what I here assert is incredible, but not less true, that of the whole seventeen parish ministers, not one could be moved by the supplications and cries of the famishing wretches to take any steps for their relief! They answered all entreaties with a cold refusal, alleging that the proprietors would, in their own good time, send the necessary relief! but, so far as I could ever learn, they took no means to hasten that relief. They said in their sermons "that the Lord had a controversy with the land for the people's wickedness; and that in his providence, and even in his mercy, he had sent this scourge to bring them to repentance," etc. Some people (wicked people, of course) may think such language, in such circumstances, savoured more of blasphemy than of religious truth. Meantime, the newspapers were keeping up the public expectations of the munificent donations the proprietors were sending. One journal had it that £9,000 worth of provisions were on the way; others £8,000, and £7,000, etc. However, the other Highlanders had received relief at least two months before anything came to Sutherland. At last it did come; the amount of relief, and the manner of its appropriation shall be explained in my next.

LETTER XV.

IN my last I quoted an expression current among the clergy at the time of the famine "that God had a controversy with the people for their sins," but I contend—and I think my readers in general will agree with me—that the poor Sutherlanders were "more sinned against than sinning". To the aspersions cast upon them by Mr. Loch, in his book (written by an interested party, and evidently for a purpose), I beg the public to contrast the important work by General Stewart before mentioned, and draw their own conclusions. The truth is, that the Sutherlanders were examples of almost all the humble virtues—a simple and uncorrupted, rural, and pastoral population; even the unexampled protracted cruelty with which they were treated, never stirred them to take wild or lawless revenge. During a period of 200 years, there had been only three capital convictions, and very few crimes of any description; the few that did occur were chiefly against the excise laws. But those who coveted the lands, which in justice were their patrimony, like Queen Jezebel of old, got false witnesses to defame them (in order that a pretext might be afforded for expelling them from the possessions which had been defended with the blood of their forefathers). It was the factors, the capitalists, and the clergy, that had a controversy with the people, and not the Almighty, as they blasphemously asserted. The Sutherlanders had always been a religious, a devout, and a praying people, and now their oppressors, and not Divine Providence, had made them a *fasting people*. I proceed to give some account of that mockery of relief which was so ostentatiously paraded before the public in the newspapers, and at public meetings.

I have already observed that the relief afforded to the Highland districts generally, by the government, and by private charity, was not only effectual in meeting the exigency, but it was a *bona-fide* charity, and was forthcoming in time; while the pittance doled out to the Sutherlanders, was destitute of those characteristics. How the poor people passed the winter and spring under the circumstances already mentioned, I must leave to the reader's imagination; suffice it to say, that though worn to the bone by cold, hunger, and nakedness, the bulk of them still survived. The Highlanders are still proverbially tenacious of life. In the latter end of April, 1837, when news reached them that the long-promised relief, consisting of meal, barley, potatoes, and seed oats, had actually arrived, and was to be immediately distributed at Tongue and other stated places, the people at once flocked to these places, but were told that nothing would be given to anyone, till they produced a certificate from their parish minister that they were proper objects of charity. Here was a new obstacle. They had to return and implore those haughty priests for certificates, which were frequently withheld from mere caprice, or for some alleged offence or lack of homage in the applicant, who if not totally refused, had to be humbled in the dust, sickened by delay, and the boon only at last yielded to the intercession of some of the more humane of the shepherds. Those who were in the fishing trade were peremptorily refused. This is the way in which man, religious man, too ! can trifle with the distress of his famishing brother.

The places appointed for distribution were distant from the homes of many of the sufferers, so that by the time they had waited on the ministers for the necessary qualification, and travelled again to places of distribution and back again, with what they could obtain, on their backs, several days were consumed, and in many cases from 50 to 100 miles traversed. And what amount of relief did they receive after all ? From 7 to 28 ℔s. of meal, with seed oats and potatoes in the same proportion ; and this not for individuals, but for whole families ! In the fields, and about the dykes adjoining the places where these pittances were doled out, groups of famishing creatures might be lying in the mornings (many of them having travelled the whole day and night previous), waiting the leisure of the factors or their clerks, and no attention was paid to them till those gentlemen had breakfasted and dressed; by which time the day was far advanced.

Several subsequent distributions of meal took place; but in every new case, fresh certificates of continued destitution had to be procured from the ministers and elders of the respective parishes. This was the kind, and quantity, of relief afforded, and the mode of dispensing it; different indeed from what was represented in the glozing falsehoods so industriously palmed on public credulity.

In the month of September, her Grace being then on a visit in the country, the following proceedings took place, reported in the public papers of the day, which afforded a specimen of groundless assertions, clerical sycophancy, and fulsome adulation, for which it would be difficult to find a parallel :—

The Presbytery of Tongue, at their last meeting, agreed to present the following address to the Duchess of Sutherland. Her Grace being then at Tongue, the Presbytery waited on her: and the address being read by the Moderator, she made a suitable reply :—

"*May it please your Grace,*

"We, the Presbytery of Tongue, beg leave to approach your Grace with feelings of profound respect, and to express our joy at your safe arrival within our bounds.

"We have met here this day for the purpose of communicating to your Grace the deep sense which we entertain of your kindness during the past season to the people under our charge.

"When it pleased Providence by an unfavourable harvest to afflict the Highlands of Scotland with a scarcity of bread, and when the clergymen of other districts appealed to public charity on behalf of their parishioners, the confidence which we placed in your Grace's liberality led us to refrain from making a similar appeal.

"When we say that this confidence has been amply realised, we only express the feelings of our people; and participating strongly in these feelings, as we do, to withhold the expression of them from your Grace, would do injustice alike to ourselves and to them.

"In their name, therefore, as well as in our own, we beg to offer to your Grace our warmest gratitude. When other districts were left to the precarious supplies of a distant benevolence, your Grace took on yourself the charge of supporting your people ; by a constant supply of meal, you not only saved them from famine, but enabled them to live in comfort ; and by a seasonable provision of seed, you were the means, under God, of securing to them the blessing of the present abundant harvest.

"That Almighty God may bless your Grace,—that he may long spare you to be a blessing to your people,—and that He may finally give you the inheritance which is incorruptible, undefiled, and that fadeth not away, is the prayer of,

"May it please your Grace,
"THE MEMBERS OF THE PRESBYTERY OF TONGUE,
(Signed) "HUGH MACKENZIE, *Moderator*."

The evident tendency of this document was to mislead her Grace, and by deluding the public, to allay anxiety, stifle inquiry, and conceal the truth. However, her Grace made a "suitable reply," and great favour was shown to the adulators. About a year before, the very clergyman whose signature is appended to this address exchanged part of his glebe for the lands of Diansad and Inshverry ; but in consenting to the change, he made an express condition that the present occupiers, amounting to eight families, should be "removed," and accordingly they were driven out in a body ! To this gentleman, then, the honour is due of having consummated the Sutherland ejections ; and hence he was admirably fitted for signing the address. I must not omit to notice "the abundant harvest," said to succeed the famine. The family "allotments" only afforded the sowing of from a half firlot to two or three firlots of oats, and a like quantity of barley, which, at an average in good seasons, yielded about three times the quantity sown ; in bad years little or nothing ; and even in the most favourable cases, along with their patches of potatoes, could not maintain the people more than three months in the year. The crop succeeding the famine was anything but an abundant one to the poor people ; they had got the seed too late, and the season was not the most favourable for bringing it

to even ordinary perfection.   Hence, that "abundance,"
mentioned in the address was like all the rest of its groundless assumption.   But I have still to add to the crowning
iniquity—the provisions distributed in charity had to be
paid for! but this point—I must postpone till my next.

LETTER XVI.

It would require a closer acquaintance with the recent
history of Sutherlandshire than I am able to communicate,
and better abilities than mine to convey to the reader an
adequate idea of the mournful contrast between the former
comfortable and independent state of the people and that
presented in my last.   They were now, generally speaking,
become a race of paupers, trembling at the very looks of
their oppressors, objects of derision and mockery to the
basest underlings, and fed by the scanty hand of those who
had been the means of reducing them to their present state ;
To their capability of endurance must, in a great measure,
be ascribed their surviving, in any considerable numbers,
the manifold inflictions they had to encounter.   During the
spring and summer many of the young and robust of both
sexes left the country in quest of employment ; some to the
neighbouring county of Caithness, but most of them went
to the Lowlands, and even into England, to serve as cattle
drivers, labourers, and in other menial occupations.   No
drudgery was too low for their acceptance, nor any means
left untried, by which they could sustain life in the most
frugal manner, and anything earned above this was carefully
transmitted to their suffering relations at home.   When
harvest commenced they were rather better employed, and
then the object was to save a little to pay the rent at the

approaching term; but there was another use they had never thought of, to which their hard and scanty earnings had to be applied.

Not long after the termination of the Duchess' visit (during which the address given in my last was presented), I think just about two months after, the people were astonished at seeing placards posted up in all public places, warning them to prepare to pay their rents, and also the meal, potatoes, and seed oats and barley they had got during the spring and summer! This was done in the name of the Duchess, by the orders of Mr. Loch and his under-factors. Ground-officers were despatched in all directions to explain and enforce this edict, and to inform the small tenants that their rents would not be received till the accounts for the provisions were first settled. This was news indeed!—astonishing intelligence this—that the pitiful mite of relief, obtained with so much labour and ceremony, and doled out by pampered underlings with more than the usual insolence of charity, was after all to be paid for! After government aid and private charity, so effectually afforded to other Highland districts had been intercepted by ostentatious promises of ample relief from the bounty of her Grace; after the clergy had lauded the Almighty, and her Grace no less, for that *bounty;* the poor creatures were to be concussed into paying for it, and at a rate too, considerably above the current prices. I know this, to persons unacquainted with Highland tyranny, extortion and oppression, will appear incredible; but I am able to substantiate its truth by clouds of living witnesses.

The plan adopted deserves particular notice. The people were told, "their rents would not be received till the provisions were first paid for". By this time those who had procured a little money by labouring elsewere, were returning with their savings to enable their relatives to meet the rents, and this was thought a good time to get the "charity" paid up.   Accordingly when the people, as usual, waited upon the factor with the rent, they were told distinctly that the meal, etc., must be paid first, and that if any lenity was shown, it would be for the rent, but none for the provisions! The meaning of this scheme seems to be, that by securing payment for the provisions in the first instance, they would avoid the odium of pursuing for what was given as charity, knowing that they could at any time enforce payment of the rent, by the usual summary means to which they were in the habit of resorting.   Some laid down their money at once, and the price of all they had got was then deducted, and a receipt handed to them for the balance, in part of their rent. Others seeing this, remonstrated and insisted on paying their rents first, and the provisions afterwards, if they must be paid; but their pleading went for nothing, their money was taken in the same manner (no receipts in any case being given for the payment of the "charity,"), and they were driven contemptuously from the counting-table.

A few refused to pay, especially unless receipts were granted for the "charity," and returned home with their money, but most of them were induced by the terror of their families to carry it back and submit like the rest.   A smaller portion, however, still continued refractory, and alternate threats and wheedlings were used by the underlings to make these comply; so that gradually all were made to pay the last shilling it was possible for them to raise.   Some who had got certificates of destitution being unable, from age or illness, to undergo the fatigue of waiting on the factors for their portion, or of carrying it home, had to obtain the charitable assistance of some of their abler fellow sufferers for that purpose, but when there was any difficulty about the payment, the carriers were made accountable the same as if they had been the receivers! Hitherto, the money collected at the church doors, had been divided among the poor, but this year it was withheld; in one parish to my personal knowledge (and as far as my information goes the refusal was general), the parish minister telling them that they could not expect to get meal and money both, signifying that the deficient payments for the provisions had to be made up from the church collections. Whether this was the truth or not, it served for a pretext to deprive the poor of this slender resource; for, ever since—now four years—they have got nothing. This is one among many subjects of inquiry. Verily there is much need for light to be thrown on this corner of the land! A rev. gentleman from the west, whose failing it was to transgress the ten commandments, had, through some special favour, obtained a parish in Sutherlandshire, and thinking probably that charity should begin at home, had rather misapplied the poor's money which was left in his hand, for on his removal to another parish, there was none of it forthcoming. The elders of his new parish being aware of this, refused to entrust him with the treasureship, and had the collection-money kept in a locked box in the church, but when it amounted to some pounds, the box was broken up and the money was taken out. The minister had the key of the church.

Owing to the complete exhaustion of the poor people's means in the manner I have been describing, the succeeding year (1838) found them in circumstances little better than its predecessor. What any of them owed in Caithness and elsewhere, they had been unable to pay, and consequently their credit was at an end, and they were obliged to live

from hand to mouth; besides, this year was unproductive in
the fishing, as the years since have also been.

In the earlier part of this correspondence, I have treated
of the large sums said to have been laid out on improvements (roads, bridges, inns, churches, manses, and mansions
for the new tenants); but I have yet to mention a poll-tax
called road-money, amounting to 4s. on every male of 18
years and upwards, which was laid on about the year 1810,
most rigorously exacted, and continues to be levied on each
individual in the most summary way, by seizure of any kind
of moveables in or about the dwelling till the money is paid.
To some poor families this tax comes to £1 and upwards
every year, and be it observed that the capitalist possessing
50,000 acres, only pays in the same proportion, and his
shepherds are entirely exempt! Those of the small tenantry
or their families, who may have been absent for two or three
years, on their return are obliged to pay up their arrears of
this tax, the same as if they had been all the time at home;
and payment is enforced by seizure of the goods of any
house in which they may reside. The reader will perceive
that the laws of Sutherlandshire are different, and differently
administered, from what they are in other parts of the
country—in fact those in authority do just what they please,
whether legal or otherwise, none daring to question what
they do. Nothwithstanding this burdensome tax, the roads,
as far as the small tenants' interests are concerned, are
shamefully neglected, while every attention is paid to suit the
convenience and pleasure of the ruling parties and the new
tenantry, by bringing roads to their very doors.

LETTER XVII.

In my last letter I mentioned something about the with-holding and misappropriation of the money collected at church doors for the poor; but let it be understood that notwithstanding the iniquitous conduct of persons so acting, the loss to the poor was not very great. The Highlander abhors to be thought a pauper, and the sum afforded to each of the few who were obliged to accept of it, varied from 1s. 6d. to 5s. a year; the congregations being much diminished, as I had before occasion to observe. It is no wonder, then, that the poor, if at all able, flee from such a country and seek employment and relief in the various maritime towns in Scotland, where they arrive broken down and exhausted by previous hardship—meatless and money-less; and when unable to labour, or unsuccessful in obtain-ing work, they become a burden to a community who have no right to bear it, while those who have reduced them to that state escape scot-free. Any person acquainted gener-ally with the statistics of pauperism in Scotland will, I am sure, admit the correctness of these statements. The Highland landlords formerly counted their riches by the number of their vassals or tenants, and were anxious to retain them; hence the poem of Burns, addressed to the Highland lairds, and signed Beelzebub, by which the ever selfish policy of those gentlemen is celebrated in their endeavouring, by force, to restrain emigration to Canada. But since then the case is reversed. First the war, and then the food monopoly has made raising of cattle for the English markets, the more eligible speculation, against which the boasted feelings of clanship, as well as the claims of common humanity have entirely lost their force. Regard-ing the poll-tax or road money, it is also necessary to state, that in every case when it is not paid on the appointed day, expenses are arbitrarily added (though no legal progress has been entered) which the defaulter is obliged to submit to without means of redress. There are no tolls in the county; the roads, etc., being kept up by this poll-tax, paid by the small tenants for the exclusive benefit of those who have superseded them. In this way very large sums are screwed out of the people, even the poorest, and from the absentees, if they ever return to reside. So that if the population are not extirpated wholesale, a considerable portion of the sums laid out on improvements will ultimately return to the proprietors, from a source whence, of all others, they have no shadow of right to obtain it.

I have now arrived at an important event in my narrative; the death of an exalted personage to whom I have often had occasion to refer—the Duchess-Countess of Sutherland.

This lady who had, during a long life, maintained a high position in courtly and aristocratic society, and who was possessed of many great qualities, was called to her account on the 29th of January, 1839, in the 74th year of her age. Her death took place in London, and her body was conveyed to Sutherland by Aberdeen, and finally interred with great pomp in the family vault, beside the late Duke, her husband, in the Cathedral of Dornoch. The funeral was attended to Blackwell by many of the first nobility in England, and afterwards by her two grandsons, Lord Edward Howard, and the Honourable Francis Egerton, and by her friend and confidential servant, Mr. Loch, with their respective suites. The procession was met by Mr. Sellars, Mr. Young, and many of her under-factors and subordinate retainers, together with the whole body of the new occupiers, while the small tenantry brought up the rear of the solemn cavalcade. She was buried with the rites of the Church of

England. Mr. George Gunn, under-factor, was the only gentleman native of the county who took a prominent part in the management of the funeral, and who certainly did not obtain that honour by the exercise of extraordinary virtues towards his poor countrymen : the rest were all those who had taken an active part in the scenes of injustice and cruelty which I have been endeavouring to represent to the reader, in the previous part of my narrative. The trump of fame has been seldom made to sound a louder blast, than that which echoed through the island, with the virtues of the Duchess; every periodical, especially in Scotland, was for a time literally crammed with them, but in those extravagant encomiums few or none of her native tenantry could honestly join. That she had many great and good qualities none will attempt to deny, but at the same time, under the sanction or guise of her name and authority, were continually perpetrated deeds of the most atrocious character, and her people's wrongs still remained unredressed. Her severity was felt, perhaps, far beyond her own intentions ; while her benevolence was intercepted by the instruments she employed, and who so unworthily enjoyed her favour and confidence. Her favours were showered on aliens and strangers; while few, indeed, were the drops which came to the relief of those from whom she sprung, and whose co-eval, though subordinate right to their native soil, had been recognised for centuries.

The same course of draining the small tenants, under one pretext or another, continued for some time after her Grace's decease; but exactions must terminate, when the means of meeting them are exhausted. You cannot starve a hen and make her lay eggs at the same time. The factors, having taken all, had to make a virtue of necessity, and advise the Duke to an act of high-sounding generosity—to remit all arrears due by the small tenantry. Due proclamation was made of his Grace's benevolent intentions, with an express condition annexed, that no future arrears would be allowed, and that all future defaulters should be instantly removed, and their holdings (not let to tenants, but) handed over to their next neighbour, and failing him, to the next again, and so on. This edict was proclaimed under the authority of his Grace and the factors, in the year 1840, about twelve months after the Duchess's decease, and continues the law of the estate as regards the unfortunate natives, or small tenantry as they are generally called.

It will be perceived that I have now brought my narrative to an end. I may, however, with your permission, trouble you with a few remarks in your next publication, by way of conclusion.

LETTER XVIII.

In concluding my narrative, allow me to express—or rather to declare my inability to express—the deep sense I enter-tain of your kindness in permitting me to occupy so large a space of your columns, in an attempt to pourtray the wrongs of my countrymen. I trust these feelings will be participated by those whose cause you have thus enabled me to bring before the public, as well as by all benevolent and enlight-ened minds, who abhor oppression, and sympathize with its victims. I am conscious that my attempt has been a feeble one. In many cases my powers of language fell short, and in others I abstained from going to the full extent, when I was not quite prepared with proof, or when the deeds of our oppressors were so horrible in their nature and consequence as to exceed belief.

Though nowhere in the North Highlands have such atrocities been practised in the wholesale way they have been in Sutherland, yet the same causes are producing like effects, more or less generally in most, if not all, the surrounding counties. Sutherland has served as a model for successfully "clearing" the land of its aboriginal inhabitants, driving them to the sea-shore, or into the sea,—to spots of barren moors—to the wilds of Canada—and to Australia ; or if unable to go so far, to spread themselves over Lowlands, in quest of menial employment among strangers, to whom their language seems barbarous, who are already overstocked with native labourers, besides those continually pouring in from Ireland. No wonder the Highland lairds combine to resist a government inquiry, which would lead to an exposure of their dark and daring deeds, and render a system of efficient poor laws (not sham, like those now existing) inevitable. Were all the paupers they have created, by "removing" the natives and substituting strangers and cattle in their places, enabled to claim that support from the soil they are justly entitled to, what would become of their estates ?

Hence their alarm and anxiety to stifle all inquiry but that conducted by themselves, their favourites and retainers, and their ever-subservient auxiliaries, the parochial clergy. Will these parties expose themselves by tracing the true causes of Highland destitution ? Oh, no ! What they cannot ascribe to Providence, they will lay to the charge of the "indolent, improvident, and intractable character," they endeavour to cover their own foul deeds by ascribing to their too passive victims. They say "the Highlanders would pay no rent ". A falsehood on the very face of it. Were not the tenants' principal effects in cattle, the article of all others most convenient of arrest ? "The Highlanders were unteachable, enemies to innovation or improvement, and incorrigibly opposed to the will of their superiors." Where are the proofs ? What methods were taken to instruct them in improved husbandry, or any other improvements? None! They were driven out of the land of their fathers, causelessly, cruelly, and recklessly. Let their enemies say what have been their crimes of revenge under the most inhumane provocation ? Where are the records in our courts of law, or in the statistics of crime, of the fell deeds laid to the charge of the expatriated Highlander ? They are nowhere to be found, except in the groundless accusations of the oppressors, who calculating on their simplicity, their patient, moral, and religious character, which even the base conduct of their clergy could not pervert, drove them unresisting, like sheep to the slaughter, or like mute fishes, unable to scream, on whom any violence could be practised with impunity. It was thought an illiterate people, speaking a lauguage almost unknown to the public press, could not make their wrongs heard as they ought to be, through the length and breadth of the land. To give their wrongs a tongue—to implore inquiry by official, disinterested parties into the cause of mal-practices which have been so long going on, so as if possible to procure some remedy in future— has been my only motive for availing myself of your kindness to throw a gleam of light on Highland misery, its causes and its consequences. And I cannot too earnestly implore all those in any authority, who take an interest in the cause of humanity, to resist that partial and close-conducted, sham inquiry to which interested parties would have recourse to screen themselves from public odium, and save their pockets. Some of these parties are great, wealthy, and influential. Several of them have talent, education, and other facilities for perverting what they cannot altogether suppress, making "the worst appear the better reason," and white-washing their blackest deeds—therefore, I say, beware! They want now a government grant, forsooth, to take away the redundant population! There is no redundant population but black cattle and sheep, and their owners, which the lairds have themselves introduced; and do they want a grant to rid of these? Verily, no! Their misdeeds are only equalled by their shameless impudence to propose such a thing. First, to ruin the people and make them paupers, and when their wrongs and miseries have made the very stones cry out, seek to get rid of them at the public expense! Insolent proposition! "Contumelious their humanity." No doubt there have been some new churches built, but where are the congregations? Some schools erected, but how can the children of parents steeped in poverty profit by them? The clergy say they dispense the bread of life, but if they do so, do they give it freely—do they not *sell it* for as much as they can get, and do the dirty work of the proprietors, instead of the behests of Him they pretend to serve? Did this precious article grow on any lands which the proprietors could turn into sheep walks, I verily believe they would do so, and the clergy would sanction the deed! They and the proprietors think the natives have no right to any of God's mercies, but what they dole out in a stinted and miserable charity. Mr. Dempster of Skibo, the orator and apologist of the Highland lairds, says he "keeps two *permanent* soup-kitchens on his estate"; if this were true (as I have reason to believe it is not), what is to be inferred but that the wholesome ruin inflicted on the natives has rendered such a degrading expedient necessary. Their forefathers, a stalwart and athletic race, needed no soup-kitchens, nor would their progeny, if they had not been inhumanely and unjustly treated. Mr. Loch says in his work, that the Sutherlanders were "in a state of nature". Well; he and his coadjutors have done what they could to put them in an unnatural state—a state from which it would take an age to reclaim them. I admit there was great need of improvement in Sutherland fifty years ago, as there was at that time in the Lothians and elsewhere; but where, except in the Highlands, do we find general expulsion and degradation of the inhabitants resorted to by way of improvement? But Mr. Loch has improved—if not in virtue, at least in station—and become a great man and a legislator, from very small beginnings; he and his coadjutors have waxed fat on the miseries of their fellow-creatures, and on the animals they have substituted for human beings. Well, I would not incur their responsibility for all their grandeur and emoluments. Mr. Dempster has improved, and his factor from being a kitchen boy, has become a very thriving gentleman. These are the kind of improvements which have taken place, and all would go merrily if they could get entirely rid of the small tenants, "the redundant population," by a grant of public money. A redundant population in an extensively exporting country! This is *Irish* political economy. The same cause (the food taxes) is in operation in that unhappy country, and producing similar results; but the Irish do not always bear it so tamely; a little Lynch law, a few-extra judicial executions is now and then administered, by way of example. This, however, is a wrong mode of proceeding, and one which I trust my countrymen will never imitate : better suffer than commit a crime. No system of poor law in the Highlands would be of any avail, but one that would confer SETTLEMENT ON EVERY PERSON BORN IN THE PARISH. The lairds will evade every other, and to save their pockets would be quite unscrupulous as to the means. They could easily resort again to their burning and hunting, but a settlement on the English plan would oblige them either to support the paupers they have made, or send them away at their own expense. This would be bare justice, and in my humble opinion nothing short of it would be of any avail. Comparatively few of the sufferers would now claim the benefit of such settlements; the greater part of them have already emigrated, and located elsewhere, and would not fancy to come back as paupers whatever their right might be. But there are still too many groaning and pining away in helpless and hopeless destitution in Sutherland, and in the surrounding counties, and I have reason to know that the West Highlands are much in the same situation. There is much need, then, for official inquiry, to prevent this mass of human misery from accumulating, as well as to afford some hope of relief to present sufferers. I have now made an end for the present; but should any contradiction appear, or any new event of importance to my countrymen occur, I shall claim your kind indulgence to resume the pen.

LETTER XIX.

I am glad to find that some of my countrymen are coming forward with communications to your paper confirming my statements, and expressing that gratitude we ought all deeply to feel for the opportunity you have afforded of bringing our case before the public, by so humble an instrument as myself.

Nothing, I am convinced, but fear of further persecution, prevents many more from writing such letters, and hence you need not wonder if some of those you receive are anonymous. They express a wish, which from various sources of information, I am inclined to think general, that my narrative should appear, as it now will, in the form of a pamphlet, and that my own particular case should form an appendage to it. I had no intention originally of bringing my particular case and family sufferings before the public, but called on, as I am, it appears a duty to the public, as well as myself, to give a brief account of it, lest withholding it might lead to suspicion as to my motives and character.

I served an apprenticeship in the mason trade to my father, and on coming to man's estate I married my present wife, the partner of my fortunes, most of which have been adverse, and she, the weaker vessel, has largely partaken of my misfortunes in a life of suffering and a ruined constitution. Our marriage took place in 1818. My wife was the daughter of Charles Gordon, a man well known and highly esteemed in the parish of Farr, and indeed throughout the county, for his religious and moral character.

For some years I followed the practice of going south during the summer months for the purpose of improving in my trade and obtaining better wages, and returning in the winter to enjoy the society of my family and friends ; and also, to my grief, to witness the scenes of devastation that were going on, to which, in the year 1820, my worthy father-in-law fell a victim. He breathed his last amid the scenes I have described, leaving six orphans in a state of entire destitution to be provided for ; for he had lost his all, in common with the other ejected inhabitants of the county.

This helpless family now fell to my care, and, in order to discharge my duty to them more effectually, I wished to give up my summer excursions, and settle and pursue my business at home.

I, therefore, returned from Edinburgh in the year 1822, and soon began to find employment, undertaking mason work by estimate, etc., and had I possessed a less independent mind and a more crouching disposition, I might perhaps have remained. But stung with the oppression and injustice prevailing around me, and seeing the contrast my country exhibited to the state of the Lowlands, I could not always hold my peace ; hence I soon became a marked man, and my words and actions were carefully watched for an opportunity to make an example of me. After I had baffled many attempts, knowing how they were set for me, my powerful enemies at last succeeded in effecting my ruin after seven years' labour in the pious work ! If any chose to say I owed them money, they had no more to do than summon me to the court, in which the factor was judge, and a decreet, right or wrong, was sure to issue. Did any owe me money, it was quite optional whether they paid me or not, they well knew I could obtain no legal redress.

In the year 1827, I was summoned for £5 8s., which I had previously paid [in this case the factor was both pursuer and judge !]. I defended, and produced receipts and other vouchers of payment having been made; all went for nothing! The factor, pursuer and judge, commenced the following dialogue :—

Judge—Well, Donald, do you owe this money ?

Donald—I would like to see the pursuer before I would enter into any defences.

Judge—I'll pursue you.

Donald—I thought you were my judge, sir.

Judge—I'll both pursue and judge you—did you not promise me on a former occasion that you would pay this debt ?

Donald—No, Sir.

Judge—John MacKay (constable), seize the defender.

I was accordingly collared like a criminal, and kept a prisoner in an adjoining room for some hours, and afterwards placed again at the bar, when the conversation continued.

Judge—Well, Donald, what have you got to say now, will you pay the money?

Donald—Just the same, sir, as before you imprisoned me; I deny the debt.

Judge—Well, Donald, you are one of the damn'dest rascals in existence, but if you have the sum pursued for betweer heaven and hell, I'll make you pay it, *whatever receipts you may hold*, and I'll get you removed from the estate.

Donald—Mind, sir, you are in a magisterial capacity.

Judge—I'll let you know that—(with another volley of execrations).

Donald—Sir, your conduct disqualifies you for your office, and under the protection of the law of the land, and in presence of this court, I put you to defiance.

I was then ordered from the bar, and the case continued undecided. Steps were, however, immediately taken to put the latter threat—my removal—my banishment!—into execution.

Determined to leave no means untried to obtain deliverance, I prepared an humble memorial in my own name, and that of the helpless orphans, whose protector I was, and had it transmitted to the Marquis and Marchioness of Stafford, praying for an investigation. In consequence of this, on the very term day, on which I had been ordered to remove, I received a verbal message from one of the under-factors, that it was the noble proprietor's pleasure that I should retain possession, repair my houses and provide my fuel as usual, until Mr. Loch should come to Sutherlandshire, and then my case would be investigated. On this announcement becoming known to my opponent, he became alarmed, and the parish minister no less so, that the man he feasted with was in danger of being disgraced ; every iron was therefore put in the fire, to defeat and ruin Donald for his presumption in disputing the will of a factor, and to make him an example to deter others from a similar rebellion.

The result proved how weak a just cause must prove in Sutherland, or anywhere, against cruel despotic factors and graceless ministers ; my case was judged and decided before Mr. Loch left London ! I, however, got Jeddart justice, for on that gentleman's arrival, I was brought before him for examination, though, I had good reason to know, my sentence had been pronounced in London six weeks before, and everything he said confirmed what I had been told. I produced the receipts and other documents, and evidence, which proved fully the statements in my memorial, and vindicated my character apparently to his satisfaction. He dismissed me courteously, and in a soothing tone of voice bade me go home and make myself easy, and before he left the country he would let me know the result. I carried home the good news to my wife, but her fears, her dreams, and forebodings were not so easily got over, and the event proved that her apprehensions were too well founded, for, on the 20th October, 1830, about a month after the investigation by Mr. Loch, the concluding scene took place.

On that day a messenger with a party of eight men following entered my dwelling (I being away about forty miles off at work), about three o'clock just as the family were rising from dinner ; my wife was seized with a fearful panic at seeing the fulfilment of all her worst forebodings about to take place. The party allowed no time for parley, but, having put out the family with violence, proceeded to fling out the furniture, bedding, and other effects in quick time, and after extinguishing the fire, proceeded to nail up the doors and windows in the face of the helpless woman, with a sucking infant at her breast, and three other children, the eldest under eight years of age, at her side.   But how shall I describe the horrors of that scene ?   Wind, rain and sleet were ushering in a night of extraordinary darkness and violence, even in that inclement region.   My wife and children, after remaining motionless a while in mute astonishment at the ruin which had so suddenly overtaken them, were compelled to seek refuge for the night under some neighbour's roof, but they found every door shut against them !   Messengers had been despatched warning all the surrounding inhabitants, at the peril of similar treatment, against affording shelter, or assistance, to wife, child, or animal belonging to Donald MacLeod.   The poor people, well aware of the rigour with which such edicts were carried into execution, durst not afford my distressed family any assistance in such a night as even an "enemy's dog" might have expected shelter. After spending most part of the night in fruitless attempts to obtain the shelter of a roof or hovel, my wife at last returned to collect some of her scattered furniture, and to erect with her own hands a temporary shelter against the walls of her late comfortable residence, but even this attempt proved in vain; the wind dispersed her materials as fast as she could collect them, and she was obliged to bide the pelting of the pitiless storm with no covering but the frowning heavens, and no sound in her ears but the storm, and the cries of her famishing children.   Death seemed to be staring them in the face, for by remaining where they were till morning, it was next to impossible that even the strongest of them could survive, and to travel any distance amid the wind, rain, and darkness, in that rugged district, seemed to afford no prospect but that of death by falling over some of the cliffs or precipices with which they were surrounded, or even into the sea, as many others had done before.

LETTER XX.

BEFORE proceeding to detail the occurrences of that memorable night in which my wife and children were driven from their dwelling, it seems necessary to guard against any misconception that might arise from my rather incredible statement, that the factor (whose name I omit for obvious reasons) was both pursuer and judge.

The pretended debt had been paid, for which I hold a receipt, but the person represented it as still due, and the factor advanced the amount, issued the summons, etc., and proceeded in court in the manner I have described in my last. But to proceed with my narrative.

The only means left my wife seemed to be the choice of perishing with her children where she was, or of making some perilous attempts to reach distant human habitations where she might hope for shelter. Being a woman of some resolution, she determined on the latter course. Buckling up her children, including the one she had hitherto held at her breast, in the best manner she could, she left them in charge of the eldest (now a soldier in the 78th regiment), giving them such victuals as she could collect, and prepared to take the road for Caithness, fifteen miles off, in such a night and by such a road as might have appalled a stout heart of the other sex ! And for a long while she had the cries of her children, whom she had slender hopes of seeing again alive, sounding in her ears. This was too much ! No wonder she has not been the same person since. She had not proceeded many miles when she met with a good Samaritan, and acquaintance, of the name of Donald MacDonald, who, disregarding the danger he incurred, opened his door to her, refreshed and consoled her, and (still under the cover of night), accompanied her to the dwelling of William Innes, Esq., of Sandside, Caithness, and through his influence, that gentlemen took her under his protection, and gave her permission to occupy an empty house of his at Armidale (a sheep farm he held of the Sutherland family), only a few miles from the dwelling she had been turned out of the day before. On arriving there she was obliged to take some rest for her exhausted frame, notwithstanding the horrible suspense she was in as to the fate of her children.

At this time I was working in Wick, and on that night had laboured under such great uneasiness and apprehension of something wrong at home that I could get no rest, and at last determined to set out and see how it fared with my family, and late in the evening I overtook my wife and her benevolent conductor proceeding from Sandside. After a brief recital of the events of the previous night, she implored me to leave her and seek the children, of whose fate she was ignorant. At that moment I was in a fit mood for a deed that would have served as a future warning to Highland tyrants, but the situation of my imploring wife, who suspected my intention, and the hope of saving my children, stayed my hand, and delayed the execution of justice on the miscreants, till they shall have appeared at a higher tribunal.

I made the best of my way to the place near our dwelling where the children were left, and to my agreeable surprise, found them alive; the eldest boy, in pursuance of his mother's instructions, had made great exertions, and succeeded in obtaining for them temporary shelter. He took the infant on his back, and the other two took hold of him by the kilt, and in this way they travelled in darkness, through rough and smooth, bog and mire, till they arrived at a grand-aunt's house, when, finding the door open, they bolted in, and the boy advancing to his astonished aunt, laid his infant burden in her lap, without saying a word, and proceeding to unbuckle the other two, he placed them before the fire without waiting for invitation. The goodman here rose, and said he must leave the house and seek a lodging for himself, as he could not think of turning the children out, and yet dreaded the ruin threatend to any that would harbour or shelter them, and he had no doubt his house would be watched to see if he should transgress against the order. His wife, a pious woman, upbraided him with cowardice, and declared that if a legion of devils were watching her, she would not put out the children or leave the house either. So they got leave to remain till I found them next day, but the man impelled by his fears, did go and obtain a lodging two miles off. I now brought the children to their mother, and set about collecting my little furniture and other effects, which had been damaged by exposure to the weather, and some of it lost or destroyed. I brought what I thought worth the trouble, to Armidale, and having thus secured them and seen the family under shelter, I began to cast about to see how they were to live, and here I found troubles and difficulties besetting us on every side.

I had no fear of being able by my work to maintain the family in common necessaries, if we could get them for money, but one important necessary, fuel, we could scarcely at all obtain, as nobody would venture to sell or give us peats (the only fuel used), for fear of the factors; but at last it was contrived that they would allow us to take them by stealth, and under cover of night !

My employment obliging me to be often from home, this laborious task fell to the lot of my poor wife. The winter came on with more than usual severity, and often amidst blinding, suffocating drifts, and tempests unknown in the lowlands, had this poor, tenderly brought-up woman to toil through snow, wind, and rain, for miles, with a burden of peats on her back! Instances, however, were not few of the kind assistance of neighbours endeavouring by various ways to mitigate her hard lot, though, of course, all by stealth, lest they should incur the vengeance of the factors.

During the winter and following spring, every means was used to induce Mr. Innes to withdraw his protection and turn us out of the house; so that I at last determined to take steps for removing myself and family for ever from those scenes of persecution and misery. With this view, in the latter end of spring, I went to Edinburgh, and found employment, intending when I had saved as much as would cover the expenses, to bring the family away. As soon as it was known that I was away, our enemies recommenced their work. Mr.————, a gentleman, who fattened on the spoils of the poor in Sutherland, and who is now pursuing the same course on the estates of Sir John Sinclair in Caithness; this manager and factor bounced into my house one day quite unexpectedly, and began abusing my wife, and threatened her if she did not instantly remove, he would take steps that would astonish her, the nature of which she would not know till they fell upon her, adding that he knew Donald MacLeod was now in Edinburgh, and could not assist her in making resistance. The poor woman, knowing she had no mercy to expect, and fearing even for her life, removed with her family and little effects to my mother's house which stood near the parish church, and was received kindly by her. There she hoped to find shelter and repose for a short time, till I should come and take her and the family away, and this being the week of the sacrament, she was anxious to partake of that ordinance, in the house where her forefathers had worshipped, before she bade it farewell for ever. But on the Thursday previous to that solemn occasion, the factor again terrified her by his appearance, and alarmed my mother to such an extent that my poor family had again to turn out in the night, and had they not a more powerful friend, they would have been forced to spend that night in the open air. Next day she bade adieu to her native country and friends, leaving the sacrament to be received by her oppressors, from the hands of one no better than themselves, and, after two days of incredible toil, she arrived with the family at Thurso, a distance of nearly forty miles !

These protracted sufferings and alarms have made fatal inroads on the health of this once strong and healthy woman—one of the best of wives—so that instead of the cheerful and active helpmate she formerly was, she is now, except at short intervals, a burden to herself, with little or no hope of recovery. She has been under medical treatment for years, and has used a great quantity of medicine with little effect ; the injuries she received in body and mind, were too deep for even her good spirits and excellent constitution to overcome, and she remains a living monument of Highland oppression.

LETTER XXI.

I beg leave, by way of conclusion, to take a retrospective glance at some of the occurrences that preceded the violent expulsion of my family, as described in my two last letters, and our final retirement from the country of our nativity.

For reasons before stated, nothing could have given more satisfaction to the factors, clergy, and all the Jacks-in-office under them, than a final riddance of that troublesome man, Donald MacLeod; and hence their extreme eagerness to make an example of him, to deter others from calling their proceedings in question.   I mentioned in letter XIX that on being unjustly and illegally imprisoned, and decerned to pay money I did not owe, I prepared and forwarded a memorial to the noble proprietors (the then Marquis and Marchioness of Stafford), setting forth the hardships of my case, and praying for investigation, alleging that I would answer the accusation of my enemies, by undeniable testimonials of honest and peaceful character.   This memorial was returned with the deliverance that Mr. Loch, on his next visit to Sutherland, would examine into my case and decide.   I then set about procuring my proposed certificate preparatory to the investigation, but here I found myself baffled and disappointed in a quarter from which I had no reason to expect such treatment.   I waited on my parish minister, the Rev. Mr. Mackenzie, requesting him to give me a certificate, and then, after him, I could obtain the signatures of the elders and as many of the other parishoners as might be necessary.   He made no objection at the time, but alleging that he was then engaged, said I could send my wife for it.   I left directions with her accordingly, and returned to my work.   The same night the factor (my pretended creditor and judge) *had the minister and his family to spend the evening with him*, and the consequence was that in the morning a messenger was dispatched from his reverence to my wife, to say, that she need not take the trouble of calling for the certificate, as he had changed his mind!   Some days after, I returned and waited on the Rev. gentleman to inquire the cause of this change.   I had great difficulty in obtaining an audience, and when at last I did, it was little to my satisfaction.   His manner was contemptuous and forbidding ; at last he told me that he could not give me a certificate as I was at variance with the factor; that my conduct was unscriptural, as I obeyed not those set in authority over me, etc. I excused and defended myself as well as I could, but all went for nothing, and at last he ordered me to be off, and shut the door in my face. This took place in June, 1830, and Mr. Loch was not expected till the September following, during which interval I had several rencounters with the minister. Many of his elders and parishioners pleaded and remonstrated with him on my behalf, well knowing that little attention would be paid in high quarters to my complaints, however just, without his sanction ; and considerable excitement prevailed in the parish about this dispute, but the minister remained im-moveable. Meantime the parish schoolmaster mentioned in confidence to one of the elders (who was a relation of my wife, and communicated it to us) that my case was already decided by Mr. Loch, though a sham trial would take place; that he had been told this, and he had it from good authority, and that the best thing I could do was to leave the place entirely. I could not believe this, but the result proved the truth of it. Matters continued in the same way till Mr. Loch's arrival, when I ventured to repeat my request to the minister, but found him still more determined, and I was dismissed with more than usual contempt. I then got a certificate prepared myself, and readily obtained the signatures of the elders and neighbouring parishioners to the number of several hundreds, which I presented to Mr. Loch, along with the before-mentioned memorial, when the following dialogue took place between that gentleman and me in presence of the factors, etc.

Mr. Loch.—Well, Mr. MacLeod, why don't you pay this £5 8s. you were summoned for ?

Donald.—Just, sir, because I don't consider myself entitled to pay it. I hold legal receipts to show that I paid it two years ago ; besides, that is a case to be legally decided before a competent court, and has no connection with my memorial.

Mr. L.—Will you pay it altogether or by instalments, if you are allowed to remain on the estate ?

D.—Let the case be withdrawn from the civil court or decided by the civil magistrate, before I answer that question.

Mr. L.—Well, can you produce the certificate of character mentioned in this memorial ?

I handed over to him the certificate mentioned above, with three or four sheets full of names attached to it. He looked at it for some time (perhaps surprised at the number of signatures) and then said,—

Mr. L.—I cannot see the minister's name here, how is this ?

D.—I applied to the minister and he would not sign it.

Mr. L.—Why ?

D.—He stated as his reason that I was at variance with the factors.

One of the Factors.—That is a falsehood.

Mr. L.—I will wait upon Mr. MacKenzie on the subject.

D.—Will you allow me, sir, to meet you and Mr. MacKenzie face to face, when he is asked to give his reasons ?

Mr. L.—Why will you not believe what he says ?

D.—I have got too much reason to doubt it; but if he attempts to deny what I have stated, I hope you will allow him to be examined on oath ?

Mr. L.—By no means, we must surely believe the minister.

After asking me some further questions which had nothing to do with the matter in hand, he dismissed me in seeming good humour.

I pressed to know his decision in my case, but he said, "you will get to know it before I leave the country; make yourself easy, I will write to your parish minister in a few days". The result was the cruel expulsion of my family and the spoliation of my goods, as detailed in my two last letters.

Mr. Loch, in his judgment on my case, alleged as his principal reason for punishing me that Mr. MacKenzie denied my assertions in regard to himself, and represented me as a turbulent character.

During our temporary residence at Armidale, I took an opportunity of again waiting on the rev. gentleman when he was catechising in a neighbouring fishing village with several of his elders in company, and asked to speak with him in their presence. He attempted to meet me outside the door, but I pushed in where the elders were sitting at breakfast; saying, " No sir, I wish what passes between you and me to be before witnesses. I want a certificate of my moral charac- ter, or an explanation from you before your elders why it is withheld." Here my worthy friend Donald MacDonald (the preserver of my wife's life on the memorable night of her expulsion) interfered and expostulated with his reverence, who driven into a corner, found no excuse for refusal, except that he had not writing materials convenient. I directly met this objection by producing the articles required, yet, strange to say, he found means to shuffle the business over by a solemn promise, in presence of his elders, to do it on a certain mentioned day. I waited on him that day, and after long delay was admitted into his parlour and accosted with, " Well, MacLeod, I am not intending to give you a certi- ficate." " Why so, sir?" " Because you have told false- hoods of me to Mr. Loch, and I cannot certify for a man that I know to be a liar," adding " Donald, I would favour you on your father's account, and much more on your father-in-law's account, but after what you have said of me, I cannot." I repelled the charge of being a liar, and said, " I do believe that if my father and father-in-law, whom you have mentioned with so much respect, stood at the gate of Heaven seeking admittance, and nothing to prevent them but a false accusation on the part of some of the factors, you would join in refusing their entrance, to all eternity". He rose up and said, "you are a Satan and not fit for human society". I retired for that time ; but ultimately forced him, by incessant applications, to write and sign the following :—

> " This certifies that the bearer, DONALD MACLEOD, is a native of this parish, a married man, free from church censure ; therefore he, his wife and family may be *admitted as Gospel hearers* wherever Providence may order their lot.
>
> Given at Farr Manse.   (Signed)

Previous to granting this certificate, the minister proposed to bind me up not to use it to the prejudice of the Marquis of Stafford, or any of his factors. This point, however, he did not carry, for when he submitted it to the session he was overruled by their votes.

This concludes the narrative of what I have myself suffered at the hands of the petty tyrants whom I had enraged by denouncing their barbarous treatment of my countrymen, and whose infamous deeds I have had the satisfaction of exposing to public reprobation. I shall not resume the pen on this subject unless I see that what I have written requires to be followed up to prevent a continuation of such atrocities as I have already recorded.

RIOTS IN DURNESS.

LETTER XXII.

When concluding that series of letters, descriptive of the woes of Sutherlandshire, which I now republish in the form of a pamphlet, I was not expecting so soon to find occasion to add important new matter to the sad detail. Another portion of my native county has fallen under the oppressor, and got into the fangs of law, which being administered by those interested, little mercy can be expected by the wretched defaulters.

All those conversant with the public papers will have seen an article, copied from the *Inverness Courier*, entitled, "Riot in Durness, Sutherlandshire," in which as usual a partial and one-sided account of the affair is given, and the whole blame laid on the unfortunate inhabitants. The violation of law, committed by the poor people, driven to desperation, and for which they will no doubt have to pay dear, is exaggerated, while their inhuman oppression and provocation are carefully left out of sight. The following facts of the case are a combination of my own knowledge, and that of trustworthy correspondents who were eye-witnesses of this unfortunate occurrence, which will yet be productive of much misery to the victims—perhaps end in causing their blood to be shed !

Mr. Anderson, the tacksman of Keenabin, and other farms under Lord Reay, which were the scene of the riot, was one of the earliest of that unhallowed crew of new tenants, or middle-men, who came in over the heads of the native farmers. He, with several others I could name, some of whom have come to an unhappy end, counting the natives as their slaves and prey, disposed without scruple of them and all that they had, just as it suited their own interest or convenience, reckless of the wrongs and misery they inflicted on these simple, unresisting people. They were removed from their comfortable houses and farms in the interior, to spots on the sea shore, to make room for the new comers with their flocks and herds, and to get their living, and pay exorbitant rents, by cultivating kelp, and deep-sea fishing. In these pursuits their persevering courage and industry enabled them to surmount appalling difficulties, though with much suffering and waste of health and life. The tacksman set up for a fish curer and *rented the sea to them* at his own pleasure, furnishing boats and implements at an exorbitant price, *while he took their fish at his own price*, and thus got them drowned in debt and consequent bondage, from which, by failures both in the kelp and fishing trades, they have never been able to relieve themselves. Seeing this, and thinking he could, after taking their all for thirty years, put their little holdings, improved by their exertions, to a more profitable use, this gentlemen *humanely* resolved to extirpate them, root and branch, after he had sucked their blood and peeled their flesh, till nothing more could be got from them, and regardless of the misery to which he doomed them, how they might fare, or which way they were to turn to procure a subsistence. To emigrate they were unable, and to repair to the manufacturing towns in quest of employment, when such multitudes are in destitution already, would afford no hope of relief. Where, then, were they to find refuge? To this question, so often urged by the poor outcasts in Sutherlandshire, the general answer of their tyrants was, "let them go to hell, but they must leave our boundaries".

Human patience and endurance have limits, and is it to be wondered at that poor creatures driven to such extremities should be tempted to turn on their oppressors, and violate the letter of the law? Hence it is true that the poor people gathered, and seized and burned the paper, which appeared as a death warrant to them (and may in one way or other prove so to them) and did their utmost, though without much personal violence, to scare away their enemies; and though law may punish, will humanity not sympathise with them? The story as represented in the papers, of severe beating and maltreatment of the officers is, to say the least, a gross exaggeration. The intention, however indefensible on the score of law, was merely to intimidate, not to injure. The military, it seems, is now to be called upon to wind up the drama in the way of their profession. I pray it may not end tragically. If the sword be unsheathed at Cape Wrath, let the Southrons look out! If the poor and destitute—made so by injustice—are to be cut down in Sutherland, it may only be the beginning; there are plenty of poor and destitute elsewhere, whose numbers the landlords, to save their monopoly, might find it convenient to curtail; and to do which they only want a colourable pretext. Meanwhile, I shall watch the progress of the affair at Durness, and beg to call on all rightly constituted minds to sympathise with the distress of the unfortunate people.

LETTER XXIII.

HAVING lately exposed the partial and exaggerated statements in the *Inverness Courier*, the organ of the oppressors
of Sutherlandshire, my attention is again called to subsequent paragraphs in that paper, and which I feel it my duty
to notice.

Since my last, I have received communications from
correspondents on whom I can rely, which, I need scarcely
say, give a very different colour to the proceedings from
what appears in the *Courier*, emanating, as it evidently does,
from the party inflicting the injury. The first notice in that
paper represents the conduct of the poor natives in the
blackest aspect, while the latter, that of the 27th October,
is calculated to mislead the public in another way, by representing them as sensible of their errors, and acknowledging
the justice of the severities practised upon them.

The *Courier* says, "We are happy to learn that the excitement that led to the disturbance by Mr. Anderson's
tenants in Durness has subsided, and that the people are
quiet, peaceful, and fully sensible of the illegality and unjustifiable nature of their proceedings. The Sheriff addressed
the people in a powerful speech, with an effect which had
the best consequences. They soon made written communications to the Sheriff and Mr. Anderson, stating their con-
trition, and soliciting forgiveness ; promising to remove voluntarily in May next, if permitted in the meantime to remain
and occupy their houses. An arrangement on this footing
was then happily accomplished, which, while it vindicates
the law, tempers justice with mercy. Subsequently, Mr.
Napier, Advocate-Depute, arrived at the place to conduct
the investigation."

Latterly, the *Courier* says—" The clergyman of the parish convinced the people, and Mr. Lumsden, the Sheriff, addressed them on the serious nature of their late proceed. ings; this induced them to petition Mr. Anderson, their landlord, asking his forgiveness ; and he has allowed them to remain till May next. We trust something will be done in the interval for the poor homeless Mountaineers." This is the subdued, though contemptuous tone of the *Courier*, owing doubtless to the noble and impartial conduct of the Advocate-Depute, Mr. Napier, who in conducting the investigation, found, notwithstanding the virulent and railing accusations brought by those who had driven the poor people to madness, that their conduct was very different from what it had been represented. The *Courier*, in his first article, called for the military "to vindicate the law " by shedding the blood of the Sutherland rebels; but now calls them "poor homeless mountaineers ". His crocodile tears accord ill with the former virulence of him and his employers, and we have to thank Mr. Napier for the change. The local authorities who assisted at the precognition did the utmost that malice could suggest to exasperate that gentleman against the people, but he went through the case in his own way, probing it to the bottom, and qualifying their rage by his coolness and impartiality.

Notwithstanding a series of injuries and provocations un-paralleled, this is the first time the poor Sutherlanders, so famous in their happier days for defending their country and its laws, have been led to transgress ; and I hope when the day of trial comes, the very worst of them will be found "more sinned against than sinning ". It is to be lamented that the law has been violated, but still more to be lamented that all the best attributes of our common nature—all the principles of justice, mercy, and religion, had been violated by the oppressors of this people, under colour of law! The poor victims, simple, ignorant, and heart-broken, have men of wealth, talent, and influence for their opponents and accusers—the very individuals who have been the authors of all their woes, are now their vindictive persecutors. Against the combination of landlords, factors, and other officials, there is none to espouse their cause. One of my correspondents says, that the only gentleman who seemed to take any interest in the people's cause was ordered by Sheriff Lumsden out of his presence. Another says, no wonder the Sheriff was so disposed, for when he arrived in Dornoch, the officials represented the people as savages in a state of rebellion, so that he at first declined proceeding without military protection, and in consequence, a detachment of the 53rd Regiment, in Edinburgh Castle, received orders to march; and could a steamboat have been procured at the time, which providence prevented, one hundred rank and file would have been landed on the shores of Sutherlandshire, and, under the direction of the people's enemies, would probably have stained their arms with innocent blood! But before a proper conveyance could be obtained, the order was countermanded, the Sheriff having found cause to alter his opinion, and the people, though goaded into momentary error, became immediately amenable to his advice. The clergyman of the parish, also made himself useful on this occasion, threatening the people with punishment here and hereafter, if they refused to bow their necks to the oppressor. According to him, all the evils inflicted upon them were ordained of God, and for their good, whereas any opposition on their part proceeded from the devil, and subjected them to just punishment here, and eternal torment hereafter. Christ says :—" Of how much more value is a man than a sheep?" The Sutherland clergy never preached this doctrine, but practically the reverse. They literally prefer flocks of sheep to their human flocks, and lend their aid to every scheme for extirpating the latter to make room for the former. They find their account in leaguing with the oppressors, following up the threatenings of fire and sword by the Sheriff with the terrors of the bottomless pit. They gained their end ; the people prostrated themselves at the feet of their oppressors, " whose tender mercies are cruel". The *Courier* says, " the law has thus been vindicated ". Is it not rather injustice and tyranny that have been vindicated, and the people made a prey ? When they were ordered, in the manner described, to put themselves entirely in the wrong, and beg mercy, they were led to believe this would procure a full pardon and kinder treatment. But their submission was immediately followed up by the precognition, in which, as I said before, every means was used to criminate them, and exaggerate their offence, and it depends on the view the Lord Advocate may be induced to take, what is to be their fate. One thing is certain, Mr. Anderson and his colleagues will be content with nothing short of their expatriation, either to Van Dieman's Land or the place the clergy consigned them to; he cares not which. For the mercy which, as the *Courier* says, has been tempered with justice, of allowing the people to possess their houses till May, while their crop has been lost by the bad weather, or destroyed by neglect during the disturbance, they are mainly indebted to Mr. Napier. Anderson found himself shamed into a consent, which he would otherwise never have given. God knows, their miserable allotments, notwithstanding the toil and money they have expended on them, are not worth contending for, did the poor creatures know where to go when banished? but this with their attachment to the soil, makes them feel it like death itself, to think of removing.

Anderson craftily turned this feeling to his advantage, for, though he obtained the decrees of ejectment in April, he postponed their execution till the herring fishing was over, in order to drain every shilling the poor people had earned, exciting the hope, that if they paid up, they would be allowed to remain! The *Courier* hopes " something will be done for the poor mountaineers ". O my late happy, high-minded countrymen, has it come to this? Represented as wild animals or savages, and hunted accordingly in your own native straths, so often defended by the sinews and blood of your vigorous ancestors !

Surely, your case must arouse the sympathy of generous Britons, otherwise the very stones will cry out! Surely, there is still so much virtue remaining in the country that your wrongs will be made to ring in the ears of your oppressors, till they are obliged to hide their heads for very shame, and tardy justice at length overtake them in the shape of public indignation.

LETTER XXIV.

Since my last communication was written, I have received letters from several correspondents in the north of Scotland, and I now proceed to lay a portion of the contents before the public. Much of the information I have received must be suppressed, from prudential considerations. Utter ruin would instantly overtake the individual, especially if he were an official, who dared to throw a gleam of light on the black deeds going on, or give a tongue to the people's wrongs. Besides, the language of some of the letters is too strong and justly indignant, to venture its publication, least I might involve myself and others in the toils of the law, with the meshes of which I am but little acquainted; hence my correspondence must, generally speaking, be suppressed or emasculated. From the mass of evidence received, I am fully satisfied that the feeble resistance to the instruments of cruelty and oppression at Durness—and which was but a solitary and momenty outbreak of feeling—owes its importance as a *riot* entirely to the inventive and colouring talents of the correspondent of the *Inverness Courier*. One of my correspondents says, "this affray must be a pre-concerted one on the part of the authorities"; another says "the Advocate-Depute asked me, why did the Duke of Sutherland's tenants join Mr. Anderson's tenants; my reply was (which he allowed to be true) that when Anderson would remove his, he and his either hand neighbours would directly use their influence to get the duke's small tenants removed likewise, as they now hate to see a poor man at all, and if any of the tenants would offer to say so much, they would not be believed. This is the way the offspring of the once valiant MacKays are now used; their condition is beyond what pen can describe, but we are here afraid to correspond with such a character as you : if it was known, we would be ruined at once." Another says, "there was not a pane of glass, a door, or railing, or any article of furniture broken within or without the inn at Durine, nor as much as a hair of the head of a Sheriff, Fiscal, or Constable touched. If it was the Sheriff or Fiscal Fraser who published the first article, entitled Durness Riot, in the *Inverness Courier*, indeed, they should be ashamed of their unpardonable conduct"; another says, "after all their ingenuity it was only one Judas they made in Durness, and if there was any one guilty of endeavouring to create disturbance, it was himself. Therefore, we may call him Donald Judas Mac an Diabhuil, fear casaid na braithrean, and the authorities should consider what credence his evidence deserved in criminating the people he was trying to mislead." Another correspondent says, "Fraser the Fiscal (a countryman himself, but an enemy, as all renegades are) inserted a most glaring and highly coloured mis-statement in the *Inverness Courier*, and is ever on the alert to publish anything that might serve his employers and injure his poor countrymen"; another says, "the Fiscal and Sheriff Lumsden were very severe on the people before the Advocate-Depute, but after he had gone through the business they found it prudent to alter their tone a good deal"; he adds, "I incurred the Fiscal's displeasure *for not giving the evidence he wanted for condemning the people,* and to punish me, he would pay me only 10s. for attending the precognition five days and a night. But when the Duke comes I will lay the case before him and tell him how Fraser was so anxious to get the people into a scrape. He is a little worth gentleman." The conduct of the Fiscal requires no comment, and his, it is said, is the *Courier's* authority for its mis-statements. The plan of the persecutors is not only to ruin and expel the natives, by any and every means, but to deprive them of public sympathy, by slandering their character, belying their actions, and harassing them in every possible way, so as to make them willing to leave their native soil before a regular authorised enquiry takes place, which would (in case their victims remain on the spot) not only expose their nefarious deeds, but also lead the way to a regular law for obliging them to provide in some way for the poor they have made.

These are now the two objects of their fears; first, lest they should be shown up, and secondly, that a real—and not, as hitherto, a sham—poor-law should be established, to make them contribute to relieve the misery they have so recklessly and wickedly created. With these preliminaries, I present you with a large extract *verbatim*, from the letter of a gentleman, with whom, though I know his highly respectable connexions, I am personally unacquainted. Coming evidently from a person of education and character, it seems justly entitled to the consideration of all who are pleased to interest themselves in the woes and wrongs of Sutherland, and the outrages there offered to our common humanity:—

"You are aware that Anderson was a pretty considerable speculator in his time (but not so great a speculator as * * *), extensively engaged in the white and herring fishings, at the time he held out the greatest inducements to the poor natives who were expelled from other places in this parish, came and built little huts on his farm, and were entirely dependent on their fishings, and earnings with him. In this humble sphere they were maintaining themselves and families, until God in just retribution turned the scales upon Anderson ; his speculations proved unsuccessful, he lost his shipping, and his cash was fast following; he broke down his herring establishments, and so the poor fishermen had to make the best of it they could with other curers. Anderson now began to turn his attention to sheep farming, and removed a great many of his former tenants and fishermen : however, he knew little or nothing of the details of sheep farming, and was entirely guided by the advice of his either hand neighbours, Alex. Clark, Erribol, and John Scobie, of Koldale (both sheep farmers); and it is notorious that it was at the instigation of these creatures that he adopted such severe measures against those remaining of his tenants —but, be this as it may, this last summer when the whole male adult population were away at the fishing in Wick, he employed a fellow of the name of C———l to summon and frighten the poor women in the absence of their husbands. The proceeding was both cowardly and illegal. However, the women (acting as it can be proved upon C———l's own suggestion!) congregated, lighted a fire, laid hands on C———l and compelled him to consign his papers to the flames! Anderson immediately reported the case to the Dornoch law-mongers, who, smelling a job, dispatched their officer;—off he set to Durness as big as a mountain, and together with one of Anderson's shepherds proceeded to finish what C———l had begun: however, he 'reckoned without his host,' for ere he got half through, the women fell in hot love with him also—and embraced him so cordially, that he left with them his waterproof Mackintosh, and 'cut' to the tune of Cabarfeidh. No sooner had he arrived in Dornoch, than the gentlemen there concluded that they themselves had been insulted and ill-used by proxy in Durness. Shortly afterwards they dispatched the same officer and a messenger-at-arms, with instructions to raise a trusty party by the way to aid them. They came by Tongue, went down to Farr on the Saturday evening, raised Donald MacKay, pensioner, and other two old veterans, whom they sent off before them on the Sabbath, *incog.;* however, they only advanced to the ferry at Hope when they were told that the Durness people were fully prepared to give them a warm reception, so they went no further, but returned to Dornoch, and told there a doleful Don Quixote tale. Immediately thereafter, a 'council of war' was held, and the sheriff-substitute, together with the fiscal and a band of fourteen special constables marched off to Durness. Before they arrived the people heard of their approach, and consulted among themselves what had best be done (the men were by this time all returned home). They allowed the whole party to pass through the parish till they reached the inn; this was on a Saturday evening about eight or nine o'clock;—the men of the parish to the amount of four dozen called at the inn, and wanted to have a conference with the sheriff. This was refused to them. They then respectfully requested an assurance from him that they would not be interfered with during the Sabbath, which was likewise refused to them. Then the people got a little exasperated, and, determined in the first place on depriving the sheriff of his sting. They took his constables one by one, and turned them out of the house *minus* their batons. There was not the least injury done, or violence shewn to the persons of any of the party. The natives now made their way to the sheriff's room and began to dictate (!) to him; however, as they could not get him to accede to their terms, they ordered him to march off; which, after some persuasion he did; they laid no hands on him or the fiscal. And, to show their civility, they actually harnessed the horses for them, and escorted them beyond the precincts of the parish ! ! !

The affair had now assumed rather an alarming aspect. The glaring and highly coloured statement already referred to, appeared in the *Inverness Courier*, and soon found its way into all the provincial and metropolitan prints; the parties referred to were threatened with a military force. The Duke of Sutherland was stormed on all hands with letters and petitions. The matter came to the ears of the Lord Advocate. Mr. Napier, the Depute-Advocate, was sent from Auld Reekie, and the whole affair investigated before him and the Sheriff, and Clerk and Fiscal of the County. How this may ultimately terminate I cannot yet say, but, one thing is certain, the investigators have discovered some informality in the proceedings on the part of the petty lawyers, which has for the present suspended all further procedure ! I am glad to understand that the Duke of Sutherland expresses great sympathy with the poor people. Indeed, I am inclined to give his Grace credit for good intentions, if he only knew how his people are harassed ; but this is religiously concealed from him.

I live at some distance from Tongue, but I satisfied myself of the certainty of the following extraordinary case which could have occurred nowhere but in Sutherland.

The present factor in Tongue is from Edinburgh. This harvest, a brother of his who is a clerk, or something in that city, came down to pay him a visit; they went out a-shooting one day in September, but could kill no birds. They, however, determined to have some sport before returning home, so, falling in with a flock of goats belonging to a man of the name of Manson, and within a few hundred yards of the man's own house, they set to, and after firing a number of ineffectual shots, succeeded at length, in taking down two of the goats, which they left on the ground ! Satisfied and delighted with this manly sport they returned to Tongue. Next day when called upon by the poor man who owned the goats, and told that they were all he had to pay his rent with, this exemplary factor told him, " he did not care should he never pay his rent,"—" he was only sorry he had not proper ammunition at the time,"— as " he would not have left one of them alive !!! " Think you, would the Duke tolerate such conduct as this, or what would he say did the fact come to his ears ? As Burns says :—

> This is a sketch of H———h's way,
> Thus does he slaughter, kill, and slay,
> And 's weel paid for 't.

The poor man durst not whisper a complaint for this act

of brutal despotism; but I respectfully ask, will the Duke of Sutherland tolerate such conduct? I ask will such conduct be tolerated by the legislature? Will Fiscal Fraser and the Dornoch law-mongers smell this job?"

LETTER XXV.

HAVING done my best to bring the wrongs of the Sutherlanders in general, and, latterly, those of Mr. Anderson's tenantry in particular, under the public eye in your valuable columns, I beg leave to close my correspondence for the present, with a few additional facts and observations. Before doing so, however, I must repeat my sense—in which I am confident my countrymen will participate—of your great kindness in allowing me such a vehicle as your excellent paper through which to vent our complaints and proclaim our wrongs. I also gratefully acknowledge the disinterested kindness of another individual, whose name it is not now necessary to mention, who has assisted me in revising and preparing my letters for the press. I hope such friends will have their reward.

It is unnecessary to spin out the story of the Durness Riot (as it is called) any longer. It evidently turns out what I believed it to be from the beginning—a humbug scheme for further oppressing and destroying the people; carrying out, by the most wicked and reckless means, the long prevailing system of expatriation, and, at the same time, by gross misrepresentations, depriving them of that public sympathy to which their protracted sufferings and present misery give them such strong claims. In my latest corres-

pondence from that quarter the following facts are contained, which further justify my previous remarks, viz. :—

A gentleman who makes a conspicuous figure in the proceedings against the people is law-agent for Mr. Anderson,
the lessee, from whose property the poor crofters were to be
ejected ; and C————l, the first officer sent to Durness, was
employed by them.   This C————l was an unqualified
officer, but used as a convenient tool by his employers, and
it was actually, as I am assured, this man who advised or
suggested to the poor women and boys, in absence of the
male adults, to kindle the fire, and lay hold of him, and
compel him to consign his papers to the flames !—acting
probably under the directions of his employers.

The next emissary sent was a qualified officer—qualified
by having served an apprenticeship as a thief-catcher in the
police establishment of Edinburgh, who, when he came in
contact with the virtuous Durness women, behaved as he
was wont to do among those of a different sort in Anchor
Close and Halkerston's Wynd ; and I am sorry to say some
of the former were inhumanly and shamefully dealt with by
him.—See *Inverness Courier* of 17th November.   And
here, I am happy to be able in a great degree to exonerate
that journal from the charge brought against it in former
letters.   The Editor has at last put the saddle on the right
horse—namely, his first informers, the advisers and actors
in the cruel and vindictive proceedings against the poor
victims of oppression.

It is lamentable to think that the Sheriff-substitute of
Sutherland should arrive in Durness, with a formidable
party and a train of carts, to carry off to Dornoch Jail the
prisoners he intended to make, on the Sabbath-day !   If this
was not his intention, what was the cause of the resistance
and defeat he and his party met with ?   Just this (according

to the *Courier* and my own correspondents), that he would not consent to give his word that he would not execute his warrant on the Sabbath-day, although they were willing to give him every assurance of peaceably surrendering on the Monday following. Provoked by his refusal, the men of Durness, noted for piety as well as forbearance, chose rather to break the laws of man on the Saturday, than see the laws of God violated in such a manner on the Sabbath. He and his party, who had bagpipes playing before them on leaving Dornoch, told inquirers, that " they were going to a wedding in Durness ". It was rather a divorce, to tear the people away from their dearly-loved, though barren, hills. Under all the circumstances, many, I doubt not will think with me that these willing emissaries of mischief got better treatment than they deserved. It is high time the law-breaking and law-wresting petifoggers of Sutherlandshire were looked after. This brings again to my mind the goat-shooting scene, described in my last, which was the more aggravated and diabolical from having been perpetrated during the late troubles, and while a military force was hourly expected to cut down such as should dare to move a finger against those in authority; knowing that, under these circumstances, no complaints of the people would be listened to. But this was not the only atrocity of the kind that took place in the country at this time. I have seen a letter from a respectable widow woman residing in Blairmore, parish of Rogart, to her son in Edinburgh, which, after detailing the harassment and misery to which the country is subject, says—" I had only seven sheep, and one of Mr. Sellar's shepherds drowned five of them in Lochsalchie, along with other five belonging to Donald MacKenzie; and many more, the property of other neighbours, sharing the same fate. We could not get so much as the skins of them." But they durst not say one word about it, or if they did no one would hearken to their complaints. God alone knows how they are used in that unfortunate country, and he will avenge it in his own time.

A correspondent of mine says—" At an early period of your narrative, you stated that the natives were refused employment at public works, even at reduced wages; but, if you believe me, sir, in the last and present year, masons, carpenters, etc., were brought here from Aberdeenshire, and employed at those works, while equally good, if not better native tradesmen were refused, and obliged to go idle. This, however, was not admitted as an excuse when house-rent, poll-tax, or road money was demanded, but the most summary and oppressive means were used for recovery. They have been paying these strangers four or five shillings a-day, when equally good workmen among the natives would be glad of eighteen-pence!"

In this way, the money drained from the natives in the most rigorous manner, is paid away to strangers before their eyes, while they themselves are refused permission to earn a share of it! My correspondent adds—"We know the late Duchess, some years before her demise, gave orders (and we cannot think the present Duke of Sutherland has annulled these orders) that no stranger should be employed, while natives could be found to execute the work. But it seems the officials, and their under-strappers, can do what they please, without being called to account; and this is but one instance among the many in which their tyranny and injustice is manifested." Every means, direct and indirect, are used to discourage the aborigines, to make them willing to fly the country, or be content to starve in it.

May I not ask, will the Duke of Sutherland never look into the state of his county? Will he continue to suffer such treatment of the people to whom he owes his greatness; proceedings so hazardous to his own real interest and safety? Is it not high time that that illustrious family should institute a searching inquiry into the past and present conduct of those who have wielded their power only to abuse it?

Their extensive domains are now, generally speaking, in the hands of a few selfish, ambitious strangers, who would laugh at any calamity that might befall the people as they do at the miseries of those faithful subjects whom they have supplanted. Many of these new tenants have risen from running about with hobnails in their shoes, and a collie dog behind them, their whole wardrobe being on their back—and all their other appointments and equipage bearing the same proportion—to be Esquires, Justices of the Peace, and gentlemen riding in carriages, or on blood-horses, and living in splendid mansions, all at the expense of his Grace's family, and of those whom they have despoiled of their inheritance. The time may come—I see it approaching already—when these gentlemen will say to his Grace, "If you do not let your land to us on our own terms, you may take it and make the best of it; who can compete with us?" This will be the case, especially when the natives are driven away, and the competition for land, caused by the food taxes, comes to an end. Let his Grace consider these things, and no longer be entirely guided by the counsels of his Ahitophel, nor adopt the system of Rehoboam towards the race of the devoted vassals of his ancestors, a portion of whose blood runs in his veins.

"Woe is me! the possessors of my people slay them, and hold themselves not guilty"; and they that sell them say, "blessed be the Lord, for I am rich; and their own shepherds pity them not". "Let me mourn and howl" for the pride of Sutherland is spoiled!"

In a former letter I put the question to the Sutherland clergy, "of how much more value is a man than a sheep?" No reply has been made.

I ask again, "You that have a thousand score of sheep feeding on the straths that formerly reared tens of thousand of as brave and virtuous men as Britain could boast of, ready to shed their blood for their country or their chief; were these not of more value than your animals, your shepherds, or yourselves? You that spend your ill-gotten gains in riotous living, in hunting, gaming, and debauchery, of how much more value were the men you have dispersed, ruined, and tortured out of existence, than you and your base companions?" But I must now cease to unpack my heart with words, and take leave of the subject for the present; assuring my kind correspondents, that their names will never be divulged by me, and pledging myself to continue exposing oppression so long as it exists in my native country.

In conclusion I implore the Government to make inquiry into the condition of this part of the empire, and not look lightly at the out-rooting of a brave and loyal people and the razing to the ground of that important portion of the national bulwarks, to gratify the cupidity of a few, to whose character neither bravery nor good feeling can be attributed.

REPLY TO MRS. BEECHER STOWE'S
"SUNNY MEMORIES".

[*Abridged.*]

MACLEOD here apologises for his style in the following terms :—" I am quite aware that great allowance must be made by readers of education and literary taste, should these pages be honoured with a perusal by any such, I am not capable of writing to please critics ; I had a higher aim, and my success in bringing out the case of my countrymen must now stand the ordeal of public opinion. For my own part, zeal and faithfulness are all I lay claim to, and if my conscience tells me true, I deserve to have both conceded to me, by both friends and foes." He then refers particularly to various acts of tyranny, one of these being the evictions from Coire-Bhuic, in Strathconan, and the case of Angus Campbell, Rogart, the particulars of which he relates thus :—

Angus Campbell possessed a small lot of land in the parish of Rogart, in the immediate neighbourhood of the parish minister, the Rev. Mr. Mackenzie. This rev. divine, it seems, had, like King Ahab, coveted this poor man's small possession, in addition to his own extensive glebe, and obtained a grant of it from the factor. Angus Campbell, besides his own numerous family, was the only support of his elder brother, who had laboured for many years under a painful and lingering disease, and had spent his all upon physicians.

Angus having got notice of the rev. gentleman's designs, had a memorial drawn up and presented to her grace the late Duchess, who, in answer, gave orders to the factor to the effect that, if Angus Campbell was to be removed for the convenience of Mr. Mackenzie, he should be provided with another lot of land equally as good as the one he possessed. But, like all the other good promised by her Grace, this was disregarded as soon as she turned her back : the process of removal was carried on, and to punish Angus for having applied to her, he was dealt with in the following manner, as stated in a memorial to his Grace the present Duke, dated 30th March, 1840.

In his absence, a messenger-at-arms, with a party, came from Dornoch to his house, and ejected his wife and family ; and having flung out their effects, locked the doors of the dwelling house, offices, etc., and carried the keys to the safe keeping of the Rev. Mr. Mackenzie, for his own behoof. These proceedings were a sufficient warning to all neighbours not to afford shelter or relief to the victims ; hence the poor woman had to wander about, sheltering her family as well as she could in severe weather, till her husband's arrival. When Angus came home, he had recourse to an expedient which annoyed his reverence very much ; he erected a booth on his own ground in the churchyard, and on the tomb of his father, and in this solitary abode he kindled a fire, endeavouring to shelter and comfort his distressed family, and showed a determination to remain, notwithstanding the wrath and threatenings of the minister and factors. But as they did not think it prudent to expel him thence by force, they thought of a stratagem, which succeeded. They spoke him fair, and agreed to allow him to resume his former possession, if he would pay the expenses, £4 13s., incurred in ejecting him. The poor man consented, but no sooner had he paid the money than he was turned out again, and good care taken this time to keep him out of the churchyard. He had then to betake himself to the open fields, where he remained with his family till his wife was seized with an alarming trouble, when some charitable friend at last ventured to afford him a temporary covering ; but no distress could soften the heart of his reverence, so as to make *him* relent !

This Campbell is a man of good and inoffensive character, to attest which he forwarded a certificate numerously signed, along with his memorial to the Duke, but received for answer, that, as the case was settled by his factor, his Grace could not interfere !

The second case is that of an aged woman of four-score— Isabella Graham, of the parish of Lairg, who was also ejected with great cruelty. She, too, sought redress at the hands of his Grace, but with no better success. A copy of the substance of her memorial, which was backed by a host of certificates, I here subjoin :—

That your Grace's humble applicant, who has resided with her husband on the lands of Toroball for upwards of fifty years, has been removed from her possession for no other reason than that Robert Murray, holding an adjoining lot, coveted her's in addition. That she is nothing in arrears of her rent, and hopes from your Grace's generosity and charitable disposition, that she will be permitted to remain in one of the houses belonging to her lot, till by some means or other she may obtain another place previous to the coming winter, and may be able to get her bed removed from the open field, where she has had her abode during the last *fifteen weeks!* Your Grace's humane interposition is most earnestly but respectfully implored on the present occasion, and your granting immediate relief will confirm a debt of never-ending gratitude, and your memorialist shall ever pray, etc.

In the enlarged edition of his work, published in Canada, in 1857, MacLeod falls foul of Mrs. Beecher Stowe, who had attacked him in her *Sunny Memories.* A great portion of the controversy is personal and now of little interest to any one. When it is not personal it is directed against classes and institutions lauded to the skies by Mrs. Beecher Stowe. Referring to her sympathies for the slaves of America, MacLeod contrasts, in feeling and eloquent language, her labours in their interest with her laudation of those in high places in this country, who had treated their dependents worse than the slaves of the Southern States. " The American slave-owners," he says, " are to be pitied, for they are the dupes or victims of false doctrine, or rather, say, of the misinterpretation of sacred records. They believe to have a divine right to sell and buy African slaves ; to flog, hang, and shoot them for disobedience ; and to chase them with bloodhounds and methodist ministers if they run away. But the English aristocracy maintain to still higher prerogatives, in direct opposition to sacred records,—they believe to have divine right to monopolise the whole creation of God in Britain for their own private use, to the exclusion of all the rest of His creatures. They have enacted laws to establish these rights, and they blush not to declare these laws sacred. And it is to be lamented that these laws and doctrines are generally believed. Let any one peruse their Parchment Rights of Property, and he will find that they include the surface of the earth, all the minerals below the surface to the centre, all that is above it up to the heavens, rivers of water, bays and creeks of mixed salt water and fresh water for one and one-fourth of a league out to sea, with all the fish of every description which spawn or feed therein, and all the fowls who lay and are raised on land,—a right to deprive the people of the least pretention of right to the creation of God but what they choose to give them,—a right to compel the people to defend their properties from invaders; to press and ballot as many of them as they choose; handcuff them if they are unwilling, and force them to swear by God to be true and faithful slaves,—a right to imprison, to flog, to hang, and shoot them, if refractory, or for the least disobedience. Yes, a right to force them away to foreign and unhealthy climes, to fight nations who never did them any injury, where they perish in thousands by disease, fatigue, and starvation, like brute beasts ; to hang, shoot, or flog them to death for even taking a morsel of food when dying for the want of it—all to gain more possessions and power for the British aristocracy.

"Slavery is damnable, and is the most disgusting word in the English or any other language ; it is to be hoped that the Americans will soon discern its deformity, pollution and iniquity, and wipe away that old English polluted stain from their character. But there is not the least shadow of hope that ever the British aristocracy will think shame, or give up *their* system of slavery—for it is the most profitable now under heaven, the most admired, and is adopted by all other nations of the earth—at least, until the promised Millenium will arrive, whatever time that blessed era will take in coming—unless the people in their might will rise some morning early, and demand their rights and liberties with the united voice of thunder which will 'make the most hardened and stubborn of the aristocratic adamant hearts tremble and ache'."

Mrs. Beecher Stowe, referring to the so-called "Sutherland Improvements," wrote:—"To my view it is an almost sublime instance of the benevolent employment of superior wealth and power in shortening the struggles of civilisation, and elevating in a few years a whole community to a point of education and material prosperity, which, unassisted, they might never have obtained". To this remarkable statement MacLeod replies :—Yes, indeed, the shortest process of civilisation recorded in the history of nations. Oh, marvellous ! From the year 1812 to 1820, the whole interior of the county of Sutherland—whose inhabitants were advancing rapidly in the science of agriculture and education, who by nature and exemplary training were the bravest, the most moral and patriotic people that ever existed—even admitting a few of them did violate the excise laws, the only sin which Mr. Loch and all the rest of their avowed enemies could bring against them—where a body of men could be raised on the shortest possible notice that kings and emperors might and would be proud of ; and where the whole fertile valleys, and straths which gave them birth were in due season waving with corn; their mountains and hill-sides studded with sheep and cattle ; where rejoicing, felicity, happiness, and true piety prevailed ; where the martial notes of the bagpipes sounded and reverberated from mountain to glen, from glen to mountain. I say, marvellous ! in eight years converted to a solitary wilderness, where the voice of man praising God is not to be heard, nor the image of God upon man to be seen; where you can set a compass with twenty miles of a radius upon it, and go round with it full stretched, and not find one acre of land within the circumference which has come under the plough for the last thirty years, except a few in the parishes of Lairg and Tongue,—all under mute brute animals. This is the advancement of civilisation, is is not, madam? Return now with me to the begining of your elaborate eulogy on the Duchess of Sutherland, and if you are open to conviction, I think you should be convinced that I never published nor circulated in the American, English, or Scotch public prints any ridiculous, absurd stories about her Grace of Sutherland. An abridgement of my lucubrations is now in the hands of the public, and you may peruse them. I stand by them as facts *(stubborn chiels)*. I can prove them to be so even in this country (Canada), by a cloud of living witnesses, and my readers will find that, instead of bringing absurd accusations against her Grace, that I have endeavoured in some instances to screen her and her predecessors from the public odium their own policy and the doings of their servants merited. Moreover, there is thirty years since I began to expostulate with the House of Sutherland for their short-sighted policy in dealing with their people as they were doing, and it is twenty years since I began to expose them publicly, with my real name, Donald MacLeod, attached to each letter, sending a copy of the public paper where it appeared, directed by post, to the Duke of Sutherland. These exposing and remonstrating letters were published in the Edinburgh papers, where the Duke and his predecessors had their principal Scotch law agent, and you may easily believe that I was closely watched, with the view to find one false accusation in my letters, but they were baffled. I am well aware that each letter I have written on

the subject would, if untrue, constitute a libel, and I knew
the editors, printers, and publishers of these papers were
as liable or responsible for libel as I was. But the House
of Sutherland could never venture to raise an action of
damages against either of us. In 1841, when I published
my first pamphlet, I paid $4 50c., for binding one of them,
in a splendid style, which I sent by mail to his Grace the
present Duke of Sutherland, with a complimentary note requesting him to peruse it, and let me know if it contained
anything offensive or untrue. I never received a reply, nor
did I expect it ; yet I am satisfied that his Grace did peruse it.
I posted a copy of it to Mr. Loch, his chief commissioner ;
to Mr. W. Mackenzie, his chief lawyer in Edinburgh ; to
every one of their underlings, to sheep-farmers, and
ministers in the county of Sutherland who abetted the de-
populators, and I challenged the whole of them, and other
literary scourges who aided and justified their unhallowed
doings, to gainsay one statement I have made. Can you
or any other believe that a poor sinner like Donald MacLeod
would be allowed for so many years to escape with impunity,
had he been circulating and publishing calumnious, absurd
falsehoods against such personages as the House of Sutherland. No, I tell you, if money could secure my punishment, without establishing their own shame and guilt, that
it would be considered well-spent long ere now,—they
would eat me in penny pies if they could get me cooked for
them.

I agree with you that the Duchess of Sutherland is a
beautiful accomplished lady, who would shudder at the idea
of taking a faggot or a burning torch in her hand to set fire
to the cottages of her tenants, and so would her predecessor,
the first Duchess of Sutherland, her good mother ; likewise
would the late and present Dukes of Sutherland, at least I

am willing to believe that they would. Yet it was done in
their name, under their authority, to their knowledge, and
with their sanction. The Dukes and Duchesses of Sutherland, and those of their depopulating order, had not, nor
have they any call to defile their pure hands in milder work
than to burn people's houses; no, no, they had, and have
plenty of willing tools at their beck to perform their dirty
work. Whatever amount of humanity and purity of heart the
late or the present Duke and Duchess may possess or be
ascribed to them, we know the class of men from whom
they selected their commissioners, factors and underlings. I
knew every one of the unrighteous servants who ruled the
Sutherland estate for the last fifty years, and I am justified
in saying that the most skilful phrenologist and physiogno-
mist that ever existed could not discern one spark of
humanity in the whole of them, from Mr. Loch down to
Donald Sgrios, or, Damnable Donald, the name by which
the latter was known. The most of those cruel executors of the atrocities I have been describing are now
dead, and to be feared but not lamented. But it seems
their chief was left to give you all the information you
required about British slavery and oppression. I have read
from speeches delivered by Mr. Loch at public dinners
among his own party, "that he would never be satisfied
until the Gaelic language and the Gaelic people would be
extirpated root and branch from the Sutherland estate; yes,
from the highlands of Scotland". He published a book,
where he stated as a positive fact, "that when he got the
management of the Sutherland estate he found 408
families on the estate who never heard the name of Jesus,"
—whereas I could make oath that there were not at that
time, and for ages prior to it, above two families within
the limits of the county who did not worship that Name

and holy Being every morning and evening. I know there are hundreds in the Canadas who will bear me out in this assertion. I was at the pulling down and burning of the house of William Chisholm. I got my hands burnt taking out the poor old woman from amidst the flames of her once comfortable though humble dwelling, and a more horrifying and lamentable scene could scarcely be witnessed. I may say the skeleton of a once tall, robust, high-cheek-boned, respectable woman, who had seen better days; who could neither hear, see, nor speak; without a tooth in her mouth, her cheek skin meeting in the centre, her eyes sunk out of sight in their sockets, her mouth wide open, her nose standing upright among smoke and flames, uttering piercing moans of distress and agony, in articulations from which could be only understood, "Oh, *Dhia, Dhia, teine, teine*—Oh God, God, fire, fire". When she came to the pure air, her bosom heaved to a most extraordinary degree, accompanied by a deep hollow sound from her lungs, comparable to the sound of thunder at a distance. When laid down upon the bare, soft, moss floor of the roofless shed, I will never forget the foam of perspiration which emitted and covered the pallid death-looking countenance. This was a scene, madam, worthy of an artist's pencil, and of a conspicuous place on the stages of tragedy. Yet you call this a specimen of the ridiculous stories which found their way into respectable prints, because Mr. Loch, the chief actor, told you that Sellar, the head executive, brought an action against the sheriff and obtained a verdict for heavy damages. What a subterfuge; but it will not answer the purpose, "*the bed is too short to stretch yourself, and the covering too narrow and short to cover you*". If you took the information and evidence upon which you founded your *Uncle Tom's Cabin* from such unreliable sources (as I said before), who can

believe the one-tenth of your novel? I cannot. I have at
my hand here the grandchild of the slaughtered old woman,
who recollects well of the circumstance. I have not far
from me a respectable man, an elder in the Free Church,
who was examined as a witness at Sellar's trial, at the Spring
assizes of Inverness, in 1816, which you will find narrated
in letters four and five of my work. Had you the opportunity, madam, of seeing the scenes which I, and hundreds
more, have seen—the wild ferocious appearance of the
infamous *gang* who constituted the burning party, covered
over face and hands with soot and ashes of the burning
houses, cemented by torch-grease and their own sweat, kept
continually drunk or half-drunk while at work; and to
observe the hellish amusements some of them would get up
for themselves and for an additional pleasure to their leaders !
The people's houses were generally built upon declivities,
and in many cases not far from pretty steep precipices. They
preserved their meal in tight-made boxes, or chests, as they
were called, and when this fiendish party found any quantity
of meal, they would carry it between them to the brink, and
dispatch it down the precipice amidst shrieks and yells.
It was considered grand sport to see the box breaking to
atoms and the meal mixed with the air.   When they would
set fire to a house, they would watch any of the domestic
animals making their escape from the flames, such as dogs,
cats, hens, or any poultry ; these were caught and thrown
back to the flames—grand sport for demons in human
form !
   As to the vaunted letter which his "Grace received from
one of the most determined opposers of the measures, who
travelled in the north of Scotland as editor of a newspaper,
regretting all that he had written on the subject, being convinced that he was misinformed," I may tell you, madam,

that this man did not travel to the north or in the north of Scotland as editor; his name was Thomas Mulock; he came to Scotland a fanatic speculator in literature in search of money, or a lucrative situation, vainly thinking that he would be a dictator to every editor in Scotland. He first attacked the immortal Hugh Miller, of the *Witness*, Edinburgh, but in him he met more than his match. He then went to the north, got hold of my first pamphlet, and by setting it up in a literary style, and in better English than I, he made a splendid and promising appearance in the northern papers for some time; but he found out that the money expected was not coming in, and that the hotels, head inns, and taverns would not keep him up any longer without the prospect of being paid for the past or for the future. I found out that he was hard up, and a few of the Highlanders in Edinburgh and myself sent him from twenty to thirty pounds sterling. When he saw that that was all he was to get, he at once turned tail upon us, and instead of expressing his gratitude, he abused us unsparingly, and regretted that ever he wrote in behalf of such a hungry, moneyless class. He smelled (like others we suspect) where the gold was hoarded up for hypocrites and flatterers, and that one apologising letter to his Grace would be worth ten times as much as he could expect from the Highlanders all his lifetime; and I doubt not it was, for his apology for the sin of mis-information got wide circulation.

He then went to France and started an English paper in Paris, and for the service he rendered Napoleon in crushing republicanism during the besieging of Rome, etc., the Emperor presented him with a *gold pin*, and in a few days afterwards sent a *gendarme* to him with a brief notice that his service was not any longer required, and a warning to quit France in a few days, which he had to do. What became of him after I know not, but very likely he is dictating to young Loch, or some other Metternich.

No feelings of hostile vindictiveness, no desire to inflict chastisement, no desire to make riches, influenced my mind, pourtraying the scenes of havoc and misery which in those past days darkened the annals of Sutherland. I write in my own humble style, with higher aims, wishing to prepare the way for demonstrating to the Dukes of Sutherland, and all other Highland proprietors, great and small, that the path of selfish aggrandisement and oppression leads by sure and inevitable results, yea to the ruin and destruction of the blind and misguided oppressors themselves. I consider the Duke himself victimised on a large scale by an incurably wrong system, and by being enthralled by wicked counsellors and servants. I have no hesitation in saying, had his Grace and his predecessors bestowed one-half of the encouragement they had bestowed upon strangers on the aborigines—a hardy, healthy, abstemious people, who lived peaceably in their primitive habitations, unaffected with the vices of a subtle civilisation, possessing little, but enjoying much; a race devoted to their hereditary chief, ready to abide by his counsels; a race profitable in peace, and loyal, available in war; I say, his Grace, the present Duke of Sutherland, and his beautiful Duchess, would be without compeers in the British dominions, their rents, at least doubled; would be as secure from invasion and annoyance in Dunrobin Castle as Queen Victoria could, or can be, in her Highland residence, at Balmoral, and far safer than she is in her English home, Buckingham Palace; every man and son of Sutherland would be ready, as in the days of yore, to shed the last drop of their blood in defence of their chief, if required. Congratulations, rejoicings, dancing to the martial notes of the pipes, would meet them at the entrance to every glen and strath in Sutherlandshire, accompanied, surrounded, and greeted, as they proceeded, by the most grateful, devotedly attached, happy, and bravest peasantry that ever existed ; yes, but alas ! where there is nothing now, but desolation and the cries of famine and want, to meet the noble pair—the ruins of once comfortable dwellings—will be seen the land-marks of the furrows and ridges which yielded food to thousands, the footprints of the arch-enemy of human happiness, and ravager—before, after, and on each side, solitude, stillness, and the quiet of the grave, disturbed only at intervals by the yells of a shepherd, or fox-hunter, and the bark of a collie dog. Surely we must admit that the Marquises and Dukes of Sutherland have been duped and victimised to a most extraordinary and incredible extent; and we have Mr. Loch's own words for it in his speech in the House of Commons, June 21st, 1845:—"I can state, as from facts, that from 1811 to 1833, not one sixpence of rent has been received from that county ; but, on the contrary, there has been sent there for the benefit and improvement of the people a sum exceeding sixty thousand pounds sterling". Now think you of this immense wealth which has been expended. I am not certain, but I think the rental of the county would exceed £60,000 a year ; you have then from 1811 to 1833, twenty-two years, leaving them at the above figures, and the sum total will amount to £1,320,000 expended upon the self-styled Sutherland improvements ; add to this £60,000 sent down to preserve the lives of the victims of those improvements from death by famine, and the sum total will turn out in the shape of £1,380,000. It surely cost the heads of the house of Sutherland an immense sum of money to convert the county into the state I have described it in a former part of this work (and I challenge contradiction). I say the expelling of the people from their glens and straths, and huddling them in motley groups on the sea-shore and barren moors, and to keep them alive there, and to make them willing to be banished from the nation when they thought proper, or when they could get a *haul* of the public money to pay their passage to America or Australia, cost them a great deal. This fabulous, incredible munificence of their Graces to the people I will leave the explanation of what it was, how it was distributed, and the manner in which payment and refunding of the whole of it was exacted from the people, to my former description of it in this work; yet I am willing to admit that a very small portion, if any, of the *refunding* of the amount sent down ever reached the Duke's or the Marquis's coffers. Whatever particle of good the present Duke might feel inclined to do will be ever frustrated by the counteracting energy of a prominent evil principle; I know the adopting and operations of the Loch policy towards the Sutherland peasantry cost the present Duke and his father many thousands of pounds, and, I predict, it will continue to cost them on a large scale while a Loch is at the head of their affairs, and is principal adviser. Besides, how may they endanger what is far more valuable than gold and silver; for those who are advised by men who never sought counsel or advice from God all their lifetime, as their work will testify, do hazard much, and are trifling with Omniscience.

You should be surprised to hear and learn, madam, for what purposes most of the money drained from the Duke's coffers yearly are expended since he became the Duke and proprietor of Sutherland, upholding the Loch policy. There are no fewer than seventeen who are known by the name of water bailiffs in the county who receive yearly salaries, what doing, think you? Protecting the operations of the Loch policy, watching day and night the freshwater lakes, rivers, and creeks, teeming with the finest salmon and trout fish in the world, guarding from the famishing people, even during the years of famine and dire distress, when many had to subsist upon weeds, sea-ware, and shellfish, yet guarded and preserved for the amusement of English anglers; and what is still more heart-rending, to prevent the dying by hunger to pick up any of the dead fish left by the sporting anglers rotting on the lake, creek, and river sides, when the smallest of them, or a morsel, would be considered by hundreds, I may say thousands, of the needy natives, a treat; but they durst not touch them, or if they did and were found out, to jail they were conducted, or removed summarily from his Grace's domains; (let me be understood, these gentlemen had no use for the fish, killing them for amusement, only what they required for their own use, and complimented to the factors; they were not permitted to cure them).

You will find, madam, that about three miles from Dunrobin Castle there is a branch of the sea which extends up the county about six miles, where shellfish, called mussels, abound. Here you will find two sturdy men, called mussel bailiffs, supplied with rifles and ammunition, and as many Newfoundland dogs as assistants, watching the mussel scalps, or beds, to preserve them from the people in the surrounding parishes of Dornoch, Rogart, and Golspie, and keep them, to supply the fishermen, on the opposite side of the Moray Firth, with bait, who come there every year and take away thousands of tons of this nutritive shellfish, when many hundreds of the people would be thankful for a diet per day of them, to pacify the cravings of nature. You will find that the unfortunate native fishermen, who pay a yearly rent to his Grace for bait, are only permitted theirs from the refuse left by the strangers of the other side of the Moray Firth, and if they violate the *iron* rule laid down to them, they are entirely at the mercy of the underlings. There has been an instance of two of the fishermen's wives going on a cold, snowy, frosty day to gather bait, but on account of the boisterous sea, could not reach the place appointed by the factors; one took what they required from the forbidden ground, and was observed by some of the bailiffs, in ambush, who pursued them like tigers. One came up to her unobserved, took out his knife and cut the straps by which the basket or creel on her back was suspended; the weight on her back fell to the ground, and she, poor woman, big in the family way, fell her whole length forward in the snow and frost. Her companion turned round to see what had happened, when she was pushed back with such force that she fell; he then trampled their baskets and mussels to atoms, took them both prisoners, ordered one of them to call his superior bailiff to assist him, and kept the other for two hours standing, wet as she was, among frost and snow, until the superior came a distance of three miles. After a short consultation upon the enormity of the crime, the two poor women were led, like convicted criminals, to Golspie, to appear before Licurgus Gunn, and in that deplorable condition were left standing before their own doors in the snow, until Marshall Gunn found it convenient to appear and pronounce judgment,— verdict: You are allowed to go into your houses this night; this day week you must leave this village for ever, and the whole of the fishermen of the village are strictly prohibited from taking bait from the Little Ferry until you leave; my bailiffs are requested to see this my decree strictly attended to. Being the middle of winter and heavy snow, they delayed a week longer: ultimately the villagers had to expel the two families from among them, so that they would get bait, having nothing to depend upon for subsistence but the fishing, and fish they could not without bait. This is a specimen of the injustice to and subjugation of the Golspie fishermen, and of the people at large; likewise of the purposes for which the Duke's money is expended in that quarter. If you go, then, to the other side of the domain, you will find another Kyle, or a branch of the sea, which abounds in cockles and other shellfish, fortunately for the poor people, not forbidden by a Loch ukase. But in the years of distress, when the people were principally living upon vegetables, sea-weeds, and shellfish, various diseases made their appearance amongst them hitherto unknown. The absence of meal of any kind being considered the primary cause, some of the people thought they would be permitted to exchange shellfish for meal with their more fortunate neighbours in Caithness, to whom such shellfish were a rarity, and so far the understanding went between them, that the Caithness boats came up loaded with meal, but the Loch embargo, through his underling in Tongue, who was watching their movements, was at once placed upon it; the Caithness boats had to return home with the meal, and the Duke's people might live or die, as they best could. Now, madam, you have steeped your brains, and ransacked the English language to find refined terms for your panegyric on the Duke, Duchess, and family of Sutherland. (I find no fault with you, knowing you have been well paid for it.) But I would briefly ask you (and others who devoted much of their time and talents in the same strain), would it not be more like a noble pair,—if they did merit such noble praise as you have bestowed upon them—if they had, especially during years of famine and distress, freely opened up all these bountiful resources which God in His eternal wisdom and goodness prepared for His people, and which should never be intercepted nor restricted by man or men. You and others have composed hymns of praise, which it is questionable if there is a tune in heaven to sing them to.

So I returned, and considered all the oppressions that are done under the sun : and behold the tears of such as were oppressed, and they had no comforter ; and on the side of their oppressors there was power ; but they had no comforter.—ECCLES. iv. 1.

The wretch that works and weeps without relief
Has one that notices his silent grief.
He, from whose hands alone all pow'r proceeds,
Ranks its abuse among the foulest deeds,
Considers *all* injustice with a frown,
But *marks* the man that treads his fellow down.
Remember Heav'n has an avenging rod—
To smite the poor is treason against God.—COWPER.

But you shall find the Duke's money is expended for most astonishing purposes ; not a little of it goes to hire hypocrites, and renowned literary flatterers, to vindicate the mal-administration of those to whom he entrusted the management of his affairs, and make his Grace (who is by nature a simple-minded man) believe his servants are innocent of all the charges brought against them, and doing justice to himself and to his people, when they are doing the greatest injustice to both ; so that instead of calling his servants to account at any time, and enquiring into the broad charges brought against them—as every wise landlord should do—it seems the greater the enormities of foul deeds they commit, and the louder their accusations may sound through the land, the farther they are received into his favour.   The fact is, that James Loch was Duke of Sutherland, and not the "tall, slender man with rather a thin face, light brown hair, and mild blue eyes" who armed you up the extraordinary elegant staircase in Stafford House.

Allow me to allude to an historical parallel. After the conquest, the Norman kings afforested a large portion of the soil of conquered England, in much the same way as the landlords are now doing in the Highlands of Scotland. To such an extent was this practice carried on, that an historian informs us, that in the reign of King John "the greater part of the kingdom" was turned into forest, and that so multiform and oppressive were the forest laws, that it was impossible for any man who lived within the boundaries to escape falling a victim to them. To prepare the land for these forests, the people were required to be driven, in many cases, as in the Highlands, at the point of the bayonet; cultivated lands were laid waste, villages were destroyed, and the inhabitants extirpated. Distress ensued, and discontent followed as natural consequences. But observe, the Norman kings did all this in virtue of their feudal supremacy; and in point of law and right, were better entitled to do it than the Highland lairds are to imitate their example in the present day. Was it, however, to be tolerated? were the people to groan for ever under this oppression? No. The English Barons gave a practical reply to these questions at Runneymede, which it is unnecessary to detail. King John did cry out *utopian* at first, but was compelled to disafforest the land, and restore it to its natural and appropriate use; and the records of that great day's proceedings are universally esteemed as one of the brightest pages in English history. With this great example before their eyes, let the most conservative pause before they yield implicit faith in the doctrine that every one of them may do with his lands as he pleases. The fundamental principle of land tenure are unchanged since the days of Magna Charta; and however much the tendency of modern ideas may have cast these principles into oblivion,

they are still deeply graven in the constitution, and if necessity called, would be found as strong and operative in
the present day as they were five centuries ago.   If the
barons could compel the sovereign to open his forests,
surely the sovereign may more orderly compel the barons to
open theirs, and restore them to their natural and appropriate
use ; and there is a power behind the throne which impels
and governs all.   These are deep questions that should be
stirred in the country, in the midst of extremities and abuse
of power.   For it is impossible for any one to travel in the
Highlands of Scotland, and cast his eyes about him without
feeling inwardly that such a crisis is approaching, and indeed consider it should have arrived long ago.   Sufferings
have been inflicted in the Highlands as severe as those occasioned by the policy of the brutal Roman kings in England;
deer have extended ranges, while men have been hunted
within a narrower and still narrower circle.   The strong have
fainted in the race for life ; the old have been left to die.
One after another of their liberties have been cloven down.
To kill a fish in the stream, or a wild beast in the hill,
is a transportable crime, even in time of famine.   To
travel through the fenceless forest is a crime ; paths which
at one time linked hamlet to hamlet for ages have been shut
and barred.   These oppressions are daily on the increase,
and if pushed much farther, (I should say if not speedily
and timely pushed back) it is obvious that the sufferings of
the people will reach a pitch, when action will be the
plainest duty, and the most sacred instinct.   To prevent
such forbidden calamity, permit me to address a few lines to
Her Majesty.

Come Victoria, Queen of Great Britain, Berwick-upon-
Tweed, and Ireland ; thou, the most beloved of all Sovereigns upon earth, in whose bosom and veins the blood of

the Stuarts, the legitimate Sovereigns of Scotland is freely circulating; who hath endeared thyself to thy Celtic lieges in a peculiar manner, stretch forth thy Royal hand to preserve that noble race from extirpation, and becoming extinct, and to protect them from the violence, oppression, and spoliation to which they have been subjected for many years. Bear in mind, that this is the race in whom your forefathers confided, trusted, and depended on so much at all times, especially when a foreign invader threatened and attempted to take possession of the Scottish throne; and never trusted to them in vain. And though they unfortunately divided upon who of the Stuart family was to rule over them, and much valuable blood shed on that account; yet the impartial investigator into that affair will find the zeal, patriotism and loyalty of each party meriting equal praise and admiration, though the *butchers* and literary scourges of the defeated party converted the praise and loyalty due to them into calumny and abuse. But these gloomy days of strife and murder are over, and the defeated consider that they sustained no loss but that they gained much; and I assure your Majesty that your name is now imprinted upon every Scotch Highlander's heart in letters more valuable than gold, and that the remnant of them still left, are as willing and as ready to shed their blood for the honour and dignity of your crown, and the safety of your person and family, as their fathers were for your grandsires. ˙ Then allow not this noble race to be extirpated, nor deteriorated in their soul, mind, chivalry, character, and persons : allow it not, your Majesty, to be told in Gath, nor published in the streets of Askelon, that other nations have to feed and keep alive your Highland Scotch warriors, while you require their service on the battle field ; while the nursery where these brave men, who carried many a laurel to the British crown from foreign strands, are now converted into game preserves, hunting parks, and lairs for wild animals. Come then, like a God-fearing, God-loving and Christian queen ; like a subject-loving and beloved sovereign, and demand the restitution of their inalienable rights for your Highland lieges, and the restoration of the Highland straths and glens to their natural and appropriate use. Examine, like *Ahasuerus*, the book of records of the chronicles, and find what service the High-landers rendered you and your forefathers, and how they were requitted. " Who knoweth whether thou art come to the kingdom for such a time as this ? " and " how can you endure to see the evil that came upon your people, or how can you endure to see the destruction of your kindred " people ? and then like good Queen Esther, declare boldly and publicly that you shall not have a Hamanite or a Hamanitess about your person, in your household, or in your counsel. Highland proprietors hold the lands and other rights they plundered from the people, on the principle that Rob Roy maintained his right to the cattle he stole from his distant neighbours in Badenoch. But the day is drawing nigh when these rank delusions in high quarters will be dispelled. It is a Satanic imposture, that the stewardship of God's soil is freely convertible into a mis-chevious power of oppressing the poor. The proper use of property is to make property useful ; where this is not done, it were better for land owners to have been born beggars, than to live in luxury while causing the wretched to want and weep. I know that if our Sovereign Lady was to make such a demand as this, that she would incur the ire and displeasure of the turf and sporting classes, a consuming not a producing body, the most destructive, vicious, cruel, dis-orderly, unvirtuous, revelling, and the most useless of all her

Majesty's subjects. On the other hand her Majesty would gain for herself the praise and admiration of all the most wise, prudent, liberal, humane, virtuous, and most exemplary of the nation; the blessings of the people and of heaven would rest upon her, and remain with her, and Highland proprietors, their children, and children's children would have cause to hold her name and memory in grateful recollection. Their estates would in a few years double their rents, and they and their heirs would be redeemed from insolvency, and secured from beggary. The poor law would become a dead letter. The poaching game law expenditure, along with many other unrighteous laws, which are hanging heavily upon the nation, would fall to disuse; the people would prosper, and nothing would be lost but hunting grounds for the younger branches of the aristocracy and English snobs, and that could be easily supplied by Her Majesty directing the attention of this cruel cowardly class to the Hudson's Bay and North West Territories, where they might have plenty useful sport, destroying animals much of their own disposition, *though not half so injurious.*

The Duchess of Sutherland pays a visit every year to Dunrobin Castle, and has seen and heard so many supplicating appeals presented to her husband by the poor fishermen of Golspie, soliciting liberty to take mussels from the Little Ferry Sands to bait their nets—a liberty of which they were deprived by his factors, though paying yearly rent for it; yet returned by his Grace, with the brief deliverance, that he could do nothing for them. Can I believe that this is the same personage who can set out from Dunrobin Castle, her own Highland seat, and after travelling from it, then can ride in one direction over thirty miles, in another direction forty-four miles, in another, by taking the necessary circuitous route, sixty miles, and that over fertile glens, valleys, and straths, bursting with fatness, which gave birth to, and where were reared for ages, thousands of the bravest, the most moral, virtuous, and religious men that Europe could boast of; ready to a man, at a moment's warning from their chiefs, to rise in defence of their king, queen, and country ; animated with patriotism and love to their chief, and irresistible in the battle contest for victory. But these valiant men had then a *country*, a *home*, and a *chief* worth the fighting for. But I can tell her that she can now ride over these extensive tracts in the interior of the county without seeing the image of God upon a man travelling these roads, with the exception of a wandering Highland shepherd, wrapped up in a gray plaid to the eyes, with a colly dog behind him as a drill serjeant to train his ewes and to marshal his tups. There may happen to travel over the dreary tract a geologist, a tourist, or a lonely carrier, but these are as rare as a pelican in the wilderness, or a camel's convoy caravan in the deserts of Arabia. Add to this a few English sportsmen, with their stag hounds, pointer dogs, and servants, and put themselves and their bravery together, and one company of French soldiers would put ten thousand of them to a disorderly flight, to save their own carcases, leaving their ewes and tups to feed the invaders ! The question may arise, where those people, who inhabited this country at one period, have gone ? In America and Australia the most of them will be found. The Sutherland family and the nation had no need of their services ; hence they did not regard their patriotism or loyalty, and disregarded their past services. Sheep, bullocks, deer, and game, became more valuable than men. Yet a remnant, or in other words a *skeleton*, of them is to be found along the sea-shore, huddled together in motley groups upon barren moors, among cliffs and precipices, in the most impoverished, degraded, subjugated, slavish, spiritless condition that human beings could exist in. If this is really the lady who has "Glory to God in the highest, peace on earth, and good will to men," in view, and who is so religiously denouncing the American statute which "denies the slave the sanctity of marriage, with all its joys, rights, and obligations —which separates, at the will of the master, the wife from the husband, the children from the parents,"—I would advise her in God's name to take a tour round the sea-skirts of Sutherland, her own estate, beginning at Brora, then to Helmsdale, Portskerra, Strathy, Farr, Tongue, Durness, Eddrachillis, and Assynt, and learn the subjugated, degraded, impoverished, uneducated condition of the spiritless people of that sea-beaten coast, about two hundred miles in length, and let her with similar zeal remonstrate with her husband, that their condition be bettered ; for the cure for all their misery and want is lying unmolested in the fertile valleys above, and all under his control ; and to advice his Grace, her husband, to be no longer guided by his Ahitophel, Mr. Loch, but to discontinue his depopulating schemes, which have separated many a wife from her husband, never to meet—which caused many a premature death, and that separated many sons and daughters, never to see each other; and by all means to withdraw that mandate of Mr. Loch, which forbids marriage on the Sutherland estate, under pains and penalties of being banished from the county ; for it has already been the cause of a great amount of prostitution, and his augmented illegitimate connections and issues fifty per cent. above what such were a few years ago—before this unnatural, ungodly law was put in force.

Let us see what the character of these ill-used people was!
General Stewart of Garth, in his "Sketches of the Highlands," says :—In the words of a general officer by whom the
93rd Sutherlanders were once reviewed, "They exhibit a
perfect pattern of military discipline and moral rectitude.
In the case of such men disgraceful punishment would be
as unnecessary as it would be pernicious."   "Indeed," says
the General "so remote was the idea of such a measure in
regard to them, that when punishments were to be inflicted
on others, and the troops in garrison assembled to witness
their execution, the presence of the Sutherland Highlanders
was dispensed with, the effects of terror as a check to crime
being in their case uncalled for, as examples of that nature
were not necessary for such honourable soldiers.   When the
Sutherland Highlanders were stationed at the Cape of
Good Hope, anxious to enjoy the advantages of religious
instruction agreeably to the tenets of their national church,
and there being no religious service in the garrison except
the customary one of reading prayers to the soldiers on
parade, the Sutherland men," says the General, "formed
themselves into a congregation, appointed elders of their
own number, engaged and paid a stipend (collected among
themselves) to a clergyman of the Church of Scotland, and
had divine service performed agreeably to the ritual of the
Established Church every Sabbath, and prayer meetings
through the week."   This reverend gentlemen, Mr. Thom,
in a letter which appeared in the *Christian Herald* of October, 1814, writes thus :—"When the 93rd Highlanders left
Cape Town last month, there were among them 156 members of the church, including three elders and three deacons,
all of whom, so far as men can know the heart from the life,
were pious men.   The regiment was certainly a pattern of
morality, and good behaviour to all other corps.   They read

their Bibles and observed the Sabbath. They saved their money to do good. 7,000 rix dollars, a sum equal to £1,200, the non-commissioned officers and privates saved for books, societies, and for the spread of the Gospel, a sum unparalleled in any other corps in the world, given in the short space of eighteen months. Their example had a general good effect on both the colonists and the heathen. If ever apostolic days were revived in modern times on earth, I certainly believe some of those to have been granted to us in Africa." Another letter of a similar kind, addressed to the Committee of the Edinburgh Gaelic School Society (fourth annual report), says:—" The 93rd Highlanders arrived in England, when they immediately received orders to proceed to North America; but, before they re-embarked, the sum collected for your society was made up and remitted to your treasurer, amounting to seventy-eight pounds sterling." " In addition to this," says the noble minded, immortal General, "such of them as had parents and friends in Sutherland did not forget their destitute condition, occasioned by the operation of the *(fire and faggot) mis-*improved state of the county." During the short period the regiment was quartered at Plymouth, upwards of £500 was lodged in one banking-house, to be remitted to Sutherland, exclusive of many sums sent through the Post-office and by officers; some of the sums exceeding £20 from an individual soldier. Men like these do credit to the peasantry of a country. " It must appear strange, and somewhat inconsistent," continues the General, " when the same men who are so loud in their profession of an eager desire to promote and preserve the religious and moral virtues of the people, should so frequently take the lead in removing them from where they imbibed principles which have attracted the notice of Europe and of measures which lead to a deterioration, placing families on patches of potato ground as in Ireland, a system pregnant with degradation, poverty, and disaffection." It is only when parents and heads of families in the Highlands are moral, happy, and contented, that they can instil sound principles into their children, who in their intercourse with the world may become what the men of Sutherland have already been, "an honourable example, worthy the imitation of all".

I cannot help being grieved at my unavoidable abbreviation of these heart-stirring and heart-warming extracts, which should ornament every mantel-piece and library in the Highlands of Scotland; but I could refer to other authors of similar weight; among the last (though not the least), Mr. Hugh Miller of the *Witness*, in his "Sutherland as it was and is : or, How a country can be ruined;" a work which should silence and put to shame every vile, malignant, calumniator of Highland religion and moral virtue in bygone years, who in their sophistical profession of a desire to promote the temporal and spiritual welfare of the people, had their own sordid cupidity and aggrandisement in view in all their unworthy lucubrations (as I will endeavour to show at a future period). Come then, ye perfidious declaimers and denouncers ; you literary scourges of Highland happiness, under whatever garb, whether political economist or theology mongers, answer for yourselves—What good have you achieved, after expending such enormous sums of money? Is it possible that the world will believe you, or put confidence in you any longer? Before I am done with you, come, you professing preachers of the everlasting Gospel of peace and of good will to men, stand alongside and on the same platform with the Highland Destitution Relief Board, exhibited before God and the world, and accused of misapplying and squandering away an enormous amount of money, and of having in your league, and combination with political economists—treacherous professing civilizers and improvers of the Highlands and Highland population,—produced the most truly deplorable results that ever were recorded in the history of any nation, the utter ruin and destruction of as brave, moral, religious, loyal, and patriotic a race of men as ever existed. Spiritual and temporal destitution in the Highlands has been a profitable field for you these many years back. Many a scheme has been tried, hitherto successful, to extract money from the pockets of the credulous benevolent public, who unfortunately believed your fabulous accusation and misrepresentation of the Highlanders, and who confided in your honesty ; and although you, yourselves, may see, the public, yea, and he that runneth may see, that the Lord, not without a cause, has discountenanced you, still you continue pour appeals to the public, that your traffic may continue likewise ; appeals from respectable quarters have lately been made for Gaelic teachers, Gaelic bibles, and psalm books, and tracts, for the poor Highlanders, who are dying for want of food. Depend upon it that there is a squad of students out of employment, and a great deal of these books unsold somewhere, that must be turned to money. We have now an association forming in Edinburgh, got up by men from whom better things should be expected, who have for their object to export these dying, penniless Highlanders to Ireland, to mix location with the poor Irish—who have gone through many a fiery ordeal for the last sixty years— that the wastes of Ireland may be reclaimed from nature, and cultivated by Highlanders ; just as if there was no waste land in the Highlands and Islands of Scotland to reclaim and cultivate ; or, as if there was something devilish

or unnatural in the Highland soil, detrimental to the progress of its inhabitants.

Britain will some day bewail the loss of her Highland
sons, Highland bravery, loyalty, patriotism, and Highland
virtue.   May God hasten the day, that I may live to see it.

At the commencement of the Russian war a correspondent wrote MacLeod as follows :—" Your predictions are
making their appearance at last, great demands are here for
men to go to Russia, but they are not to be found.   It
seems that the Secretary of War has corresponded with all
our Highland proprietors, to raise as many men as they
could for the Crimean war, and ordered so many officers of
rank to the Highlands to assist the proprietors in doing so
—but it has been a complete failure as yet.   The nobles
advertised, by placards, meetings of the people ; these pro-
clamations were attended to, but when they came to understand what they were about, in most cases the recruiting
proprietors and staff were saluted with the ominous cry of
' Maa ! maa ! boo ! boo !' imitating sheep and bullocks, and,
' Send your deer, your roes, your rams, dogs, shepherds, and
gamekeepers, to fight the Russians, they have never done
us any harm '.   The success of his Grace the Duke of
Sutherland was deplorable ; I believe you would have
pitied the poor old man had you seen him.

" In my last letter I told you that his head commissioner,
Mr. Loch, and military officer, was in Sutherland for the
last six weeks, and failed in getting one man to enlist ; on
getting these doleful tidings, the Duke himself left London
for Sutherland, arriving at Dunrobin about ten days ago,
and after presenting himself upon the streets of Golspie
and Brora, he called a meeting of the male inhabitants of
the parishes of Clyne, Rogart, and Golspie ; the meeting
was well attended ; upwards of 400 were punctual at the

hour; his Grace in his carriage, with his military staff and factors appeared shortly after; the people gave them a hearty cheer; his Grace took the chair. Three or four clerks took their seats at the table, and loosened down bulky packages of bank notes, and spread out platefuls of glittering gold. The Duke addressed the people very seriously, and entered upon the necessity of going to war with Russia, and the danger of allowing the Czar to have more power than what he holds already; of his cruel, despotic reign in Russia, etc.; likewise praising the Queen and her government, rulers and nobles of Great Britain, who stood so much in need of men to put and keep down the tyrant of Russia, and foil him in his wicked schemes to take possession of Turkey. In concluding his address, which was often cheered, the Duke told the young able-bodied men that his clerks were ready to take down the names of all those willing to enlist, and everyone who would enlist in the 93rd Highlanders, that the clerk would give him, there and then, £6 sterling; those who would rather enter any other corps, would get £3, all from his own private purse, independently of the government bounty. After advancing many silly flattering decoyments, he sat down to see the result, but there was no movement among the people; after sitting for a long time looking at the clerks, and they at him, at last his anxious looks at the people assumed a somewhat indignant appearance, when he suddenly rose up and asked what was the cause of their non-attention to the proposals he made, but no reply; it was the silence of the grave. Still standing, his Grace suddenly asked the cause; but no reply; at last an old man leaning upon his staff, was observed moving towards the Duke, and when he approached near enough, he addressed his Grace something as follows:—" I am sorry for the response your Grace's pro-

posals are meeting here to-day, so near the spot where your
maternal grand-mother, by giving forty-eight hours' notice,
marshalled fifteen hundred men to pick out of them the nine
hundred she required, but there is a cause for it, and a
grievous cause, and as your Grace demands to know it, I
must tell you, as I see no one else are inclined in this
assembly to do it. Your Grace's mother and predecessors
applied to our fathers for men upon former occasions, and
our fathers responded to their call ; they have made liberal
promises, which neither them nor you performed ; we are,
we think, a little wiser than our fathers, and we estimate
your promises of to-day at the value of theirs, besides you
should bear in mind that your predecessors and yourself
expelled us in a most cruel and unjust manner from the
land which our fathers held in lien from your family, for
their sons, brothers, cousins, and relations, which were
handed over to your parents to keep up their dignity, and
and to kill the Americans, Turks, French, and the Irish ;
and these lands are devoted now to rear dumb brute
animals, which you and your parents consider of far more
value than men.   I do assure your Grace that it is the prevailing opinion in this county, that should the Czar of
Russia take possession of Dunrobin Castle and of Stafford
House next term, that we could not expect worse treatment
at his hands, than we have experienced at the hands of
your family for the last fifty years.   Your parents, yourself,
and your commissioners, have desolated the glens and
straths of Sutherland, where you should find hundreds, yea,
thousands of men to meet you, and respond cheerfully to
your call, had your parents and yourself kept faith with
them.   How could your Grace expect to find men where
they are not, and the few of them which are to be found
among the rubbish or ruins of the county, has more sense

an to be decoyed by chaff to the field of slaughter ; but one comfort you have, though you cannot find men to fight, you can supply those who will fight with plenty of mutton, beef, and venison." The Duke rose up, put on his hat and left the field.

Whether my correspondent added to the old man's reply to his Grace or not, I cannot say, but one thing is evident, it was the very reply his Grace deserved.

I know for a certainty this to be the prevailing feeling throughout the whole Highlands of Scotland, and who should wonder at it ? How many thousands of them who served out their 21, 22, 25 and 26 years, fighting for the British aristocracy, and on their return—wounded, maimed, or worn out—to their own country, promising themselves to spend the remainder of their days in peace, and enjoying the blessings and comfort their fathers enjoyed among their Highland, healthy, delightful hills, but found to their grief, that their parents were expelled from the country to make room for sheep, deer, and game, the glens where they were born desolate, and the abodes which sheltered them at birth, and where they were reared to manhood, burnt to the ground ; and instead of meeting the cheers, shaking-hands, hospitality, and affections of fathers, mothers, brothers, sisters, and relations, met with desolated glens, bleating of sheep, barking of dogs ; and if they should happen to rest their worn-out frame upon the green sod which has grown upon their father's hearth, and a game-keeper, factor, or water bailiff, to come round, he would very unceremoniously tell them to absent themselves as smart as they could, and not to annoy the deer. No race on record has suffered so much at the hands of those who should be their patrons, and proved to be so tenacious of patriotism as the Celtic race, but I assure you it has found its level now, and will disappear soon altogether; and as soon as patriotism shall disappear in any nation, so sure that nation's glory is tarnished, victories uncertain, her greatness diminished, and decaying consumptive death will be the result. If ever the old adage, which says, " Those whom the gods deter-mine to destroy, they first deprive them of reason," was verified, it was, and is, in the case of the British aristocracy, and Highland proprietors in particular. I am not so void of feeling as to blame the Duke of Sutherland, his parents, or any other Highland absentee proprietor for all the evil done in the land, but the evil was done in their name, and under the authority they have invested in wicked, cruel servants. For instance, the only silly man who enlisted from among the great assembly which his Grace addressed, was a married man, with three of a family and his wife ; it was generally believed that his bread was baked for life, but no sooner was he away to Fort George to join his regiment, than his place of abode was pulled down, his wife and family turned out, and only permitted to live in a hut, from which an old female pauper was carried a few days before to the church-yard ; there the young family were sheltered, and their names registered upon the poor roll for support ; his Grace could not be guilty of such low rascality as this, yet he was told of it, but took no cognisance of those who did it in his name. It is likewise said that this man got a furlough of two weeks to see his wife and family before going abroad, and that when the factor heard he was coming, he ordered the ground-officer of the parish of Rogart, named MacLeod, to watch the soldier, and not allow him to see nor speak to his wife, but in his (the officer's) pre-sence. We had at the same time, in the parish an old bachelor of the name of John Macdonald, who had three idiot sisters, whom he upheld, independent of any source of relief; but a favourite of George, the notorious factor, envied this poor bachelor's farm, and he was summoned to remove at next term. The poor fellow petitioned his Grace and Loch, but to no purpose; he was doomed to walk away on the term day, as the factor told him, "to America, Glasgow, or to the devil if he choosed". Seeing he had no other alternative, two days before the day of his removal he yoked his cart, and got neighbours to help him to haul the three idiots into it, and drove away with them to Dunrobin Castle. When he came up to factor Gunn's door, he capsized them out upon the green, and wheeled about and went away home. The three idiots finding themselves upon the top of one another so sudden, they raised an inhuman-like yell, fixed into one another to fight, and scratched, yelled, and screeched so terrific that Mr. Gunn, his lady, his daughters, and all the clerks and servants were soon about them; but they hearkened to no reason, for they had none themselves, but continued their fighting and inharmonious music. Messenger after messenger was sent after John, but of no use; at last the great Gunn himself followed and overtook him, asked him how did he come to leave his sisters in such a state? He replied, "I kept them while I had a piece of land to support them; you have taken that land from me, then take them along with the land, and make of them what you can; I must look out for myself, but I cannot carry them to the labour market". Gunn was in a fix, and had to give John assurance that he would not be removed if he would take his sisters, so John took them home, and has not been molested as yet.

I have here beside me (in Canada) a respectable girl of the name of Ann Murray, whose father was removed during the time of the wholesale *faggot* removals, but got a

lot of a barren moor to cultivate. However barren-like it
was, he was raising a family of industrious young sons, and
by dint of hard labour and perseverance, they made it a
comfortable home; but the young sons one by one left the
country (and four of them are within two miles of where I
sit); the result was, that Ann was the only one who remained
with the parents. The mother, who had an attack of palsy,
was left entirely under Ann's care after the family left; and
she took it so much to heart that her daughter's attention
was required day and night, until death put an end to her
afflictions, after twelve years' suffering. Shortly after the
mother's death, the father took ill, and was confined to bed
for nine months; and Ann's labour re-commenced until
his decease. Though Ann Murray could be numbered
among the most dutiful of daughters, yet her incessant
labour, for a period of more than thirteen years, made
visible inroads upon her tender constitution; yet by the
liberal assistance of her brothers, who did not loose sight
of her and their parent (though upon a foreign strand), Ann
Murray kept the farm in the best of order, no doubt expecting that she would be allowed to keep it after her parent's
decease, but this was not in store for her; the very day
after her father's funeral, the officer came to her, and told
her that she was to be removed in a few weeks, that the
farm was let to another, and that Factor Gunn wished to
see her. She was at that time afflicted with jaundice,
and told the officer she could not undertake the journey,
which was only ten miles. Next day the officer was at her
again, more urgent than before, and made use of extraordinary threats; so she had to go. When she appeared
before this Bashaw, he swore like a trooper, and damned
her soul, why she disobeyed his first summons; she excused
herself, trembling, that she was unwell; another volley of

oaths and threats met her response, and told her to remove herself from the estate next week, for her conduct; and with a threat, which well becomes a Highland tyrant, not to take away, nor sell a single article of furniture, implements of husbandry, cattle, or crop; nothing was allowed but her own body clothes; everything was to be handed over to her brother, who was to have the farm. Seeing there was neither mercy nor justice for her, she told him the crop, house, and every other thing belonging to the farm, belonged to her and brothers in America, and that the brother to whom he (the factor) intended to hand over the farm and effects never helped her father or mother while in trouble; and that she was determined that he should not enjoy what she laboured for, and what her other brothers paid for. She went and got the advice of a man of business, advertised a sale, and sold off, in the face of threats of interdict, and came to Canada, where she was warmly received by brothers, sisters, and friends, now in Woodstock, and can tell her tale better than I can. No one could think, nor believe that his Grace would ever countenance such doings as these; but it was done in his name.

I have here within ten miles of me, Mr. William Ross, once taxman of Achtomleeny, Sutherlandshire, who occupied the most convenient farm to the principal deer-stalking hills in the county. Often have the English and Irish lords, connected in marriage with the Sutherlands, dined and took their lunch at William Ross's table, and at his expense; and more than once passed the night under his roof. Mr. Ross being so well acquainted among the mountains and haunts of the deer, was often engaged as a guide and instructor to these noblemen on their deer-stalking and fishing excursions, and became a real favourite with the Sutherland family, which enabled him to erect

superior buildings to the common rule, and improve his
farm in a superior style ; so that his mountain-side farm
was nothing short of a Highland paradise. But unfortunately for William, his nearest neighbour, one Major
Gilchrist, a sheep-farmer, coveted Mr. Ross's vineyard, and
tried many underhand schemes to secure the place for
himself, but in vain. Ross would hearken to none of his
proposals. But Ahab was a chief friend of Factor Gunn ;
and William Ross got notice of removal. Ross prepared
a memorial to the first and late Duchess of Sutherland,
and placed it in her own hand. Her Grace read it, instantly went into the factor's office, and told him that
William Ross was not to be removed from Achtomleeny
while he lived ; and wrote the same on the petition, and
handed it back to Ross, with a graceful smile, saying, " You
are now out of the reach of factors ; now, William, go
home in peace ". William bowed, and departed cheerfully ;
but the factor and ground-officer followed close behind
him, and while Ross was reading her Grace's deliverance,
the officer, David Ross, came and snapped the paper out of
his hand, and ran to Factor Gunn with it. Ross followed,
but Gunn put it in his pocket, saying, " William, you would
need to give it to me afterwards, at any rate, and I will
keep it till I read it, and then return it to you," and with a
tiger-like smile on his face, said, " I believe you came good
speed to-day, and I am glad of it " ; but William never got
it in his hand again. However, he was not molested during
her Grace's life. Next year she paid a visit to Dunrobin, when
Factor William Gunn advised Ross to apply to her for a
reduction of rent, under the mask of favouring him. He
did so, and it was granted cheerfully. Her Grace left
Dunrobin that year never to return ; in the beginning of the
next spring, she was carried back to Dunrobin a corpse,

and a few days after was interred in Dornoch. William Ross was served with a summons of removal from Achtomleeny, and he had nothing to show. He petitioned the present Duke, and his commissioner, Mr. Loch, and related the whole circumstances to them, but to no avail, only he was told that Factor Gunn was ordered to give him some other lot of land, which he did : and having no other resource, William accepted of it to his loss ; for between loss of cattle, building and repairing houses, he was minus one hundred and fifty pounds sterling, of his means and substance, from the time he was removed from Achtomleeny till he removed himself to Canada. Besides, he had a written agreement or promise for melioration or valuation for all the farm improvements and house building at Achtomleeny, which was valued by the family surveyor at £250. William was always promised to get it, until they came to learn that he was leaving for America, then they would not give him a cent. William Ross left them with it to join his family in Canada ; but he can in his old age sit at as comfortable a table, and sleep on as comfortable a bed, with greater ease of mind and a clearer conscience, among his own dutiful and affectionate children, than the tyrant factor ever did, or ever will among his. I know as well as any one can tell me, that this is but one or two cases out of the thousand I could enumerate, where the liberality and benevolence of his Grace, and of his parents, were abused, and that to their patron's loss. You see in the above case that William was advised to plead for a reduction of rent, so that the factor's favourite, Ahab Gilchrist, would have the benefit of Naboth Ross's improvement, and the reduction he got on his rent, which would not be obtained otherwise. The unhallowed crew of factors and officials, from the highest to the lowest grade, employed by the family of Sutherland, got the corrupt portion of the public press on their side, to applaud their wicked doings and schemes, as the only mode of improvement and civilisation in the Highlands of Scotland. They have got what is still more to be lamented, all the Established ministers, with few exceptions, on their side; and in them they found faithful auxiliaries in crushing the people. Any of them could hold a whole congregation by the hair of their heads over hell-fire, if they offered to resist the powers that be, until they submitted. If a single individual resisted, he was denounced from the pulpit, and considered afterwards a dangerous man in the community; and he might depart as quick as he could. Any man, or men, may violate the laws of God, and violate the laws of heaven, as often as he chooses; he is never heeded, and has nothing to fear; but if he offends the Duke's factor, the lowest of his minions, or violates the least of their laws and regulations, it is an unpardonable sin. The present Duke's mother was no doubt a liberal lady of many good parts, and seemed to be much attached to the natives, but unfortunately for them, she employed for her factors, a vile, unprincipled crew, who were their avowed enemies; she would hearken to the complaints of the people, and would write to the ministers of the Gospel to ascertain the correctness of complaints, and the factor was justified, however gross the outrage was that he committed—the minister dined with the factor, and could not refuse to favour him. The present Duke is a simple, narrow-minded gentleman, who concerns himself very little even about his own pecuniary affairs; he entrusts his whole affairs to his factors, and the people are enslaved so much, that it is now considered the most foolish thing a man can do to petition his Grace, whatever is done to him, for it will go hard with the factor, or he will punish and make an example of him to deter others.

To detail what I knew myself personally, and what I have learned from others of their conduct, would, as I said before, fill a volume. For instance :—When a marriage in the family of Sutherland takes place, or the birth of an heir, a feast is ordered for the Sutherland people, consisting of whisky, porter, ale, and plenty of eatables. The day of feasting and rejoicing is appointed, and heralded throughout the country, and the people are enjoined in marshal terms to assemble—barrels of raw and adulterated whisky are forwarded to each parish, some raw adulterated sugar, and that is all. Bonfires are to be prepared on the tops of the highest mountains. The poorest of the poor are warned by family officers to carry the materials, consisting of peats and tar barrels, upon their backs ; the scene is lamentable to see groups of these wretched, half-clad and ill-shod, climbing up these mountains with their loads ; however, the work must be done, there is no denial, the evening of rejoicing is arrived, and the people are assembled at their different clachans. The barrels of whisky are taken out to the open field, poured into large tubs, a good amount of abominable-looking sugar is mixed with it, and a sturdy favourite is employed to stir it about with a flail handle, or some long cudgel—all sorts of drinking implements are produced, tumblers, bowls, ladles, and tin jugs. Bag-pipers are set up with great glee. In the absence of the factor, the animal called the ground-officer, and in some instances the parish minister, will open the jollification, and show an example to the people how to deal with this coarse beverage. After the first round, the respectable portion of the people will depart, or retire to an inn, where they can enjoy themselves ; but the *drouthies*, and ignorant youthful, will keep the field of revelling until tearing of clothes and faces comes to be the rule ; fists and cudgels supplant jugs and ladles, and this will continue until king Bacchus enters the field and hushes the most heroic brawlers, and the most ferocious combatants to sound snoring on the field of rejoicing, where many of them enter into contracts with death, from which they could never extricate themselves. With the co-operation and assistance of factors, ministers, and editors, a most flourishing account is sent to the world, and to the absentee family in London, who knows nothing about how the affair was conducted. The world will say how happy must the people be who live under such good and noble, liberal-minded patrons ; and the patrons themselves are so highly-pleased with the report, that however extraordinary the bill that comes to them on the rent day, in place of money, for roast beef and mutton, bread and cheese, London porter and Edinburgh ale, which was never bought, nor tasted by the people, they will consider their commissioners used great economy ; no cognizance is taken, the bill is accepted and discharged, the people are deceived, and the proprietors injured.

JOHN MACKIE.

Donald MacLeod continues his remarks on the Sutherland thus :—

"I am sorry that for the present I must lay aside many important communications bearing upon the clearing system of the Highlanders which corroborates and substantiates my description of it, such as letters published by Mr. Somers and Mr. Donald Ross, Glasgow, Mr. Donald Sutherland, which appeared in the *Woodstock Sentinel*, a few weeks ago; but above all I regret how little I can take from the pen of Mr. Mackie, editor of the *Northern Ensign*, Wick, Caithness, a gentleman who, since the appearance of his valuable paper, proved himself the faithful friend of the oppressed, the indefatigable exposer of their wrongs, the terror of their oppressors, and chastiser of their tools, apologisers and abettors, though his pecuniary benefits would be to sail in the same boat with his unprincipled contemporaries in the north of Scotland; but he chose the better part, and there is a higher promise of reward for him than worm Dukes, Lords, Esquires, and their vile underlings could bestow. The following is among the last of Mr. Mackie's productions on the subject" :—

WILLING HANDS FOR INDIA.

Over this title *Punch* of last week gives a very exciting illustration. A towering cart-load of ingathered grain, with a crowing cock on its summit, forms the background; while in front a recruiting officer and a party are cheered by the excited harvesters, coming forward with reaping-hooks in their hands, to volunteer for India, the banner borne by the officer representing the British lion in the act of springing on the Bengal tiger. The recruits, not yet returned from the harvest field, are all enthusiasm, and are eagerly rushing to enrol themselves among the avengers of the butcheries that have been perpetrated in our Indian empire.

The newspapers of the south report that the recruiting in certain districts had been most successful, and that already many thousand young men of promise have entered the line. It is remarkable, however, particularly so, that all reference to the districts from which the main strength of our regular army was formerly obtained is most studiously avoided.   May we ask the authorities what success the recruiting officer has now met with in the Highlands of Scotland?   Time was, in former exigencies, when all eyes were turned in that direction, and not in vain.   Time was when, in only five days, the county of Sutherland alone contributed one thousand young men ; and when, in four- teen days, no fewer than eleven times that number were enrolled as recruits from the various Highland districts. Time was when the immortal Chatham boasted that " he had found upon the mountains of Caledonia a gallant though oppressed race of heroes, who had triumphantly carried the British banner into every quarter of the globe ". Time was when *Punch* would, in such an illustration as that of last week, have included in his representation some half- dozen kilted Celts, shoulder to shoulder, issuing from their mountain homes, and panting to be let loose on the Indian bloodhounds.

Why not now?   Answer the question, my Lord Duke of Sutherland.   Tell Her Majesty, my Lord, why the bagpipes of the recruiting party are silent in Sutherland, and why no "willing hands for India" are found in your Grace's vast Highland domain.   Tell her how it happens that the pat- riotic enthusiasm which at the close of the last century was shown in the almost magical enrolment of thousands of brawny Sutherlanders, who gained wide-world renown at Corunna, at Fuentes d'Onor, at Vittoria, at Waterloo, and elsewhere, is now unknown in Sutherland, and how the enrolment of one man in that large county is a seven years' wonder.   If your Grace is silent, the answer is not wanting, nor is Her Majesty ignorant of it.

And yet the cursed system which has disheartened and well-nigh destroyed that " race of heroes," is pertinaciously persevered in by the very men who, of all others, should be the first to come forward and denounce it. "Willing hands for India," says *Punch.* "No," says high-bred lords and coroneted peers; "give us game preserves, deer forests, and sheep walks. Perish your bold peasantry! and life to the pleasures of the forest and the mountain heath." And thus it is that landlord after landlord is yearly weeding out the aborigines, and converting Scotland into one ponderous deer forest. Not a year passes without seeing hundreds of unoffending men, women, and children, from Cape Wrath to Mull of Galloway, remorselessly unhoused, and their little crofts added to the vast waste. And now that Britain for the second time in four years has again to invoke the patriotism of her sons, and to call for aid in the eventful crisis in India, the blast of the recruiter's bugle evokes only the bleat of sheep, or the pitiful bray of the timid deer, in the greater part of these wide regions which formerly contributed their tens of thousands of men to fight their country's battles. Oh, had Chatham been alive now, what a feeling would have been awakened in his manly breast as he surveyed the wreck which the Loch policy had occasioned; and with what crushing eloquence would he have invoked the curse of heaven on that system. Meanwhile, Britain misses her Highland heroes, and the imperilled troops in India, with the unoffending women and children, must wait the tardy arrival of "willing hands" to assist them, while, had the Highlanders of Scotland been as they once were, in one week more men would have been raised for India than would have sufficed to have effectually crushed the Indian revolt, had it spread itself from the foot of the Himalaya mountains to the most distant district of our Indian empire.

Let Highland evictors, from Dukes to the meanest squires, beware. Popular patience has a limit; and it

seems to me that the time is rapidly nearing when, if
Parliament remains longer silent, the people of the country
will arouse themselves, and, by one united expression of
their will, drive back to its native den the foul and disastrous
policy which has depeopled the Scottish Highlands.

MacLeod continues :—To detail individual deaths, sufferings, and oppressions in the Highlands of Scotland, would
be an endless work.   A few months ago a letter from Donald
Sutherland, farmer, West Lorra, Canada West, appeared in
the *Woodstock Sentinel,* detailing what his father and family
suffered at the hands of the Sutherlandshire landlords ; all
the offence his father was guilty of was that he, along with
others, went and remonstrated with the house burners and
made them desist until the people could remove their
families and chattels out of their houses ; for this offence he
would not be allowed to remain on the estate.   He took
shelter with his family under the roof of his father-in-law ;
from this abode he was expelled, and his father-in-law made
a narrow escape from sharing the same fate for affording him
shelter.   He was thus persecuted from one parish to another,
until ultimately another proprietor, Skibo, took pity upon
him, and permitted him, in the beginning of an extraordinary
stormy winter, to build a house in the middle of a bog or
swamp, during the building of which, he having no assistance,
his family being all young, and far from his friends, and
having all materials to carry on his back, the stance of his new
house being inaccessible by horses or carts, he, poor fellow,
fell a victim to cold and fever, and a combination of other
troubles, and died before the house was finished, leaving a
widow and six fatherless children in this half-finished hut,
in the middle of a swamp, to the mercy of the world.   Well
might Donald Sutherland, who was the oldest of the family,
and who recollects what his father suffered, and his death,

I say, charge the Sutherland family and their tools with his death.

But many were the hundreds who suffered alike, and died similar deaths in Sutherlandshire during the wholesale evictions and house-burnings of the County. But I must now cease to unpack my heart upon these revolting scenes and gloomy memories. I know many will say that I have dealt too hard with the House of Sutherland,—that such disclosures as I have made cannot be of any public service,—that the present Duke of Sutherland is a good man, and that in England he is called the Good Duke. I have in my own unvarnished way brought to light a great amount of inhumanity, foul, unconstitutional, and barbarous atrocities, committed and perpetrated in his name, and in the name of his parents, and by their authority. I stand by these as stern facts.

The preceding pages are a reproduction of the Canadian edition of Donald MacLeod's "Gloomy Memories of the Highlands," published at Woodstock, in 1857. The "Letters" are, with very slight alterations, re-printed entire; but the author's Appendix, written in reply to Mrs. Beecher Stowe's "Sunny Memories" is considerably abridged and otherwise modified.

We shall next give the opinions of such eminent authors as General Stewart of Garth, Hugh Miller, Professor John Stuart Blackie, John Mackay C.E., born and bred in the County; and others.

GENERAL STEWART OF GARTH,

REFERRING to the Sutherland evictions, in his first edition, writes :—On the part of those who instituted similar improvements, in which so few of the people were to have a share, conciliatory measures, and a degree of tenderness, beyond what would have been shown to strangers, were to have been expected towards the hereditary supporters of their families. It was, however, unfortunately the natural consequences of the measures which were adopted, that few men of liberal feelings could be induced to undertake their execution. The respectable gentlemen, who, in so many cases, had formerly been entrusted with the management of Highland property, resigned, and their places were supplied by persons cast in a coarser mould, and, generally, strangers to the country, who, detesting the people, and ignorant of their character, capability, and language, quickly surmounted every obstacle, and hurried on the change, without reflecting on the distress of which it might be productive, or allowing the kindlier feelings of landlords to operate in favour of their ancient tenantry. To attempt a new system, and become acceptable tenants, required a little time and a little indulgence, two things which it was resolved should not be conceded them : they were immediately removed from the fertile and cultivated farms ; some left the country, and others were offered limited portions of land on uncultivated moors, on which they were to form a settlement ; and thus, while particular districts have been desolated, the gross numerical population has, in some manner, been preserved. Many judicious men, however, doubt the policy of these measures, and dread their consequences on the condition and habits of the people. The following account of their situation is from the respectable and intelligent clergyman of an extensive parish in that county :—" When the valleys and higher grounds were let to the shepherds, the whole population was drawn down to the sea-shore, where they were crowded on small lots of land, to earn their subsistence by labour (where all are labourers and few employers) and by sea-fishing, the latter so little congenial to their former habits. This cutting down farms into lots was found so profitable, that over the whole of this district, the sea-coast, where the shore is accessible, is thickly studded with wretched cottages, crowded with starving inhabitants. Ancient respectable tenants, who passed the greater part of life in the enjoyment of abundance, and in the exercise of hospitality and charity, possessing stocks of ten, twenty, and thirty breeding cows, with the usual proportion of other stock, are now pining on one or two acres of bad land, with one or two starved cows, and, for this accommodation, a calculation is made, that they must support their families and pay the rent of their lots, which the land cannot afford. When the herring fishery (the only fishery prosecuted on this coast) succeeds, they generally satisfy the landlords, whatever privations they may suffer, but when the fishing fails, they fall in arrears, and are sequestrated, and their stock sold to pay the rents, their lots given to others, and they and their families turned adrift on the world. The herring fishery, always precarious, has, for a succession of years, been very defective, and this class of people are reduced to extreme misery. At first, some of them possessed capital, from converting their farm stock into cash, but this has been long

exhausted.   It is distressing to view the general poverty of
this class of people, aggravated by their having once enjoyed
abundance and independence; and we cannot sufficiently
admire their meek and patient spirit, supported by the
powerful influence of religious and moral principle.   There
are still a few small tenants on the old system, occupying
the same farm jointly, but they are falling fast to decay, and
sinking into the new class of cottars."

    This mode of sub-dividing small portions of inferior land
is bad enough certainly, and to propose the establishment
of villages, in a pastoral country, for the benefit of men who
can neither betake themselves to the cultivation of the land
nor to commerce for earning the means of subsistence, is
doubtless a refinement in policy solely to be ascribed to the
enlightened and enlarged views peculiar to the new system.
But, leaving out of view the consideration that, from the
prevalence of turning corn lands into pasture, the demand
for labour is diminished, while the number of labourers is
increased, it can scarcely be expected that a man who had
once been in the condition of a farmer, possessed of land,
and of considerable property in cattle, horses, sheep, and
money, often employing servants himself, conscious of his
independence, and proud of his ability to assist others, should,
without the most poignant feelings, descend to the rank of a
hired labourer, even where labour and payment can be
obtained, more especially if he must serve on the farms or
in the country where he formerly commanded as a master.
It is not easy for those who live in a country like England,
where so many of the lower orders have nothing but what
they acquire by the labour of the passing day, and possess
no permanent property or share in the agricultural produce
of the soil, to appreciate the nature of the spirit of independence, which is generated in countries where the free cultivators

of the soil constitute the major part of the population. It can scarcely be imagined how proudly a man feels, however small his property may be, when he has a spot of arable land and pasture, stocked with corn, horses, and cows, a species of property which, more than any other, binds him, by ties of interest and attachment, to the spot with which he is connected. He considers himself an independent person, placed in a station in society far above the day-labourer, who has no stake in the permanency of existing circumstances, beyond the prospect of daily employment; his independence being founded on permanent property, he has an interest in the welfare of the state, by supporting which he renders his own property more secure, and, although the value of the property may not be great, it is every day in his view; his cattle and horses feed around him; his grass and corn he sees growing and ripening; his property is visible to all observers, which is calculated to raise the owner in general consideration; and when a passing friend or neighbour praises his thriving crops and his cattle, his heart swells with pleasure, and he exerts himself to support and to preserve that government and those laws which render it secure. Such is the case in many parts of the world; such was formerly the case in Scotland, and is still in many parts of the Highlands. Those who wish to see only the two castes of capitalists and day-labourers, may smile at this union of independence and poverty. But, that the opposite system is daily quenching the independent spirit of the Highlanders, is an undoubted fact, and gives additional strength to the arguments of those who object to the reduction of the agricultural population, and regret their removal to the great towns, and to the villages in preparation in some parts of the country.

It is painful to dwell on this subject, but as information, communicated by men of honour, judgment, and perfect veracity, descriptive of what they daily witness, affords the best means of forming a correct judgment, and as these gentlemen, from their situations in life, have no immediate interest in the determination of the question, beyond what is dictated by humanity and a love of truth, their authority may be considered as undoubted.

The following extract of a letter from a friend, as well as the extract already quoted, is of this description. Speaking of the settlers on the new allotments, he says :—" I scarcely need tell you that these wretched people exhibit every symptom of the most abject poverty, and the most helpless distress. Their miserable lots in the moors, notwithstanding their utmost labour and strictest economy, have not yielded them a sufficient crop for the support of their families for three months. The little money they were able to derive from the sale of their stock, has, therefore, been expended in the purchase of necessaries, and is now wholly exhausted. Though they have now, therefore, overcome all their scruples about leaving their native land, and possess the most ardent desire to emigrate, in order to avoid more intolerable evils of starvation, and have been much encouraged by the favourable accounts they have received from their countrymen already in America, they cannot possibly pay the expense of transporting themselves and their families thither."

It has been said that an old Highlander warned his countrymen " to take care of themselves, for the law had reached Ross-shire ". When his fears were excited by vague apprehensions of change, he could not well anticipate that the introduction of civil order, and the extension of legal authority, which in an enlightened age, tend to advance the prosperity as well as promote the security of a nation, should have been to his countrymen either the signals of banishment from their native country, or the means of lowering the condition of those who were permitted to remain. With more reason it might have been expected that the principles of an enlightened age would have gradually introduced beneficial changes among the ancient race ; that they would have softened down the harsher features of their character, and prepared them for habits better suited to the cultivation of the soil, than the indolent freedom of a pastoral life. Instead of this, the new system, whatever may be its intrinsic merits or defects, has, in too many cases, been carried into execution, in a manner which has excited the strongest and most indignant sensations in the breasts of those who do not overlook the present inconvenience and distress of the many, in the eager pursuit of a prospective advantage to the few. The consequences which have resulted, and the contrast between the present and past condition of the people, and between their present and past disposition and feelings toward their superiors, show, in the most striking light, the impolicy of attempting, with such unnatural rapidity, innovations, which it would require an age, instead of a few years, to accomplish in a salutary manner, and the impossibility of effecting them without inflicting great misery, endangering morals, and undermining loyalty to the king, and respect for constituted authority.

A love of change, proceeding from the actual possession of wealth, or from the desire of acquiring it, disturbs, by an ill-directed influence, the gradual and effectual progress of those improvements which, instead of benefiting the man of capital alone, should equally distribute their advantages to all. In the prosecution of recent changes in the north, it would appear that the original inhabitants were never thought of, nor included in the system which was to be productive of such wealth to the landlord, the man of capital, and the country at large,—and that no native could be intrusted with, or, perhaps, none was found hardy enough to act a part in the execution of plans which commenced with the ejectment of their unfortunate friends and neighbours. Strangers were, therefore, called in, and whole glens cleared of their inhabitants, who, in some instances, resisted these mandates (although legally executed), in the hope of preserving to their families their ancient homes, to which all were enthusiastically attached. These people, blameless in every respect, save their poverty and ignorance of modern agriculture, could not believe that such harsh measures proceeded from their honoured superiors, who had hitherto been kind, and to whom they themselves had ever been attached, and faithful. The whole was attributed to the acting agents, and to them, therefore, their indignation was principally directed ; and, in some instances, their resistance was so obstinate, that it became necessary to enforce the orders " vi et armis," and to have recourse to a mode of ejectment, happily long obsolete, by setting their houses on fire. This last species of legal proceeding was so peculiarly conclusive and forcible, that even the stubborn Highlanders, with all their attachment to the homes of their fathers, were compelled to yield.

In the first instances of this mode of removing refractory tenants, a small compensation (six shillings), in two separate sums, was allowed for the houses destroyed. Some of the ejected tenants were also allowed small allotments of land, on which they were to build houses at their own expense, no assistance being given for that purpose. Perhaps it was owing to this that they were the more reluctant to remove till they had built houses on their new stations. The compensations allowed in the more recent removals are stated to have been more liberal; and the improvements which have succeeded those summary ejectments of the ancient inhabitants are highly eulogised both in pamphlets and newspapers. Some people may, however, be inclined to doubt the advantages of improvements which called for such frequent apologies; for, if more lenient measures had been pursued, vindication would have, perhaps, been unnecessary, and the trial of one of the acting agents might have been avoided. This trial was brought forward at the instance of the Lord Advocate, in consequence of the loud cry of indignation raised in the country against proceedings characterised by the sheriff of the county as "conduct which has seldom disgraced any country". But the trial ended (as was expected by every person who understood the circumstances) in the acquittal of the acting agent, the verdict of the jury proceeding on the principle that he acted under legal authority. This acquittal, however, did by no means diminish the general feeling of culpability; it only transferred the offence from the agent to a quarter too high and too distant to be directly affected by public indignation, if, indeed there be any station so elevated, or so distant, that public indignation, justly excited, will not, sooner or later, reach, so as to touch the feelings, however obtuse, of the transgressor of that law of humanity written on every upright mind, and deeply engraved on every kind and generous heart.

It must, however, be a matter of deep regret, that such a line of proceeding was pursued with regard to these brave, unfortunate, and well-principled people, as excited a sensation of horror, and a conviction of culpability, so powerful as only to be removed by an appeal to a criminal court. It is no less to be deplored, that any conduct sanctioned by authority, even although productive of ultimate advantage (and how it can produce any advantage beyond what might have been obtained by pursuing a scheme of conciliation and encouragement is a very questionable point), should have, in the first instance, inflicted such general misery. More humane measures would undoubtedly have answered every good purpose; and had such a course been pursued, as an enlightened humanity would have suggested, instead of depopulated glens, and starving peasantry, alienated from their superiors, and, in the exacerbation of their feelings, too ready to imbibe opinions hostile to the best interests of their country, we should still have seen a high-spirited and loyal people, ready, at the nod of their respected chiefs, to embody themselves into regiments, with the same zeal as in former times; and when enrolled among the defenders of their country, to exhibit a conduct honourable to that country and to their profession. Such is the acknowledged character of the men of these districts as soldiers, when called forth in the service of their country, although they be now described as irregular in their habits, and a burthen on the lands which gave them birth, and on which their forefathers maintained the honour, and promoted the wealth and prosperity, of the ancestors of those who now reject them. But is it conceivable that the people at home should be so degraded, while their brothers and sons who become soldiers maintain an honourable character? The people ought not to be reproached with incapacity or immorality without better evidence than that of their prejudiced and unfeeling calumniators. If it be so, however, and if this virtuous and honourable race, which has contributed to raise and uphold the character of the British peasantry in the eyes of all Europe, are thus fallen, and so suddenly fallen; how great and powerful must be the cause, and how heavy the responsibility of its authors?

But if at home they are thus low in character, how un-paralleled must be the improvement which is produced by difference of profession, as for example, when they become soldiers, and associate in barracks with troops of all char-acters, or in quarters, or billets, with the lowest of the people, instead of mingling with such society as they left in their native homes? Why should these Highlanders be at home so degenerate as they are represented, and as in recent instances they would actually appear to be? And why, when they mount the cockade, are they found to be so virtuous and regular, that one thousand men of Sutherland have been embodied four and five years together, at different and distant periods, from 1759 to 1763, from 1779 to 1783, and from 1793 to 1798, without an instance of military punishment? These men performed all the duties of soldiers to the perfect satisfaction of their commanders, and continued so unexceptionable in their conduct down to the latest period, when embodied into the 93rd regiment, that, according to the words of a distinguished general officer, "Although the youngest regiment in the service, they might form an example to all" : and on general parades for punishment, the Sutherland Highlanders have been ordered to their quarters, as "examples of this kind were not necess-ary for such honourable soldiers ".*

The same author adds the following, in the third edition of the same work, published in 1825 :—

"The great changes which have taken place in the above parishes of Sutherland, and some others, have excited a warm and general interest. While the liberal expenditure of capital was applauded by all, many intelligent persons

*Sketches of the Character, Manners, and Present State of the High-landers of Scotland, with details of the Military Service of the Highland Regiments, by Colonel David Stewart, 1822.

lamented that its application was so much in one direction ;
that the ancient tenantry were to have no share in this expenditure ; and that so small a portion was allotted for the
future settlement of the numerous population who had been
removed from their farms, and were placed in situations so
new, and in many respects so unsuitable,—certain that, in
the first instance, great distress, disaffection, and hostility
towards the landlords and government, with a diminution of
that spirit of independence, and those proper principles
which had hitherto distinguished them, would be the inevitable result.   So sudden and universal a change of station,
habits, and circumstances, and their being reduced from the
state of independent tenants to that of cottagers and day-
labourers, could not fail of arresting the notice of the
public.

Anxious to obtain the best information on this interesting
subject, I early made the most minute inquiry, careful, at
the same time, to form no opinion on intelligence communicated by the people of the district, or by persons connected
with them, and who would naturally be interested in, and
prejudiced against, or in favour of those changes.   I was the
more desirous for the best information, as the statements
published with regard to the character, capability, and principles of the people, exhibited a perfect contrast to my own
personal experience and knowledge of the admirable character and exemplary conduct of that portion of them that
had left their native country ; and I believe it improbable,
nay impossible, that the sons of worthless parents, without
religious or moral principle—as they have been described—
could conduct themselves in such an honourable manner as
to be held up as an example to the British army.   But,
indeed, as to information, so much publicity had been
given, by various statements explanatory of, and in vindi-

cation of these proceedings, that little more was necessary, beyond what these publications afforded, to show the nature of the plans, and the manner in which they were carried into execution.

Forming my opinions, therefore, from those statements, and from information communicated by persons not immediately connected with that part of the country, I drew the conclusions which appeared in the former editions of these Sketches. But, with a strong desire to be correct and well informed in all I state, and with an intention of correcting myself, in this edition, should I find that I had been misinformed, or had taken up mistaken views of the subject, in the different statements I had produced, I embraced the first spare time I could command, and in autumn 1823, I travelled over the " improved " districts, and a large portion of those parts which had been depopulated and laid out in extensive pastoral farms, as well as the stations in which the people are placed. After as strict an examination as circumstances permitted, and a careful inquiry among those who, from their knowledge and judgment were enabled to form the best opinions, I do not find that I have one statement to alter, or one opinion to correct ; though I am fully aware that many hold very different opinions. But however much I may differ in some points, there is one in which I warmly and cordially join ; and that is, in expressing my high satisfaction and admiration at the liberality displayed in the immense sums expended on buildings, in enclosing, clearing, and draining land, in forming roads and communications, and introducing the most improved agricultural implements. In all these, the generous distribution of such exemplary encouragement stands unparalleled and alone. Equally remarkable is the great abatement of rents given to the tenants of capital —

abatements which it was not to be expected they would ask, considering the preference and encouragement given them, and the promises they had held out of great and unprecedented revenue, from their skill and exertions. But these promises seem to have been early forgotten; the tenants of capital were the first to call for relief; and so great and generous has this relief been, that the rents are reduced so low as to be almost on a level with what they were when the great changes commenced. Thus while upwards of £210,000 have been expended on improvements, no return is to be looked for from this vast expenditure; and in the failure of their promised rents, the tenants have sufficiently proved the unstable and fallacious nature of the system which they, with so much plausibility and perseverance, got established by delusions practised on a high minded, honourable individual, not aware of the evils produced by so universal a movement of a whole people. Every friend to a brave and valuable race, must rejoice that these evils are in progress of alleviation by a return of that kindness and protection which had formerly been so conspicuous towards that race of tenantry, and which could never have been interrupted had it not been for those delusions to which I have more than once alluded, and which have been prosecuted, within the last twenty years, in many parts of the Highlands, with a degree of assiduity and antipathy to the unfortunate inhabitants altogether remarkable.

But in the county in question, no antipathy to the people is now to be dreaded; a return of ancient kindness will cement with ancient fidelity and attachment; and if the people are rendered comfortable and contented, they will be kept loyal, warlike, and brave.

HUGH MILLER.

So MUCH has been already said about these disastrous Sutherland evictions that we greatly fear the reader is already sickened with the horrid narrative, but as it is intended to make the present record of these atrocious proceedings not only in Sutherland but throughout the whole Highlands, as complete as it is now possible to make it, we shall yet place before the reader at considerable length Hugh Miller's observations on this National Crime—especially as his remarks largely embody the philosophical views and conclusions of the able and far-seeing French writer Sismondi, who in his great work declares,—" It is by a cruel use of legal—it is by an unjust usurpation—that the tacksman and the tenant of Sutherland are considered as having no right to the land which they have occupied for so many ages. . . . A count or earl has no more right to expel from their homes the inhabitants of his county, than a king to expel from his country the inhabitants of his kingdom." Hugh Miller introduces his remarks on Sutherland by a reference to the celebrated Frenchman's work, and his opinion of the Sutherland Clearances, thus :—There appeared at Paris, about five years ago, a singularly ingenious work on political economy, from the pen of the late M. de Sismondi, a writer of European reputation. The greater part of the first volume is taken up with discussions on territorial wealth, and the condition of the cultivators of the soil ; and in this portion of the work there is a prominent place

assigned to a subject which perhaps few Scotch readers
would expect to see introduced through the medium of a
foreign tongue to the people of a great continental state.
We find this philosophic writer, whose works are known far
beyond the limits of his language, devoting an entire essay
to the case of the Duchess of Sutherland and her tenants,
and forming a judgment on it very unlike the decision of
political economists in our own country, who have not hesi-
tated to characterise her great and singularly harsh experiment, whose worst effects we are but beginning to see, as at
once justifiable in itself and happy in its results.   It is
curious to observe how deeds done as if in darkness and in
a corner, are beginning, after the lapse of nearly thirty years,
to be proclaimed on the house-tops.   The experiment of
the late Duchess was not intended to be made in the eye of
Europe.   Its details would ill bear the exposure.   When
Cobbett simply referred to it, only ten years ago, the noble
proprietrix was startled, as if a rather delicate family secret
was on the eye on being divulged ; and yet nothing seems
more evident now than that civilised man all over the world
is to be made aware of how the experiment was accomplished, and what it is ultimately to produce.

In a time of quiet and good order, when law, whether in
the right or the wrong, is all-potent in enforcing its findings,
the argument which the philosophic Frenchman employs in
behalf of the ejected tenantry of Sutherland is an argument
at which proprietors may afford to smile.   In a time of
revolution, however, when lands change their owners, and
old families give place to new ones, it might be found
somewhat formidable,—sufficiently so, at least, to lead a
wise proprietor in an unsettled age rather to conciliate than
oppress and irritate the class who would be able in such
circumstances to urge it with most effect.   It is not easy

doing justice in a few sentences to the facts and reasonings of an elaborate essay; but the line of the argument runs thus:—

Under the old Celtic tenures—the only tenures, be it remembered, through which the Lords of Sutherland derive their rights to their lands,—the *Klaan*, or children of the soil, were the proprietors of the soil;—"the whole of Sutherland," says Sismondi, belonged to "the men of Sutherland". Their chief was their monarch, and a very absolute monarch he was. "He gave the different *tacks* of land to his officers, or took them away from them, according as they showed themselves more or less useful in war. But though he could thus, in a military sense, reward or punish the clan, he could not diminish in the least the property of the clan itself";—he was a chief, not a proprietor, and had "no more right to expel from their homes the inhabitants of his county, than a king to expel from his country the inhabitants of his kingdom". "Now, the Gaelic tenant," continues the Frenchman, "has never been conquered; nor did he forfeit, on any after occasion, the rights which he originally possessed";—in point of right, he is still a co-proprietor with his captain. To a Scotchman acquainted with the law of property as it has existed among us, in even the Highlands, for the last century, and everywhere else for at least two centuries more, the view may seem extreme; not so, however, to a native of the Continent, in many parts of which prescription and custom are found ranged, not on the side of the chief, but on that of the vassal. "Switzerland," says Sismondi, "which in so many respects resembles Scotland,—in its lakes, its mountains,—its climate,—and the character, manners, and habits of its children,—was likewise at the same period parcelled out among a small number of lords. If the

Counts of Kyburgh, of Lentzburg, of Hapsburg, and of Gruyeres, had been protected by the English laws, they would find themselves at the present day precisely in the condition in which the Earls of Sutherland were twenty years ago. Some of them would perhaps have had the same taste for *improvements*, and several republics would have been expelled from the Alps, to make room for flocks of sheep. But while the law has given to the Swiss peasant a guarantee of perpetuity, it is to the Scottish laird that it has extended this guarantee in the British empire, leaving the peasant in a precarious situation. The clan,—recognised at first by the captain, whom they followed in war, and obeyed for their common advantage, as his friends and relations, then as his soldiers, then as his vassals, then as his farmers,—he has come finally to regard as hired labourers, whom he may perchance allow to remain on the soil of their common country for his own advantage, but whom he has the power to expel so soon as he no longer finds it for his interest to keep them."

Arguments like those of Sismondi, however much their force may be felt on the Continent, would be formidable at home, as we have said, in only a time of revolution, when the very foundations of society would be unfixed, and opinions set loose, to pull down or re-construct at pleasure. But it is surely not uninteresting to mark how, in the course of events, that very law of England which, in the view of the Frenchman, has done the Highland peasant so much less, and the Highland chief so much more than justice, is bidding fair, in the case of Sutherland at least, to carry its rude equalising remedy along with it. Between the years 1811 and 1820, fifteen thousand inhabitants of this northern district were ejected from their snug inland farms, by means

for which we would in vain seek a precedent, except, perchance, in the history of the Irish massacre.

But though the interior of the county was thus improved
into a desert, in which there are many thousands of sheep,
but few human habitations, let it not be supposed by the
reader that its general population was in any degree less-
ened. So far was this from being the case, that the census
of 1821 showed an increase over the census of 1811 of more
than two hundred ; and the present population of Sutherland exceeds, by a thousand, its population before the
change. The county has not been depopulated—its population has been merely arranged after a new fashion. The
late Duchess found it, spread equally over the interior and
the sea-coast, and in very comfortable circumstances ;—she
left it compressed into a wretched selvage of poverty and
suffering that fringes the county on its eastern and western
shores, and the law which enabled her to make such an
arrangement, maugre the ancient rights of the poor Highlander, is now on the eve of stepping in, in its own clumsy
way, to make her family pay the penalty. The southern
kingdom must and will give us a poor-law ; and then shall
the selvage of deep poverty which fringes the sea-coasts of
Sutherland avenge on the titled proprietor of the county
both his mother's error and his own. If our British laws,
unlike those of Switzerland, failed miserably in her day in
protecting the vassal, they will more than fail, in those of
her successor, in protecting the lord. Our political economists shall have an opportunity of reducing their arguments regarding the improvements in Sutherland, into a few
arithmetical terms, which the merest tyro will be able to
grapple with.

There is but poor comfort, however, to know, when one
sees a country ruined, that the perpetrators of the mischief

have not ruined it to their own advantage. We purpose
showing how signal in the case of Sutherland this ruin has
been, and how very extreme the infatuation which continues to
possess its hereditary lord. We are old enough to remember the county in its original state, when it was at once the
happiest and one of the most exemplary districts in Scotland, and passed, at two several periods, a considerable
time among its hills; we are not unacquainted with it now,
nor with its melancholy and dejected people, that wear out
life in their comfortless cottages on the sea-shore. The
problem solved in this remote district of the kingdom is not
at all unworthy the attention which it seems but beginning
to draw, but which is already not restricted to one kingdom,
or even one continent.

But what, asks the reader, was the economic condition—
the condition with regard to circumstances and means of
living—of these Sutherland Highlanders? How did they
fare? The question has been variously answered: much
must depend on the class selected from among them as
specimens of the whole,—much, too, taking for granted
the honesty of the party who replies, on his own condition
in life, and his acquaintance with the circumstances of the
poorer people of Scotland generally. The county had its
less genial localities, in which, for a month or two in the
summer season, when the stock of grain from the previous
year was fast running out, and the crops on the ground not
yet ripened for use, the people experienced a considerable
degree of scarcity—such scarcity as a mechanic in the
South feels when he has been a fortnight out of employment.
But the Highlander had resources in these seasons which
the mechanic has not. He had his cattle and his wild pot-
herbs, such as the mug-wort and the nettle. It has been
adduced by the advocates of the change which has ruined

Sutherland, as a proof of the extreme hardship of the Highlander's condition, that at such times he could have eaten as food broth made of nettles, mixed up with a little oatmeal, or have had recourse to the expedient of bleeding his cattle, and making the blood into a sort of pudding. And it is quite true that the Sutherlandshire Highlanders was in the habit, at such times, of having a recourse to such food. It is not less true, however, that the statement is just as little conclusive regarding his condition, as if it were alleged that there must always be famine in France when the people eat the hind legs of frogs, or in Italy when they make dishes of snails. With regard to the general comfort of the people in their old condition, there are better tests than can be drawn from the kind of food they occasionally ate. The country hears often of dearth in Sutherland now! every year in which the crop falls a little below average in other districts, is a year of famine there: but the country never heard of dearth in Sutherland then. There were very few among the holders of its small inland farms who had not saved a little money. Their circumstances were such, that their moral nature found full room to develop itself, and in a way the world has rarely witnessed. Never were there a happier or more contented people, or a people more strongly attached to the soil; and not one of them now lives in the altered circumstances on which they were so rudely precipitated by the landlord, who does not look back on this period of comfort and enjoyment with sad and hopeless regret.

But we have not yet said how this ruinous revolution was effected in Sutherland,—how the aggravations of the *mode*, if we may so speak, still fester in the recollections of the people,—or how thoroughly that policy of the lord of the soil, through which he now seems determined to complete the work of ruin which his predecessor began, harmonizes with its worst details. We must first relate, however, a disastrous change which took place, in the providence of God, in the noble family of Sutherland, and which, though it dates fully eighty years back, may be regarded as pregnant with the disasters which afterwards befell the county.

The marriage of the young countess into a noble English family was fraught with further disaster to the county. There are many Englishmen quite intelligent enough to perceive the difference between a smoky cottage of turf, and a whitewashed cottage of stone, whose judgment on their respective inhabitants would be of but little value. Sutherland, as a county of men, stood higher at this period than perhaps any other district in the British Empire; but, as our descriptions have shown,—it by no means stood high as a county of farms and cottages. The marriage of the countess brought a new set of eyes upon it,—eyes accustomed to quite a different face of things. It seemed a wild, rude county, where all was wrong, and all had to be set right,—a sort of Russia on a small scale, that had just got another Peter the Great to civilize it,—or a sort of barbarous Egypt, with an energetic Ali Pasha at its head. Even the vast wealth and great liberality of the Stafford family militated against this hapless county ! it enabled them to treat it as the mere subject of an interesting experiment, in which gain to themselves was really no object,—nearly as little so, as if they had resolved on dissecting a dog alive for the benefit of science. It was a still farther disadvantage, that they had to carry on their experiment by the hands, and to watch its first effects with the eyes, of others. The agonies of the dog might have had their softening influence on a dissecter who held the knife himself ; but there could be no such influence exerted over him, did he merely issue orders to his footman that the dissection should be completed, remaining himself, meanwhile, out of sight and out of hearing. The plan of improvement sketched out by his English family was a plan exceedingly easy of conception. Here is a vast tract of land, furnished with two distinct sources of wealth. Its shores may be made the seats of extensive fisheries, and the whole of its interior parcelled out into productive sheep farms. All is waste in its present state ; it has no fisheries, and two-thirds of its internal produce is consumed by the inhabitants. It had contributed, for the use of the community and the landlord, its large herds of black cattle; but the English family saw, and, we believe, saw truly, that for every one pound of beef which it produced, it could be made to produce two pounds of mutton, and perhaps a pound of fish in addition. And it was resolved, therefore, that the inhabitants of the central districts, who, as they were mere Celts, could not be transformed, it was held, into store farmers, should be marched down to the sea-side, there to convert themselves into fishermen, on the shortest possible notice, and that a few farmers of capital, of the industrious Lowland race, should be invited to occupy the new sub-divisions of the interior.

And, pray, what objections can be urged against so liberal and large-minded a scheme ? The poor inhabitants of the interior had very serious objections to urge against it. Their humble dwellings were of their own rearing; it was they themselves who had broken in their little fields from the waste ; from time immemorial, far beyond the reach of history, had they possessed their mountain holdings,—they had defended them so well of old that the soil was still virgin ground, in which the invader had found only a grave ; and their young men were now in foreign lands, fighting, at the command of their chieftainess, the battles of their country, not in the character of hired soldiers, but of men who regarded these very holdings as their stake in the quarrel. To them, then, the scheme seemed fraught with the most flagrant, the most monstrous injustice. Were it to be suggested by some Chartist convention in a time of revolution, that Sutherland might be still further improved —that it was really a piece of great waste to suffer the revenues of so extensive a district to be squandered by one individual—that it would be better to appropriate them to the use of the community in general—that the community in general might be still further benefited by the removal of the one said individual from Dunrobin to a road-side, where he might be profitably employed in breaking stones— and that this new arrangement could not be entered on too soon—the noble Duke would not be a whit more aston- ished, or rendered a whit more indignant, by the scheme, than were the Highlanders of Sutherland by the scheme of his predecessor.

The reader must keep in view, therefore, that if atrocities unexampled in Britain for at least a century were perpet- rated in the clearing of Sutherland, there was a species of at least passive resistance on the part of the people (for active resistance there was none), which in some degree provoked them. Had the Highlanders, on receiving orders, marched down to the sea-coast, and become fishermen, with the readiness with which a regiment deploys on review day, the atrocities would, we doubt not, have been much fewer. But though the orders were very distinct, the High- landers were very unwilling to obey; and the severities formed merely a part of the means though which the ne- cessary obedience was ultimately secured. We shall instance a single case, as illustrative of the process.

In the month of March, 1814, a large proportion of the

Highlanders of Farr and Kildonan, two parishes in Sutherland, were summoned to quit their farms in the following
May. In a few days after, the surrounding heaths on which
they pastured their cattle, and from which at that season,
the sole supply of herbage is derived (for in those northern
districts the grass springs late, and the cattle-feeder in the
spring months depends chiefly on the heather), were set on
fire and burnt up. There was that sort of policy in the stroke
which men deem allowable in a state of war. The starving
cattle went roaming over the burnt pastures, and found
nothing to eat. Many of them perished, and the greater
part of what remained, though in miserable condition, the
Highlanders had to sell perforce. Most of the able-bodied
men were engaged in this latter business at a distance from
home, when the dreaded term-day came on. The pasturage
had been destroyed before the legal term, and while in
even the eye of the law, it was still the property of the poor
Highlanders ; but ere disturbing them in their dwellings,
term-day was suffered to pass. The work of demolition
then began. A numerous party of men, with a factor at
their head, entered the district, and commenced pulling
down the houses over the heads of the inhabitants. In an
extensive tract of country not a human dwelling was left
standing, and then, the more effectually to prevent their
temporary re-erection, the destroyers set fire to the wreck.
In one day were the people deprived of home and shelter,
and left exposed to the elements. Many deaths are said to
have ensued from alarm, fatigue, and cold.

Our author then corroborates in detail the atrocities,
cruelties, and personal hardships already described by
Donald MacLeod and proceeds :—But to employ the language of Southey,

> Things such as these, we know, must be
> At every famous victory.

And in this instance the victory of the lord of the soil over the children of the soil was signal and complete. In little more than nine years a population of fifteen thousand individuals were removed from the interior of Sutherland to its sea-coasts or had emigrated to America. The inland districts were converted into deserts, through which the traveller may take a long day's journey, amid ruins that still bear the scathe of fire, and grassy patches betraying when the evening sun casts aslant its long deep shadows, the half-effaced lines of the plough.

After pointing out how at the Disruption sites for churches were refused, Hugh Miller proceeds:—We have exhibited to our readers, in the *clearing* of Sutherland a process of ruin so thoroughly disastrous, that it might be deemed scarcely possible to render it more complete. And yet with all its apparent completeness, it admitted of a supplementary process. To employ one of the striking figures of Scripture, it was possible to grind into powder what had been previously broken into fragments,—to degrade the poor inhabitants to a still lower level than that on which they had been so cruelly precipitated,—though persons of a not very original cast of mind might have found it difficult to say how the Duke of Sutherland has been ingenious enough to fall on exactly the one proper expedient for supplementing their ruin. All in mere circumstance and situation that could lower and deteriorate had been present as ingredients in the first process; but there still remained for the people, however reduced to poverty or broken in spirit, all in religion that consoles and ennobles. Sabbath-days came round with their humanising influences; and, under the teachings of the gospel, the poor and the oppressed looked longingly forward to a future scene of being, in which there is no poverty or oppression. They still posessed, amid their misery, something positively good, of which it was impossible to deprive them ; and hence the ability derived to the present lord of Sutherland of deepening and rendering more signal the ruin accomplished by his predecessor.

These harmonise but too well with the mode in which the interior of Sutherland was cleared, and the improved cottages of its sea-coasts erected. The plan has its two items. No sites are to be granted in the district for Free Churches, and no dwelling-houses for Free Church ministers. The climate is severe,—the winters prolonged and stormy, —the roads which connect the chief seats of population with the neighbouring counties, dreary and long. May not ministers and people be eventually worn out in this way? Such is the portion of the plan which his Grace and his Grace's creatures can afford to present to the light. But there are supplementary items of a somewhat darker kind. The poor cotters are, in the great majority of cases, tenants-at-will ; and there has been much pains taken to inform them, that to the crime of entertaining and sheltering a Protesting minister, the penalty of ejection from their holdings must inevitably attach. The laws of Charles have again returned in this unhappy district, and free and tolerating Scotland has got, in the nineteenth century, as in the seventeenth, its intercommuned ministers. We shall not say that the intimation has emanated from the Duke. It is the misfortune of such men, that there creep around them creatures whose business it is to anticipate their wishes ; but who, at times, doubtless, instead of anticipating misinterpret them ; and who, even when not very much mistaken, impart to whatever they do the impress of their own low and menial natures, and thus exaggerate in the act, the intention of their masters. We do not say, therefore, that the intimation has emanted from the Duke; but this we say, that an exemplary Sutherlandshire minister of the Protesting Church, who resigned his worldly all for the sake of his principles, had lately to travel, that he might preach to his attached people, a long journey of forty-four miles outwards, and as much in return, and all this without taking shelter under cover of a roof, or without partaking of any other refreshment than that furnished by the slender store of provisions which he had carried with him from his new home.   Willingly would the poor Highlanders have received him at any risk; but knowing from experience what a Sutherlandshire removal means he preferred enduring any amount of hardship rather than that the hospitality of his people should be made the occasion of their ruin.   We have already adverted to the case of a lady of Sutherland threatened with ejection from her home because she had extended the shelter of her roof to one of the Protesting clergy,—an aged and venerable man, who had quitted the neighbouring manse, his home for many years, because he could no longer enjoy it in consistency with his principles; and we have shown that that aged and venerable man was the lady's own father.   What amount of oppression of a smaller and more petty character may not be expected in the circumstances, when cases such as these are found to stand but a very little over the ordinary level?

The meanness to which ducal hostility can stoop in this hapless district, impress with a feeling of surprise.   In the parish of Dornoch for instance, where his Grace is fortunately not the sole landowner, there has been a site procured on the most generous terms from Sir George Gunn Munro of Poyntzfield; and this gentleman, believing himself possessed of a hereditary right to a quarry, which, though on the Duke's ground, had been long resorted to by the proprietors of the district generally, instructed the builder to take from it the stones which he needed. Never had the quarry been prohibited before, but on this occasion, a stringent interdict arrested its use. If his Grace could not prevent a hated Free Church from arising in the district, he could at least add to the expense of its erection. We have even heard that the portion of the building previously erected had to be pulled down and the stones returned.

How are we to account for a hostility so determined, and that can stoop so low? In two different ways, we are of opinion, and in both have the people of Scotland a direct interest. Did his Grace entertain a very intense regard for Established Presbytery, it is probably that he himself would be a Presbyterian of the Establishment. But such is not the case. The church into which he would so fain force the people has been long since deserted by himself. The secret of the course which he pursues can have no connection therefore with religious motive or belief. It can be no proselytising spirit that misleads his Grace. Let us remark, in the first place, rather however, in the way of embodying a fact, than imputing a motive, that with his present views, and in his present circumstances, it may not seem particularly his Grace's interest to make the county of Sutherland a happy or desirable home to the people of Scotland. It may not be his Grace's interest that the population of the district should increase. The clearing of the sea-coast may seem as little prejudicial to his Grace's welfare now, as the clearing of the interior seemed adverse to the interests of his predecessor thirty years ago; nay, it is quite possible that his Grace may be led to regard the clearing of the coast as the better and more important clearing of the two. Let it not be forgotten that a poor-law hangs over Scotland,—that the shores of Sutherland are covered with

what seems one vast straggling village, inhabited by an impoverished and ruined people,—and that the coming assess-
ment may yet fall so weighty that the extra profits accruing
to his Grace from his large sheep-farms, may go but a small
way in supporting his extra paupers. It is not in the least
improbable that he may live to find the revolution effected
by his predecessor taking to itself the form, not of a crime,—
for that would be nothing,—but of a disastrous and very
terrible blunder.

There is another remark which may prove not unworthy
the consideration of the reader. Ever since the completion
of the fatal experiment which ruined Sutherland, the noble
family through which it was originated and carried on have
betrayed the utmost jealousy of having its real results made
public. Volumes of special pleading have been written on
the subject,—pamphlets have been published, laboured
articles have been inserted in widely-spread reviews,—
statistical accounts have been watched over with the most
careful surveillance. If the misrepresentations of the press
could have altered the matter of fact, famine would not be
gnawing the vitals of Sutherland in a year a little less abundant than its predecessors, nor would the dejected and
oppressed people be feeding their discontent, amid present
misery, with the recollections of a happier past. If a
singularly well-conditioned and wholesome district of
country has been converted into one wide ulcer of
wretchedness and woe, it must be confessed that the sore
has been carefully bandaged up from the public eye,—that
if there has been little done for its cure, there has at least
been much done for its concealment. Now, be it remembered, that a Free Church threatened to insert a *tent* into
this wound, and so keep it open. It has been said that the
Gaelic language removes a district more effectually from the

influence of English opinion than an ocean of three thousand miles, and that the British public know better what is doing in New York than what is doing in Lewis or Skye. And hence one cause, at least, of the thick obscurity that has so long enveloped the miseries which the poor High-lander has had to endure, and the oppressions to which he has been subjected. The Free Church threatens to translate her wrongs into English, and to give them currency in the general mart of opinion. She might possibly enough be no silent spectator of conflagrations such as those which characterised the first general improvement of Sutherland,— nor yet of such Egyptian schemes of house-building as that which formed part of the improvements of a later plan. She might be somewhat apt to betray the real state of the district, and thus render laborious misrepresentation of little avail. She might effect a diversion in the cause of the people, and shake the foundations of the hitherto despotic power which has so long weighed them down. She might do for Sutherland what Cobbett promised to do, but what Cobbett had not character enough to accomplish, and what he did not live even to attempt. A combination of circum-stances have conspired to vest in a Scottish proprietor, in this northern district, a more despotic power than even the most absolute monarchs of the Continent possess; and it is, perhaps, no great wonder that that proprietor should be jealous of the introduction of an element which threatens, it may seem, materially to lessen it. And so he struggled hard to exclude the Free Church, and, though no member of the Establishment himself, declares warmly in its behalf. Certain it is, that from the Establishment, as now constituted, he can have nothing to fear, and the people nothing to hope.

After what manner may his grace the Duke of Sutherland

be most effectually met in this matter, so that the case of toleration and freedom óf conscience may be maintained in the extensive district which God, in his providence, has consigned to his stewardship? We are not unacquainted with the Celtic character, as developed in the Highlands of Scotland. Highlanders, up to a certain point, are the most docile, patient, enduring of men; but that point once passed, endurance ceases, and the all too gentle lamb starts up an angry lion. The spirit is stirred and maddens at the sight of the naked weapon, and that in its headlong rush upon the enemy, discipline can neither check nor control. Let our oppressed Highlanders of Sutherland beware. They have suffered much; but, so far as man is the agent, their battles can be fought on only the arena of public opinion, and on that ground which the political field may be soon found to furnish.

Such of our readers as are acquainted with the memoir of Lady Glenorchy, must remember a deeply melancholy incident which occurred in the history of this excellent woman, in connection with the noble family of Sutherland. Her only sister had been married to William, seventeenth Earl of Sutherland,—" the first of the good Earls "; " a nobleman," says the Rev. Dr. Jones in his Memoir, " who to the finest person united all the dignity and amenity of manners and character which give lustre to greatness ". But his sun was destined soon to go down. Five years after his marriage, which proved one of the happiest, and was blessed with two children, the elder of the two, the young Lady Catherine, a singularly engaging child, was taken from him by death, in his old hereditary castle of Dunrobin. The event deeply affected both parents, and preyed on their health and spirits. It had taken place amid the gloom of a severe northern winter, and the soli-

tude of the Highlands; and, acquiescing in the advice of
friends, the Earl and his lady quitted the family seat, where
there was so much to remind them of their bereavement,
and sought relief in the more cheerful atmosphere of Bath.
But they were not to find it there. Shortly after their
arrival, the Earl was seized by a malignant fever, with which,
upheld by a powerful constitution, he struggled for fifty-four
days, and then expired. "For the first twenty-one days and
nights of these," says Dr. Jones, " Lady Sutherland never
left his bedside; and then, at last, overcome with fatigue,
anxiety, and grief, she sank an unavailing victim to an
amiable but excessive attachment, seventeen days before the
death of her lord." The period, though not very remote,
was one in which the intelligence of events travelled
slowly; and in this instance the distraction of the family
must have served to retard it beyond the ordinary time.
Her ladyship's mother, when hastening from Edinburgh to
her assistance, alighted one day from her carriage at an inn,
and on seeing two hearses standing by the wayside, inquired of an attendant whose remains they contained? The
reply was, the remains of Lord and Lady Sutherland, on
their way for interment to the Royal Chapel of Holyrood
House. And such was the first intimation of which the
lady received of the death of her daughter and son-in-
law.

The event was pregnant with disaster to Sutherland,
though many years elapsed ere the ruin which it involved
fell on that hapless country. The sole survivor and heir of
the family was a female infant of but a year old. Her
maternal grandmother, an ambitious, intriging woman of
the world, had the chief share in her general training and
education; and she was brought up in the south of Scotland, of which her grandmother was a native, far removed

from the influence of those genial sympathies with the
people of her clan, for which the old lords of Sutherland
had been so remarkable, and, what was a sorer evil still,
from the influence of the vitalities of that religion which,
for five generations together, her fathers had illustrated and
adorned.   The special mode in which the disaster told first,
was through the patronage of the county, the larger part of
which was vested in the family of Sutherland.   Some of the
old Earls had been content, as we have seen, to place themselves on the level of the Christian men of their parishes,
and thus to unite with them in calling to their churches the
ministers of their choice.   They know,—what regenerated
natures can alone know, with the proper emphasis, that in
Christ Jesus the vassal ranks with his lord, and they con-
scientiously acted on the conviction.   But matters were now
regulated differently.   The presentation supplanted the
call, and ministers came to be placed in the parishes of
Sutherland without the consent, and contrary to the will of
the people.   Churches, well-filled hitherto, were deserted by
their congregations, just because a respectable woman of the
world, making free use of what she deemed her own, had
planted them with men of the world, who were only tolerably
respectable ; and in houses and barns, the devout men of
the district learned to hold numerously-attended Sabbath
meetings for reading the Scriptures, and mutual exhortation
and prayer, as a sort of substitute for the public services, in
which they found they could no longer join with profit.
The spirit awakened by the old Earls had survived themselves, and ran directly counter to the policy of their
descendant.   Strongly attached to the Establishment, the
people, though they thus forsook their old places of worship,
still remained members of the national Church, and
travelled far in the summer season to attend the better

ministers of their own and the neighbouring counties. We have been assured, too, from men whose judgment we respect, that, under all their disadvantages, religion continued peculiarly to flourish among them;—"a deep-toned evangelism prevailed; so that perhaps the visible Church throughout the world at the time could furnish no more striking contrast than that which obtained between the cold, bald, common-place service of the pulpit in some of these parishes, and the fervid prayers and exhortations which give life and interest to these humble meetings of the people." What a pity it is that differences such as these the Duke of Sutherland cannot see!

Let us follow, for a little, the poor Highlanders of Sutherland to the sea-coast. It would be easy dwelling on the terrors of their expulsion, and multiplying facts of horror; but had there been no permanent deterioration effected in their condition, these, all harrowing and repulsive as they were, would have mattered less. Sutherland would have soon recovered the burning up of a few hundred hamlets, or the loss of a few bed-ridden old people, who would have died as certainly under cover, though perhaps a few months later, as when exposed to the elements in the open air. Nay, had it lost a thousand of its best men in the way in which it lost so many at the storming of New Orleans, the blank ere now would have been completely filled up. The calamities of fire or of decimation even, however distressing in themselves, never yet ruined a country: no calamity ruins a country that leaves the surviving inhabitants to develop, in their old circumstances, their old character and resources.

In one of the eastern eclogues of Collins, where two shepherds are described as flying for their lives before the troops of a ruthless invader, we see with how much of the terrible the imagination of a poet could invest the evils of war, when aggravated by pitiless barbarity. Fertile as that imagination was, however, there might be found new circumstances to heighten the horrors of the scene—circumstances beyond the reach of invention—in the retreat of the Sutherland Highlanders from the smoking ruins of their cottages to their allotments on the coast. We have heard of one man, named Mackay, whose family, at the time of the greater conflagration referred to by Macleod, were all lying ill of fever, who had to carry two of his sick children on his back a distance of twenty-five miles. We have heard of the famished people blackening the shores, like the crew of some vessel wrecked on an inhospitable coast, that they might sustain life by the shell-fish and sea-weed laid bare by the ebb. Many of their allotments, especially on the western coast, were barren in the extreme—unsheltered by bush or tree, and exposed to the sweeping sea-winds, and in time of tempest, to the blighting spray; and it was found a matter of the extremest difficulty to keep the few cattle which they had retained, from wandering, especially in the night-time into the better sheltered and more fertile interior. The poor animals were intelligent enough to read a practical comment on the nature of the change effected; and, from the harshness of the shepherds to whom the care of the interior had been entrusted, they served materially to add to the distress of their unhappy masters. They were getting continually impounded; and vexatious fines, in the form of trespass-money, came thus to be wrung from the already impoverished Highlanders. Many who had no money to give were obliged to relieve them by depositing some of their few portable articles of value, such as bed or body-clothes, or, more distressing still, watches, and rings, and pins,—the only relics, in not a few instances, of brave men whose bones were mouldering under the fatal rampart at New Orleans, or in the arid sands of Egypt—on that spot of proud recollection, where the invincibles of Napoleon went down before the Highland bayonet. Their first efforts as fishermen were what might be expected from a rural people unaccustomed to the sea. The shores of Sutherland, for immense tracts together, are iron-bound, and much exposed —open on the Eastern coast to the waves of the German Ocean, and on the North and West to the long roll of the Atlantic. There could not be more perilous seas for the unpractised boatmen to take his first lessons on ; but though the casualties were numerous, and the loss of life great, many of the younger Highlanders became expert fisher-men. The experiment was harsh in the extreme, but so far, at least, it succeeded. It lies open, however, to other objections than those which have been urged against it on the score of its inhumanity.*

PROFESSOR JOHN STUART BLACKIE.

PROFESSOR BLACKIE in his recently published and splen-did work, "Altavona," sums up his chapter on the Sutherland Clearances in appropriate terms. Having listened to the leading character in the book—the Professor himself—giving both sides of the question at length, Bücherblume, the German scholar, exclaimed :—

"If all this is true, the power of a factor, under one of your gigantic landowners in Scotland, and wielding laws, made for the most part by landlords in their own interests, and manipulated by lawyers and judges, who were them-

* Hugh Miller's leading articles on " *Sutherland as it was and is* ",

selves mostly landowners, must have been tremendous, not
a whit less galling than the domination of the police in
Prussia, under the Government of the old unqualified bureau-
cracy."

MAC.—"Tremendous, indeed. Even now the factor of
an absentee landlord, or of a resident landlord, who may be
feeble, or careless, or asleep, is the most absolute of
despots. In many matters of vital importance to the poor
peasant there is neither law nor public opinion to lay a
check on his high-handedness."

The Professor then reproduces the conversation which
took place between Donald Macleod and his judge at
Dornoch, already printed at pp. 81-82 of this work, when
Bücherblume again exclaims :—

"Good heavens ! And this is British liberty in the year
1827. Our Teutonic Michel must learn to admire the glorious
British Constitution less from a moral point of view."

MAC.—"Very wise. There are rats sometimes in the
biggest palaces, as well as in the lowest hovels ;" and he
sums up by laying down the following propositions :—

I. I hold it to be quite certain, as a consequence of the
altered relation of the Highlands to the Government occasioned by the rebellion of '45, and the gradual opening up
of "the rough boundaries" to Lowland influences thereupon
following, that some very considerable changes would require
to take place in the management of Highland properties.

II. Among these changes, I consider it proven that the
introduction of sheep-farming was one of the most obvious,
and has proved one of the most beneficial.

III. I lay it down as an axiom of social science, that all
changes affecting the welfare and comfort of large classes
of men ought not to be made hastily, and in the way of a
sharp revolution, but gradually, moderately, and with great

tenderness : and this especially when the sufferers by any
social changes are not to be the few rich and prosperous,
but the many poor and industrious of the land.

IV. As a deduction from this axiom, it is plain that the
introduction of sheep-farming in the wholesale manner
practised by the managers of the Sutherland estates at the
commencement of the present century was harsh, cruel, and
tyrannical, and in the circumstances altogether unjustifiable.

V. I hold it proven, that by the use and wont of clan
law, and the practice of their recognised chiefs, the Highland peasantry had a right to expect, that, unless convicted
of gross misconduct, they were not to be ejected from their
holdings : certainly not in favour of strangers, who had no
interest in the country, but to extrude the native population, and make money by the wholesale substitution of
sheep for men.

VI. I hold it *not* proven, that for the introduction of sheep-
farming into the Sutherland estates, it was necessary to
hand over the whole glens to the tender mercies of Lowland
adventurers, and men of business eager to make money;
and that it would have been more politic and more wise,
not to say more human, to have gradually enlarged the
holdings, as the holders might die out, or, at all events, to
have attached to each new sheep farm of more moderate dimensions, a certain number of small crofts for the supply of
labour, or finally to have kept the peasantry on the property
by the introduction of club-farms, or otherwise, according to
circumstances ; *not* proven also, that sheep-farming cannot
be carried on beneficially in conjunction with the other
forms of rural economy ; but generally rather proven, that
eagerness to make money, combined with a fashionable
doctrinaire mania for large farms, and a natural desire in the
factors to get clear returns with as little trouble as possible,

was the real cause of the atrocious proceedings commonly known as the Sutherland Clearances.

VII. I hold it proven that in Sutherland, as in other parts of the Highlands, there existed a large population, beyond what the district could profitably support, who dragged on their tenure from father to son without any capacity of progress; but, as this population had been allowed to grow up under the eye and even with the encouragement of the proprietor and the Goverment, it was not the people who ought to have been made to suffer from the neglect and the misconduct of their natural heads; and this state of the case furnished an additional reason why any changes that took place should have been made with peculiar tenderness and delicacy.

VIII. I hold it proven that the government of large Highland estates by absentee landlords, English Commissioners, and Lowland factors, utterly ignorant of the language, the feelings, and the consuetudinary rights of the people from whom they draw their rents, is the form of economical administration naturally the best calculated to produce those harsh, inhuman, and impolitic agrarian changes commonly called the Sutherland Clearances.

Are you satisfied? asks the Professor, and the German replies:—

"I am: so far, at least, as one may be, who has not, like you, carefully read all the documents. I must say, however, that my own convictions on the general question are so strongly on your side, arising partly from my practical knowledge of the condition of rural economy in Westphalia and other parts of my fatherland, partly from the recollections I have of the admirable prelections on this subject delivered by Professor Roscher in Leipzig, that no evidence that I am likely to get from the detailed consideration of the documents from which you have quoted so copiously, would have any power to rebut the moral and political presumptions, which from the beginning have led me to condemn the whole ugly process by which your selfish, anti-social, or ignorant and short-sighted oligarchs have turned the green glens of Alba, smoking with rows of bonnie white cottages, into banks of investment for Dumfriesshire farmers, and braes of browsing ground for wild beasts. My German opinion on this big British blunder is expressed in one short classical sentence—

LATIFUNDIA PERDIDERE CALEDONIAM!"

The Professor, *alias* "Macdonald," expresses the following "sentiments," as he terms them, to which the philosophical German, in each case, adds his hearty AMEN :—

If there be any person who maintains that money, rather than men, constitutes the wealth of a healthy and well-ordered State, let him be anathema-maranatha !

If there be any person who maintains that it is better to make one big Lowland farmer rich than a hundred Highlanders happy and prosperous in a Highland glen, let him be anathema-maranatha !

If any man maintain that landlords have no duties but to gather rents, and that they may, without sin before God, and without injury to society, neglect the condition and the distribution of the people, from whom they draw their rents, let him be anathema-maranatha !

If any say that cash payment is and ought to be the only bond of cement between the different classes of society, let him be anathema-maranatha !

If any one maintain that it is better for the land of a country to be held by a few large proprietors, than to be distributed into many properties, of various sizes and qualities, let him be anathema-maranatha !

If any man maintain that a lord of the soil is justified in extruding an old and faithful tenantry, and making a deer forest of their cultivable lots, merely because he can make more money of it, or indulge himself in a wild pleasure, let him be anathema-maranatha!

If any man maintain that the distinctive glory of a landed proprietor in Scotland consists in the number of grouse which he can shoot, the number of deer which he can stalk, and the number of salmon which he can hook during the season, let him be anathema-maranatha!

If any man maintain that Scotland is only a northern province of England, and the sooner all local distinctions between the two peoples are merged in the universal dominance of purely English manners, customs, and institutions, let him be anathema-maranatha!

If any man maintain that the Highlands of Scotland are fit for nothing but being hired out as hunting-ground to the English aristocracy and plutocracy, let him be anathema-maranatha!*

To all of which we also say—AMEN!

The Sutherland Clearances Professor Blackie finally condemns as "a social crime and a blunder" for which he holds the land laws principally to blame.

JOHN MACKAY, C.E.,

REFERRING to the Sutherland Clearances, Mr. John Mackay, C.E., Hereford, said at a recent meeting of the Edinburgh Sutherland Association :—

* *Altavona; Fact and Fiction from my Life in the Highlands.* By John Stuart Blackie, F.R.S.E., Professor of Greek, Edinburgh : David Douglas, 1882.

We still helplessly condemn the fatuity that caused the m
we hopelessly deplore the national blunder that permitted
such barbaric acts to be perpetrated upon such a generous,
loyal, and unoffending people, the most moral, the most
religious population in the Highlands of Scotland, leaving
the remnant of it that could not take itself away, struck and
benumbed with a terror from which it has not yet recovered,
and never will.

Gus an till an gràdh 's an t-iochd
'S dual do athair thoirt d'a shliochd
'S gu'm faic na triath gur fearr na treun
Na milte uan am mile treud.

Thrust out of their ancient homes in fertile plains and
sheltered valleys on to sterile hill-sides, or equally sterile
sea shores, to make new habitations for themselves, if they
could or would, out of moory, mossy, heathery hillsides, or
lead an amphibious life on sandy, rocky, stormy sea shores,
without aid, without even encouragement being given or
extended to them, to live or not to live, to dig or not to dig,
to improve or not to improve, often without sufficient sustenance, need it be surprising that the population has dwarfed
and dwindled away? The greater surprise is that it has not
died out of existence altogether, and that it has in spite of
oppression, repression, contumely, and neglect, maintained
itself as it has. Surely such facts as these speak volumes
for the tenacity and morals of that people. What was the
condition of the population thus treated in so barbarous a
manner in a civilized country, vaunting so much of its civilization? I will give it you in the words of a Sutherland
lady, put by her on record upwards of fifty years ago. She
says :—" I have of late frequently heard strangers coming
amongst us express their surprise at the marked intelligence
evinced by the old people of this district, devoid of any

degree of early cultivation. To this it may be answered that the state of society was very different then from what it is now, progressively retrograding as it has been for the last few years, at least in this part of the country. At the time I allude to the lords, lairds, and gentleman of the county not only interested themselves in the welfare and happiness of their clan and dependants, but they were always solicitous that their manners, and customs, and intelligence, should keep pace with their personal appearance. The fact was the chief knew his clansmen, and it was deemed no inconsiderable part of duty in the higher classes of the community to elevate the minds as well as to assist in increasing the means of their humbler relatives and clansmen. I am aware that many unacquainted with the close ties of such a system argue largely that the distinction of rank appointed by God could not be maintained by such indiscriminate intercourse—still the habits of that day never produced a contrary effect. The chiefs here for many generations had been 'men fearing God and hating covetousness'. Iniquity was ashamed and obliged to hide its face. A dishonourable action excluded the guilty person from the invaluable privilege enjoyed by his equals in the kind notice and approbation of their superiors. Grievances of any kind were minutely inquired into and redressed, and the humble orders of the community had a degree of external polish and manly mildness of deportment in domestic life that few of the present generation have attained to, much as had been said of modern improvements." That is a picture to you of the civilization and morality existing and reigning in Sutherland, and other districts of the Highlands, at the beginning of this century, before the dark and dread days of the evictions were seen or thought of, and it may be asked what was the result of such kind and considerate conduct on the part of chiefs, lords, and lairds? History has a ready reply. From 1760 to 1810, a period of only half a century, the Highlands of Scotland, under the regime which the Sutherland lady so graphically described, sent forth 80,000 of its best and bravest men to defend the country, and fight its battles, and when they did go forth, they restored the prestige of the country, retrieved its laurels, and brought victory to crown British banners in every quarter of the globe. There is not a village round Paris, nor round Brussels, in which I have been, and conversed with their oldest inhabitants, but still revere the conduct of those Highland soldiers; so different it was to that of the other regiments of the British army. Were this the time and place, I could keep you long relating anecdotes I gathered from French and Belgians of the grand " *soldats Ecossais,*" lambs in the house, lions in the field of battle. It was from that grand population in the Highlands, nurtured and reared in the way the Sutherland lady describes so truly, that those gallant, brave soldiers went forth in legions to conquer or to die. What has Sutherland itself done in that eventful period of our history, before sheep became to be of greater value in the estimation of lairds, than a brave and loyal population of happy, contented, and hardy peasantry ! In the '45 the chiefs of Sutherland had 2550 men under arms in the defence of the Throne and the country. In 1760, in the short space of nine days, 1100 Sutherland men responded to the call of their chiefs and served their country for four years. In 1777, when the country was in dire need of men, gallant and true, an equal number answered the call to arms, and served under their chiefs for five years. In 1794, the Sutherland chiefs again appealed to their clansmen, and 1800 men followed them into the field, Sutherlands and Mackays. These men, sons of crofters and tacksmen, behaved themselves in England, Ireland, and the Channel Islands in a manner that drew forth from commanding generals the highest enconiums for their good conduct and military bearing in quarters, and in the field. General Lake, on his defeat by the French at Castlebar, said of the Mackay Regiment of Fencibles, "If I had my brave and honest Reays here this would not have happened". In 1800, the 93rd Highlanders was raised, 1000 strong; 800 of them were Sutherland men, and how that regiment comported itself whenever it had an opportunity of showing the stern stuff of which it was composed, its history nobly tells. In the Cape Colony all the Dutchmen spoke of it with raptures. By its conciliatory and gentle, and considerate conduct, it alleviated conquest to the conquered. Such were the sons and brothers of the evicted of Sutherland.

> Where are they now? Tell us where are thy sons and daughters,
>   Sutherland! sad mother! no more in thy bosom they dwell;
> Far, far away, they have found a new home o'er the waters,
>   Yearning for thee with a love that no language can tell.
> Nimrods and hunters are now lords of the mount and forest.
>   Men but encumber the soil where their forefathers trod;
> Tho' for their country they fought when its need was the sorest,
>   Forth they must wander, their hope not in man, but in God.

I need not enlarge upon this theme, but I may be permitted to ask what are loyalty and affection? Are they virtues to be held cheap by the country? It is said that loyalty in the subject is the stability and safety of the throne, the palace, and the castle; but after all, loyalty and affection are simply the development of our best sentiments, which can be cultivated, which can be increased or diminished by kind or harsh treatment, by good or bad government, exactly as the Sutherland lady described in the past, and as we ourselves, most unfor-

tunately, see in our own day in the Highlands and in
Ireland—grievances unheeded and unredressed, till agitation
and outrage bring them to the light of day. Then remedies
more or less drastic have to be applied, and loud complaints
heard of confiscation and cries for compensation. Was any
compensation ever heard of for the evicted of the Highlands?
Highlanders carried the spirit of loyalty with them even
when evicted. They were proud of the sentiment, and
maintained it, from the furnace of fire on the field of
Culloden, so glorious to the vanquished, so humiliating to
the conquerors, to the fires of the evictions and through
them to the present day, in spite of the divorce from their
chiefs, in spite of the want of sympathy that might reason-
ably have been expected from chiefs whom they so implicitly
trusted, and whom they so well served, little conscious of
what was their own due for such elevated services, and in
spite, too, of after neglect, harsh treatment, and want of any
encouragement when the evil day overtook them. Greed
of gold, love of display in the hearts and minds of Highland chiefs, led to the national disaster of the extirpation of
the heroic population of the Highlands of seventy years ago,
the boast and the pride of Scotland, the safety of England
and the terror of her foes. Shall we see its like again?
No, not for another century or more. Wealth, with its
concomitant vices—pride, luxury, tyranny, oppression, and
disregard of the golden rule—lead to nihilism, socialism,
communism, as it has led to the decline and fall of empires
and kingdoms, ancient and modern. Well will it be for us
and for themselves if our aristocracy and plutocracy,
imitating the bright and grand example of the best and most
beloved monarch that ever ruled the destinies of our country, to exercise the rights conferred upon them by the
Crown, and by Acts of Parliament framed by themselves,

that from them to us might flow a stream of affection, pure and unalloyed, and from us to them course its way back in veins of true loyalty and attachment, as a return for the proper exercise of duties implied and understood in the conferring of rights. This done and observed, the throne and the castle are secure; this not done, both are insecure—a breath can unmake them, as a breath has made. Both are in danger of being swept away here as elsewhere, and in other countries :

> Remember, man, the universal cause
> Acts not by partial, but by general laws.

The eternal law of right and justice to all classes and between all classes must ultimately prevail. The British Government is no longer at the dictation of the rich and powerful. Was not the great principle of National Education in Scotland wrung from rapacious noblemen by John Knox? Was not political power wrenched from an unwilling oligarchy half a century ago? Has not free trade in corn been made the law of the land in spite of the opposition of the landed interest? Were not civil and religious freedom secured to us by the best blood of our countrymen, in the face of much opposition and bloodshed? Frequently evil is done by want of thought as much as by want of heart. I have attempted to describe what was the happy and contented condition of the Highland people, and the state of civilization that ruled at the beginning of this century, before the terrible change came that tore them from their homes, and thrust them out totally unprepared for such a dire catastrophe. Humanity shudders at the scene. Need it be surprising that a people so accustomed to gentle, kind, considerate treatment and cultivation from former chiefs, were absolutely stunned by such a sudden and terrible revolutionary visitation. No wonder that the people reeled and staggered like ships caught in a storm and about to sink into an unknown abyss. Bowing to their fate with despair in their looks and terror in their hearts, without striking a blow in self-defence, or in the preservation of what they considered almost their own, they have not yet recovered from the shock, and never will, if left to the tender mercies of ruthless factors, strangers to them, ignorant of their language, their character, their capabilities, and their idiosyncrasies. These men in the past were, as we know, ruthless; they may be better now, yet many of them are still accused of exceeding their authority, and provoking the kindlier feelings of landlords from operating in favour of their ancient tenantry. The Highland crofter has been accused, is now accused, of indolence and want of industrious habits. What was? what is the premium offered him for industry? Where is there now, even in this day, an inducement held out to him to be industrious? The terror frequently inspired by factors unmans him. The fear of eviction and rent-raising represses him. Is this a state of things, a condition of tenantry worthy of Highland lords and lairds—worthy of the benign rule of Victoria? How different from the period when chiefs knew their men, lived amongst them, and guided them in the way they should go? No man may be more independent with generous and judicious treatment, though comparatively poor, than the crofter on a good croft, with his horses, and his cows, and his sheep, and his rent paid. He rightly considers himself placed in a situation and in a station of life and society far above the day labourer. Those who wish to see only two castes—capitalists and day labourers—may smile at this union of independence and comparative poverty; but it is established beyond a doubt that the opposite system has quenched the independent spirit of the

Highlanders, and it gives additional strength to the argument of those who object to reduction of the agricultural population, and regret their removal to the centres of population and seats of industry, seats of misery, vice, and immorality. It would really appear that the eviction of rural populations, and forcing them to leave the country for the purpose of adding field to field, has brought about its own retribution at last. The evicted, after enduring severe hardships, many struggles, and untold misery, now produce a surplus, send it to this country, and thereby force down prices to an extent unequal to pay the rents exacted for large farms, thus showing that in the long run there is a compensation for all evils ; and many regard the present condition of agricultural affairs as a retribution for past misdeeds.

So much, and, in many respects, it is more than enough, about the Sutherland Clearances ! We shall next record instances, many of them exhibiting equal ingratitude and brutality, though not so well-known, in other places, and by different people, throughout the Highlands.

GLENCALVIE.

GREAT cruelties were perpetrated at Glencalvie, Ross-shire, where the evicted had to retire into the parish churchyard, where for more than a week they found the only shelter obtainable in their native land, no one daring to succour them, under a threat of receiving similar treatment to those whose hard fate had driven them thus among the tombs. Many of them, indeed, wished that their lot had landed them under the sod with their ancestors and friends, rather than be treated and driven out of house and home in such a ruthless manner. A special Commissioner sent down by the London *Times* describes the circumstances as follows :—

ARDGAY, NEAR TAIN, ROSS-SHIRE,
15th May, 1845.

Those who remember the misery and destitution to which large masses of the population were thrown by the system- atic " Clearances " (as they are here called) carried on in Sutherlandshire some 20 years ago, under the direction and on the estate of the late Marchioness of Stafford—those who have not forgotten to what an extent the ancient ties which bound clansmen to their chiefs were then torn asunder—will regret to learn the heartless source with all its sequences of misery, of destitution, and of crime, is again being resorted to in Ross-shire. Amongst an imaginative people like the Highlanders, who, poetic from dwelling amongst wild and romantic scenery, shut out from the world and clinging to the traditions of the past, it requires little, with fair treatment, to make them almost idolise their heritor. They would spend the last drop of their blood in his service. But this feeling of respectful attachment to the landowners, which money cannot buy, is fast passing away. This change is not without cause; and perhaps if the dark deeds of calculating "feelosophy" transacted through the instrumentality of factors in some of these lonely glens; if the almost inconceivable misery and hopeless destitution in which, for the expected acquisition of a few pounds, hundreds of peaceable and generally industrious and contented peasants are driven out from the means of self-support to become wanderers and starving beggars, and in which a brave and valuable population is destroyed—are exposed to the gaze of the world, general indignation and disgust may effect what moral obligations and humanity cannot. One of these clearances is about to take place in the parish of Kincardine, from which I now write; and throughout the whole district it has created the strongest feeling of indignation. This parish is divided into two districts each of great extent; one is called the parliamentary district of Croick. The length of this district is about 20 miles, with a breadth of from 10 to 15 miles. It extends amongst the most remote and unfrequented parts of the country, consisting chiefly of hills of heather and rock, peopled only in a few straths and glens. This district was formerly thickly peopled; but one of those clearances many years ago nearly swept away the population, and now the whole number of its inhabitants amounts, I am told, to only 370 souls. These are divided into three straths or glens, and live in a strath called Amatnatua, another strath called Greenyard, and in Glencalvie. It is the inhabitants of Glencalvie, in number 90 people, whose turn it is now to be turned out of their homes, all at once, the aged and the helpless as well as the young and strong; nearly the whole of them without hope or prospect for the future. The proprietor of this glen is Major Charles Robertson of Kindeace, who is at present out with his regiment in Australia; and his factor or steward who acts for him in his absence is Mr. James Gillanders of Highfield Cottage, near Dingwall. Glencalvie is situated about 25 miles from Tain, eastward. Bleak rough hills, whose surface are almost all rock and heather, closed in on all sides, leaving in the valley a gentle declivity of arable land of a very poor description, dotted over by cairns of stone and rock, not, at the utmost computation, of more than 15 to 20 acres in extent. For this piece of indifferent land with a right of pasturage on the hills impinging upon it—and on which, if it were not a fact that sheep do live, you would not credit that they could live, so entirely does it seem so devoid of vegetation beyond the brown heather, whilst its rocky nature makes it dangerous and impossible even for a sheep walk—the almost increditable rent of £55 10s., has been paid. I am convinced that for the same land no farmer in England would give £15 at the utmost.

Even respectable farmers here say they do not know how the people raise the rent for it. Potatoes and barley were grown in the valley, and some sheep and a few black cattle find provender amongst the heather. Eighteen families have each a cottage in the valley; they have always paid their rent punctually, and they have contrived to support themselves in all ordinary seasons. They have no poor on the poor roll, and they help one another over the winter. I am told that not an inhabitant of this valley has been charged with any offence for years back. During the war it furnished many soldiers; and an old pensioner, 82 years of age, who has served in India, is now dying in one of these cottages, where he was born. For the convenience of the proprietor, some ten years ago, four of the principal tenants became bound for the rest, to collect all the rents and pay the whole in one sum.

The clearance of this valley, having attracted much notice, has been thoroughly enquired into, and a kind of defence has been entered upon respecting it, which I am told has been forwarded to the Lord Advocate. Through the politeness of Mr. Mackenzie, writer, Tain, I have been favoured with a copy of it. The only explanation or defence of the clearance, that I can find in it, is that shortly after Mr. Gillanders assumed the management of Major Robertson's estate, he found that it became absolutely necessary to adopt a different system, in regard to the lands of Glencalvie " from that hitherto pursued ".

The " different system " as it appears was to turn the barley and potato grounds into a sheep walk ; and the " absolute necessity " for it is an alleged increase of rent.

It was accordingly, in 1843, attempted to serve summonses of removal upon the tenants. They were in no arrears of rent, they had no burdens in poor ; for 500 years their fathers had peaceably occupied the glen, and the people were naturally indignant. Who can be surprised that on the constables going amongst them with the summonses, they acted in a manner which, while it showed their excitement, not the less evinced their wish to avoid breaking the law. The women met the constables beyond the boundaries, over the river, and seized the hand of the one who held the notices : whilst some held it out by the wrist, others held a live coal to the papers and set fire to them. They were afraid of being charged with destroying the notices, and they sought thus to evade the consequences.

This act of resistance on their part has been made the most of. One of the men told me, hearing they were to be turned out because they did not pay rent enough, that they offered to pay £15 a-year more, and afterwards to pay as much rent as any other man would give for the place. The following year (1844) however, the four chief tenants were decoyed to Tain, under the assurance that Mr. Gillanders was going to settle with them, they believing that their holdings were to be continued to them. The notices were then, as they say, in a treacherous and tricky manner, served upon them, however. Having been served, "a decreet of removal" was obtained against them under which, of course, if they refused to turn out they would be put out by force. Finding themselves in this position, they entered into an arrangement with Mr. Gillanders, in which after several propositions on either side, it was agreed that they should remain until the 12th of May, to give them time to provide themselves with holdings elsewhere, Mr. Gillanders agreeing to pay them £100 on quitting, and to take their stock on at a valuation. They were also to have liberty to carry away the timber of their houses, which was really worthless except for firewood. On their part they agreed to leave peaceably, and not to lay down any crop. Beyond the excessive harshness of removing the people at all, it is but right to say that the mode of proceeding in the removal hitherto has been temperate and considerate.

Two respectable farmers became bound for the people that they would carry out their part of the agreement, and the time of removal has since been extended to the 25th of this month. In the defence got up for this proceeding it is stated that all have been provided for; this is not only not the case, but seems to be intentionally deceptive. In speaking of all, the four principal tenants only are meant; for, accord-

ing to the factor, these were all he had to do with; but this
is not the case even in regard to the four principal tenants.
Two only, a father and son, have got a piece of black
moor, near Tain, 25 miles off, without any house or shed on
it, out of which they hope to obtain subsistence. For this
they are to pay £1 rent for 7 acres the first year; £2 for
the second year; and £3 for a continuation. Another old
man with a family has got a house and a small lot of land
in Edderton, about 20 miles off. These three, the whole
who have obtained places where they may hope to make a
living. The old pensioner, if removing does not kill him, has
obtained for himself and family, and for his son's family, a
house at a rent of £3 or £4, some ten miles off, without
any land or means of subsistence attached to it. This old
soldier has been offered 2s. a-week by the factor to support
him while he lived. He was one of the four principal
tenants bound for the rent; and he indignantly refused to
be kept as a pauper.

A widow with four children, two imbecile, has obtained
two small apartments in a bothie or turf hut near Bonar
Bridge, for which she is to pay £2 rent, without any land
or means of subsistence. Another, a man with a wife and
four children, has got an apartment at Bonar Bridge, at £1
rent. He goes there quite destitute, without means of
living. Six only of eighteen households therefore have been
able to obtain places in which to put their heads; and of
these, three only have any means of subsistence before them.
The rest are hopeless and helpless. Two or three of the
men told me they have been round to every factor and
proprietor in the neighbourhood, and they could obtain no
place, and nothing to do, and they did not know where to
go to, nor what to do to live.

Speaking of the cottages the Commissioner says :—The

fire is on a stone in the middle of the family or centre room, and warms the whole cottage. Though the roofs and sides are blackened with the peat smoke, everything within is clean and orderly.

And for what are all these people to be reduced from comfort to beggary? For what is this virtuous and contented community to be scattered? I confess I can find no answer. It is said that the factor would rather have one tenant than many, as it saves him trouble! But so long as the rent is punctually paid as this has been, it is contrary to all experience to suppose that one large tenant will pay more rent than many small ones, or that a sheep walk can pay more rent than cultivated land.

Let me add that so far from the clearance at Glencalvie being a solitary instance in this neighbourhood, it is one of many. The tenants of Newmore, near Tain, who I am told, amount to 16 families, are to be weeded out (as they express it here) on the 25th, by the same Mr. Gillanders. The same factor manages the Strathconon estate, about 30 miles from Newmore, from which during the last four years, some hundreds of families have been weeded. The Government Church of that district, built eighteen years ago, to meet the necessities of the population, is now almost unnecessary from the want of population. At Black Isle, near Dingwall, the same agent is pursuing the same course, and so strong is the feeling of the poor Highlanders at these outrageous proceedings, so far as they are concerned wholly unwarranted from any cause whatever, that I am informed on the best authority, and by those who go amongst them and hear what they say, that it is owing to the influence of religion alone that they refrain from breaking out into open and turbulent resistance of the law. I enclose you the defence of this proceeding, with a list of the names and numbers of each family in Glencalvie—in all 92 persons.*

Mr. Gillanders has been severely hit off for his conduct here, in Strathconon, and elsewhere, by Duncan Mackenzie, the Kenlochewe Bard, in a long Gaelic poem, from which we extract the following stanzas :—

'S dhearbh Seumas a dhuthchas,
A bhi na shiamarlan bruideal,
Mar bha sheanair bho thus,
A creach, 's a rusgadh nam bochd.
Am fior-anmhaidh, gun churam,
Gun Dia, gun chreideamh, gun umhlachd,
Gun chliu, gun tuigse, gun diulam,
Ach na ùmaidh gun tlachd ;
Gheibh e bhreitheanas dubailt,
Air son na Rosaich a sgiursadh,
A Gleann-a-Chalbhaidh le dhurachd,
Na daoine ionraic gun lochd,
Bha riamh onarach, sumhail,
Gun sgilig fhiachan air chul orr',
'S na màil paight' aig gach aon diubh,
'S gach cis shaoghalt bha orr'.

Bu truagh, cianail, a dh-fhag e,
Gleann-a-Chalbhaidh na fhasach,
An sluagh sgaipte anns gach aite,
Gun cheo, gun larach, gun tigh,
Air an ruagadh le tamailt,
'S olc a fhuair iad an caradh,
Gun aite fuirich na tamh ac',
Gun truas, gun chairdeas, gun iochd.
Chaidh cuid a chomhnuidh fuidh sgail dhiubh,
Ann an cladh Chinn a-Chairdin ;
Thug sud masladh, 'us taire,
Dha 'n t-Siorr'achd ghaidh'leach so 'm feasd ;
'S bi' Seumas mor air a phaigheadh,
An lath a' ghairmeas am bàs e,
'S cha bhi bron air na Gaidheil,
Nuair theid a charadh fuidh lic.

*London *Times* of Tuesday, 20th of May, 1845.

Rinn am buamasdair grannda,
Obair eile, bha graineil,
A chur air ruaig Cloinn-'ic-Thearlaich,
Bha paigheadh mal Choirre-bhuic,
An tuath chothromach, laidir,
Nach dh-fhuair masladh, no taire,
Gus an d-thainig an namhaid
Nach deanadh fabhar air bith.
Chaidh an Sgaoileadh 's gach aite ;
Cha robh trocair 'na nadurs',
Fear gun choguis, gun naire,
Air an laidh an càineadh is mios',
'S iomadh athchuimhnich araidh,
'Chaidh a ghuidhe d' a chnaimhean ;
'S cha 'n urrainn es' a bhi sabhailt
Ann an aite sam bith.

THE EVICTION OF THE ROSSES.

In a "Sermon for the Times," the Rev. Richard Hibbs, of the Episcopal Church, Edinburgh, referring to these evictions says :—" Take first, the awful proof how far in oppression men can go—men highly educated and largely gifted in every way—property, talents, all ; for the most part indeed, they are so-called noblemen. What, then, are they doing in the Highland districts, according to the testimony of a learned professor in this city ? Why, depopulating those districts in order to make room for red deer. And how ? by buying off the cottars, and giving them money to emigrate ? Not at all, but by starving them out ; by rendering them absolutely incapable of procuring subsistence for themselves and families ; for they first take away from them their apportionments of poor lands, although they may have paid their rents ; and if that don't suffice to eradicate from their hearts that love of the soil on which they have been born and bred—a love which

the great Proprietor of all has manifestly implanted in our
nature—why, then, these inhuman landlords, who are far
more merciful to their very beasts, take away from these
poor cottars the very roofs above their defenceless heads,
and expose them, worn down with age and destitude of
of everything, to the inclemencies of a northern sky ; and
this, forsooth, because they must have plenty of room for
their dogs and deer. For plentiful instances of the most
wanton barbarities under this head we need only point to
the Knoydart evictions. Here were perpetrated such
enormities as might well have caused the very sun to hide
his face at noon-day." Macleod, referring to this sermon,
says :—

"It has been intimated to me by an individual who heard
this discourse on the first occasion that the statements
referring to the Highland landlords have been controverted.
I was well aware, long before the receipt of this intimation,
that some defence had appeared ; and here I can truly say,
that none would have rejoiced more than myself to find
that a complete vindication had been made. But, unhappily, the case is far otherwise. In order to be fully
acquainted with all that had passed on the subject, I have
put myself during the week in communication with the
learned professor to whose letter, which appeared some
months ago in the *Times*, I referred. From him I learn
that none of his statements were invalidated—nay, not even
impugned ; and he adds, that to do this was simply impossible, as he had been at great pains to verify the facts. All
that could be called in question was the theory that he had
based upon those facts—namely, that evictions were made
for the purpose of making room for more deer. This, of
course, was open to contradiction on the part of those landlords who had not openly avowed their object in evicting

the poor Highland families. As to the evictions themselves —and this was the main point—no attempt at contradiction was made."

In addition to all that the benevolent Professor [Black] has made known to the world under this head, who has not heard of "The Massacre of the Rosses," and the clearing of the glens. "I hold in my hand," Mr. Hibbs continued, "a little work thus entitled, which has passed into the second edition. The author, Mr. Donald Ross—a gentleman whom all who feel sympathy for the down-trodden and oppressed must highly esteem. What a humiliating picture of the barbarity and cruelty of fallen humanity does this little book present! The reader, utterly appalled by its horrifying statements finds it difficult to retain the recollection that he is perusing the history of his own times, and country too. He would fain yield himself to the tempting illusion that the ruthless atrocities which are depicted were enacted in a fabulous period, in ages long past ; or at all events, if it be contemporaneous history, that the scene of such heart-rending cruelties, the perpetrators of which were regardless alike of the innocency of infancy and the helplessness of old age, is some far distant, and as yet not merely unchristianized, but wholly savage and uncivilized region of of our globe. But alas ! it is Scotland, in the latter half of the nineteenth century, of which he treats. One feature of the heart-harrowing case is the shocking and barbarous cruelty that was practised on this occasion upon the female portion of the evicted clan. Mr. D. Ross, in a letter addressed to the Right Hon. the Lord Advocate, Edinburgh, dated April 19, 1854, thus writes in reference to one of those clearances and evictions which had just then taken place, under the authority of a certain sheriff of the district, and by means of a body of policemen as executioners :—

" The feeling on this subject, not only in the district, but in Sutherlandshire and Ross-shire is, among the great majority of the people, one of universal condemnation of the Sheriff's reckless conduct, and of indignation and disgust at the brutality of the policemen. Such, indeed, was the sad havoc made on the females on the banks of the Carron, on the memorable 31st March last, that pools of blood were on the ground—that the grass and earth were dyed red with it—that the dogs of the district came and licked up the blood ; and at last, such was the state of feeling of parties who went from a distance to see the field, that a party (it is understood by order or instructions from head-quarters) actually harrowed the ground during the night to hide the blood !

" The affair at Greenyard, on the morning of the 31st March last, is not calculated to inspire much love of country, or rouse the martial spirit of the already ill-used Highlanders. The savage treatment of innocent females on that morning, by an enraged body of police, throws the Sinope butchery into the shade; for the Ross-shire Haynaus have shown themselves more cruel and more blood-thirsty than the Austrian women-floggers. What could these poor men and women—with their wounds, and scars, and broken bones, and disjointed arms, stretched on beds of sickness, or moving on crutches, the result of the brutal treatment of them by the police at Greenyard—have to dread from the invasion of Scotland by Russia ? "

Commenting on this incredible atrocity, committed in the middle of the nineteenth century! Donald Macleod says truly that :—It was so horrifying and so brutal that he did not wonder at the rev. gentleman's delicacy in speaking of it, and directing his hearers to peruse Mr. Ross's pamphlet for full information. Mr. Ross went from Glasgow to Greenyard,

all the way to investigate the case upon the spot, and found
that Mr. Taylor, a native of Sutherland, well educated in the
evicting schemes and murderous cruelty of that county,
and Sheriff-substitue of Ross-shire, marched from Tain upon
the morning of the 31st March, at the head of a strong
party of armed constables, with heavy bludgeons and fire
arms, conveyed in carts and other vehicles, allowing them as
much ardent drink as they chose to take before leaving and
on their march, so as to qualify them for the bloody work
which they had to perform ; fit for any outrage, fully
equipped, and told by the Sheriff to show no mercy to any
one who would oppose them, and not allow themselves to
be called cowards, by allowing these mountaineers victory
over them. In this excited, half-drunken state, they came
in contact with the unfortunate women of Greenyard, who
were determined to prevent the officers from serving the
summonses of removal upon them, and keep their holding of
small farms where they and their forefathers lived and died
for generations. But no time was allowed for parley ; the
Sheriff gave the order to clear the way, and, be it said to his
everlasting disgrace, he struck the first blow at a woman,
the mother of a large family, and large in the family way at
the time, who tried to keep him back ; then a general
slaughter commenced ; the women made noble resistance,
until the bravest of them got their arms broken ; then they
gave way. This did not allay the rage of the murderous
brutes, they continued clubbing at the protectless creatures
until every one of them was stretched on the field, weltering
in their blood, or with broken arms, ribs, and bruised limbs.
In this woful condition many of them were hand-cuffed
together, others tied with coarse ropes, huddled into carts,
and carried prisoners to Tain. I have seen myself
in the possession of Mr. Ross, Glasgow, patches or scalps

of the skin with the long hair adhering to them, which was found upon the field a few days after this inhuman affray. I did not see the women, but I was told that gashes were found on the heads of two young female prisoners in Tain jail, which exactly corresponded with the slices of scalps which I have seen, so that Sutherland and Ross-shire may boast of having had the Nana Sahib and his chiefs some few years before India, and that in the persons of some whose education, training, and parental example should prepare their minds to perform and act differently. Mr. Donald Ross placed the whole affair before the Lord Advocate for Scotland, but no notice was taken of it by that functionary, further than that the majesty of the law would need to be observed and attended to.

In this unfortunate country, the law of God and humanity may be violated and trampled under foot, but the law of wicked men which sanctions murder, rapine, and robbery must be observed. From the same estate (the estate of Robertson of Kindeace, if I am not mistaken in the date) in the year 1843 the whole inhabitants of Glencalvie were evicted in a similar manner, and so unprovided and unprepared were they for removal at such an inclement season of the year, that they had to shelter themselves in a Church and a burying-ground. I have seen myself nineteen families within this gloomy and solitary resting abode of the dead, they were there for months. The London *Times* sent a commissioner direct from London to investigate into this case, and he did his duty; but like the Sutherland cases, it was hushed up in order to maintain the majesty of the law, and in order to keep the right, the majesty of the people, and the laws of God in the dark.

In the year 1819 or '20, about the time when the depopulation of Sutherlandshire was completed, and the annual conflagration of burning the houses ceased, and when there was not a glen or strath in the county to let to a sheep farmer, one of these insatiable monsters of Sutherlandshire sheep farmers fixed his eyes upon a glen in Ross-shire, inhabited by a brave race, hardy for time immemorial. Summonses of removal were served upon them at once. The people resisted—a military force was brought against them —the military and the women of the glen met at the entrance to the glen—a bloody conflict took place; without reading the riot act or taking any other precaution, the military fired (by the order of Sheriff MacLeod) ball cartridge upon the women; one young girl of the name of Mathieson was shot dead on the spot; many were wounded. When this murder was observed by the survivors, and some young men concealed in the background, they made a heroic sudden rush upon the military, when a hand-to-hand melee or fight took place. In a few minutes the military were put to disorder by flight; in their retreat they were unmercifully dealt with, only two of them escaping with whole heads. The Sheriff's coach was smashed to atoms, and he made a narrow escape himself with a whole head. But no legal cognisance was taken of this affair, as the Sheriff and the military were the violators. However, for fear of prosecution, the Sheriff settled a pension of £6 sterling yearly upon the murdered girl's father, and the case was hushed up likewise. The result was that the people kept possession of the glen, and that the proprietor, and the oldest and most insatiable of Sutherlandshire scourges went to law, which ended in the ruination of the latter, who died a pauper.

Hugh Miller, describing a " Highland Clearing," in one of his able leading articles in the *Witness*, since published in volume form, quotes freely from an article by John Robertson, which appeared in the *Glasgow National* in August, 1844, on the evictions of the Rosses of Glencalvie. When the article from which Hugh Miller quotes was written, the inhabitants of the glen had just received notices of removal, but the evictions had not yet been carried out. Commenting on the proceedings our authority says :—

"In an adjacent glen (to Strathcarron), through which the Calvie works its headlong way to the Carron, that terror of the Highlanders, a summons of removal, has been served within the last few months on a whole community: and the graphic sketch of Mr. Robertson relates both the peculiar circumstances in which it has been issued, and the feelings which it has excited. We find from his testimony that the old state of things which is so immediately on the eve of being broken up in this locality, lacked not a few of those sources of terror to the proprietary of the county, that are becoming so very formidable to them in the newer states."

The constitution of society in the Glen, says Mr. Robertson, is remarkably simple. Four heads of families are bound for the whole rental. The number of souls was about ninety, sixteen cottages paid rent ; they supported a teacher for the education of their own children ; they supported their own poor. "The laird has never lost a farthing of rent in bad years, such as 1836 and 1837, the people may have required the favour of a few weeks' delay, but they are not now a single farthing in arrears ; " that is, when they are in receipt of summonses of removal. "For a century," Mr. Robertson continues, speaking of the Highlanders, "their privileges have been lessening ; they dare not now hunt the deer, or shoot the grouse or the blackcock ; they have no longer the range of the hills for their cattle and their sheep ; they must not catch a salmon in the stream : in earth, air, and water, the rights of the laird are greater, and the rights of the people are smaller, than they were in the days of their forefathers." The same writer eloquently concludes :—

" The father of the laird of Kindeace bought Glencalvie. It was sold by a Ross two short centuries ago. The swords of the Rosses of Glencalvie did their part in protecting this little glen, as well as the broad lands of Pitcalvie, from the ravages and the clutches of hostile septs. These clansmen bled and died in the belief that every principle of honour and morals secured their descendants a right to subsisting on the soil. The chiefs and their children had the same charter of the sword. Some Legislatures have made the right of the people superior to the right of the chief ; British law-makers made the rights of the chief everything, and those of their followers nothing. The ideas of the morality of property are in most men the creatures of their interests and sympathies. Of this there cannot be a doubt, however, the chiefs would not have had the land at all, could the clansmen have foreseen the present state of the Highlands— their children in mournful groups going into exile—the faggot of legal myrmidons in the thatch of the feal cabin— the hearths of their homes and their lives the green sheep-walks of the stranger. Sad it is, that it is seemingly the will of our constituencies that our laws shall prefer the few to the many. Most mournful will it be, should the clansmen of the Highlands have been cleared away, ejected, exiled, in deference to a political, a moral, a social, and an economical mistake,—a suggestion not of philosophy, but of mammon,— a system in which the demon of sordidness assumed the shape of the angel of civilization and of light."

That the Eviction of the Rosses was of a most brutal character is amply corroborated by the following account, extracted from the *Inverness Courier :*—"We mentioned last week that considerable obstruction was anticipated in the

execution of the summonses of removal upon the tenants of
Major Robertson of Kindeace, on his property of Greenyards, near Bonar Bridge.   The office turned out to be of a
very formidable character.   At six o'clock on the morning
of Friday last, Sheriff Taylor proceeded from Tain, accompanied by several Sheriff's officers, and a police force of
about thirty more, partly belonging to the constabulary
force of Ross-shire, and partly to that of Inverness-shire,—
the latter under the charge of Mr. Mackay, inspector, Fort-
William.   On arriving at Greenyards, which is nearly four
miles from Bonar Bridge, it was found that about three
hundred persons, fully two-thirds of whom were women, had
assembled from the county round about, all apparently prepared to resist the execution of the law.   The women
stood in front, armed with stones, and the men occupied the
background, all, or nearly all, furnished with sticks.

"The Sheriff attempted to reason with the crowd, and to
show them the necessity of yielding to the law: but his
efforts were fruitless ; some of the women tried to lay hold
of him and to strike him, and after a painful effort to effect
the object in view by peaceable means—which was renewed
in vain by Mr. Cumming, the superintendent of the Ross-
shire police—the Sheriff was reluctantly obliged to employ
force.   The force was led by Mr. Cumming into the crowd,
and after a sharp resistance, which happily lasted only a few
minutes, the people were dispersed, and the Sheriff was
enabled to execute the summonses upon the four tenants.
The women, as they bore the brunt of the battle, were the
principal sufferers.   A large number of them—fifteen or
sixteen, we believe, were seriously hurt, and of these several
are under medical treatment ; one woman, we believe, still
lies in a precarious condition.   The policemen appear to
have used their batons with great force, but they escaped

themselves almost unhurt. Several correspondents from the district, who do not appear, however, to make sufficient allowance for the critical position of affairs, and the necessity of at once impressing so large a multitude with the serious nature of the case, complain that the policemen used their batons with wanton cruelty. Others state that they not only did their duty, but that less firmness might have proved fatal to themselves. The instances of violence are certainly, though very naturally, on the part of the attacking force; several batons were smashed in the melee, a great number of men and women were seriously hurt, especially about the head and face, while not one of the policemen, so far as we can learn, suffered any injury in consequence. As soon as the mob was fairly dispersed, the police made active pursuit, in the hope of catching some of the ringleaders. The men had, however, fled, and the only persons apprehended were some women, who had been active in the opposition, and who had been wounded. They were conveyed to the prison at Tain, but liberated on bail next day, through the intercession of a gallant friend, who became responsible for their appearance."

" A correspondent writes," continues the *Courier*, "ten young women were wounded in the back of the skull and other parts of their bodies. . . . . . The wounds on these women show plainly the severe manner in which they were dealt with by the police when they were retreating. It was currently reported last night that one of them was dead ; and the feeling of indignation is so strong against the manner in which the constables have acted, that I fully believe the life of any stranger, if he were supposed to be an officer of the law, would not be worth twopence in the district. This unfortunate affair reminds me of an Irishman who was successful in a law suit, and after all, said he had only 'gained a loss'; and truly the authority of the law has fared in a similar way in the parish of Kincardine. The fact is that the authority of the law has served to clear an estate of paupers at the public expense; for if the relation that ought to exist between landlord and tenant existed in this case, neither law nor blows would be required in the removal of the poor crofters. If we refer to your paper in the spring of 1845 we shall find summonses peaceably served on 70 or 80 tenants in Glencalvie. Repeated applications were then made for the military and refused. Could not our Lord-Advocate introduce some short measure that would do away with these harrowing Clearances?"

The *Northern Ensign*, referring to the same case, says:—
"One day lately a preventive officer with two cutter men made their appearance on the boundaries of the estate and were taken for Tain Sheriff-officers. The signals were at once given, and in course of half-an-hour the poor gauger and his men were surrounded by 300 men and women, who would not be remonstrated with, either in English or Gaelic; the poor fellows were taken and denuded of their clothing, all papers and documents were extracted and burnt, amongst which was a purse with a considerable quantity of money. In this state they were carried shoulder-high off the estate, and left at the Braes of Downie, where the great Culrain riot took place thirty years ago."

THE HEBRIDES.

The people of Skye and the Uist, where the Macdonalds for centuries ruled in the manner of princes over a loyal and devoted people, were treated not a whit better than those on the mainland, when their services were no longer required to fight the battles of the Lords of the Isles, or to secure to them their possessions, their dignity, and power. *Bha latha eile ann!* There was another day! When possessions were held by the sword, those who wielded them were highly valued, and well cared for. Now that sheep-skins are found sufficient, what could be more appropriate in the opinion of some of the sheepish chiefs of modern times than to displace the people who anciently secured and held the lands for real chiefs worthy of the name, and replace them by the animals that produced the modern sheep-skins by which they hold their lands; especially when these were found to be better titles than the old ones—the blood and sinew of their ancient vassals.

Prior to 1849, the manufacture of kelp in the Outer Hebrides had been for many years a large source of income to the proprietors of those islands, and a considerable revenue to the inhabitants; the lairds, in consequence, for many years encouraged the people to remain, and it is alleged that they multiplied to a degree quite out of proportion to the means of subsistance within reach when kelp manufacture failed. To make matters worse for the poor tenants, the rents were meanwhile raised by the proprietors to more than double—not because the land was considered worth more by itself, but because the possession of it enabled the poor tenants to earn a certain sum a year from kelp made out of the sea-ware to which their holdings entitled them, and out of which the proprietor pocketed a profit of from £3 to £4 per ton, in addition to the en-chanced rent obtained from the crofter for the land. In these circumstances one would have thought that some consideration would have been shown to the people, who, it may perhaps be admitted, were found in the altered cir-cumstances, too numerous to obtain a livelihood in those islands; but such consideration does not appear to have been given—indeed the very reverse.

NORTH UIST.

IN 1849, Lord Macdonald determined to evict between 600 and 700 persons from Sollas, in North Uist, of which he was then proprietor. They were at the time in a state of great misery from the failure of the potato crop for several years previously in succession, many of them having had to work for ninety-six hours a week for a pittance of two stones of Indian meal once a fortnight. Sometimes even that miserable dole was not forthcoming, and families had to live for weeks solely on shell-fish picked up on the sea-shore. Some of the men were employed on drainage works, for which public money was advanced to the pro-prietors; but here, as in most other places throughout the Highlands, the money earned was applied by the factors to wipe off old arrears, while the people were permitted generally to starve. His lordship having decided that they must go, notices of ejectment were served upon them, to take effect on the 15th of May, 1849. They asked for delay, to enable them to dispose of their cattle and other effects to the best advantage at the summer markets, and offered to work meanwhile making kelp, on terms which would prove remunerative to the proprietors, if only, in the altered circumstances, they might get their crofts on equitable terms—for their value, as such—apart from the kelp manufacture, on account of which the rents had previously been raised. Their petitions were ignored. No answers were received, while at the same time they were directed to sow as much corn and potatoes as they could during that spring, and for which they were told, they would be fully compensated, whatever happened. They sold much of their effects to procure seed, and continued to work and sow up to and even after the 15th of May. They then began to cut their peats as usual, thinking they were after all to be allowed to get the benefit. They were, however, soon disappointed—their goods were hypothecated. Many of them were turned out of their houses, the doors locked, and everything they possessed—cattle, crops, and peats—seized. Even their bits of furniture were thrown out of doors in the manner which had long become the fashion in such cases. The season was too far advanced—towards the end of July —to start for Canada. Before they could arrive there the cold winter would be upon them, without means or money to provide against it. They naturally rebelled, and the principal Sheriff-Substitute, Colquhoun, with his officers and a strong body of police left Inverness for North Uist, to eject them from their homes. Naturally unwilling to proceed to extremes, on the arrival of the steamer at Armadale, they sent a messenger ashore to ask for instructions to guide them in case of resistance, or if possible to obtain a modification of his lordship's views. Lord Macdonald had no instructions to give, but referred the Sheriff to Mr.

Cooper, his factor, whose answer was that the whole population of Sollas would be subject to eviction if they did not at once agree to emigrate. A few men were arrested who obstructed the evictors on a previous occasion. They were marched off to Lochmaddy by the police. The work of destruction soon commenced. At first no opposition was made by the poor people. An eye-witness, whose sympathies were believed to be favourable to the proprietor, describes some of the proceedings as follows :—" In evicting Macpherson, the first case taken up, no opposition to the law officers was made. In two or three minutes the few articles of furniture he possessed—a bench, a chair, a broken chair, a barrel, a bag of wool, and two or three small articles, which comprised his whole household of goods and gear— were turned out to the door, and his bothy left roofless. The wife of the prisoner Macphail (one of those taken to Lochmaddy on the previous day) was the next evicted. Her domestic plenishing was of the simplest character—its greatest, and by far its most valuable part, being three small children, dressed in nothing more than a single coat of coarse blanketing, who played about her knee, whilst the poor woman, herself half-clothed, with her face bathed in tears, and holding an infant in her arms, assured the Sheriff that she and her children were totally destitute and without food of any kind. The Sheriff at once sent for the Inspector of Poor, and ordered him to place the woman and her family on the poor's roll." The next house was occupied by very old and infirm people, whom the Sheriff positively refused to evict. He also refused to eject eight other families, where an irregularity was discovered by him in the notices served upon them. The next family ejected led to the almost solitary instance hitherto in the history of Highland evictions where the people made anything like real resistance.

This man was a crofter and weaver, having a wife and nine children to provide for. At this stage a crowd of men and women gathered on an eminence a little distance from the house, and gave the first indications of a hostile intention by raising shouts, as the police advanced to help in the work of demolition, accompanied by about a dozen men who came to their assistance in unroofing the houses from the other end of the island. The crowd, exasperated at the conduct of their own neighbours, threw some stones at the latter. The police were then drawn up in two lines. The furniture was thrown outside, the web was cut out of the loom, and the terrified woman rushed to the door with an infant in her arms, exclaiming in a passionate and wailing voice—"Tha mo chlann air a bhi' air a muirt" (My children are to be murdered). The crowd became excited, stones were thrown at the officers, their assistants were driven from the roof of the house, and they had to retire behind the police for shelter. Volleys of stones and other missiles followed. The police charged in two divisions. There were some cuts and bruises on both sides. The work of demolition was then allowed to go on without further opposition from the crowd.

Several heart-rending scenes followed, but we shall only give a description of the last which took place on that occasion, and which brought about a little delay in the cruel work. In one case it was found necessary to remove the women out of the house by force. "One of them threw herself upon the ground and fell into hysterics, uttering the most doleful sounds, and barking and yelling like a dog for about ten minutes. Another, with many tears, sobs, and groans put up a petition to the Sheriff that they would leave the roof over part of her house, where she had a loom with cloth in it, which she was weaving ; and a third woman, the

eldest of the family made an attack with a stick on an officer,
and, missing him, she sprang upon him, and knocked off his
hat. So violently did this old woman conduct herself that two
stout policemen had great difficulty in carrying her outside
the door. The excitement was again getting so strong that
the factor, seeing the determination of the people, and
finding that if he continued and took their crops away from
those who would not leave, even when their houses were
pulled down about their ears, they would have to be fed
and maintained at the expense of the parish during the
forthcoming winter, relaxed and agreed to allow them to
occupy their houses until next spring, if the heads of families
undertook and signed an agreement to emigrate any time
next year, from the 1st of February to the end of June.
Some agreed to these conditions, but the majority declined;
and, in the circumstance, the people were permitted to go
back to their unroofed and ruined homes for a few months
longer. Their cattle were, however, mostly taken possession
of, and applied to the reduction of old arrears."

Four of the men were afterwards charged with deforcing
the officers, and sentenced at Inverness Court of Justiciary
each to four months' imprisonment. The following year
the district was completely and mercilessly cleared of all its
remaining inhabitants, numbering 603 souls.*

The Sollas evictions did not satisfy the evicting craze
which his lordship afterwards so bitterly regretted, In 1851-
53 he, or rather his trustee, determined to evict the people
from the villages of

BORERAIG AND SUISINISH, ISLE OF SKYE.

His Lordship's position in regard to the proceedings was

* A very full account of these proceedings, written on the spot, appeared
at the time in the *Inverness Courier*, to which we are indebted for the above
facts.

most unfortunate. Donald Ross, writing as an eye-witness of these evictions, says—"Some years ago Lord Macdonald incurred debts on his property to the extent of £200,000 sterling, and his lands being entailed, his creditors could not dispose of them, but they placed a trustee over them in order to intercept certain portions of the rent in payment of the debt. Lord Macdonald, of course, continues to have an interest and a surveillance over the property in the matter of removals, the letting of the fishings and shootings, and the general improvement of his estates. The trustee and the local factor under him have no particular interest in the property, nor in the people thereon, beyond collecting their quota of the rents for the creditors; consequently the property is mismanaged, and the crofter and cottar population are greatly neglected. The tenants of Suisinish and Boreraig were the descendants of a long line of peasantry on the Macdonald estates, and were remarkable for their patience, loyalty, and general good conduct." The only plea made at the time for evicting them was that of over population. Ten families received the usual summonses, and passages were secured for them in the *Hercules*, an unfortunate ship which sailed with a cargo of passengers under the auspices of a body calling itself " The Highland and Island Emigration Society ". A deadly fever broke out among the passengers, the ship was detained at Cork in consequence, and a large number of the passengers died of the epidemic. After the sad fate of so many of those previously cleared out, in the ill-fated ship, it was generally thought that some compassion would be shown for those who had still been permitted to remain. Not so, however. On the 4th of April, 1853, they were all warned out of their holdings. They petitioned and pleaded with his Lordship to no purpose. They were ordered to remove their cattle from the pasture, and themselves from their houses and lands. They again petitioned his Lordship for his merciful consideration. For a time no reply was forthcoming. Subsequently, however, they were informed that they would get land on another part of the estate—portions of a barren moor, quite unfit for cultivation.

In the middle of September following, Lord Macdonald's ground-officer, with a body of constables, arrived, and at once proceeded to eject, in the most heartless manner, the whole population, numbering thirty-two families, and that at a period when the able-bodied male members of the families were away from home trying to earn something by which to pay their rents, and help to carry their families through the coming winter. In spite of the wailing of the helpless women and children, the cruel work was proceeded with as rapidly as possible, and without the slightest apparent compunction. The furniture was thrown out in what had now become the orthodox fashion. The aged and infirm, some of them so frail that they could not move, were pushed or carried out. "The scene was truly heart-rending. The women and children went about tearing their hair, and rending the heavens with their cries. Mothers with tender infants at the breast looked helplessly on, while their effects, and their aged and infirm relatives, were cast out, and the doors of their houses locked in their faces." The young children, poor, helpless, little creatures, gathered in groups, gave vent to their feelings in loud and bitter wailings. "No mercy was shown to age or sex—all were indiscriminately thrust out and left to perish on the hills." Untold cruelties were perpetrated on this occasion on the helpless creatures during the absence of their husbands and other principal bread-winners. Donald Ross in his pamphlet, "Real Scottish Grievances," published in

1854, and who not only was an eye-witness, but generously supplied the people with a great quantity of food and clothing, describes several of the cases. I can only find room here, however, for his first, that of

Flora Robertson or Matheson, a widow, aged ninety-six years, then residing with her son, Alexander Matheson, who had a small lot of land in Suisinish. Her son was a widower, with four children; and shortly before the time for evicting the people arrived, he went away to labour at harvest in the south, taking his oldest boy with him. The grandmother and the other three children were left in the house. "When the evicting officers and factor arrived, the poor old woman was sitting on a couch outside the house. The day being fine, her grandchildren lifted her out of her bed and brought her to the door. She was very frail; and it would have gladdened any heart to have seen how the two youngest of her grandchildren helped her along; how they seated her where there was most shelter; and then, how they brought her some clothing and clad her, and endeavoured to make her comfortable. The gratitude of the old woman was unbounded at these little acts of kindness and compassion; and the poor children, on the other hand, felt highly pleased at finding their services so well appreciated. The sun was shining beautifully, the air was refreshing, the gentle breeze wafted across the hills, and, mollified by passing over the waters of Loch Slapin, brought great relief and vigour to poor old Flora. Often with eyes directed towards heaven, and with uplifted hands, did she invoke the blessings of the God of Jacob on the young children who were ministering so faithfully to her bodily wants. Nothing could now exceed the beauty of the scene. The sea was glittering with millions of little waves and globules, and looked like a lake of silver, gently agitated.   The hills, with the heather in full bloom, and with the wild flowers in their beauty, had assumed all the colours of the rainbow, and were most pleasant to the eye to look upon.   The crops of corn in the neighbourhood were beginning to get yellow for the harvest; the small patches of potatoes were under flower, and promised well; the sheep and cattle, as if tired of feeding had lain down to rest on the face of the hills; and the dogs, as if satisfied their services were not required for a time, chose for themselves pleasant, well-sheltered spots and lay basking at full length in the sun; even the little boats on the loch, though their sails were spread, made no progress, but lay at rest, reflecting their own tiny shadows on the bosom of the deep and still waters.   The scene was most enchanting; and although old Flora's eyes were getting dim with age, she looked on the objects before her with great delight.   Her grandchildren brought her a cup of warm milk and some bread from a neighbour's house, and tried to feed her as if she had been a pet bird; but the old woman could not take much, although she was greatly invigorated by the change of air.   Nature seemed to take repose.   A white fleecy cloud now and then ascended, but the sun soon dispelled it; thin wreaths of cottage smoke went up and along, but there was no wind to move them, and they floated on the air; and, indeed, with the exception of a stream which passed near the house, and made a continuous noise in its progress over rocks and stones, there was nothing above or around to disturb the eye or the ear for one moment. While the old woman was thus enjoying the benefit of the fresh air, admiring the beauty of the landscape, and just when the poor children had entered the house to prepare a frugal meal for themselves and their aged charge, a sudden barking of dogs gave signal intimation of the approach of strangers. The native inquisitiveness of the young ones was immediately set on edge, and off they set across the fields, and over fences, after the dogs. They soon returned, however, with horror depicted in their countenances; they had a fearful tale to unfold; the furniture and other effects of their nearest neighbours, just across the hill, they saw thrown out; they heard the children screaming, and they saw the factor's men putting bars and locks on the doors. This was enough. The heart of the old woman, so recently revived and invigorated, was now like to break within her. What was she to do? What could she do? Absolutely nothing! The poor children, in the plenitude of their knowledge of the humanity of lords and factors, thought that if they could only get their aged grannie inside before the evicting officers arrived, that all would be safe,—as no one, they thought, would interfere with an old creature of ninety-six, especially when her son was not there to take charge of her; and, acting upon this supposition, they began to remove their grandmother into the house. The officers, however, arrived before they could get this accomplished; and in place of letting the old woman in, they threw out before the door every article that was inside the house, and then they placed large bars and padlocks on the door! The grandchildren were horror-struck at this procedure—and no wonder. Here they were, shut out of house and home, their father and elder brother several hundred miles away from them, their mother dead, and their grandmother, now aged, frail, and unable to move, sitting before them, quite unfit to help herself,—and with no other shelter than the broad canopy of heaven. Here then was a crisis, a predicament, that would have twisted the strongest nerve and tried the stoutest heart and healthiest frame,—with nothing but helpless infancy and

old age and infirmities to meet it. We cannot compre-
hend the feelings of the poor children on this occasion;
and cannot find language sufficiently strong to express
condemnation of those who rendered them houseless.
Shall we call them savages ? That would be paying them
too high a compliment, for among savages conduct such as
theirs is unknown. But let us proceed. After the grandchildren had cried until they were hoarse, and after their
little eyes had emptied themselves of the tears which
anguish, sorrow, and terror had accumulated within them,
and when they had exhausted their strength in the general
wail, along with the other children of the district, as house
after house was swept of its furniture, the inmates evicted,
and the doors locked,—they returned to their poor old
grandmother, and began to exchange sorrows and consola-
tions with her. But what could the poor children do ?
The shades of evening were closing in, and the air, which
at mid-day was fresh and balmy, was now cold and freezing.
The neighbours were all locked out, and could give no shelter,
and the old woman was unable to travel to where lodgings
for the night could be got. What were they to do? We
may rest satisfied that their minds were fully occupied with
their unfortunate condition, and that they had serious con-
sultations as to future action. The first consideration,
however, was shelter for the first night, and a sheep-cot
being near, the children prepared to remove the old woman
to it. True, it was small and damp, and it had no door,
no fire-place, no window, no bed,—but then, it was better
than exposure to the night air ; and this they represented to
their grandmother, backing it with all the other little bits of
arguments they could advance, and with professions of
sincere attachment which, coming from such a quarter, and
at such a period, gladdened her old heart. There was a

difficulty, however, which they at first overlooked. The grandmother could not walk, and the distance was some hundreds of yards, and they could get no assistance, for all the neighbours were similarly situated, and were weeping and wailing for the distress which had come upon them. Here was a dilemma; but the children helped the poor woman to creep along, sometimes she walked a few yards, at other times she crawled on her hands and knees, and in this way, and most materially aided by her grandchildren, she at last reached the cot.

The sheep-cot was a most wretched habitation, quite unfit for human beings, yet here the widow was compelled to remain until the month of December following. When her son came home from the harvest in the south, he was amazed at the treatment his aged mother and his children had received. He was then in good health; but in a few weeks the cold and damp of the sheep-cot had a most deadly effect upon his health, for he was seized with violent cramps, then with cough; at last his limbs and body swelled, and then he died! When dead, his corpse lay across the floor, his feet at the opposite wall, and his head being at the door, the wind waved his long black hair to and fro until he was placed in his coffin.

The inspector of poor, who, be it remembered, was ground-officer to Lord Macdonald, and also acted as the chief officer in the evictions, at last appeared, and removed the old woman to another house; not, however, until he was threatened with a prosecution for neglect of duty. The grand-children were also removed from the sheep-cot, for they were ill; Peggy and William were seriously so, but Sandy, although ill, could walk a little. The inspector for the poor gave the children, during their illness, only 14 lbs. of meal and 3 lbs. of rice, as aliment for three weeks, and nothing else.   To the grandmother he allowed two shillings and sixpence per month, but made no provision for fuel, lodgings, nutritious diet, or cordials—all of which this old woman much required.

When I visited the house where old Flora Matheson and her grand-children reside, I found her lying on a miserable pallet of straw, which, with a few rags of clothing, are on the bare floor.   She is reduced to a skeleton, and from her own statement to me, in presence of witnesses, coupled with other inquiries and examinations, I have no hesitation in declaring that she was then actually starving.   She had no nourishment, no cordials, nothing whatever in the way of food but a few wet potatoes and two or three shell-fish. The picture she presented, as she lay on her wretched pallet of black rags and brown straw, with her mutch as black as soot, and her long arms thrown across, with nothing on them but the skin, was a most lamentable one—and one that reflects the deepest discredit on the parochial authorities of Strath.   There was no one to attend to the wants or infirmities of this aged pauper but her grandchild, a young girl, ten years of age.   Surely in a country boasting of its humanity, liberty, and Christianity, such conduct should not be any longer tolerated in dealing with the infirm and help-less poor.   The pittance of 2s 6d a month is but a mockery of the claims of this old woman ; it is insulting to the com-monsense and every-day experience of people of feeling, and it is a shameful evasion of the law.   But for accidental charity, and that from a distance, Widow Matheson would long ere this have perished of starvation.

Three men were afterwards charged with deforcing the officers of the law, before the Court of Justiciary at Inver-ness.   They were first imprisoned at Portree, and afterwards marched on foot to Inverness, a distance of over a 100 miles, where they arrived two days before the date of their trial. The factor and sheriff-officers came in their conveyances, at the public expense, and lived right royally, never dreaming but they would obtain a victory, and get the three men sent to the Penitentiary, to wear hoddy, break stones, or pick oakum for at least twelve months. The accused, through the influence of charitable friends, secured the services of Mr. Rennie, solicitor, Inverness, who was able to show to the jury the unfounded and farcical nature of the charges made against them. His eloquent and able address to the jury in their behalf was irresistible, and we cannot better explain the nature of the proceedings than by quoting it in part from the report given of it, at the time, in the *Inverness Advertiser*:—

" Before proceeding to comment on the evidence in this case, he would call attention to its general features. It was one of a fearful series of ejectments now being carried through in the Highlands ; and it really became a matter of serious reflection, how far the pound of flesh allowed by law was to be permitted to be extracted from the bodies of the Highlanders. Here were thirty-two families, averaging four members each, or from 130 to 150 in all, driven out from their houses and happy homes, and for what ? For a tenant who, he believed, was not yet found. But it was the will of Lord Macdonald and of Messrs. Brown and Ballingal, that they should be ejected ; and the civil law having failed them, the criminal law with all its terrors, is called in to overwhelm these unhappy people. But, thank God, it has come before a jury—before you, who are sworn to return, and will return, an impartial verdict ; and which verdict will, I trust, be one that will stamp out with ignominy the cruel actors in it. The Duke of Newcastle had querulously asked, ' Could he not do as he liked with his own ? ' but a greater

man had answered, that 'property had its duties as well as
its rights,' and the concurrent opinion of an admiring age
testified to this truth. Had the factor here done his duty?
No! He had driven the miserable inhabitants out to the
barren heaths and wet mosses. He had come with the
force of the civil power to dispossess them, and make way
for sheep and cattle. But had he provided adequate refuge?
The evictions in Knoydart, which had lately occupied the
attention of the press and all thinking men, were cruel
enough; but there a refuge was provided for a portion of
the evicted, and ships for their conveyance to a distant land.
Would such a state of matters be tolerated in a country
where a single spark of Highland spirit existed? No!
Their verdict that day would proclaim, over the length and
breadth of the land, an indignant denial. Approaching the
present case more minutely, he would observe that the
prosecutor, by deleting from this libel the charge of obstruction, which was passive, had cut away the ground from under
his feet. The remaining charge of deforcement being active,
pushing, shoving, or striking, was essential. But he would
ask, What was the character of the village and the household
of Macinnes? There were mutual remonstrances; but was
force used? The only things the officer, Macdonald, seized
were carried out. A spade and creel were talked of as being
taken from him, but in this he was unsupported. The
charge against the panel, Macinnes, only applied to what
took place inside his house. As to the other panels, John
Macrae was merely present. He had a right to be there; but
he touched neither man nor thing, and he at any rate must
be acquitted. Even with regard to Duncan Macrae, the
evidence *quoad* him was contemptible. According to Alison
in order to constitute the crime of deforcement, there must be
such violence as to intimidate a person of ordinary firmness

of character. Now, there was no violence here, they did not even speak aloud, they merely stood in the door; that might be obstruction, it was certainly no deforcement. Had Macdonald, who it appeared combined in his single person the triple offices of sheriff-officer, ground-officer, and inspector of poor, known anything of his business, and gone about it in a proper and regular manner, the present case would never have been heard of. As an instance of his irregularity, whilst his execution of deforcement bore that he read his warrants, he by his own mouth stated that he only read part of them. Something was attempted to be made of the fact of Duncan Macrae seizing one of the constables and pulling him away; but this was done in a good-natured manner, and the constable admitted he feared no violence. In short, it would be a farce to call this a case of deforcement. As to the general character of the panels, it was unreproached and irreproachable, and their behaviour on that day was their best certificate."

The jury immediately returned a verdict of "Not guilty," and the poor Skyemen were dismissed from the bar, amid the cheers of an Inverness crowd. The families of these men were at the next Christmas evicted in the most spiteful and cruel manner, delicate mothers, half-dressed, and recently-born infants, having been pushed out into the drifting snow. Their few bits of furniture, blankets and other clothing lay for days under the snow, while they found shelter themselves as best they could in broken-down, dilapidated out-houses and barns. These latter proceedings were afterwards found to have been illegal, the original summonses, on which the second proceedings were taken, having been exhausted in the previous evictions, when the Macinneses and the Macraes were unsuccessfully charged with deforcing the sheriff-officers. The proceedings were universally condemned by every right-thinking person who knew the district, as quite uncalled for, most unjustifiable and improper, as well as for "the reckless cruelty and inhumanity with which they were carried through". Yet, the factor issued a circular in defence of such horrid work in which he coolly informed the public that these evictions were "prompted by motives of benevolence, piety, and humanity," and that the cause for them all was "because they (the people) were too far from Church". Oh God! what crimes have been committed in Thy name, and in that of religion? Preserve us from such piety and humanity as were exhibited by Lord Macdonald and his factor on this and other occasions.

A Contrast.

Before leaving Skye, it will be interesting to see the difference of opinion which existed among the chiefs regarding the eviction of the people at this period and a century earlier. We have just seen what a Lord Macdonald has done in the present century, little more than thirty years ago. Let us compare his proceedings and feelings to those of his ancestor, in 1739, a century earlier. In that year a certain Norman Macleod managed to get some islanders to emigrate, and it was feared that Government would hold Sir Alexander Macdonald of Sleat reponsible, as he was reported to have encouraged Macleod. The baronet being from home, his wife, Lady Margaret, wrote to Lord Justice-Clerk Milton on the 1st of January, 1740, pleading with him to use all his influence against a prosecution of her husband, which, "tho' it cannot be dangerouse to him, yett it cannot faill of being both troublsome and expensive". She begins her letter by stating that she was informed " by different hands from Edinburgh that there is a currant report of a ships haveing gon from thiss country with a greate many people designed for America, and that Sir Alexander is thought to have concurred in forceing these people away ". She then declares the charge against her husband to be " a falsehood," but she " is quite acquainted with the danger of a report " of that nature. Instead of Sir Alexander being a party to the proceedings of this " Norman Macleod, with a number of fellows that he had picked up to execute his intentions," he " was both angry and concern'd to hear that some of his oune people were taken in thiss affair". What a contrast between the sentiments here expressed and those which carried out the modern evictions ; and yet it is well known that, in other respects no more humane man ever lived than he who was nominally responsible for the cruelties in Skye and at Sollas. He allowed himself to be imposed upon by others, and completely abdicated his high functions as landlord and chief of his people. We have the most conclusive testimony and assurance from one who knew his lordship intimately, that, to his dying day, he never ceased to regret what had been done in his name, and at the time, with his tacit approval, in Skye and in North Uist. This should be a warning to other proprietors, and induce them to consider carefully proposals submitted to them by heartless or inexperienced subordinates. It is very generally believed that to this same dependence on and belief in subordinates some of the more recent evictions in the Highlands can be traced; but matters had proceeded so far that it was found impossible to retrace without an appearance of giving way to the clamour raised by outsiders. These are only specimens of the proceedings carried out on an extensive scale in the Western Islands.

South Uist and Barra.

Napoleon Bonaparte, at one time, took 500 prisoners and was unable to provide food for them; let them go he would not, though he saw that they would perish by famine. His ideas of mercy suggested to him to have them all shot. They were by his orders formed into a square, and 2000 French muskets with ball cartridge was simultaneously levelled at them, which soon put the disarmed mass of human beings out of pain. Donald Macleod refers to this painful act as follows :—" All the Christian nations of Europe were horrified, every breast was full of indignation at the perpetrator of this horrible tragedy, and France wept bitterly for the manner in which the tender mercies of their wicked Emperor were exhibited. Ah! but guilty Christian, you Protestant law-making Britain, tremble when you look towards the great day of retribution. Under the protection of your law, Colonel Gordon has consigned 1500 men, women, and children, to a death a hundred-fold more agonising and horrifying. With the sanction of your law he (Colonel Gordon) and his predecessors, in imitation of His Grace the Duke of Sutherland and his predecessors, removed the people from the land created by God, suitable for cultivation, and for the use of man, and put it under brute animals ; and threw the people upon bye-corners, precipices, and barren moors, there exacting exorbitant rack-rents, until the people were made penniless, so that they could neither leave the place nor better their condition in it. The potato-blight blasted their last hopes of retaining life upon the unproductive patches—hence they became clamourous for food. Their distress was made known through the public press ; public meetings were held, and it was managed by some known knaves to saddle the God of providence with the whole misery—a job in which many of God's professing and well-paid servants took a very active part. The generous public responded; immense sums of money were placed in the hands of Government agents and other individuals, to save the people from death by famine on British soil. Colonel Gordon and his worthy allies were silent contributors, though terrified. The gallant gentleman solicited Government, through the Home Secretary, to purchase the Island of Barra for a penal colony, but it would not suit; yet our humane Government sympathised with the Colonel and his coadjutors, and consulted the honourable and brave MacNeil, the chief pauper gauger of Scotland, upon the most effective and speediest scheme to relieve the gallant Colonel and colleagues from this clamour and eye-sore, as well as to save their pockets from able-bodied paupers. The result was, that a liberal grant from the public money, which had been granted a twelvemonth before for the purpose of improving and cultivating the Highlands, was made to Highland proprietors to assist them to drain the nation of its best blood, and to banish the Highlanders across the Atlantic, there to die by famine among strangers in the frozen regions of Canada, far from British sympathy, and far from the resting place of their brave ancestors, though the idea of mingling with kindred dust, to the Highlanders, is a consolation at death, more than any other race of people I have known or read of under heaven. Oh! Christian people, Christian people, Christian fathers and mothers, who are living at ease, and never experienced such treatment and concomitant sufferings; you Christian rulers, Christian electors, and representatives, permit not Christianity to blush and hide her face with shame before heathenism and idolatry any longer. I speak with reverence when I say, permit not Mahomet Ali to deride our

Saviour with the conduct of His followers—allow not demons
to exclaim in the face of heaven, 'What can you expect of us,
when Christians, thy chosen people, are guilty of such deeds
of inhumanity to their own species?'   I appeal to your
feelings, to your respect for Christianity and the cause of
Christ in the world, that Christianity may be redeemed
from the derision of infidels, Mahomedans, idolaters, and
demons—that our beloved Queen and constitutional laws
may not be any longer a laughing stock and derision to the
despots of the Continent, who can justly say, 'You interfere
with us for our dealings with our people; but look at your cruel
conduct toward your own.   Ye hypocrites, first cast out the
beam out of your own eye, before you meddle with the mote
in ours.'   Come, then, for the sake of neglected humanity
and prostrated Christianity, and look at this helpless,
unfortunate people ; place yourselves for a moment in their
hopeless condition at their embarkation, decoyed, in the
name of the British Government, by false promises of
assistance, to procure homes and comforts in Canada, which
were denied to them at home—decoyed I say, to an unwilling and partial consent—and those who resisted or recoiled
from this conditional consent, and who fled to the caves and
mountains to hide themselves from the brigands, look at
them, chased and caught by policemen, constables, and other
underlings of Colonel Gordon, handcuffed, it is said, and
huddled together with the rest on an emigrant vessel.   Hear
the sobbing, sighing, and throbbings of their guileless, warm
Highland hearts, taking their last look, and bidding a final
adieu to their romantic mountains and valleys, the fertile
straths, dales, and glens, which their forefathers from time
immemorial inhabited, and where they are now lying in un-
disturbed and everlasting repose, in spots endeared and sacred
to the memory of their unfortunate offspring, who must now

bid a mournful farewell to their early associations, which were as dear and as sacred to them as their very existence, and which had hitherto made them patient in suffering. But follow them on their six weeks' dreary passage, rolling upon the mountainous billows of the Atlantlc, ill fed, ill clad, among sickness, disease and excrements. Then come a-shore with them where death is in store for them—hear the Captain giving orders to discharge the cargo of live stock—see the confusion, hear the noise, the bitter weeping and bustle ; hear mothers and children asking fathers and husbands, where are we going ? hear the reply, 'cha neil fios againn'—we know not ; see them in groups in search of the Government Agent, who, they were told, was to give them money ; look at their despairing countenances when they come to learn that no agent in Canada is authorised to give them a penny ; hear them praying the Captain to bring them back that they might die among their native hills, that their ashes might mingle with those of their forefathers ; hear this request refused, and the poor helpless wanderers bidding adieu to the Captain and crew, who showed them all the kindness they could, and to the vessel to which they formed something like an attachment during the voyage ; look at them scantily clothed, destitute of food, without implements of husbandry, consigned to their fate, carrying their children on their backs, begging as they crawl along in a strange land, unqualified to beg or buy their food for want of English, until the slow moving and mournful company reach Toronto and Hamilton, in Upper Canada, where according to all accounts, they spread themselves over their respective burying-places, where famine and frost-bitten deaths were awaiting them. Mothers in Christian Britain, look, I say, at these Highland mothers, who conceived and gave birth, and who are equally as fond of their offspring as you can be ; look at them by this time, wrapping their frozen remains in rags and committing them to a frozen hole— fathers, mothers, sons, and daughters, participants of similar sufferings and death, and the living who are seeking for death (yet death fleeing from them for a time) performing a similar painful duty. This is a painful picture, the English language fails to supply me with words to describe it. I wish the spectrum would depart from me to those who could describe it and tell the result. But how can Colonel Gordon, the Duke of Sutherland, James Loch, Lord Macdonald, and others of the unhallowed league and abettors, after looking at this sight, remain in Christian communion, ruling elders in Christian Churches, and partake of the emblems of Christ's broken body and shed blood ? But the great question is, Can we as a nation be guiltless, and allow so many of our fellow creatures to be treated in such a manner, and not exert ourselves to put a stop to it and punish the perpetrators ? Is ambition, which attempted to dethrone God, become omnipotent, or so powerful, when incarnated in the shape of Highland dukes, lords, esquires, colonels, and knights, that we must needs submit to its revolting deeds? Are parchment rights of property so sacred that thousands of human beings must be sacrificed year after year, till there is no end of such, to preserve them inviolate ? Are sheep walks, deer forests, hunting parks, and game preserves, so beneficial to the nation that the Highlands must be converted into a hunting desert, and the aborigines banished and murdered ? I know that thousands will answer in the negative; yet they will fold their arms in criminal apathy until the extirpation and destruction of my race shall be completed. Fearful is the catalogue of those who have already become the victims of the cursed clearing system in the Highlands, by famine, fire, drowning, banishment, vice, and crime."

He then publishes the following communication from an eye-witness, of the enormities perpetrated in South Uist and in the Island of Barra in the summer of 1851 :—The un-feeling and deceitful conduct of those acting for Colonel Gordon cannot be too strongly censured. The duplicity and art which was used by them in order to entrap the unwary natives, is worthy of the craft and cunning of an old slave-trader. Many of the poor people were told in my hearing, that Sir John McNeil would be in Canada before them, where he would have every necessary prepared for them. Some of the officials signed a document binding themselves to emigrate, in order to induce the poor people to give their names ; but in spite of all these stratagems, many of the people saw through them and refused out and out to go. When the transports anchored in Loch Boisdale these tyrants threw off their masks, and the work of devas-tation and cruelty commenced. The poor people were commanded to attend a public meeting at Loch Boisdale, where the transports lay, and, according to the intimation, any one absenting himself from the meeting was to be fined in the sum of two pounds sterling. At this meeting some of the natives were seized and, in spite of their entreaties, sent on board the transports. One stout Highlander, named Angus Johnston, resisted with such pith that they had to hand-cuff him before he could be mastered ; but in con-sequence of the priest's interference his manacles were removed, and he was marched between four officers on board the emigrant vessel. One morning, during the trans-porting season, we were suddenly awakened by the screams of a young female who had been re-captured in an adjoining house ; she having escaped after her first capture. We all rushed to the door, and saw the broken-hearted creature, with dishevelled hair and swollen face, dragged away by two constables and a ground-officer. Were you to see the racing and chasing of policemen, constables, and ground-officers, pursuing the outlawed natives, you would think, only for their colour, that you had been, by some miracle, transported to the banks of the Gambia, on the slave cqast of Africa.

The conduct of the Rev. H. Beatson on that occasion is deserving of the censure of every feeling heart. This ' wolf in sheep's clothing,' made himself very officious, as he always does, when he has an opportunity of oppressing the poor Barra-men, and of gaining the favour of Colonel Gordon. In fact, he is the most vigilant and assiduous officer Colonel Gordon has. He may be seen in Castle Bay, the principal anchorage in Barra, whenever a sail is hoisted, directing his men, like a game-keeper with his hounds, in case any of the doomed Barra-men should escape. He offered one day to board an Arran boat, that had a poor man concealed, but the master, John Crawford, lifted a hand-spike and threatened to split the skull of the first man who would attempt to board his boat, and thus the poor Barra-man escaped their clutches.

I may state in conclusion that, two girls, daughters of John Macdougall, brother of Barr Macdougall, whose name is mentioned in Sir John McNeill's report, have fled to the mountains to elude the grasp of the expatriators, where they still are, if in life. Their father, a frail, old man, along with the rest of the family, has been sent to Canada. The respective ages of these girls are 12 and 14 years. Others have fled in the same way, but I cannot give their names just now.

We shall now take the reader after these people to

Canada, and witness their deplorable and helpless condition and privations in a strange land. The following is extracted from a Quebec newspaper :—

We noticed in our last the deplorable condition of the 600 paupers who were sent to this country from the Kilrush Unions. We have to-day a still more dismal picture to draw. Many of our readers may not be aware that there lives such a personage as Colonel Gordon, proprietor of large estates in South Uist and Barra, in the Highlands of Scotland ; we are sorry to be obliged to introduce him to their notice, under circumstances which will not give them a very favourable opinion of his character and heart.

It appears that his tenants on the above-mentioned estates were on the verge of starvation, and had probably become an eye-sore to the gallant Colonel ! He decided on shipping them to America. What they were to do there? was a question he never put to his conscience. Once landed in Canada, he had no further concern about them. Up to last week, some 1100 souls from his estates had landed at Quebec, and begged their way to Upper Canada ; when in the summer season, having only a daily morsel of food to procure, they probably escaped the extreme misery which seems to be the lot of those who followed them.

On their arrival here, they voluntarily made and signed the following statement :—" We the undersigned passengers per *Admiral*, from Stornoway, in the Highlands of Scotland, do solemnly depose to the following facts :—that Colonel Gordon is proprietor of estates in South Uist and Barra ; that among many hundreds of tenants and cottars whom he has sent this season from his estates to Canada, he gave directions to his factor, Mr. Fleming of Cluny Castle, Aberdeenshire, to ship on board of the above-named vessel a number of nearly 450 of said tenants and cottars, from the

estate in Barra ; that accordingly, a great majority of these
people, among whom were the undersigned, proceeded
voluntarily to embark on board the *Admiral*, at Loch
Boisdale, on or about the 11th August, 1851 ; but that
several of the people who were intended to be shipped for
this port, Quebec, refused to proceed on board, and, in fact,
absconded from their homes to avoid the embarkation.
Whereupon Mr. Fleming gave orders to a policeman, who
was accompanied by the ground-officer of the estate in Barra,
and some constables, to pursue the people, who had run
away, among the mountains ; which they did, and succeeded
in capturing about twenty from the mountains and islands
in the neighbourhood ; but only came with the officers on
an attempt being made to handcuff them ; and that some
who ran away were not brought back, in consequence of
which four families at least have been divided, some having
come in the ships to Quebec, while the other members of
the same families are left in the Highlands.

"The undersigned further declare, that those who voluntarily embarked, did so under promises to the effect, that
Colonel Gordon would defray their passage to Quebec ; that
the Government Emigration Agent there would send the
whole party free to Upper Canada, where, on arrival, the
Government agents would give them work, and furthermore,
grant them land on certain conditions.

"The undersigned finally declare, that they are now
landed in Quebec so destitute, that if immediate relief be
not afforded them, and continued until they are settled in
employment, the whole will be liable to perish with want."

(Signed)   " HECTOR LAMONT,
and 70 others."

This is a beautiful picture ! Had the scene been laid in

Russia or Turkey, the barbarity of the proceeding would have shocked the nerves of the reader ; but when it happens in Britain, emphatically the land of liberty, where every man's house, even the hut of the poorest, is said to be his castle, the expulsion of these unfortunate creatures from their homes—the man-hunt with policemen and bailiffs—the violent separation of families—the parent torn from the child, the mother from her daughter, the infamous trickery practised on those who did embark—the abandonment of the aged, the infirm, women, and tender children, in a foreign land—forms a tableau which cannot be dwelt on for an instant without horror. Words cannot depict the atrocity of the deed. For cruelty less savage, the slave-dealers of the South have been held up to the execration of the world.

And if, as men, the sufferings of these our fellow-creatures find sympathy in our hearts, as Canadians their wrongs concern us more dearly. The fifteen hundred souls whom Colonel Gordon has sent to Quebec this season, have all been supported for the past week at least, and conveyed to Upper Canada at the expense of the colony ; and on their arrival in Toronto and Hamilton, the greater number have been dependent on the charity of the benevolent for a morsel of bread. Four hundred are in the river at present, and will arrive in a day or two, making a total of nearly 2000 of Colonel Gordon's tenants and cottars whom the province will have to support. The winter is at hand, work is becoming scarce in Upper Canada. Where are these people to find food ? *

We take the following from an Upper Canadian paper describing the position of the same people after finding their way to Ontario :—We have been pained beyond measure for some time past, to witness in our streets so

* *Quebec Times.*

many unfortunate Highland emigrants, apparently destitute of any means of subsistence, and many of them sick from want and other attendant causes. It was pitiful the other day, to view a funeral of one of these wretched people. It was, indeed, a sad procession. The coffin was constructed of the rudest material; a few rough boards nailed together, was all that could be afforded to convey to its last resting-place the body of the homeless emigrant. Children followed in the mournful train; perchance they followed a brother's bier, one with whom they had sported and played for many a healthful day among their native glens. Theirs were looks of indescribable sorrow. They were in rags; their mourning weeds were the shapeless fragments of what had once been clothes. There was a mother, too, among the mourners, one who had tended the departed with anxious care in infancy, and had doubtless looked forward to a happier future in this land of plenty. The anguish of her countenance told too plainly these hopes were blasted, and she was about to bury them in the grave of her child.

There will be many to sound the fulsome noise of flattery in the ear of the generous landlord, who had spent so much to assist the emigration of his poor tenants. They will give him the misnomer of a *benefactor*, and for what? Because he has rid his estates of the encumbrance of a pauper population.

Emigrants of the poorer class, who arrive here from the Western Highlands of Scotland, are often so situated, that their emigration is more cruel than banishment. Their last shilling is spent probably before they reach the upper province—they are reduced to the necessity of begging. But again, the case of those emigrants of which we speak, is rendered more deplorable from their ignorance of the

English tongue. Of the hundreds of Highlanders in and around Dundas at present, perhaps not half-a-dozen understand anything but Gaelic.

In looking at these matters, we are impressed with the conviction, that so far from emigration being a panacea for Highland destitution, it is fraught with disasters of no ordinary magnitude to the emigrant whose previous habits, under the most favourable circumstances, render him unable to take advantage of the industry of Canada, even when brought hither free of expense. We may assist these poor creatures for a time, but charity will scarcely bide the hungry cravings of so many for a very long period. Winter is approaching, and then—but we leave this painful subject for the present.*

THE ISLAND OF RUM.

THIS Island, at one time, had a large population, all of whom were weeded out in the usual way. The Rev. Donald Maclean, Minister of the Parish of Small Isles, informs us in *The New Statistical Account*, that "in 1826 all the inhabitants of the Island of Rum, amounting at least to 400 souls, found it necessary to leave their native land, and to seek for new abodes in the distant wilds of our Colonies in America. Of all the old residenters, only one family remained upon the island. The old and the young, the feeble and the strong were all united in this general emigration— the former to find tombs in a foreign land—the latter to encounter toils, privations, and dangers, to become familiar with customs, and to acquire that to which they had been

* *Dundas Warder*, 2nd October, 1851.

entire strangers. A similar emigration took place in 1828, from the Island of Muck, so that the parish has now become much depopulated."

In 1831, the population of the whole parish was 1015, while before that date it was much larger. In 1851, it was 916. In 1881, it was reduced to 550. The total population of Rum, in 1881, was 89 souls.

Hugh Miller, who visited the Island afterwards, describes it and the evictions thus :—The evening was clear, calm, golden-tinted ; even wild heaths and rude rocks had assumed a flush of transient beauty ; and the emerald-green patches on the hill-sides, barred by the plough lengthwise, diagonally, and transverse, had borrowed an aspect of soft and velvety richness, from the mellowed light and the broadening shadows. All was solitary. We could see among the deserted fields the grass-grown foundations of cottages razed to the ground ; but the valley, more desolate than that which we had left, had not even its single inhabited dwelling : it seemed as if man had done with it for ever. The Island eighteen years before, had been divested of its inhabitants, amounting at the time to rather more than four hundred souls, to make way for one sheep-farmer and eight thousand sheep. All the aborigines of Rum crossed the Atlantic ; and, at the close of 1828, the entire population consisted of but the sheep-farmer, and a few shepherds, his servants : the Island of Rum reckoned up scarce a single family at this period for every five square miles of area which it contained. But depopulation on so extreme a scale was found inconvenient ; the place had been rendered too thoroughly a desert for the comfort of the occupant ; and on the occasion of a clearing which took place shortly after in Skye, he accommodated some ten or twelve of the ejected families with sites for cottages, and pasturage for a

few cows, on the bit of morass beside Loch Scresort, on
which I had seen their humble dwellings. But the whole
of the once peopled interior remains a wilderness, without
inhabitants,—all the more lonely in its aspect—from the
circumstance that the solitary valleys, with their plough-
furrowed patches, and their ruined heaps of stone, open upon
shores every whit as solitary as themselves, and that the
wide untrodden sea stretches drearily around. The armies
of the insect world were sporting in the light this evening by
the million ; a brown stream that runs through the valley
yielded an incessant poppling sound, from the myriads of
fish that were ceaselessly leaping in the pools, beguiled by
the quick glancing wings of green and gold that fluttered
over them : along a distant hillside there ran what seemed
the ruins of a gray-stone fence, erected, says tradition, in a
remote age, to facilitate the hunting of the deer ; there were
fields on which the heath and moss of the surrounding
moorlands were fast encroaching, that had borne many a
successive harvest ; and prostrate cottages, that had been
the scenes of christenings, and bridals, and blythe new-year's
days ;—all seemed to bespeak the place of fitting habitation
for man, in which not only the necessaries, but also a few of
the luxuries of life, might be procured ; but in the entire
prospect, not a man nor a man's dwelling could the eye
command. The landscape was one without figures. I do
not much like extermination carried out so thoroughly and
on system ;—it seems bad policy ; and I have not succeeded
in thinking any the better of it though assured by the
economists that there are more than people enough in
Scotland still. There are, I believe, more than enough in
our workhouses—more than enough on our pauper-rolls—
more than enough muddled up, disreputable, useless, and
unhappy, in their miasmatic valleys and typhoid courts of

our large towns ; but I have yet to learn how arguments for local depopulation are to be drawn from facts such as these. A brave and hardy people, favourably placed for the development of all that is excellent in human nature, form the glory and strength of a country ;—a people sunk into an abyss of degradation and misery, and in which it is the whole tendency of external circumstances to sink them yet deeper, constitute its weakness and its shame ; and I cannot quite see on what principle the ominous increase which is taking place among us in the worse class, is to form our solace or apology for the wholesale expatriation of the better.   It did not seem as if the depopulation of Rum had tended mnch to anyone's advantage.   The single sheep-farmer who had occupied the holdings of so many had been unfortunate in his speculations, and had left the island ; the proprietor, his landlord, seemed to have been as little fortunate as the tenant, for the island itself was in the market, and a report went current at the time that it was on the eve of being purchased by some wealthy Englishman, who purposed converting it into a deer-forest.   How strange a cycle !   Uninhabited originally, save by wild animals, it became at an early period a home of men, who, as the gray wall on the hillside testified, derived in part at least, their sustenance from the chase.   They broke in from the waste the furrowed patches on the slopes of the valleys,—they reared herds of cattle and flocks of sheep,—their number increased to nearly five hundred souls,—they enjoyed the average happiness of human creatures in the present imperfect state of being,—they contributed their portion of hardy and vigorous manhood to the armies of the country, and a few of their more adventurous spirits, impatient of the narrow bounds which confined them, and a course of life little varied by incident, emigrated to America.   Then came the change of system so general in the Highlands ; and the island lost all its original inhabitants, on a wool and mutton speculation,—inhabitants, the descendants of men who had chased the deer on its hills five hundred years before, and who, though they recognised some wild island lord as their superior, and did him service, had regarded the place as indisputably their own. And now yet another change was on the eve of ensuing, and the island was to return to its original state, as a home of wild animals, where a few hunters from the mainland might enjoy the chase for a month or two every twelvemonth, but which could form no permanent place of human abode. Once more a strange, and surely most melancholy cycle ! *

In another place the same writer asks, " Where was the one tenant of the island, for whose sake so many others had been removed ? " and he answers, " We found his house occupied by a humble shepherd, who had in charge the wreck of his property,—property no longer his, but held for the benefit of his creditors. The great sheep-farmer had gone down under circumstances of very general bearing, and on whose after development, when in their latent state, improving landlords had failed to calculate."

HARRIS and the other Western Islands suffered in a similar manner. Mull, Tiree, and others in Argyleshire, will be noticed when we come to deal with that county.

GLENGARRY.

GLENGARRY was peopled down to the end of last century with a fine race of men. In 1745, six hundred stalwart vassals followed the chief of Glengarry to the battle of

* Leading Articles from the *Witness.*

Culloden. Some few years later they became so disgusted
with the return made by their chief that many of them
emigrated to the United States, though they were almost all
in comfortable, some indeed, in affluent circumstances.
Notwithstanding this semi-voluntary exodus, Major John
Macdonell of Lochgarry, was able in 1777, to raise a fine
regiment—the 76th, or Macdonald Highlanders—numbering 1086 men, 750 of whom were Highlanders mainly from
the Glengarry property.   In 1794, Alexander Macdonell of
Glengarry, raised a Fencible regiment, described as "a handsome body of men," of whom one-half were enlisted on the
same estate.   On being disbanded in 1802, these men were
again so shabbily treated, that they followed the example of
the men of the " Forty-five," and emigrated in a body, with
their families, to Canada, taking two Gaelic-speaking ministers
along with them to their new home.   They afterwards
distinguished themselves as part of the " Glengarry Fencibles " of Canada, in defence of their adopted country,
and called their settlement there after their native glen in
Scotland.   The chiefs of Glengarry drove away their people,
only, as in most other cases in the Highlands, to be themselves ousted soon after them.

The Glengarry property at one time covered an area of
nearly 200 square miles, and to-day, while many of their
expatriated vassals are landed proprietors and in affluent
circumstances in Canada, not an inch of the old possessions
of the ancient and powerful family of Glengarry remains to
the descendants of those who caused the banishment of a
people who, on many a well-fought field, shed their blood
for their chief and country.   In 1853, every inch of the
ancient heritage was possessed by the stranger, except
Knoydart in the west, and this has long ago become the
property of one of the Bairds.   In the year named, young

Glengarry was a minor, his mother, the widow of the late chief, being one of his trustees. She does not appear to have learned any lesson of wisdom from the past misfortunes of her house. Indeed, considering her limited power and possessions, she was comparatively the worst of them all.

The tenants of Knoydart, like all other Highlanders, had suffered severely during and after the potato famine in 1846 and 1847, and some of them got into arrear with a year and some with two years' rent, but they were fast clearing it off. Mrs. Macdonell and her factor determined to evict every crofter on her property, to make room for sheep. In the spring of 1853, they were all served with summonses of removal, accompanied by a message that Sir John Macneil, chairman of the Board of Supervision, had agreed to convey them to Australia. Their feelings were not considered worthy of the slightest consideration. They were not even asked whether they would prefer to follow their countrymen to America and Canada. They were to be treated as if they were nothing better than Africans, and the laws of their country on a level with those which regulated South American slavery. The people, however, had no alternative but to accept any offer made to them. They could not get an inch of land on any of the neighbouring estates, and any one who would give them a night's shelter was threatened with eviction.

It was afterwards found not convenient to transport them to Australia, and it was then intimated to the poor creatures, as if they were nothing but common slaves to be disposed of at will, that they would be taken to North America, and that a ship would be at Isle Ornsay, in the Isle of Skye, in a few days, to receive them, and that they *must* go on board. The *Sillery* soon arrived. Mrs. Macdonell and her factor

came all the way from Edinburgh to see the people hounded
across in boats, and put on board this ship whether they
would or not.   An eye-witness who described the proceeding at the time, in a now rare pamphlet, and whom we
met a few years ago in Nova Scotia, characterises the
scene as heart-rending.   "The wail of the poor women and
children as they were torn away from their homes would
have melted a heart of stone."   Some few families, principally cottars, refused to go, in spite of every influence brought
to bear upon them ; and the treatment they afterwards
received was cruel beyond belief.   The houses, not only of
those who went, but of those who remained, were burnt and
levelled to the ground.   The Strath was dotted all over with
black spots, showing where yesterday stood the habitations
of men.   The scarred, half-burned wood—couples, rafters,
and cabars—were strewn about in every direction.   Stooks of
corn and plots of unlifted potatoes could be seen on all
sides, but man was gone.   No voice could be heard.   Those
who refused to go aboard the *Sillery* were in hiding among
the rocks and the caves, while their friends were packed off
like so many African slaves to the Cuban market.

No mercy was shown to those who refused to emigrate ;
their few articles of furniture were thrown out of their houses
after them—beds, chairs, tables, pots, stoneware, clothing,
in many cases, rolling down the hill.   What took years to
erect and collect were destroyed and scattered in a few
minutes.   "From house to house, from hut to hut, and from
barn to barn, the factor and his menials proceeded carrying
on the work of demolition, until there was scarcely a human
habitation left standing in the district.   Able-bodied men
who, if the matter would rest with a mere trial of physical
force, would have bound the factor and his party hand and
foot, and sent them out of the district, stood aside as dumb

spectators. Women wrung their hands and cried aloud, children ran to and fro dreadfully frightened ; and while all this work of demolition and destruction was going on no opposition was offered by the inhabitants, no hand was lifted, no stone cast, no angry word was spoken." The few huts left undemolished were occupied by the paupers, but before the factor left for the south even they were warned not to give any shelter to the evicted, or their huts would assuredly meet with the same fate. Eleven families, numbering in all over sixty persons, mostly old and decrepit men and women, and helpless children, were exposed that night, and many of them long afterwards, to the cold air, without shelter of any description beyond what little they were able to save out of the wreck of their burnt dwellings.

We feel unwilling to inflict pain on the reader by the recitation of the untold cruelties perpetrated on the poor Highlanders of Knoydart; but doing so may, perhaps, serve a good purpose. It may convince the evil-doer that his work shall not be forgotten, and any who may be disposed to follow the example of past evictors may hesitate before they proceed to immortalise themselves in such a hateful manner. We shall therefore quote a few cases from the pamphlet already referred to :—

John Macdugald, aged about 50, with a wife and family, was a cottar, and earned his subsistence chiefly by fishing. He was in bad health, and had two of his sons in the hospital, at Elgin, ill of smallpox, when the *Sillery* was sent to convey the Knoydart people to Canada. He refused to go on that occasion owing to the state of his health, and his boys being at a distance under medical treatment. The factor and the officers, however, arrived, turned Macdugald and his family adrift, put their bits of furniture out on the field, and in a few minutes levelled their house to the ground. The whole family had now no shelter but the broad canopy of heaven. The mother and the youngest of the children could not sleep owing to the cold, and the father, on account of his sickness, kept wandering about all night near where his helpless family lay down to repose. After the factor and the officers left the district Macdugald and his wife went back to the ruins of their house, collected some of the stones and turf into something like walls, threw a few cabars across, covered them over with blankets, old sails, and turf, and then, with their children, crept underneath, trusting that they would be allowed, at least for a time, to take shelter under this temporary covering. But, alas! they were doomed to bitter disappointment. A week had not elapsed when the local manager, accompanied by a *posse* of officers and menials, traversed the country and levelled to the ground every hut or shelter erected by the evicted peasantry. Macdugald was at this time away from Knoydart; his wife was at Inverie, distant about six miles, seeing a sick relative; the oldest children were working at the shore; and in the hut, when the manager came with the 'levellers,' he found none of the family except Lucy and Jane, the two youngest. The moment they saw the officers they screamed and fled for their lives. The demolition of the shelter was easily accomplished—it was but the work of two or three minutes; and, this over, the officers and menials of the manager amused themselves by seizing hold of chairs, stools, tables, spinning-wheels, or any other light articles, by throwing them a considerable distance from the hut. The mother, as I said, was at Inverie, distant about six or seven miles, and Lucy and Jane proceeded in that direction hoping to meet her. They had not gone far, however, when they missed the footpath and wandered far out of the way. In the interval the mother returned from Inverie and found the hut razed to the ground, her furniture scattered far and near, her bedclothes lying under turf, clay, and *debris*, and her children gone ! Just imagine the feelings of this poor Highland mother on the occasion ! But, to proceed, the other children returned from the shore, and they too stood aside, amazed and grieved at the sudden destruction of their humble refuge, and at the absence of their two little sisters. At first they thought they were under the ruins, and creeping down on their knees they carefully removed every turf and stone, but found nothing except a few broken dishes. A consultation was now held and a search resolved upon. The mother, brothers and sisters set off in opposite directions, among the rocks, over hills, through moor and moss, searching every place, and calling aloud for them by name, but they could discover no trace of them. Night was now approaching and with it all hopes of finding them, till next day, were fast dying away. The mother was now returning 'home' (alas ! to what a *home*), the shades of night closed in, and still she had about three miles to travel. She made for the footpath, scrutinized every bush, and looked round every rock and hillock, hoping to find them. Sometimes she imagined that she saw her two lasses walking before her at some short distance, but it was an illusion caused by bushes just about their size. The moon now emerged from behind a cloud and spread its light on the path and surrounding district. A sharp frost set in, and ice began to form on the little pools. Passing near a rock and some bushes, where the children of the tenants used to meet when herding the cattle, she felt as if something beckoned her to search there ; this she did and found her two little children fast asleep, beside a favourite bush, the youngest with her head resting on the breast of the eldest ! Their own version of their mishap is this :

that when they saw the officers they creeped out and ran in the direction of Inverie to tell their mother; that they missed the footpath, then wandered about crying, and finally returned, they knew not how, to their favourite herding ground, and, being completely exhausted, fell asleep. The mother took the young one on her back, sent the other on before her, and soon joined her other children near the ruins of their old dwelling. They put a few sticks up to an old fence, placed a blanket over it, and slept on the bare ground that night. Macdugald soon returned from his distant journey, found his family shelterless, and again set about erecting some refuge for them from the wreck of the old buildings. Again, however, the local manager appeared with levellers, turned them all adrift, and in a few moments pulled down and destroyed all that he had built up. Matters continued in this way for a week or two until Macdugald's health became serious, and then a neighbouring farmer gave him and his family temporary shelter in an out-house; and for this act of disinterested humanity he has already received some most improper and threatening letters from the managers on the estate of Knoydart. It is very likely that in consequence of this interference Macdugald is again taking shelter among the rocks, or amid the wreck of his former residence.

John Mackinnon, a cottar, aged 44, with a wife and six children, had his house pulled down, and had no place to put his head in, consequently he and his family, for the first night or two, had to burrow among the rocks near the shore! When he thought that the factor and his party had left the district, he emerged from the rocks, surveyed the ruins of his former dwelling, saw his furniture and other effects exposed to the elements, and now scarcely worth the lifting. The demolition was so complete that he considered it utterly impossible to make any use of the ruins of the old house. The ruins of an old chapel, however, were near at hand, and parts of the walls were still standing; thither Mackinnon proceeded with his family, and having swept away some rubbish and removed some grass and nettles, they placed a few cabars up to one of the walls, spread some sails and blankets across, brought in some meadow hay, and laid it in a corner for a bed, stuck a piece of iron into the wall in another corner, on which they placed a crook, then kindled a fire, washed some potatoes, and put a pot on the fire and boiled them, and when these and a few fish roasted on the embers were ready, Mackinnon and his family had *one* good diet, being the first regular meal they tasted since the destruction of their house !

Mackinnon is a tall man, but poor and unhealthy-looking. His wife is a poor weak woman, evidently struggling with a diseased constitution and dreadful trials. The boys, Ronald and Archibald, were lying in ' bed '—(may I call a ' pickle hay on the bare ground a bed ?)—suffering from rheumatisms and cholic. The other children are apparently healthy enough as yet, but very ragged. There is no door to their wretched abode, consequently every breeze and gust that blow have free ingress to the inmates. A savage from Terra-del-Fuego, or a Red Indian from beyond the Rocky Mountains, would not exchange huts with these victims, nor humanity with their persecutors. Mackinnon's wife was pregnant when she was turned out of her house among the rocks. In about four days after she had a premature birth ; and this and her exposure to the elements, and the want of proper shelter and nutritious diet, has brought on consumption, from which there is no chance whatever of her recovery.

There was something very solemn indeed in this scene.

Here, amid the ruins of the old sanctuary, where the swallows fluttered, where the ivy tried to screen the grey moss-covered stones, where nettles and grass grew up luxuriously, where the floor was damp, the walls sombre and uninviting, where there were no doors nor windows nor roof, and where the owl, the bat, and the fox used to take refuge, a Christian family was obliged to take shelter! One would think that as Mackinnon took refuge amid the ruins of this most singular place that he would be let alone, that he would not any longer be molested by man. But, alas! that was not to be. The manager of Knoydart and his minions appeared, and invaded this helpless family, even within the walls of the sanctuary. They pulled down the sticks and sails he set up within its ruins—put his wife and children out on the cold shore—threw his tables, stools, chairs, etc., over the walls—burnt up the hay on which they slept—put out the fire—and then left the district. Four times have these officers broken in upon poor Mackinnon in this way, destroying his place of shelter, and sent him and his family adrift on the cold coast of Knoydart. When I looked in upon these creatures last week I found them in utter consternation, having just learned that the officers would appear next day, and would again destroy the huts. The children looked at me as if I had been a wolf; they creeped behind their father, and stared wildly, dreading I was a law officer. The sight was most painful. The very idea that, in Christian Scotland, and in the 19th century, these tender infants should be subjected to such gross treatment reflects strongly upon our humanity and civilization. Had they been suffering from the ravages of famine, or pestilence, or war, I could understand it and account for it, but suffering to gratify the ambition of some unfeeling speculator in brute beasts, I think it most unwarranted, and deserving the em-

phatic condemnation of every Christian man. Had Mackinnon been in arrears of rent, which he was not, even this
would not justify the harsh, cruel, and inhuman conduct
pursued towards himself and his family. No language of
mine can describe the condition of this poor family, exaggeration is impossible. The ruins of an old chapel is the last
place in the world to which a poor Highlander would resort
with his wife and children unless he was driven to it by dire
necessity. Take another case :—

Elizabeth Gillies, a widow, aged 60 years.—This is a most
lamentable case. Neither age, sex, nor circumstance saved
this poor creature from the most wanton and cruel aggres-
sion. Her house was on the brow of a hill, near a stream
that formed the boundary between a large sheep farm and
the lands of the tenants of Knoydart. Widow Gillies was
warned to quit like the rest of the tenants, and was offered a
passage first to Australia and then to Canada, but she refused
to go, saying she could do nothing in Canada. The widow,
however, made no promises, and the factor went away. She
had then a nice young daughter staying with her, but, ere
the vessel that was to convey the Knoydart people away
arrived at Isle Ornsay, this young girl died, and poor
Widow Gillies was left alone. When the time for pulling
down the houses arrived, it was hoped that some mercy
would have been shown to this poor, bereaved widow, but
there was none. Widow Gillies was sitting inside her house
when the factor and officers arrived. They ordered her to
remove herself and effects instantly, as they were, they said,
to pull down the house ! She asked them where she would
remove to ; the factor would give no answer, but continued insisting on her leaving the house. This she at last
positively refused. Two men then took hold of her, and
tried to pull her out by force, but she sat down beside the

fire and would not move an inch.   One of the assistants
threw water on the fire and extinguished it, and then joined
the other two in forcibly removing the poor widow from the
house.   At first she struggled hard, seized hold of every post
or stone within her reach, taking a death grasp of each to
keep possession.   But the officers were too many and too
cruel for her.   They struck her over the fingers, and compelled her to let go her hold, and then all she could do was
to greet and cry out murder !   She was ultimately thrust
out at the door, from where she creeped on her hands and
feet to a dyke side, being quite exhausted and panting for
breath, owing to her hard struggle with three powerful
men.   Whenever they got her outside, the work of destruction immediately commenced.   Stools, chairs, tables,
cupboard, spinning-wheel, bed, blankets, straw, dishes, pots,
and chest, were thrown out in the gutter.   They broke down
the partitions, took down the crook from over the fire-place,
destroyed the hen roosts, and then beat the hens out through
the broad vent in the roof of the house.   This done, they
set to work on the walls outside with picks and iron levers.
They pulled down the thatch, cut the couples, and in a
few minutes the walls fell out, while the roof fell in with a
dismal crash !

When the factor and his party were done with this house,
they proceeded to another district, pulling down and destroying dwelling-places as they went along.   The shades of
night at last closed in, and here was the poor helpless
widow sitting like a pelican, alone and cheerless.   Allan
Macdonald, a cottar, whose house was also pulled down,
however, ran across the hill to see how the poor widow had
been treated, and found her moaning beside the dyke.   He
led her to where his own children had taken shelter, treated

her kindly, and did all he could to comfort her under the circumstances.

When I visited Knoydart I found the poor widow at work repairing her shed, and such a shed, and such a dwelling, I never before witnessed. The poor creature spoke remarkably well, and appeared to me to be a very sensible woman. I expressed my sympathy for her, and my disapprobation of the conduct of those who so unmercifully treated her. She said it was indeed most ungrateful on the part of the representatives of Glengarry to have treated her so cruelly—that her predecessors were, from time immemorial, on the Glengarry estates—that many of them died in defence of, or fighting for, the old cheftains—and that they had always been true and faithful subjects. I asked why she refused to go to Canada ? ' For a very good reason,' she said, ' I am now old and not able to clear a way in the forests of Canada ; and, besides, I am unfit for service ; and, farther, I am averse to leave my native country, and rather than leave it, I would much prefer that my grave was opened beside my dear daughter, although I should be buried alive ! ' I do think she was sincere in what she said. Despair and anguish were marked in her countenance, and her attachment to her old habitation and its associations were so strong that I believe they can only be cut asunder by death ! I left her in this miserable shed which she occupied, and I question much if there is another human residence like it in Europe. The wigwam of the wild Indian, or the cave of the Greenlander, are palaces in comparison with it ; and even the meanest dog-kennel in England would be a thousand times more preferable as a place of residence. If this poor Highland woman will stand it out all winter in this abode it will be indeed a great wonder. The factor has issued an *ukase*, which aggravates all these cases of eviction with peculiar hardship; he has warned all and sundry on the Knoydart estates from receiving or entertaining the evicted peasantry into their houses under pain of removal.

Allan Macdonald, aged 54, a widower, with four children, was similarly treated. Our informant says of him :—" When his late Majesty George IV. visited Scotland in 1823, and when Highland lairds sent up to Edinburgh specimens of the bone and sinew—human produce—of their properties, old Glengarry took care to give Allan Macdonald a polite invitation to this ' Royal exhibition '. Alas ! how matters have so sadly changed. Within the last 30 years *man* has fallen off dreadfully in the estimation of Highland proprietors. Commercially speaking, Allan Macdonald has now no value at all. Had he been a roe, a deer, a sheep, or a bullock, a Highland laird in speculating could estimate his 'real' worth to within a few shillings, but Allan is *only* a man. Then his children ; they are of no value, nor taken into account in the calculations of the sportsman. They cannot be shot at like hares, blackcocks, or grouse, nor yet can they be sent south as game to feed the London market." Another case is—

Archibald Macisaac's, crofter, aged 66 ; wife 54, with a family of ten children. Archibald's house, byre, barn, and stable, were levelled to the ground. The furniture of the house was thrown down the hill, and a general destruction then commenced. The roof, fixtures, and wood work were smashed to pieces, the walls razed to the very foundation, and all that was left for poor Archibald to look upon was a black dismal wreck. Twelve human beings were thus deprived of their home in less than half an hour. It was grossly illegal to have destroyed the barn, for, according even to the law of Scotland, the outgoing or removing tenant is entitled to the use of the barn until his crops are disposed of. But, of course, in a remote district, and among simple and primitive people like the inhabitants of Knoydart, the laws that concern them and define their rights are unknown to them.

Archibald had now to make the best shift he could. No mercy or favour could be expected from the factor. Having convened his children beside an old fence where he sat looking on when the destruction of his home was accomplished, he addressed them on the peculiar nature of the position in which they were placed, and the necessity of asking for wisdom from above to guide them in any future action. His wife and children wept, but the old man said, ' neither weeping nor reflection will now avail; we must prepare some shelter'. The children collected some cabars and turf, and in the hollow between two ditches, the old man constructed a rude shelter for the night, and having kindled a fire and gathered in his family, they all engaged in family worship and sung psalms as usual. Next morning they examined the ruins, picked up some broken pieces of furniture, dishes, etc., and then made another addition to their shelter in the ditch. Matters went on this way for about a week, when the local manager and his men came down upon them, and after much abuse for daring to take shelter on the lands of Knoydart, they destroyed the shelter and put old Archy and his people again out on the hill.

I found Archibald and his numerous family still at Knoydart and in a shelter beside the old ditch. Any residence more wretched, or more truly melancholy, I have never witnessed. A feal, or turf erection, about 3 feet high, 4 feet broad, and about 5 feet long, was at the end of the shelter, and this formed the sleeping place of the mother and her five daughters! They creep in and out on their knees, and their bed is just a layer of hay on the cold earth of the ditch!

There is surely monstrous cruelty in this treatment of British females, and the laws that sanction or tolerate such flagrant and gross abuses are a disgrace to the statute-book and to the country that permits it. Macisaac and his family are, so far as I could learn, very decent, respectable, and well-behaved people, and can we not perceive a monstrous injustice in treating them worse than slaves because they refuse to allow themselves to be packed off to the Colonies just like so many bales of manufactured goods? Again :—

Donald Maceachan, a cottar at Arar, married, with a wife and five children. This poor man, his wife, and children were fully twenty-three nights without any shelter but the broad and blue heavens. They kindled a fire and prepared their food beside a rock, and then slept in the open air. Just imagine the condition of this poor mother, Donald's wife, nursing a delicate child, and subjected to merciless storms of wind and rain during a long October night. One of these melancholy nights the blankets that covered them were frozen and white with frost. The next is,

Charles Macdonald, aged 70 years, a widower, having no family. This poor man was also 'keeled' for the Colonies, and, as he refused to go, his house or cabin was levelled to the ground. What on earth could old Charles do in America? Was there any mercy or humanity in offering *him* a free passage across the Atlantic? In England, Charles would have been considered a proper object of parochial protection and relief, but in Scotland no such relief is afforded except to ' sick folks ' and tender infants. There can be no question, however, that the factor looked forward to the period when Charles would become charge-able as a pauper, and, acting as a ' prudent man,' he re-solved to get quit of him at once. Three or four pounds would send the old man across the Atlantic, but if he remained in Knoydart, it would likely take four or five pounds to keep him each year that he lived. When the factor and his party arrived at Charles's door they knocked and demanded admission ; the factor intimated his object, and ordered the old man to quit. ' As soon as I can,' said Charles, and, taking up his plaid and staff and adjusting his blue bonnet, he walked out, merely remarking to the factor that the man who could turn out an old, inoffensive Highlander of seventy, from such a place, and at such a season, could do a great deal more if the laws of the country permitted him. Charles took to the rocks, and from that day to this he has never gone near his old habitation. He has neither house nor home, but receives occasional supplies of food from his evicted neighbours, *and he sleeps on the hill !* Poor old man, who would not pity him—who would not share with him a crust or a covering—who ?

Alexander Macdonald, aged 40 years, with a wife and family of four children, had his house pulled down. His wife was pregnant; still the levellers thrust her out, and then put the children out after her. The husband argued, remonstrated, and protested, but it was all in vain ; for in a few minutes all he had for his (to him once comfortable) home was a lot of rubbish, blackened rafters, and heaps of stones. The levellers laughed at him and at his protests, and when their work was over, moved away, leaving him to find refuge the best way he could. Alexander had, like the rest of his evicted brethren, to burrow among the rocks and in caves until he put up a temporary shelter amid the wreck of his old habitation, but from which he was repeatedly driven away. For three days Alexander Macdonald's wife lay sick beside a bush, where, owing to terror and exposure to cold, she had a miscarriage. She was then removed to the shelter of the walls of her former house, and for three

days she lay so ill that her life was despaired of.   These are
facts as to which I challenge contradiction.   I have not inserted them without the most satisfactory evidence of their
accuracy.

Catherine Mackinnon, aged about 50 years, unmarried ;
Peggy Mackinnon, aged about 48 years, unmarried ; and
Catherine Macphee (a half-sister of the two Mackinnons),
also unmarried; occupied one house. Catherine Mackinnon
was for a long time sick, and she was confined to bed when
the factor and his party came to beat down the house.   At
first they requested her to get up and walk out, but her
sisters said she could not, as she was so unwell.   They
answered, ' Oh, she is scheming ; ' the sisters said she was
not, that she had been ill for a considerable time, and the
sick woman herself, who then feebly spoke, said she was
quite unfit to be removed, but if God spared her and bestowed upon her better health that she would remove of her
own accord.   This would not suffice ; *they forced her out of
bed, sick as she was, and left her beside a ditch from 10 a.m.,
to 5 p.m.*, when, afraid that she would die, as she was
seriously unwell, they removed her to a house and provided
her with cordials and warm clothing.   Let the reader
imagine the sufferings of this poor female, so ruthlessly torn
from a bed of sickness and laid down beside a cold ditch
and there left exposed for seven long hours, and then say if
such conduct does not loudly call for the condemnation of
every lover of human liberty and humanity.   Peggy and
her half-sister Macphee are still burrowing among the ruins
of their old home.   When I left Knoydart last week there
were no hopes whatever of Catharine Mackinnon's recovery.

I challenge the factor to contradict one sentence in this
short narrative of the poor females.   The melancholy truth
of it is too palpable, too well-known in the district to admit

of even a tenable explanation. Nothing can palliate or excuse such gross inhumanity, and it is but right and proper that British Christians should be made aware of such unchristian conduct—such cruelty towards helpless fellow-creatures in sickness and distress. The last, at present, is

Duncan Robertson, aged 35 years, with wife aged 32 years, and a family of three children. Very poor ; the eldest boy is deformed and weak in mind and body, requiring almost the constant care of one of his parents. Robertson was warned out like the rest of the tenants, and decree of removal was obtained against him. At the levelling time the factor came up with his men before Robertson's door, and ordered the inmates out. Robertson pleaded for mercy on account of his sick and imbecile boy, but the factor appeared at first inexorable ; at last he sent in one of the officers to see the boy, who, on his return, said that the boy was really and truly an object of pity. The factor said he could not help it, that he must pull down. Some pieces of furniture were then thrown out, and the picks were fixed in the walls, when Robertson's wife ran out and implored delay, asking the factor, for heaven's sake, to come in and see her sick child. He replied, ' I am sure I am no doctor'. 'I know that,' she said, ' but God might have given you Christian feelings and bowels of compassion notwithstanding '. ' Bring him out here,' said the factor ; and the poor mother ran to the bed and brought out her sick boy in her arms. When the factor saw him, he admitted that he was an object of pity, but warned Robertson that he must quit Knoydart as soon as possible, or that his house would be pulled down about his ears. The levellers peep in once a-week to see if the boy is getting better, so that the house may be razed.

We could give additional particulars of the cruelties which

had to be endured by the poor wretches who remained—cruelties which would never be tolerated in any other civilized country than Britain, and which in Britain would secure instant and severe punishment if inflicted on a dog or a pig, but the record would only inflict further pain, and we have said enough. In the words of our informant—"There is something melancholy in connection with the entire removal of a people from an inhabited and cultivated district—when a whole country-side is at one fell swoop cleared of its population to make room for sheep—when all the ties, affections, and associations that bind the inhabitants to their country and homes are struck at and cut asunder by one unflinching blow. When the march of improvement and cultivation is checked ; and when the country is transformed into a wilderness, and the land to perpetual barrenness, not only are the best feelings of our common humanity violated, but the decree is tantamount to interdicting the command of the Most High, who said to man—" Go, replenish the earth and subdue it ".

Retribution has overtaken the evictors, and is it a wonder that the chiefs of Glengarry are now as little known, and own as little of their ancient domains in the Highlands as their devoted clansmen. There is now scarcely one of the name of Macdonald in the wide district once inhabited by thousands. It is a huge wilderness in which barely anything is met but wild animals and sheep, and the few keepers and shepherds necessary to take care of them.

STRATHGLASS.

It has been shown, under " Glengarry," that a chief's widow, during her son's minority, was responsible for the

Knoydart evictions in 1853. Another chief's widow, *Marsali Bhinneach*—Marjory, daughter of Sir Ludovick Grant of Dalvey, widow of Duncan Macdonnel of Glengarry, who died in 1788—gave the whole of Glencuaich as a sheep farm to one south country shepherd, and to make room for him she evicted over 500 people from their ancient homes. The late Edward Ellice stated before a Committee of the House of Commons, in 1873, that about the time of the rebellion in 1745, the population of Glengarry amounted to between 5000 and 6000. At the same time the glen turned out an able-bodied warrior in support of Prince Charles for every pound of rental paid to the proprietor. To-day it is questionable if the same district could turn out twenty men —certainly not that number of Macdonalds. The bad example of this heartless woman was unfortunately imitated afterwards by her daughter Elizabeth, who, in 1795, married William Chisholm of Chisholm, and to whose evil influence may be traced the great eviction which, in 1801, cleared Strathglass almost to a man of its ancient inhabitants. The Chisholm was delicate, and often in bad health, so that the management of the estate fell into the hands of his strong-minded and hard-hearted wife. In 1801, no less than 799 took ship at Fort-William and Isle Martin from Strathglass, the Aird, Glen-Urquhart, and the neighbouring districts, all for Pictou, Nova Scotia; while in the following year, 473 from the same district left Fort-William, for Upper Canada, and 128 for Pictou. 550 went aboard another ship at Knoydart, many of whom were from Strathglass. In 1803, four different batches of 120 souls each, by four different ships, left Strathglass, also for Pictou; while not a few went away with emigrants from other parts of the Highlands. During these three years we find that no less than 5390 were driven out of these Highland glens, and it will be seen that a very large portion of them were evicted from Strathglass by the daughter of the notorious *Marsali Bhinneach*. From among the living cargo of one of the vessels which sailed from Fort-William no less than fifty-three souls died, on the way out, of an epidemic ; and, on the arrival of the living portion of the cargo at Pictou, they were shut in on a narrow point of land, from whence they were not allowed to communicate with any of their friends who had gone before them, for fear of communicating the contagion.   Here they suffered indescribable hardships.

By a peculiar arrangement between the Chisholm who died in 1793, and his wife, a considerable portion of the people were saved for a time from the ruthless conduct of *Marsali Bhinneach's* daughter and her co-adjutors.   Alexander Chisholm married Elizabeth, daughter of a Dr. Wilson in Edinburgh.   He made provision for his wife in case of her outliving him, by which it was left optional with her to take a stated sum annually, or the rental of certain townships, or club farms.   Her husband died in 1793, when the estate reverted to his half-brother, William, and the widow, on the advice of her only child, Mary, who afterwards became Mrs. James Gooden of London, made choice of the joint farms, instead of the sum of money named in her marriage settlement ; and though great efforts were made by *Marsali Bhinneach's* daughter and her friends, the widow, Mrs. Alexander Chisholm, kept the farms in her own hands, and took great pleasure in seeing a prosperous tenantry in these townships, while all their neighbours were heartlessly driven away.   Not one of her tenants was disturbed or interfered with in any way from the death of her husband, in February, 1793, until her own death in January, 1826, when, unfortunately for them, their farms all came into the hands of the young heir (whose sickly father died in

1817), and his cruel mother. For a few years the tenants were left in possession, but only waiting an opportunity to make a complete clearance of the whole Strath. Some had a few years of their leases to run on other parts of the property, and could not just then be expelled.

In 1830 every man who held land on the property was requested to meet his chief at the local inn of Cannich. They all obeyed, and were there at the appointed time, but no chief came to meet them. The factor soon turned up, however, and informed them that the laird had determined to enter into no negotiation or any new arrangements with them that day. They were all in good circumstances, without any arrears of rent, but were practically banished from their homes in the most inconsiderate and cruel manner, and it afterwards became known that their farms had been secretly let to sheep-farmers from the south, without the knowledge of the native population in possession.

Mr. Colin Chisholm, who was present at the meeting at Cannich, writes :—" I leave you to imagine the bitter grief and disappointment of men who attended with glowing hopes in the morning, but had to tell their families and dependants in the evening that they could see no alternative before them but the emigrant ship, and choose between the scorching prairies of Australia, and the icy regions of North America." It did not, however, come to that. The late Lord Lovat, hearing of the harsh proceedings, proposed to one of the large sheep-farmers on his neighbouring property to give up his farm, his lordship offering to give full value for his stock, so that he might divide it among those evicted from the Chisholm estate. This arrangement was amicably carried through, and at the next Whitsunday—1831—the evicted tenants from Strathglass came into possession of the large sheep-farm of Glenstrathfarrar, and paid over to the

late tenant of the farm every farthing of the value set upon
the stock by two of the leading valuators in the country ;
a fact which conclusively proved that the Strathglass tenants
were quite capable of holding their own, and perfectly able
to meet all claims that could be made upon them by their
old proprietor and unnatural chief.   They became very
comfortable in their new homes ; but about fifteen years
after their eviction from Strathglass they were again removed
to make room for deer.   On this occasion the late Lord
Lovat gave them similar holdings on other portions of his
property, and the sons and grandsons of the evicted tenants
of Strathglass are now, on the Lovat property, among the
most respectable and comfortable middle-class farmers in
the county.

The result of the Strathglass evictions was that only two
of the ancient native stock remained in possession of an
inch of land on the estate of Chisholm.   When the present
Chisholm came into possession he found, on his return from
Canada, only that small remnant of his own name and clan
to receive him.   He brought back a few Chisholms from
the Lovat property, and re-established on his old farm a
tenant who had been evicted nineteen years before from the
holding in which his father and grandfather died.   The
great-grandfather was killed at Culloden, having been shot
while carrying his commander, young Chisholm, mortally
wounded, from the field.   The gratitude òf that chief's
successors had been shown by his ruthless eviction from the
ancient home of his ancestors ; but it is gratifying to find
the present chief making some reparation by bringing back
and liberally supporting the representatives of such a devoted follower of his forbears.   The present Chisholm, who
has the character of being a good landlord, is descended from
a distant collateral branch of the family.   The evicting

Chisholms, and their offspring have, however, every one of them, disappeared, and Mr. Colin Chisholm informs us that there is not a human being now in Strathglass of the descendants of the chief, or of the south country farmers, who were the chief instruments in evicting the native population.

To give the reader an idea of the class of men who occupied this district, it may be stated that of the descendants of those who lived in Glen Canaich, one of several smaller glens, at one time thickly populated in the Strath, but now a perfect wilderness—there lived in the present generation no less than three colonels, one major, three captains, three lieutenants, seven ensigns, one bishop, and fifteen priests.

Earlier in the history of Strathglass and towards the end of last century, an attempt was made by south country sheep-farmers to persuade Alexander Chisholm to follow the example of Glengarry, by clearing out the whole native population. Four southerners, among them Gillespie, who took the farm of Glencuaich, cleared by Glengarry, called upon the Chisholm, at Comar, and tried hard to convince him of the many advantages which would accrue to him by the eviction of his tenantry, and turning the largest and best portions of his estate into great sheep walks, for which they offered to pay him large rents. His daughter, Mary, already referred to as Mrs. James Gooden, was then in her teens. She heard the arguments used, and having mildly expressed her objection to the heartless proposal of the greedy southerners, she was ordered out of the room, crying bitterly. She, however, found her way to the kitchen, called all the servants together, and explained the cause of her trouble. The object of the guests at Comar was soon circulated through the Strath, and early the following morning over a thousand men met together in front of

Comar House, and demanded an interview with their chief. This was at once granted, and the whole body of the people remonstrated with him for entertaining, even for a moment, the cruel proceedings suggested by the strangers, whose conduct the frightened natives characterised as infinitely worse than that of the freebooting Lochaber men who, centuries before, came with their swords and other instruments of death to rob his ancestors of their patrimony, but who were defeated and driven out of the district by the ancestors of those whom it was now proposed to evict, out of their native Strath, to make room for the greedy freebooters of modern times and their sheep. The chief counselled quietness, and suggested that the action they had taken might be construed as an act of inhospitality to his guests, not characteristic, in any circumstances, of a Highland chief.

The sheep-farmers, who stood inside the open drawing-room window, heard all that had passed, and, seeing the unexpected turn events were taking, and the desperate resolve shown by the objects of their cruel purpose, they adopted the better part of valour, slipped quietly out by the back door, mounted their horses, galloped away as fast as their steeds could carry them, and crossed the river Glass among the hooting and derision of the assembled tenantry, heard until they crossed the hill which separates Strathglass from Corriemony. The result of the interview with their laird was a complete understanding between him and his tenants ; and the flying horsemen, looking behind them for the first time when they reached the top of the Maol-Bhuidhe, saw the assembled tenantry forming a procession in front of Comar House, with pipers at their head, and the Chisholm being carried, mounted shoulder-high, by his stalwart vassals, on their way to Invercannich. The pleasant outcome of the whole was that chief and clan expressed renewed confidence in each other, a determination to continue in future in the same happy relationship, and to maintain, each on his part, all—modern and ancient—bonds of fealty ever entered into by their respective ancestors.

This, in fact, turned out to be one of the happiest days that ever dawned on the glen. The people were left unmolested so long as this Chisholm survived—a fact which shows the wisdom of chief and people meeting face to face, and refusing to permit others—whether greedy outsiders or selfish factors—to come and foment mischief and misunderstanding between parties whose interests are so closely bound together, and who, if they met and discussed their differences, would seldom or ever have any disagreements of a serious character. Worse counsel prevailed after Alexander's death, and the result under the cruel daughter of the notorious *Marsali Bhinneach*, has been already described.

Reference has been made to the clearance of Glenstrathfarrar by the late Lord Lovat, but for the people removed from there and other portions of the Lovat property, he allotted lands in various other places on his estates, so that, although these changes were most injurious to his tenants, his lordship's proceedings can hardly be called evictions in the ordinary sense of the term. His predecessor, Archibald Fraser of Lovat, however, evicted, like the Chisholms, hundreds from the Lovat estates.

GUISACHAN.

The modern clearances which took place within the last quarter of a century in Guisachan, Strathglass, by Sir Dudley Marjoribanks, have been described in all their phases before a Committee of the House of Commons in 1873. The Inspector of Poor for the parish of Kilterlitz wrote a

letter which was brought before the Committee, with a statement from another source that, "in 1855, there were 16
farmers on the estate; the number of cows they had was 62,
and horses 24; the principal farmer had 2000 sheep, the
next 1000, and the rest between them 1200, giving a total
of 4200. Now (1873) there is but one farmer, and he leaves
at Whitsunday; all these farmers lost the holdings on which
they ever lived in competency; indeed it is well known that
some of them were able to lay by some money. They
have been sent to the four quarters of the globe, or to
vegetate in Sir Dudley's dandy cottages at Tomich, made
more for show than convenience, where they have to depend
on his employment or charity. To prove that all this is
true, take at random, the smith, the shoemaker, or the
tailor, and say whether the poverty and starvation were then
or now? For instance, under the old *regime*, the smith
farmed a piece of land which supplied the wants of his
family with meal and potatoes; he had two cows, a horse,
and a score or two of sheep on the hill; he paid £7 of
yearly rent; he now has nothing but the bare walls of his
cottage and smithy, for which he pays £10. Of course he
had his trade then as he has now. Will he live more comfortably now than he did then?" It was stated, at the
same time, that when Sir Dudley Marjoribanks bought the
property, there was a population of 255 souls upon it, and
Sir Dudley, in his examination, though he threw some
doubt upon that statement, was quite unable to refute it.
The proprietor, on being asked, said that he did not evict
any of the people. But Mr. Macombie having said, "Then
the tenants went away of their own free will," Sir Dudley
replied, "I must not say so quite. I told them that when
they had found other places to go to, I wished to have
their farms."

They were, in point of fact, evicted as much as any others
of the ancient tenantry in the Highlands, though it is but
fair to say that the same harsh cruelty was not applied in
their case as in many of the others recorded in these pages.
Those who had been allowed to remain in the new cottages,
are without cow or sheep, or an inch of land, while those
alive of those sent off are spread over the wide world, like
those sent, as already described, from other places.

GLENELG.

IN 1849 more than 500 souls left Glenelg. These
petitioned the proprietor, Mr. Baillie of Dochfour, to
provide means of existence for them at home by means
of reclamation and improvements in the district, or, failing
this, to help them to emigrate. Mr. Baillie, after repeated
communications, made choice of the latter alternative, and
suggested that a local committee should be appointed to
procure and supply him with information as to the number
of families willing to emigrate, their circumstances, and the
amount of aid necessary to enable them to do so. This was
done, and it was intimated to the proprietor that a sum of
£3000 would be required to land those willing to emigrate
at Quebec. This sum included passage money, free-rations,
a month's sustenance after the arrival of the party in
Canada, and some clothing for the more destitute. Ultimately, the proprietor offered the sum of £2000, while
the Highland Destitution Committee promised £500. A
great deal of misunderstanding occurred before the *Liscard*
finally sailed, in consequence of misrepresentations made as
to the food to be supplied on board, while there were loud
protests against sending the people away without any
medical man in charge. Through the activity and generous
sympathy of the late Mr. Stewart of Ensay, then tenant of

Ellanreach, on the Glenelg property, who took the side of the people, matters were soon rectified. A doctor was secured, and the people satisfied as to the rations to be served out to them during the passage, though these did not come up to one-half what was originally promised. On the whole, Mr. Baillie behaved liberally, but, considering the suitability of the beautiful valley of Glenelg for arable and food-producing purposes, it is to be regretted that he did not decide upon utilizing the labour of the natives in bringing the district into a state of cultivation, rather than have paid so much to banish them to a foreign land. That they would themselves have preferred this is beyond question.

Mr. Mulock, father of the author of " John Halifax, Gentleman," an Englishman who could not be charged with any preconceived prejudices or partiality for the Highlanders, travelled at this period through the whole North, and ultimately published an account of what he had seen. Regarding the Glenelg business, he says, as to their willingness to emigrate—" To suppose that numerous families would as a matter of choice sever themselves from their loved soil, abolish all the associations of local and patriotic sentiment, fling to the winds every endearing recollection connected with the sojourneying spot of vanished generations, and blot themselves, as it were, out of the book of ' home-borne happiness,' is an hypothesis too unnatural to be encouraged by any sober, well-regulated mind." To satisfy himself, he called forty to fifty heads of families together at Glenelg, who had signed an agreement to emigrate, but who did not find room in the *Liscard*, and were left behind, after selling off everything they possessed, and were consequently reduced to a state of starvation. " I asked," he says, " these poor perfidiously treated creatures if, notwithstanding all their hardships, they were willing emigrants from their native land. With one voice they assured me that nothing short of the impossibility of obtaining land or employment at home could drive them to seek the doubtful benefits of a foreign shore. So far from the emigration being, at Glenelg, or Lochalsh, or South Uist, a spontaneous movement springing out of the wishes of the tenantry, I aver it to be, on the contrary, the product of desperation, the calamitous light of hopeless oppression visiting their sad hearts." We have no hesitation in saying that this is not only true of those to whom Mr. Mulock specially refers, but to almost every soul who have left the Highlands for the last sixty years. Only those who know the people intimately, and the means adopted by factors, clergy, and others to produce an appearance of spontaneity on the part of the helpless tenantry, can understand the extent to which this statement is true. If a judicious system had been applied of cultivating excellent land, capable of producing food in abundance, in Glenelg, there was not another property in the Highlands on which it was less necessary to send the people away than in that beautiful and fertile valley.

GLENDESSERAY AND LOCHARKAIG.

GREAT numbers were evicted from the Cameron country of Lochaber, especially from Glendesseray and Locharkaig side. Indeed it is said that there were so few Camerons left in the district, that not a single tenant of the name attended the banquet given by the tenantry when the present Lochiel came into possession. The details of Cameron evictions would be found pretty much the same as those in other places, except that an attempt has been made in this case to hold the factor entirely and solely responsible for the removal of this noble people, so renowned in

the martial history of the country.   That is a question, however, which it is no part of our present purpose to discuss.
What we wish to expose is the unrighteous system which
allowed such cruel proceedings to take place here and
elsewhere, by landlord or factor.

Principal Shairp of St. Andrews, and Professor of Poetry
in the University of Oxford, has described the evictions
from the country of the Camerons in a fine poem of seven
cantos, entitled, " The Clearing of the Glens," published in
Vol. II. of the *Celtic Magazine*, 1876-77.   It would be impossible to describe them so completely as has been done
in this excellent poem, and we shall therefore leave Principal
Shairp to do so himself, by quoting, at some length, from
his sixth and seventh cantos, though, to get the pathetic
picture complete, the reader must peruse the whole poem.

In an introductory note, the Principal informs us that he
attempts, in the poem, " to reproduce facts heard, and
impressions received, during the wanderings of several
successive summers among the scenes " which he describes.
" Whatever view political economists may take of these
events, it can hardly be denied that the form of human
society, and the phase of human suffering, here attempted
to be described, deserve at least some record. . . .   Of
the main outlines and leading events of the simple story, it
may well be said, ' It's an over true tale '."   After some
beautiful and touching descriptions of the state, physically
and socially, of the Cameron country, some years earlier,
Angus Cameron, who had been away for seven years in the
service of his country, returns, and is horror-stricken at
seeing the desolation brought about during his absence, in
Lochaber and the vicinity.   As he comes in sight of his
own native place, the poet describes the scene thus—

There far below, inlaid between
Steep mountain walls, lay calm and green
Glen Desseray, bright in morning sheen.
As down the rough track Angus trode
The path that led to his old abode,
Calm as of old the lone green glen
Lay stretched before him long miles ten ;
He looked, the braes as erst were fair,
But smoke none rose on the morning air :
He listened, came no blithe cock-crowing
From wakening farms, no cattle lowing,
No voice of man, no cry of child,
Blent with the loneness of the wild ;
Only the wind thro' the bent and ferns,
Only the moan of the corrie-burns. ·
Can it be ? doth this silence tell
   The same sad tale as yester-eve ?
My clansmen here who wont to dwell
   Have they too ta'en their last long leave ?
Adown this glen too, hath there been
The besom of destruction keen
Sweeping it of its people clean ?
That anxious tremour in his breast
One half-hour onward set at rest ;
Where once his home had been, now stare
Two gables roofless, gaunt, and bare ;
Two gables, and a broken wall,
Are all now left of Sheniebhal.
The huts around of the old farm-toun,
   Wherein the poorer tenants dwelt,
Moss-covered stone-heaps, crumbling down,
   Into the wilderness slowly melt.
The slopes below, where had gardens been,
Lay thick with rushes darkly green,
The furrows on the braes above
Where erst the flax and the barley throve,
With ferns and heather covered o'er,
To Nature had gone back once more.
And there beneath, the meadow lay,
   The long smooth reach of meadowy ground,
Where intertwining east away
   In loop on loop the river wound :

There, where he heard a former day
The blithe, loud shouting, shinty play,
  Was silence now as the grave profound.
.   .   .   .
Then looking back with one wide ken,
Where stood the Farms, each side the glen—
Tome-na-hua, Cuil, Glac-fern,
Each he clearly could discern ;
Once groups of homes, wherein did dwell
The people he had known so well,
These stood blank skeletons, one and all,
Like his own home, Sheniebhal :
And he sighed as he gazed on the pathways untrodden,
"These be the homes of the men of Culloden !"

  "This desolation ! whence hath come ?
What power hath hushed this living glen,
Once blithe with happy sounds of men,
  Into a wilderness blank and dumb ?
Alas for them ! leal souls and true !
Kindred and clansmen whom I knew !
Their homes stand roofless on the brae,
And the hearts that loved them, where are they !
Ah me ! what days with them I've seen
On the summer braes at the shielings green !
What nights of winter, dark and long,
Made brief and bright by the joy of song !
The men in peace so gentle and mild,
In battle onset lion-wild,
When the pibroch of Donald Dhu
  Sounded the summons of Lochiel,
From these homes to his standard flew,
  By him stood through woe and weal,
Against Clan-Chattan, age by age
Held his ancient heritage :
And when the Stuart cause was down,
And Lochiel rose for King and Crown,
Who like these same Cameron men
  Gave their gallant heart-blood pure
At Inverlochy, Killiecrankie,
  Preston-pans, Culloden Moor ?
And when red vengeance on the Gael

Fell bloody, did their fealty fail ?
Did they not screen with lives of men
Their outlawed Prince in desert and den ?
And when their chief fled far away,
Who were his sole support but they ?
Alas for them ! those faithful men !
  And this is all reward they have !
These unroofed homes, this emptied glen,
  A forlorn exile, then the grave."

That night, as October winds were tirling
  The birchen woods down Lochiel's long shore,
The wan, dead leaves on the rain-blast whirling,
  A low knock came to our cottage door.
"Lift the latch, bid him welcome," cried my sire,
  Straight a plaided stranger entered in,
And we saw by the light of the red peat fire,
  A long, lank form, and visage thin.
We children stared—as tho' a ghost
  Had crossed the door—on that face unknown ;
But my father cried—"O loved and lost !
  That voice, my brother, is thine own."
Then each on the other's neck they fell,
  And long embraced, and wept aloud ;
We children stood—I remember well—
  Our heads in wondering silence bowed.
But when our uncle raised his head,
Gazing round the house, he said—
" I've travelled down Glendesseray bare,
  Looked on our desolate home to-day,
But those my heart most longed for, where ?
  Father and mother, where are they ?
For them has their own country found
No home, save underneath the ground."
  " Too truly has your heart divined,"
My father answered him, "for they
Came hither but not long to stay—
With the fall o' the year away they dwined,
Not loth another home to find,
  Where none could say them nay.

Above their heads to-night the sward
Is green in Kilmallie's old kirkyard."

In vain for him the board we strewed,
He little cared for rest or food—
On this alone intent—to know,
Whence had come the ruin and woe.
"Tell me, O tell me whence," he cried,
" Hath spread this desolation wide ;
What ministers of dark despair—
From neither pit or upper air—
On the poor country of the Gael,
Hath breathed this blasting blight and bale.
By lone Lochourn, too, I have been,
And Runieval in ruin seen :
I know that home is desolate—
Tell me the dweller's earthly fate."
" Ah, these are gone, with many more,"
My father said, " to a far-off shore,
By some great lake, whereof we know
Only the name – Ontario.
They tell us there are broad lands there,
Whereof whoever will may share,
Great forests—trees of giant stem—
Glen-mallie pines are naught to them.
But of all that we nothing know,
Save the great name, Ontario."
" But whence came all this ruin ?   Tell
From whom the cruel outrage fell,
On our poor people."   With a sigh
My father fain had put him by ;
" A tale so full of sorrow and wrong,
To-night to tell were all too long,
Weary and hungry thou need'st must be—
Sit down at the board we have spread for thee !"
I wot we had spread it of our best,
But for him our dainties had little zest ;
Nor would he eat or drink until,
Of that dark tale he had heard his fill.

" Since then it must be, I will try,
Rehearse that cruel history,"

My father said, "but why remount
Up to the first full-flowing fount,
Of misery? From whence it came,
That ruin, or with whom the blame,
These things I know not—only know
It fell with a crushing weight of woe,
And broke in twain those hearts for grief,
Who would have died for King and Chief.
Is inborn loyalty that could keep
Its troth to death, a thing so cheap—
Clan-love and honour, that would give
Their life-blood that the Chief might live—
So vile a growth, so little worth,
That men do well to sweep from earth,
Or trample under careless feet,
The truest hearts that ever beat.
As though they were of count no more
Than sea-weed on the wreck-strewn shore?"

Rememberest not how brightly burned
Our beacon-fires when the Chiefs returned?
When clansmen hailed Clanranald's lord,
    Glengarry, and our own Lochiel,
As fathers to their own restored—
    All wrongs to right, all wounds to heal?
They dreamed again 'neath Chiefs as kings,
    To live lives happy and secure?
They knew not that old form of things
    Had perished on Culloden Moor.
Like lairds or English squires—no more,
    As fathers of their people—they
Handed their kindly tenants o'er
    To factor's grinding sway,
And left their castles and lone glens,
To dwell as dainty citizens.
And 'mid the smiles of court and town,
Air their high names of old renown ;
While we with ceaseless toil and moil,
    Hard-struggling, scarce could win,
From drenching skies and niggard soil,
    Enough to keep life in.

Claymore and targe forever cast
  Behind them, foray and raid—
Their thoughts were changed, their days were passed
  'Mid mattock, plough, and spade.
Launched sudden on the industrial race
  'Gainst lowland thrift and trade,
If chance they sought the factor's face,
  For guidance, counsel, aid,
As well they might to the rocks have turned,
So rudely from his presence spurned,
Our people home with taunts were sent,
' Ye are idle, idle—rent, more rent '.

At length, poor souls, in their despair,
They looked around for help elsewhere.

.   .   .   .

Far down the loch I watched the sail,
  Round the last headland disappear,
But long the pibroch's moaning wail—
Knell of the broken-hearted Gael—
  Came back upon my ear,
Echoing to crag, and cave, and shore,
' We return no more—return no more '.

Three summers more went by—the third
Brought to our glen the warning word,
That from their homes at Martinmas,
The tenants, every man, must pass—
Must leave the glen their fathers held,
As clansmen, from an unknown eld,
To make room for some Sassenach loon
Who, from the Borders coming soon,
With flocks of long-woolled sheep would fill
The emptied country, glen, and hill.
Nor less dismayed Glenkinzie heard—
Glen-Pean, too—that startling word,
And all the lesser glens that hide
Down long Loch Arkaig, either side,
Then 'gan our men, in sore dismay,
Look each in other's face, and say—

"What have we done, that we should reap
    For all that's past, but this reward?
Is it that we have failed to keep
    All service due to our liege lord?
Is it because o'er seas abroad,
    We sent for years a second rent,
To succour our dear Chiefs outlawed,
    And pining lone in banishment?
Was it for this our beacons burned,
So brightly when Lochiel returned?"

But when November, bleak and wan,
    With moaning winds wound up the year,
Then rose the dim and dripping dawn,
    That saw our people disappear—
Saw thirty families close their door,
And leave the Glen for evermore.
Ah! then the grief, long inly pent,
From many a breaking heart found vent,
In one wild agony of lament;
Old men, and bairns of tender years,
Mingling their crying and their tears,
The wail of a forlorn leave-taking,
As though an hundred hearts were breaking,
And love and hope the world forsaking.
By afternoon our people crept
Past Achnacarry slow, and wept.
Lochiel was gentle and humane,
    As all his race before—
To see aught living suffer pain,
    It grieved his kind heart sore.
And he, the Chief, was by that day,
As our poor people wound their way
Down the Pass called 'The Darksome Mile,'
And when from out the deep defile,
The sounds of men and cattle brake,
He to the factor turned and spake—
"Whose lowing kine are these I hear?
What means this bleating in mine ear?"
But when the factor answered, "They
Are the people from Glendesseray,"

Lochiel, though mild, with anger burned,
And on the factor sternly turned—
" You told me they were abjects all,
Leading a squalid, hopeless life—
I never paupers knew withal,
Have store of sheep and kine so rife ;
Would that I ne'er thy face had known,
        Ere thus with all the past I broke,
And drove from homes that were their own,
        These leal and simple-hearted folk !
This deed, which you have made me do,
Until my dying day I'll rue."

Well might he rue it, he had driven,
        Forth from the homes to which they clave,
Without a home or hope but heaven,
Two hundred hearts that would have given
        Their lives his life to save.
Sad thoughts that night were with the Chief,
        But these the people could not know—
They only knew that no relief
        Came to their utter woe.
Our fate was fixed, the deed was done,
        Nor Chief nor factor could repeal ;—
We wandered on—that setting sun
        Sank o'er Loch-Linnhe and Lochiel,
As we that night, on cold shore bare,
Encamped beneath the frosty air.
To all who would were crofts assigned—
        Small, meagre crofts of moory lea—
Within this narrow marge confined,
        Between the mountains and the sea.
But all the strong, who would not brook
That day of ruin and rebuke—
Whose sturdy souls could not endure
To sink down 'mid the helpless poor,
They spurned the crofts, and launched away,
To seek new homes in Canada—
The flower of all the glens they bore,
Unwilling to that unknown shore,
Hearts warm with Highland love and lore,

There with home-yearnings sad to beat,
Such hearts as here no more we meet.

But we—our parents all too frail,
Too overdone with age to sail
On that far voyage—were constrained
To take the refuge that remained
Hard by, and on this croft to raise
A rooftree o'er their latest days.
   Not long they needed it—soon they found
A surer shelter, safely laid
   Within yon ancient kirkyard ground,
'Neath the old beech trees' shade.
While we, poor remnant, left behind,
Like the last leaves which autumn wind
Spares when it strips the forest bare—
   We still to poor Lochaber cling,
Content if ceaseless toil and care,
   Scant living from these rocks may wring,
Confined to this lean strip of shore,
The Mountains free to range no more,
All gone—our goats and bonny kye,
That were so bounteous to supply
Alike the children's wants and ours ;
We drudge through late and early hours,
And for our toiling hardly win,
Of fuel, food, and raiment thin,
Enough to keep this poor life in.
How different from the easeful wealth
   Of mountain-living, those old days,
When we drank freedom, joy, and health,
   High on Glendesseray braes !
But that dear Glen, as thou hast seen,
   To-day is silent as the grave,
No songs at the high shealings green,
   No voices in the valley, save
The bleating of the thousand sheep,
   Which o'er our fields and gardens feed,
That Lowland drover thence may reap,
   O'erflowing gain to glut his greed.
The floors on which we kneeled in prayer,

The hearths round which we wont to meet,
Lie roofless and forsaken—bare
    To Saxon shepherd's careless feet.
Enough of this ! why linger o'er,
    Old homes gone back to wilderness ?
A heavenly home lies on before—
    Thereto we'll forward press.

Not many days my father's roof
    That soldier-brother could retain ;
To wander to far lands aloof
    His heart was on the strain.
But while within our home he stayed,
    He turned him every day,
To where, in sombre beech trees' shade,
His parents both are lowly laid,
    'Neath mountain flag-stone grey,
The last time that he lingered there,
    Some moss he gathered from the grave,
The one memorial he could bear,
Where'er his wandering feet might fare,
    Beyond the western wave.
And then he left my father's door,
And bidding farewell evermore
To dwellers on this mountain shore,
He sets his face to that world afar,
On which descends the evening star.

.   .   .   .   .   .

WESTER ROSS.

Kintail.

DURING the first years of the century a great many were cleared from Kintail by Seaforth at the instigation of his Kintail factor, Duncan Mor Macrae, and his father, who themselves added the land taken from the ancient tenantry to their own sheep farms, already far too extensive. In Glengarry, Canada, a few years ago, we met one man, 93 years of age, who was among the evicted. He was in excellent circumstances, his three sons having three valuable farms of their own, and considered wealthy in the district. In the same county there is a large colony of Kintail men, the descendants of those cleared from that district, all comfortable, many of them very well off, one of them being then member for his county in the Dominion Parliament. While this has been the case with many of the evicted from Kintail and their descendants in Canada, the grasping sheep farmer who was the original cause of their eviction from their native land, died ruined and penniless; and the Seaforths, not long after, had to sell the last inch of their ancient inheritance in Lochalsh and Kintail. Shortly after these Glenelchaig evictions, about fifiy families were banished in the same way and by the same people from the district of Letterfearn. This property has also changed hands since, and is now in possession of Sir Alexander Matheson, Baronet of Lochalsh. Letter of Lochalsh was cleared by Sir Hugh Innes, almost as soon as he came into possession by purchase of that portion of the ancient heritage of Seaforth and Kintail. The property has since passed into the hands of the Lillingstones.

COIGEACH.

The attempt to evict the Coigeach crofters must also be mentioned. Here the people made a stout resistance, the women disarming about twenty policemen and sheriff-officers, burning the summonses in a heap, throwing their batons into the sea, and ducking the representatives of the law in a neighbouring pool. The men formed the second line of defence, in case the women should receive any ill-treatment. They, however, never put a finger on the officers of the law, all of whom returned home without serving a single summons or evicting a single crofter. The proceedings of her subordinates fortunately came to the ears of the noble proprietrix, with the result that the Coigeach tenants are still where they were, and are to-day among the most comfortable crofters in the north of Scotland.

STRATHCONON.

From 1840 to 1848 Strathconon was almost entirely cleared of its ancient inhabitants to make room for sheep and deer, as in other places ; and also for the purposes of extensive forest plantations. The property was under trustees when the harsh proceedings were commenced by the factor, Mr. Rose, a notorious Dingwall solicitor. He began by taking away, first, the extensive hill-pasture, for generations held as club-farms by the townships, thus reducing the people from a position of comfort and independence; and secondly, as we saw done elsewhere, finally evicting them from the arable portion of the strath, though they were not a single penny in arrear of rent.   Coirre-Bhuic and Scard-Roy were first cleared, and given, respectively, as sheep-farms to Mr. Brown, from Morayshire, and Colin Munro, from Dingwall. Mr. Balfour, when he came of age, cleared Coirre-Feola and Achadh-an-eas ; Carnach was similarly treated, while no less than twenty-seven families were evicted from Glen-Meine alone.   Baile-a-Mhuilinn and Baile-na-Creige were cleared in 1844, no less than twenty-four families from these town-ships removing to the neighbourhood of Knock-farrel and Loch Ussie, above Dingwall, where they were provided with holdings by the late John Hay Mackenzie of Cromartie, father of the present Duchess of Sutherland, and where a few of themselves and many of their descendants are now in fairly comfortable circumstances.   A great many more found shelter on various properties in the Black Isle—some at Drynie Park, Maol-Bui ; others at Kilcoy, Allangrange, Cromarty, and the Aird.   It is computed that from four to five hundred souls were thus driven from Strathconon, and cast adrift on the world, including a large number of persons quite helpless, from old age, blindness, and other infirmities. The scenes were much the same as we have described in connection with other places.   There is, however, one aspect of the harshness and cruelty of the fates to be recorded in the case of many of the Strathconon people, not applicable in many other cases, namely, that in most instances where they settled down and reclaimed land, they were afterwards re-evicted, and the lands brought into culti-vation by themselves, taken from them, without any compen-sation whatever, and given at enhanced rents to large farmers.

This is specially true of those who settled down in the Black
Isle, where they reclaimed a great deal of waste now making
some of the best farms in that district.   Next after Mr. Rose
of Dingwall, the principal instrument in clearing Strathconon, was the late James Gillanders of Highfield, already so
well and unfavourably known to the reader in connection
with the evictions at Glencalvie, and elsewhere.

   It may be remarked that the Strathconon evictions are
worthy of note for the forcible illustration they furnish of
how, by these arbitrary and unexpected removals, hardships
and ruin have frequently been brought on families and communities who were at the time in contented and comfortable
circumstances.   At one time, and previous to the earlier
evictions, perhaps no glen of its size in the Highlands had a
larger population than Strathconon.   The club farm system,
once so common in the North, seems to have been peculiarly successful here.   Hence a large proportion of the people
were well to do, but when suddenly called upon to give up
their hill pasture, and afterwards their arable land, and in
the absence of other suitable places to settle in, the means
they had very soon disappeared, and the trials and difficulties
of new conditions had to be encountered.   As a rule, in most
of these Highland evictions, the evicted were lost sight of,
they having either emigrated to foreign lands or become
absorbed in the ever-increasing unemployed population of
the large towns.   In the case of Strathconon it was different,
as has been already stated ; many of the families evicted
were allowed to settle on some of the wildest unreclaimed
land in the Black Isle.   Their subsequent history there, and
the excellent agricultural condition into which they in after
years brought their small holdings, is a standing refutation of
the charge so often made against the Highland people, that
they are lazy and incapable of properly cultivating the land.

THE BLACK ISLE.

Respecting the estates of Drynie and Kilcoy, a correspondent, who says, " I well remember my excessive grief when my father had to leave the farm which his forefathers had farmed for five generations," writes :—

"Within recent times all the tenants to the east of Drynie, as far as Craigiehow, were turned out, one by one, to make room for one large tenant, Mr. Robertson, who had no less than four centres for stackyards. A most prosperous tenantry were turned out to make room for him, and what is the end of it all! Mr. Robertson has come to grief as a farmer, and now holds a very humble position in the town of Inverness. Drumderfit used to be occupied by fifteen or sixteen tenants who were gradually, and from time to time, evicted, during the last fifty years. Balnakyle was tenanted by five very comfortable and respectable farmers, four of whom were turned out within the last thirty years; Balnaguie was occupied by three; Torr by six; and Croft-cruive by five; the once famous names of Drum-na-marg and Moreton are now extinct, as well as the old tenantry whose forefathers farmed these places for generations. The present farm of Kilcoy includes a number of holdings whose tenants were evicted to make room for one large farmer;" and this is equally true of many others in the district. Nothing can better illustrate the cruel manner in which the ancient tenantry of the country have been treated than these facts; and special comment on the evictions from Strathconon and the Black Isle, after what has been said about others of a similar character would be superfluous.

The Island of Lews.

No one was evicted from the Island of Lews, in the strict sense of the term, but 2231 souls had to leave it between 1851 and 1863. To pay their passage money, their inland railway fares on arrival, and to provide them with clothing and other furnishings, the late Sir James Matheson paid a sum of £11,855. But notwithstanding all this expenditure, many of these poor people would have died from starvation on their arrival without the good offices of friends in Canada.

In 1841, before Mr. Matheson bought it, a cargo of emigrants from the Lews arrived at Quebec late in the autumn, accompanied by a Rev. Mr. Maclean, sent out to minister to their spiritual wants, but it appears that no provision had been made for the more pressing demands of a severe Canadian winter; and were it not for the Saint Andrew's Society of Montreal, every soul of them would have been starved to death that winter in a strange land. The necessities of the case, and how this patriotic Society saved their countrymen from a horrid death will be seen on perusal of the following minutes, extracted from the books of the Society, during the writer's recent tour in Canada :—

"A special meeting of the office-bearers was summoned on the 20th September, 1841, to take into consideration an application made by Mr. Morris, President of the Emigration Association of the district of St. Francis, for some pecuniary aid to a body of 229 destitute emigrants who had recently arrived from the Island of Lews (Scotland), and who were then supported chiefly by the contributions of the charitable inhabitants of the town of Sherbrooke and its neighbourhood. Mr. Morris' letter intimated that unless other assistance was received, it would be impossible for these emigrants to outlive the winter, as they were in a state of utter destitution, and the inhabitants of the township could not support so large a number of persons from their own unaided resources. The meeting decided that the Constitution of the Society prohibited them from applying its funds to an object like the one presented—it did not appear to authorise the granting of relief from its funds except to cases of destitution in the city ; but as this case appeared of an urgent nature, and one particularly calling for assistance, Messrs. Hew Ramsay and Neil M'Intosh were appointed to collect subscriptions on behalf of the emigrants. This committee acquitted itself with great diligence and success, having collected the handsome sum of £234 14s. 6d., the whole of which was, at different times, remitted to Mr. Morris, and expended by him in this charity. Letters were received from Mr. Morris, expressing the gratitude of the emigrants for this large and timely aid, which was principally the means of keeping them from starvation." The whole of these emigrants are now in easy circumstances.

Comment on the conduct of those in power, who sent out their poor tenantry totally unprovided for, is unnecessary. The idea of sending out a minister and nothing else, in such circumstances, makes one shudder to think of the uses which are sometimes made of the clergy, and how, in such cases, the Gospel they are supposed not only to preach but to practise, is only in many instances caricatured. The provisions sent by the Society had to be forwarded to where these starving emigrants were, a distance of 80 miles from Sherbrooke, on sledges, through a trackless and dense forest. The descendants of these people now form a happy and prosperous community at Lingwick and Winslow.

LECKMELM.

This small property, in the Parish of Lochbroom, changed hands in 1879, Mr. A. C. Pirie, Paper Manufacturer, Aberdeen, having purchased it for £19,000 from Colonel Davidson, now of Tulloch. No sooner did it come into Mr. Pirie's possession than a notice, dated 2nd November, 1879, in the following terms, was issued to all the tenants :—

I am instructed by Mr. Pirie, proprietor of Leckmelm, to give you notice that the present arrangements by which you hold the cottage, byre, and other buildings, together with lands on that estate, will cease from and after the term of Martinmas, 1880 ; and further, I am instructed to intimate to you that at the said term of Martinmas, 1880, Mr. Pirie purposes taking the whole arable and pasture lands, but that he is desirous of making arrangements whereby you may continue tenant of the cottage upon terms and conditions yet to be settled upon. I have further to inform you that unless you and the other tenants at once prevent your sheep and other stock from grazing or trespassing upon the enclosures and hill and other lands now in the occupation or possession of the said Mr. Pirie, he will not, upon any conditions, permit you to remain in the cottage you now occupy, after the said term of Martinmas, 1880, but will clear all off the estate, and take down the cottages.

This notice affected twenty-three families, numbering about one hundred souls. Sixteen tenants paid between them a rent of £96 10s.—ranging from £3 to £12 each, per annum. The stock allowed them was 72 head of cattle, 8 horses, and 320 sheep. The arable portion of Leckmelm was about the best tilled and the most productive land in possession of any crofters in the parish. It could all be worked with the plough, now a very uncommon thing in the Highlands ; for almost invariably land of that class is in the hands of the proprietors themselves, when not let to sheep-farmers or sportsmen. The intention of the new proprietor was strictly carried out. At Martinmas, 1880, he took every inch of land—arable and pastoral—into his own hands, and thus by one cruel stroke, reduced a comfortable tenantry from comparative affluence and independence to the position of mere cottars and day labourers, absolutely dependent for subsistence on his own will and the likes or dislikes of his subordinates, who may perhaps, for a short time, be in a position to supply the remnant that will remain, in their altered circumstances, with such common labour as trenching, draining, fencing, carrying stones, lime, and mortar, for the laird's mansion-house and outhouses. With the exception of one, all the tenants who remained are still permitted to live in their old cottages, but they are not permitted to keep a living thing about them—not even a hen. They are existing in a state of abject dependence on Mr. Pirie's will and that of his servants; and in a constant state of terror that next they will even be turned out of their cottages. As regards work and the necessaries of life, they have been reduced to that of common navvies. In place of milk, butter, and cheese in fair abundance, they have now to be satisfied with sugar, treacle, or whatever else they can buy, to their porridge and potatoes, and their supply of meat, grown and fed hitherto by themselves, is gone for ever. Two, a man and his wife, if not more, have since been provided for by the Parochial authorities, and, no doubt, that will ultimately be the fate of many more of this once thriving and contented people.

An agitation against Mr. Pirie's conduct was raised at the time, and the advantage which he had taken of his position was universally condemned by the press (excepting the *Scotsman* of course), and by the general public voice of the country; but conscious of his strength, and that the present law, made by the landlords in their own interest, was on his side, he relentlessly and persistently carried out his cruel purpose to the bitter end, and evicted from their lands and

hill grazings every soul upon his property; but in the meantime allowed them to remain in their cottages, with the
exception of Donald Munro, to whose case reference will
be made hereafter, and two other persons whose houses were
pulled down, and themselves evicted.

When the notices of removal were received, the Rev.
John MacMillan, Free Church Minister of the Parish, called
public attention to Mr. Pirie's proceedings, in the Northern
newspapers, and soon the eye of the whole country was
directed to this modern evictor—a man, in other respects,
reputed considerate and even kind to those under him in
his business of paper manufacturing in Aberdeen.   People,
in their simplicity, for years back, thought that evictions on
such a large scale, in the face of a more enlightened public
opinion, had become mere unpleasant recollections of a
barbarous past; forgetting that the same laws which permitted the clearances of Sutherland and other portions of the
Scottish Highlands during the first half of the present
century were still in force, ready to be applied by any tyrant
who had the courage, for personal ends, to outrage the more
advanced and humane public opinion of the present
generation.

The noble conduct of the Rev. Mr. MacMillan, in connection with those evictions, deserves commemoration in a
work in which the name of his prototype in Sutherland, the
Rev. Mr. Sage, shows to such advantage during the infamous
clearances in that county, already described at length.   At
the urgent request of many friends of the Highland crofters,
resident in Inverness, Mr. MacMillan agreed to lay the case
of his evicted parishioners before the public.   Early in
December, 1880, he delivered an address in the Music Hall
to one of the largest and most enthusiastic meetings which
has ever been held within its walls, and we cannot do better

here than quote at considerable length from his instructive, eloquent, and rousing appeal on that occasion. Though his remarks do not seem to have influenced Mr. Pirie's conduct, or to have benefited his unfortunate subjects, the Inverness meeting was the real beginning in earnest of the present movement throughout the Highlands in favour of Land Reform, and the curtailment of landlord power over their unfortunate tenants. Mr. Pirie can thus claim to have done our poorer countrymen no small amount of good, though probably, quite contrary to his intentions, by his cruel and high-handed conduct in dealing with the ancient tenants of Leckmelm. He has set the heather on fire, and it is likely to continue burning until such proceedings as those for which he is responsible at Leckmelm will be finally made impossible in Scotland. Mr. MacMillan after informing his audience that Mr. Pirie "is now in a fair way of reaching a notoriety which he little dreamt of when he became owner of the Leckmelm estate," proceeds to tell how the harsh proceedings were gone about, and says :—

As the public are aware, Mr. Pirie's first step after becoming owner of the estate, was to inform the tenantry, by the hands of Mr. Manners, C.E., Inverness, that at Martinmas following they were to deliver their arable land and stock, consisting of sheep and cattle, into his hands, but that some of them, on conditions yet to be revealed, and on showing entire submission to the new *regime* of things, and, withal, a good certificate of character from his factotum, William Gould, might remain in their cottages to act as serfs or slaves on his farm. On this conditional promise they were to live in the best of hope for the future and all at the mercy of the absolute master of the situation, with a *summum jus* at his back to enable him to effect all the purposes of his heart. As a prologue to the drama which was to follow, and to give a sample of what they might expect in the sequel, two acts were presented, or properly speaking, one act in two parts. These were to prepare them for what was to come, reminding us of what we read somewhere in our youth, of a husband who on marrying his fair spouse wished to teach her prompt obedience to all his commands, whatever their character. His first lesson in this direction was one assuredly calculated to strike terror into her tender breast. It was the shooting on the spot of the horse which drew his carriage or conveyance, on showing some slight restiveness. The second lesson was of a similar nature ; we can easily imagine that his object was gained. Then, after coming home, he commanded his spouse to untie his boots and shoes and take them off, and to engage in the most servile acts. Of course prompt obedience was given to all these commands and his end was gained. His wife was obedient to him to the last degree. Of the wisdom and propriety of such a procedure in a husband towards his lawful wife, I shall not here and now wait to enquire, but one thing is plain to us all ; there was a species of earthly and carnal wisdom in it which was entirely overshadowed by its cruelty. Now this illustrates exactly how Mr. Pirie acted towards the people of Leckmelm. To strike terror into their hearts, first of all, two houses were pulled down, I might say about the ears of their respective occupants, without any warning whatever, except a verbal one of the shortest kind. The first was a deaf pauper woman, about middle life, living alone for years in a bothy of her own, altogether apart from the other houses, beside a purling stream, where she had at all seasons pure water to drink if her bread was at times somewhat scanty. After this most cruel eviction no provision was made for the helpless woman, but she was allowed to get shelter elsewhere or anywhere, as best she could. If any of you ever go the way of Leckmelm you can see a gamekeeper's house, the gentry of our land, close to the side of Iseabal Bheag's bothy, and a dog kennel quite in its neighbourhood, or, as I said in one of my letters, adorning it. This then is act the first of this drama. Act second comes next. Mrs. Campbell was a widow with two children; after the decease of her husband she tried to support herself and them by serving in gentlemen's families as a servant. Whether she was all the time in Tulloch's family I cannot say, but, at all events, it was from that family she returned to Leckmelm, in failing health, and on getting rather heavy for active service. Of course her father had died since she had left, and the house in which he lived and died, and in which in all likelihood he had reared his family, and in which she was born and bred, was now tenantless. It was empty, the land attached to it being in the hands of another person. Here Widow Campbell turned aside for a while until something else would in kind providence turn up. But behold during her sojourn from her native township, another king arose, who knew not Joseph, and the inexorable edict had gone forth to raze her habitation to the ground. Her house also was pulled down about her ears. This woman has since gone to America, the asylum of many an evicted family from hearth and home. Such tragedies as I have mentioned roused some of us to remonstrate with the actors engaged in them, and to the best of our ability to expose their conduct, and, furthermore, we have brought them to the bar of public judgment to pass their verdict, which I hope before all is over will be one of condemnation and condign punishment.

Behold how great a matter a little fire kindleth. Leckmelm and its inhabitants are a small matter, but it may be as the spark which sets on fire the vast prairie. It may prove to be Janet Geddes's ghost again, which once caused an entire revolution in Scotland—a revolution which bears its mark and produces its fruits to this moment, and, I hope, for ever, while sun and season endure, while men and women remain on its soil. And here I would say without pretending to be a prophet, that whatever becomes of Leckmelm and its interests, whose fate so far as I can apprehend is already sealed (I must say through the supineness of the country and the indifference of our representatives in Parliament), I confidently hope that a campaign has been inaugurated which shall not be abandoned until the cruel and ravaging foe is routed for ever off the field, and a yoke of iron which neither we nor our fathers were able to bear, will be wrenched and snapped asunder and removed from the necks of our peasantry never more to be replaced, until the civilisation of the 19th century will give place to the barbarism of the original Britons.

Having referred at some length to the worst classes of evictions throughout the Highlands in the past, and already described in this work, the Reverend Lecturer proceeded :—

But there is another way, a more gentle, politic, and insinuating way at work which depopulates our country quite as effectually as the whole-sale clearances of which we have been speaking and against which we protest, and to which we must draw your attention for a little. There are many proprietors who get the name of being good and kind to their tenants, and who cannot be charged with evicting any of them save for misbehaviour—a deserving cause at all times—who are never-theless inch by inch secretly and stealthily laying waste the country and undermining the well-being of our people. I have some of these gentlemen before my mind at this moment. When they took possession of their estates all promised fair and well, but by-and-bye the fatal blow was struck, to dispossess the people of their sheep. Mark that *first move* and resist it to the utmost. As long as tenants have a hold of the hill pasture by sheep, and especially if it be what we term a com-monage or club farm, it is impossible to lay it waste in part. But once you snap this tie asunder, you are henceforth at the mercy of the owner to do with you as he pleases. This then is how the business is transacted and in the most business-like fashion too. To be sure none are to be forcibly evicted from their holdings : that would be highly impolitic, because it would bring public condemnation on the sacred heads of the evictors, which some of them could in no way confront, for they have a character and a name to sustain, and also because they are more susceptible to the failings common to humanity. They are moving too in the choicest circles of society. It would not do that their names should be figuring in every newspaper in the land, as cruel and oppressive landlords, or that the Rev. this and the Rev. that should excommunicate them from society and stigmatise them as tyrants and despots. But all are not so sensitive as this of name and character, as we see abundantly demonstrated, because they have none to lose. You might expose them upon a gibbet before the gaze of an assembled universe and they would hardly blush, "they are harder than the nether mill stone". But the more sensitive do their work, all the same, after all, and it is done in this fashion. When a tenant dies, or removes otherwise, the order goes forth that his croft or lot is to be laid waste. It is not given to a neighbouring tenant, except in some instances, nor to a stranger, to occupy it. In this inch by inch clearance, the work of depopulation is effected in a few years, or in a generation at most, quite as effectually as by the more glaring and reprehensible method. This more secret and insinuating way of depopulating our native land should be as stoutly resisted as the more open and defiant one, the result it produces being the same.

Describing the character of the Highlanders, as shown by their conduct in our Highland regiments, and the impossibility of recruiting from them in future, if harsh evictions are not stopped, the reverend gentleman continued :—

Let me give you words more eloquent than mine on this point, which will show the infatuation of our Government in allowing her bravest soldiers to be driven to foreign lands and to be crushed and oppressed by the tyrant's rod. After having asked, What have these people done against the state, when they were so remorselessly driven from their native shores, year by year in batches of thousands? What class have they wronged that they should suffer a penalty so dreadful? this writer gives the answer :—"They have done no wong. Yearly they have sent forth their thousands from their glens to follow the battle flag of Britain wherever it flew. It was a Highland *rearlorn* hope that followed the broken wreck of Cumberland's army after the disastrous day at Fontenoy when more British soldiers lay dead upon the field than fell at Waterloo itself. It was another Highland regiment that scaled the rock-face over the St. Lawrence, and first formed a line in the September dawn on the level sward of Abraham. It was a Highland line that broke the power of the Maharatta hordes and gave Wellington his maiden victory at Assaye. Thirty-four battalions marched from these glens to fight in America, Germany, and India ere the 18th century had run its course; and yet, while abroad over the earth, Highlanders were the first in assault and the last in retreat, their lowly homes in far away glens were being dragged down, and the wail of women and the cry of children went out on the same breeze that bore too upon its wings the scent of heather, the freshness of gorse blossom, and the myriad sweets that made the lowly life of Scotland's peasantry blest with health and happiness. These are crimes done in the dark hours of strife, and amid the blaze of man's passions, that sometimes make the blood run cold as we read them; but they are not so terrible in their red-handed vengeance as the cold malignity of a civilised law, which permits a brave and noble race to disappear by the operation of its legalised injustice. To convert the Highland glens into vast wastes untenanted by human beings; to drive forth to distant and inhospitable shores men whose forefathers had held their own among these hills, despite Roman legion, Saxon archer, or Norman chivalry, men whose sons died freely for England's honour through those wide dominions their bravery had won for her. Such was the work of laws formed in a cruel mockery of name by the Commons of England. Thus it was, that about the year 1808 the stream of Highland soldiery which had been gradually ebbing, gave symptoms of running completely dry. Recruits for Highland regiments could not be obtained for the simple reason that the Highlands had been depopulated. Six regiments which from the date of their foundation had worn the kilt and bonnet were ordered to lay aside there distinctive uniform and henceforth became merged into the ordinary line corps. From the mainland the work of destruction passed rapidly to the isles. These remote resting places of the Celt were quickly cleared, during the first ten years of the great war, Skye had given 4000 of its sons to the army. It has been computed that 1600 Skyemen stood in the ranks at Waterloo. To-day in Skye, far as the eye can reach nothing but a bare brown waste is to be seen, where still the mounds and ruined gables rise over the melancholy landscapes, sole vestiges of a soldier race for ever passed away."

Again the same writer in speaking of the strength of the

rank and file of Irishmen and Scotchmen who were engaged
in the Russian war in the year 1854, says :—

"Victorious in every fight, the army perished miserably from want.
Then came frantic efforts to replace that stout rank and file that lay
beneath the mounds on Cathcart's Hill, and at Scutari, but it could not
be done.   Men were indeed got together, but they were as unlike the
stuff that had gone, as the sapling is unlike the forest tree."   "Has the
nation," he asks, "ever realised the full meaning of the failure to carry
the Redan on the 8th of September ?   'The old soldiers behaved admirably and stood by their officers to the last, but the young,' writes an
onlooker, 'were deficient in discipline and in confidence in their officers.'
He might have added more : They were the sweepings of the large
crowded cities.   It is in moments such as this, that the cabin on the
hillside, the shieling in the Highland glen, become towers of strength
to the nation that possesses them.   It is in moments such as this that
between the peasant-born soldier and the man who first saw light in a
crowded court, between the coster and the cottier there comes that
gulf which measures the distance between victory and defeat.   Alma and
Inkerman on the one side, the Redan on the 18th June and 8th September on the other." *

The question which confronts us now is, Is there any remedy for all
this ?   Can the work of depopulation in the Highlands be reversed ?
We believe there is a remedy and that in a great measure the evil which
has been done can be reversed.   It was the opinion of a few far-seeing
men among us, when the mania for monster sheep farms began, that
they would have their day and that again the hand of providence would
take another turn for the better.   This was especially the opinion of old
Lachlan Mackenzie, Lochcarron, a household name in the Highlands,
who raised his powerful voice against the system of depopulation which
then began by preaching a series of sermons from the 5th chapter of
Isaiah, 8th v., "Woe unto them that join house to house and lay field to
field, till there be no place that they may be placed alone in the midst
of the earth.   In mine ears said the Lord of Hosts of a truth many
houses shall be desolate even great and fair without inhabitant."   He
said that the system would be altered, or that the sheep would be
destroyed in a way that was not expected in Scotland.   He did not
take upon himself to determine the times or the seasons of the great
alteration which he predicted.   But when one, in private conversation,
mentioned to him that many thousands of sheep had been lost in a snow

* Major W. S. Butler, in *MacMillan's Magazine* for May, 1878.

storm, and took occasion to say that Mr. Lachlan's predictions were thus in the way of being fulfilled, he replied, that it was not in this way that he anticipated a change ; he was not looking to present appearances—it was neither the snow of winter nor such heat as would dry the tongue of the raven that would bring deliverance from the system of oppression and grinding the face of the poor. But added he, if the people would be earnest and faithful in prayer, the deliverance will come sooner than it arrived to the children of Israel in Babylon. This was said in the year 1816, when the new leases were making great changes in Lochcarron.

These words which seem to have been delivered in a prophetic strain are now beginning to be fulfilled. It is felt on every side that monster farms are not the thing after all, and that smaller holdings are more profitable to the owner of the soil, as well as more beneficial to the nation at large. The hand of Him who guides the stars seems to fight against them in the seasons and in various ways ; among others in the competition of foreign markets—in the increased quantities of preserved meat from America and Australia. From all these causes, it is evident that the days of unwieldy farms are numbered, and as for the deer forests, I hope they have received their death blow, as a certain member of Parliament remarked, in the Hares and Rabbits Bill.

Mr. MacMillan concluded by an eloquent appeal to his brother ministers of religion to rouse themselves and oppose their influence to the tyranny of the strong and powerful in their grinding and heartless conduct towards the poor and the weak ; after which he received the unanimous thanks of one of the largest, as well as one of the most enthusiastic meetings ever held in the capital of the Highlands.

In January, 1882, news had reached Inverness that Murdo Munro, one of the most comfortable tenants on the Leckmelm property had been turned out, with his wife and young family in the snow; whereupon the writer started to enquire into the facts, and spent a whole day among the people. What he had seen proved to be as bad as any of the evictions of the past, except that it applied in this instance only to one family. Murdo Munro was too independent for the local managers, and to some extent led the people in their

opposition to Mr. Pirie's proceedings : he was first persecuted
and afterwards evicted in the most cruel fashion.   Other
reasons were afterwards given for the manner in which this
poor man and his family were treated, but it has been shown
conclusively, in a report published at the time, that these
reasons were an after-thought.*   From this report we shall
quote a few extracts : —

So long as the laws of the land permit men like Mr. Pirie to drive
from the soil, without compensation, the men who, by their labour and
money, made their properties what they are, it must be admitted that
he is acting within his legal rights, however much we may deplore the
manner in which he has chosen to exercise them.   We have to deal
more with the system which allows him to act thus, than with the
special reasons which he considers sufficient to justify his proceedings ;
and if his conduct in Leckmelm will, as I trust it may, hasten on a
change in our land legislation, the hardships endured by the luckless
people who had the misfortune to come under his unfeeling yoke, and
his ideas of moral right and wrong, will be more than counterbalanced
by the benefits which will in consequence ultimately accrue to the
people at large.   This is why I, and, I believe, the public take such an
interest in this question of the evictions at Leckmelm.

I have made the most careful and complete inquiry possible among
Mr. Pirie's servants, the tenants, and the people of Ullapool.   Mr.
Pirie's local manager, after I had informed him of my object, and put him
on his guard as to the use which I might make of his answers, informed
me that he never had any fault to find with Munro, that he always
found him quite civil, and that he had nothing to say against him.
The tenants, without exception, spoke of him as a good neighbour.
The people of Ullapool, without exception, so far as I could discover,
after inquiries from the leading men in every section of the community,
speak well of him, and condemn Mr. Pirie.   Munro is universally
spoken of as one of the best and most industrious workmen in the whole
parish, and, by his industry and sobriety, he has been able to save a
little money in Leckmelm, where he was able to keep a fairly good
stock on his small farm, and worked steadily with a horse and cart.
The stock handed over by him to Mr. Pirie consisted of 1 bull, 2 cows,

---

* See Pamphlet published at the time entitled *Report on the Leckmelm
Evictions, by Alexander Mackenzie, F.S.A. Scot., Editor of the " Celtic
Magazine," and Dean of Guild of Inverness.*

1 stirk, 1 Highland pony, and about 40 sheep, which represented a considerable saving. Several of the other tenants had a similar stock, and some of them had even more, all of which they had to dispense with under the new arrangements, and consequently lost the annual income in money and produce available therefrom. We all know that the sum received for this stock cannot last long, and cannot be advantageously invested in anything else. The people must now live on their small capital, instead of what it produced, so long as it lasts, after which they are sure to be helpless, and many of them become chargeable to the parish.

The system of petty tyranny which prevails at Leckmelm is scarcely credible. Contractors have been told not to employ Munro. For this I have the authority of some of the contractors themselves. Local employers of labour were requested not to employ any longer people who had gone to look on among the crowd, while Munro's family, goods, and furniture, were being turned out. Letters were received by others complaining of the same thing from higher quarters, and threatening ulterior consequences. Of all this I have the most complete evidence, but in the interests of those involved I shall mention no names, except in Court, where I challenge Mr. Pirie and his subordinates to the proof if they deny it.

. . . .

The extract in the action of removal was signed only on the 24th of January last in Dingwall. On the following day the charge is dated, and two days after, on the 27th of January, the eviction is complete. When I visited the scene on Friday morning I found a substantially built cottage, and a stable at the end of it, unroofed to within three feet of the top on either side, and the whole surroundings a perfect scene of desolation ; the thatch, and part of the furniture, including portions of broken bedsteads, tubs, basins, teapots, and various other articles, strewn outside. The cross-beams, couples, and cabars were still there, a portion of the latter bought from Mr. Pirie's manager, and paid for within the last three years. The Sheriff-officers had placed a padlock on the door, but I made my way to the inside of the house through one of the windows from which the frame and glass had been removed.   I found that the house, before the partitions had been removed, consisted of two good sized rooms and a closet, with a fireplace and chimney in each gable, the crook still hanging in one of them, the officer having apparently been unable to remove it after a considerable amount of wrenching. The kitchen window, containing eight panes of glass, was still whole, but the closet window, with four panes, had been smashed ; while the one in the "ben" end of the house had been removed. The cottage, as crofters' houses go, must have been fairly comfortable. Indeed, the cottages in Leckmelm are altogether superior to the usual run of crofters' houses on the West Coast, and the tenants are allowed to have been the most comfortable in all respects in the parish, before the land was taken from them. They are certainly not the poor, miserable creatures, badly housed, which Mr. Pirie and his friends led the public to believe within the last two years.

The barn, in which the wife and infant had to remain all night, had the upper part of both gables blown out by the recent storm, and the door was scarcely any protection from the weather. The potatoes, which had been thrown out in showers of snow, were still there, gathered, and a little earth put over them by the friendly neighbours.

The mother and children wept piteously during the eviction, and many of the neighbours, afraid to succour or shelter them, were visibly affected to tears ; and the whole scene was such that, if Mr. Pirie could have seen it, I feel sure that he would never consent to be held responsible for another. His humanity would soon drive his stern ideas of legal right out of his head, and we would hear no more of evictions at Leckmelm.

Those of the tenants who are still at Leckmelm are permitted to remain in their cottages as half-yearly tenants on payment of 12s. per annum, but liable to be removed at any moment that their absolute lord may take it into his head to evict them; or, what is much more precarious, when they may give the slightest offence to any of his meanest subordinates.

LOCHCARRON.

The following account was written in April, 1882, after a most careful enquiry on the spot :—So much whitewash has been distributed in our Northern newspapers of late by " Local Correspondents," in the interest of personal friends who are responsible for the Lochcarron evictions—the worst and most indefensible that have ever been attempted even in the Highlands—that we consider it a duty to state the actual

facts. We are really sorry for those more immediately concerned, but our friendly feeling for them otherwise cannot
be allowed to come between us and our plain duty. A few
days before the famous "Battle of the Braes," in the Isle of
Skye, we received information that summonses of ejectment
were served on Mackenzie and Maclean, Lochcarron. The
writer at once communicating with Mr. Dugald Stuart, the
proprietor, intimating to him the statements received, and
asking him if they were accurate, and if Mr. Stuart had anything to say in explanation of them. Mr. Stuart immediately
replied, admitting the accuracy of the statements generally,
but maintaining that he had good and valid reasons for
carrying out the evictions, which he expressed himself
anxious to explain to us on the following day, while passing
through Inverness on his way South. Unfortunately, his
letter reached us too late, and we were unable to see him.
The only reason which he vouchsafed to give in his letter
was to the following effect :—"Was it at all likely that he, a
Highlander, born and brought up in the Highlands, the son
of a Highlander, and married to a Highland lady, would be
guilty of evicting any of his tenants without good cause?"
We replied that, unfortunately, all these reasons could be
urged by most of those who had in the past depopulated the
country, but expressing a hope that, in his case, the facts
stated by him would prove sufficient to restrain him from
carrying out his determination to evict parents admittedly
innocent of their sons' proceedings, even if those proceedings were unjustifiable. The day immediately preceding
the "Battle of the Braes" we proceeded to Lochcarron to
make enquiry on the spot, and the writer on his return
from Skye a few days later, reported as follows to the Highland Land Law Reform Association :—

"Of all the cases of eviction which have hitherto come

under my notice I never heard of any so utterly unjustifiable as those now in course of being carried out by Mr. D. Stuart in Lochcarron. The circumstances which led up to these evictions are as follows :—In March, 1881, two young men, George Mackenzie and Donald Maclean, masons, entered into a contract with Mr. Stuart's ground-officer for the erection of a sheep fank, and a dispute afterwards arose as to the payment for the work. When the factor, Mr. Donald Macdonald, Tormore, was some time afterwards collecting the rents in the district, the contracters approached him and related their grievance against the ground-officer, who, while the men were in the room, came in and addressed them in libellous and defamatory language, for which they have since obtained substantial damages and expenses, in all amounting to £22 13s. 8d., in the Sheriff Court of the County. I have a certified copy of the whole proceedings in Court in my possession, and, without going into the merits, what I have just stated is the result, and Mr. Stuart and his ground-officer became furious.

"The contractors are two single men who live with their parents, the latter being crofters on Mr. Stuart's property, and as the real offenders—if such can be called men who have stood up for and succeeded in establishing their rights and their characters in Court—could not be got at, Mr. Stuart issued summonses of ejection against their parents— parents who, in one of the cases at least, strongly urged his son not to proceed against the ground-officer, pointing out to him that an eviction might possibly ensue, and that it was better even to suffer in character and purse than run the risk of eviction from his holding at the age of eighty. We have all heard of the doctrine of visiting the sins of the parents upon the children, but it has been left for Mr. Dugald Stuart of Lochcarron and his ground-officer, in the present generation—the highly-favoured nineteenth century—to reverse all this, and to punish the unoffending parents, for proceedings on the part of their children which the Sheriff of the County and all unprejudiced people who know the facts consider fully justifiable.

"Now, so far as I can discover, after careful enquiry among the men's neighbours and in the village of Lochcarron, nothing can be said against either of them. Their characters are in every respect above suspicion. The ground-officer, whom I have seen, admits all this, and makes no pretence that the eviction is for any other reason than the conduct of the young men in prosecuting and succeeding against himself in the Sheriff Court for defamation of character. Maclean paid rent for his present holding for the last 60 years, and never failed to pay it on the appointed day. His father, grandfather, and great-grandfather occupied the same place, and so did their ancestors before them. Indeed, his grand-father held one-half of the township, now occupied by more than a hundred people. The old man is in his 81st year, and bed-ridden—on his death-bed in fact—since the middle of January last, he having then had a paralytic stroke from which it is quite impossible he can ever recover. It was most pitiable to see the aged and frail human wreck as I saw him that day, and to have heard him talking of the cruelty and hard-heartedness of those who took advantage of the existing law to push him out of the home which he has occupied so long, while he is already on the brink of eternity. I quite agreed with him, and I have no hesitation in saying that if Mr. Stuart and his ground-officer only called to see the miserable old man, as I did, their hearts, however adamantine, would melt, and they would at once declare to him that he would be allowed to end his days and die in peace, under the roof which for generations had sheltered himself and his ancestors. The wife is over 70 years of age, and the frail old couple have no one to succour them but the son who has been the cause, by defending his own character, of their present misfortunes. Whatever Mr. Stuart and his ground-officer may do, or attempt to do, the old man will not, and cannot be evicted until he is carried to the churchyard; and it would be far more gracious on their part to relent and allow the old man to die in peace.

"Mackenzie has paid rent for over 40 years, and his ancestors have done so for several generations before him. He is nearly sixty years of age, and is highly popular among his neighbours all of whom are intensely grieved at Mr. Stuart's cruel and hard-hearted conduct towards him and Maclean, and they still hope that he will not proceed to extremities.

"The whole case is a lamentable abuse of the existing law, and such as will do more to secure its abolition, when the facts are fully known, than all the other cases of eviction which have taken place in the Highlands during the present generation. There is no pretence that the case is anything else than a gross and cruel piece of retaliation against the innocent parents for conduct on the part of the sons which must have been very aggravating to this proprietor and his ground-officer, who appear to think themselves fully justified in perpetuating such acts of grossest cruelty and injustice—acts which indeed I dare not characterise as they deserve—but conduct which on the part of the young men has been fully justified and sustained by the courts of the country, and for which the son of a late Vice-Chancellor of England ought to have some respect."

This report was slightly noticed at the time in the local and Glasgow newspapers, and attention was thus directed to

Mr. Stuart's proceedings. His whole conduct appeared so cruelly tyrannical that most people expected him to relent before the day of eviction arrived. But not so : a sheriff-officer and his assistants from Dingwall duly arrived, and proceeded to turn Mackenzie's furniture out of the house. People congregated from all parts of the district, some of them coming more than twenty miles. The sheriff-officer sent for the Lochcarron policemen to aid him, but, notwithstanding, the law which admitted of such unmitigated cruelty and oppression was set at defiance ; the sheriff-officers were deforced, and the furniture returned to the house by the sympathising crowd. What was to be done next ? The Procurator-Fiscal for the county was Mr. Stuart's law agent in carrying out the evictions. How could he criminally prosecute for deforcement in these circumstances ? The Crown authorities found themselves in a dilemma, and through the tyranny of the proprietor on the one hand, and the interference of the Procurator-Fiscal in civil business which has ended in public disturbance and deforcement of the Sheriff's officers, on the other, the Crown authorities found themselves helpless to vindicate the law. This is a pity ; for all right thinking people have almost as little sympathy for law breakers, even when that law is unjust and cruel, as they have for those cruel landlords who, like Mr. Stuart of Lochcarron, bring the law and his own order into disrepute by the oppressive application of it against innocent people. The proper remedy is to have the law abolished, not to break it ; and to bring this about such conduct as that of Mr. Stuart and his ground officer is more potent than all the Land Leagues and Reform Associations in the United Kingdom.*

Mr. William Mackenzie of the *Free Press*, who was on the

* *Celtic Magazine* for July, 1882.

ground, writes, next morning, after the deforcement of the sheriff-officers :—

"During the encounter the local police constable drew his baton, but he was peremptorily ordered to lay it down, and he did so. The officers then gave up the contest ; and left the place about three in the morning. Yesterday, before they left, and in course of the evening, they were offered refreshments, but these they declined. The people are this evening in possession as before.

"When every article was restored to its place, the song and the dance were resumed, the native drink was freely quaffed —for ' freedom an' whisky gang thegither '—the steam was kept up throughout the greater part of yesterday, and Mackenzie's mantelpiece to-day is adorned with a long tier of empty bottles, standing there as monuments of the eventful night of the 29th-30th May, 1882.

> A chuirm sgaoilte chualas an ceòl
> Ard-shòlas an talla nan treun !

"While these things were going on in the quiet township of Slumbay, the Fiery Cross appears to have been despatched over the neighbouring parishes ; and from Kintail, Lochalsh, Applecross, and even Gairloch, the Highlanders began to gather yesterday with the view of helping the Slumbay men, if occasion should arise. Few of these reached Slumbay, but they were in small detachments in the neighbourhood ready at any moment to come to the rescue on the appearance of any hostile force. After all the trains had come and gone for the day, and as neither policemen nor Sheriff's officers had appeared on the scene, these different groups retired to their respective places of abode. The Slumbay men, too, resolved to suspend their festivities. A procession was formed, and, being headed by the piper, they marched triumphantly through Slumbay and Jeantown, and escorted some of the strangers on their way to their homes, returning to Slumbay in course of the night."

As a contrast to Mr. Stuart's conduct we are glad to record the noble action of Mr. C. J. Murray, M.P. for Hastings, who has fortunately for the oppressed tenants on the Lochcarron property, just purchased the estate. He has made it a condition that Maclean and Mackenzie shall be allowed to remain; and a further public scandal has thus been avoided. This is a good beginning for the new proprietor, and we trust to see his action as widely circulated and commended as the tyrannical proceedings of his predecessor have been condemned.

It is also fair to state what we know on the very best authority, namely, that the factor on the estate, Mr. Donald Macdonald, Tormore, strongly urged upon Mr. Stuart not to evict these people, and that his own wife also implored and begged of him not to carry out his cruel and vindictive purpose. Where these agencies failed, it is gratifying to find that Mr. Murray has succeeded; and all parties—landlords and tenants—throughout the Highlands are to be congratulated on the result.

THE 78TH HIGHLANDERS.

IN connection with the evictions from the County of Ross, the following will appropriately come in at this stage. Referring to the glorious deeds of the 78th Highlanders in India, under General Havelock, the editor of the *Northern Ensign* writes :—All modern history, from the rebellion in 1715, to the Cawnpore massacre in 1857, teems with the record of Highland bravery and prowess. What say our Highland evicting lairds to these facts, and to the treatment of the Highlanders ?   What reward have these men received for saving their country, fighting its battles, conquering its enemies, turning the tide of revolt, rescuing women and children from the hands of Indian fiends, and establishing order, when disorder and bloody cruelty have held their murderous carnival ?   And we ask, in the name of men who have, ere now, we fondly hope, saved our gallant country-men and heroic countrywomen at Lucknow ; in the name of those who fought in the trenches of Sebastopol, and proudly planted the British standard on the heights of the Alma, how are they, their fathers, brothers, and little ones treated? Is the mere shuttle-cocking of an irrepressible cry of admira-tion from mouth to mouth, and the setting to music of a song in their praise, all the return the race is to get for such noble acts ?   We can fancy the expression of admiration of High-land bravery at the Dunrobin dinner table, recently, when the dukes, earls, lairds, and other aristocratic notables en-joyed the princely hospitality of the Duke.   We can imagine the mutual congratulations of the Highland lairds as they prided themselves on being proprietors of the soil which gave birth to the race of " Highland heroes ".   Alas, for the blush that would cover their faces if they would allow them-selves to reflect that, in their names, and by their authority, and at their expense, the fathers, mothers, brothers, wives, of the invincible " 78th " have been remorselessly driven from their native soil ; and that, at the very hour when Cawnpore was gallantly retaken, and the ruffian Nana Sahib was obliged to leave the bloody scene of his fiendish massacre, there were Highlanders, within a few miles of the princely Dunrobin, driven from their homes and left to starve and to die in the open field.   Alas, for the blush that would reprint its scarlet dye on their proud faces as they thought in one county alone, since Waterloo was fought,

more than 14,000 of this same "race of heroes" of whom
Canning so proudly boasted, have been haunted out of their
native homes; and that where the pibroch and the bugle
once evoked the martial spirit of thousands of brave hearts,
razed and burning cottages have formed the tragic scenes
of eviction and desolation; and the abodes of a loyal and a
liberty-loving people are made sacred to the rearing of
sheep, and sanctified to the preservation of game! Yes;
we echo back the cry, "Well done, brave Highlanders!"
But to what purpose would it be carried on the wings of the
wind to the once happy straths and glens of Sutherland?
Who, what, would echo back our acclaims of praise?
Perhaps a shepherd's or a gillie's child, playing amid the
unbroken wilds, and innocent of seeing a human face but
that of its own parents, would hear it; or the cry might
startle a herd of timid deer, or frighten a covey of partridges,
or call forth a bleat from a herd of sheep; but men, would
not, could not, hear it. We must go to the backwoods of
Canada, to Detroit, to Hamilton, to Woodstock, to Toronto,
to Montreal; we must stand by the waters of Lake Huron,
or Lake Ontario, where the cry—"Well done, brave Highlanders!" would call up a thousand brawny fellows, and
draw down a tear on a thousand manly cheeks. Or we
must go to the bare rocks that skirt the sea-coast of Sutherland, where the residuary population were generously
treated to barren steeps and inhospitable shores, on which
to keep up the breed of heroes, and fight for the men who
dared—*dared*—to drive them from houses for which they
fought, and from land, which was purchased with the blood
of their fathers. But the cry, "Well done, brave Highlanders," would evoke no effective response from the race.
Need the reader wonder? Wherefore should they fight?
To what purpose did their fathers climb the Peninsular

heights, and gloriously write in blood the superiority of
Britain, when their sons were rewarded by extirpation, or
toleration to starve, in sight of fertile straths and glens
devoted to beasts? These are words of truth and sober-
ness. They are but repetitions in other forms of arguments,
employed by us for years; and we shall continue to ring
changes on them so long as our brave Highland people are
subjected to treatment to which no other race would have
submitted. We are no alarmists. But we tell Highland
proprietors that were Britain some twenty years hence to
have the misfortune to be plunged into such a crisis as the
present, there will be few such men as the Highlanders of
the 78th to fight her battles, and that the country will find
when too late, if another policy towards the Highlanders is
not adopted, that sheep and deer, ptarmigan and grouse,
can do but little to save it in such a calamity.

The Rev. Dr. JOHN KENNEDY.

DR. JOHN KENNEDY, the highly, deservedly respected, and
eminent minister of Dingwall, so long resident among the
scenes which he describes, and so intimately acquainted
with all classes of the people in his native County of Ross,
informs us that it was at a time when the Highlanders
became most distinguished as the most peaceable and
virtuous peasantry in the world—"at the climax of their
spiritual prosperity," in Ross-shire—"that the cruel work of
eviction began to lay waste the hill-sides and the plains of
the north. Swayed by the example of the godly among
them, and away from the influences by which less seques-
tered localities were corrupted, the body of the people in the
Highlands became distinguished as the most peaceable and

virtuous peasantry in Britain. It was just then that they began to be driven off by ungodly oppressors, to clear their native soil for strangers, red deer, and sheep. With few exceptions, the owners of the soil began to act, as if they were also owners of the people, and, disposed to regard them as the vilest part of their estate, they treated them without respect to the requirements of righteousness or to the dictates of mercy. Without the inducement of gain, in the reckless-ness of cruelty, families by hundreds were driven across the sea, or gathered, as the sweepings of the hill-sides, into wretched hamlets on the shore. By wholesale evictions, wastes were formed for the red deer, that the gentry of the nineteenth century might indulge in the sports of the savages of three centuries before. Of many happy households sheep walks were cleared for strangers, who, fattening amidst the ruined homes of the banished, corrupted by their example the few natives who remained. Meanwhile their rulers, while deaf to the Highlanders' cry of oppression, were wasting their sinews and their blood on battle-fields, that, but for their prowess and their bravery, would have been the scene of their country's defeat." *

Mr. CHARLES INNES.

MR. CHARLES INNES is a Tory of the bluest type. He is the Conservative agent for the county of Inverness, Sheriff-Clerk for the County of Ross ; Secretary for the Northern Tory Newspaper and Printing Company ; and general Organiser for the Tory landowners of the North of Scotland. Such a position gives peculiar interest to any

*The Days of the Fathers in Ross-shire, 1861, pp. 15-16.

opinions he may express on a question like this. In July, 1874, he had occasion to defend some of the Bernera crofters, in the Lews, who were tried on a charge of deforcing a sheriff-officer. A Report of the trial was afterwards published, in pamphlet form, containing the speech delivered by Mr. Innes on the occasion, and, it is understood, revised and edited by his own hand. The late Chamberlain of the Lews, it will be remembered, resolved to evict the tenants, since known as "the Bernera Rioters". The sheriff-officer who went to serve the notices of ejectment on them met with a reception which the Crown authorities in the person of the Chamberlain himself, who was also Procurator-Fiscal of the district, construed into the serious charge of deforcement, and the crofters were duly tried for that grave offence. Addressing the jury on their behalf, Mr. Innes eloquently declared that :—

" Love of Fatherland is a feeling which is implanted in the breasts of all men, and in none more so than those in whose veins Celtic blood flows. If, then, gentlemen, that sentiment and that feeling animates you—as I am sure it does—you can, when you think of it, readily understand that love of country not only may be, but is, as strongly felt by these poor men. You can understand what a wrench their heartstrings must receive when 'notice to quit' is served upon them without good cause. Their houses may be mere mud huts, but still they are their homes, and were the homes of their forefathers for many generations ; and, however humble they are, there is, and ever will be, for them a venerated halo of fond and loving memories floating around them. So long as such men pay their rents with regularity ; so long as they conduct themselves decently and with propriety ; so long as they are wishful to remain in possession—I say that the man who summarily, without cause, and, in the face of an under-standing to the contrary, removes them, or attempts to remove them, from the soil on which they were reared, and which they cultivate, and turns them adrift on the cold world, IS NOT A FRIEND OF HIS COUNTRY."

The result was that the so-called "rioters" were dis-missed; their proposed eviction was brought under the notice of their humane proprietor, the late Sir James Matheson of the Lews, Baronet, and they are still in pos-session of their holdings; while the Chamberlain who tried to evict them was shortly after dismissed from his position as virtual king of the Island principality of the Lews, and soon after deprived of the office of Procurator-Fiscal for the district.

COUNTY OF PERTH.

ATHOL.

DONALD MACLEOD, referring to the evictions from this district, says:—"A Duke of Athol can, with propriety, claim the origin of the Highland clearances. Whatever merit the family of Sutherland may take to themselves for the fire and the faggot expulsion of the people from the glens of Sutherland, they cannot claim the merit of originality. The present [6th] Duke of Athol's grandfather cleared Glen Tilt, so far as I can learn, in 1784. This beautiful valley was occupied in the same way as other Highland valleys, each family possessing a piece of arable land, while the pasture was held in common. The people held a right and full liberty to fish in the Tilt, an excellent salmon river, and the pleasure and profits of the chase, with their chief; but the then Duke acquired a great taste for deer. The people were, from time immemorial, accustomed to take their cattle, in the summer season, to a higher glen, which is watered by the river Tarf; but the Duke appointed Glen Tarf for a deer-forest, and built a high dyke at the head of Glen Tilt. The people submitted to this encroachment on their ancient rights. The deer increased and did not pay much regard to the march; they would jump over the dyke and destroy the people's crops; the people complained, and his grace rejoiced; and to gratify the raving propensities of these light-footed animals, he added another slice of some thousand acres of the people's land to the grazing ground of his favourite deer. Gradually the forest extended, and the marks of civilisation were effaced, till the last of the brave Glen Tilt men, who fought and often confronted and defeated the enemies of Scotland and her kings upon many a bloody battle-field were routed off, and bade a final farewell to the beautiful Glen Tilt, which they and their fathers had considered their own healthy and sweet home. An event occurred at this period, according to history, which afforded a pretext to the Duke for this heartless extirpation of the aborigines of Glen Tilt. Highland chieftains else-where were exhibiting their patriotism by raising regiments to serve in the American War, and the Duke of Athol could not be indifferent in such a cause. Great efforts were made to enlist the Glen Tilt people, who are still remem-bered in the district as a strong, athletic race. Perpetual possession of their lands, at their existing rents, was pro-mised them, if they would raise a contingent force equal to a man from each family. Some consented, but the majority, with a praiseworthy resolution not to be dragged at the tail of a chief into a war of which they knew neither the begin-ning nor the end, refused. The Duke flew into a rage, and press-gangs were sent up the glen to carry off the young men by force. One of these companies seized a cripple tailor, who lived at the foot of Beneygloe, and afraid lest he might carry intelligence of their approach up the glen, they bound him, hand and foot, and left him lying on the cold hill-side, where he contracted disease from which he never recovered. By impressment and violence the regiment was at length raised ; and when peace was proclaimed, instead of restoring the soldiers to their friends and their homes, the Duke, as if he had been a trafficker in slaves, was only pre-vented from selling them to the East Indian Company by the mutiny of the regiment. He afterwards pretended great offence at the Glen Tilt people for their obstinacy in refusing to enlist, and it may now be added—to be sold. Their conduct in this affair was given out as the reason why he cleared them out from the glen—an excuse which, in the present day, may increase our admiration of the people, but can never palliate the heartlessness of his conduct. His ireful policy, however, has taken full effect. The romantic Glen Tilt, with its fertile holms and verdant steeps, is little better than a desert. The very deer rarely visit it, and the wasted grass is burned like heather, at the beginning of the year, to make room for the new verdure. On the spot where I found the grass most luxuriant, I traced the seats of thirty cottages, and have no hesitation in saying, that under skill, the industrious habits, and the agricultural facilities, of the present day, the land, once occupied by the tenants of Glen Tilt, is capable of maintaining a thousand people and have a large proportion of sheep and cattle for exportation besides. In the meantime it serves no better purpose than the occasional playground of the Duke, to whom Pope's lines are most appropriate :—

> Proud Nimrod first the bloody chase began,
> A mighty hunter—and his prey was man.
> Our haughty Norman boasts the barbarous name,
> And makes his trembling slaves the royal game,
> The fields are ravished from industrious swains,
> From men their cities, and from gods their fanes.
> In vain kind seasons swell the beaming grain,
> Soft showers, distilled, and suns grow warm in vain ;
> The swain with tears, his prostrate labours yields,
> And, famished, dies amidst his ripening fields.
> What wonder then a beast or subject slain
> Were equal crimes in a despotic reign ?
> Both, doomed alike, for sportive tyrants bled ;
> But while the subject starved, the beast was fed.

" The Glens of Athol are intersected by smaller valleys, presenting various aspects, from the most fertile carse to the
bleakest moorland. But man durst not be seen there. The
image of God is forbidden unless it be stamped upon the
Duke, his foresters, and gamekeepers, that the deer may
not be disturbed."

In 1841 the Parish of Blair Athol had a population of
2231 ; in 1881 it was reduced to 1742, notwithstanding
the great increase in Blair Athol and other rising villages.

———

RANNOCH.

Regarding the state of matters in this district a correspondent writes us as follows :—I am very glad to learn that
you are soon to publish a new edition of your " Highland
Clearances," with Macleod's " Gloomy Memories " included.
You have done good work already in rousing the conscience
of the public against the conduct of certain landlords in the
Highlands, who long ere now should have been held up to
public scorn and execration, as the best means of deterring
others from pursuing a policy which has been so fatal to the
best interests of our beloved land. . . . . And now, if
I am not too late, I should like to direct your attention to a
few authenticated facts connected with two districts in the
Highlands that I am familiar with, and which facts you may
utilise, though I shall merely give notes.

In 1851, the population of the district known as the
Quod Sacra parish of Rannoch numbered altogether 1800 ;
at last Census it was below 900. Even in 1851 it was not
nearly what it was earlier. Why this constant decrease ?

Several no doubt left the district voluntarily; but the great bulk of those who left were evicted.

Take the Slios Mìn, north side of Loch Rannoch, first. Fifty years ago the farm of Ardlarich, near the west end, was tenanted by three farmers who were in good circumstances. These were turned out, to make room for one large farmer, who was rouped out last year, penniless; and the farm is now tenantless. The next place, further east, is the township of Killichoan, containing about thirty to forty houses, with small crofts attached to each. The crofters here are very comfortable and happy, and their houses and crofts are models of what industry, thrift, and good taste can effect. Further east is the farm of Liaran, now tenantless. Fifty years ago it was farmed by seven tenants who were turned out to make room for one man, and that at a lower rent than was paid by the former tenants. Further, in the same direction, there are Aulich, Craganour, and Annat, every one of them tenantless. These three farms, lately in the occupation of one tenant, and for which he paid a rental of £900, at one time maintained fifty to sixty families in comfort, all of whom have vanished, or were virtually banished from their native land.

It is only right to say that the present proprietor is not responsible for the eviction of any of the smaller tenants; the deed was done before he came into possession. On the contrary, he is very kind to his crofter tenantry, but unfortunately for him he inherits the fruits of a bad policy, which has been the ruin of the Rannoch estates.

Then take the Slios Garbh, south-side of Loch Rannoch. Beginning in the west-end, we have Georgetown, which, about fifty years ago, contained twenty-five or twenty-six houses, every one of which were knocked down by the late Laird of Struan, and the people evicted. The crofters of

Finnart were ejected in the same way. Next comes the township of Camghouran, a place pretty similar to Killichoan, but smaller. The people are very industrious, cleanly, and fairly comfortable, reflecting much credit upon themselves and the present proprietor. Next comes Dall, where there used to be a number of tenants, but now in the hands of the proprietor, an Englishman. The estate of Innerhaden, comes next. It used to be divided into ten lots—two held by the laird, and eight by as many tenants. The whole is now in the hands of one family. The rest of Bun-Rannoch includes the estates of Dalchosnie, Lassintullich, and Crossmount, where there used to be a large number of small tenants—most of them well-to-do—but now held by five.

Lastly, take the north side of the river Dubhag, which flows out from Loch Rannoch, and is erroneously called the Tummel. Kinloch, Druimchurn, and Druimchaisteil, always in the hands of three tenants, are now held by one. Drumaglass contains a number of small holdings, with good houses on many of them. Balmore, which always had six tenants in it, has now only one, the remaining portion of it being laid out in grass parks. Ballintuim, with a good house upon it, is tenantless. Auchitarsin, where there used to be twenty houses, is now reduced to four. The whole district from, and including, Kinloch to Auchitarsin belongs to General Sir Alastair Macdonald of Dalchosnie, Commander of Her Majesty's Forces in Scotland. His father, Sir John, during his life, took a great delight in having a numerous, thriving, and sturdy tenantry on the estates of Dalchosnie, Kinloch, Lochgarry, Dunalastair, and Morlaggan. On one occasion his tenant of Dalchosnie offered to take from Sir John on lease all the land on the north side of the river. " Ay man," said he, "You would take all that land, would you, and

turn out all my people! Who would I get, if my house took
fire, to put it out?"

The present proprietor has virtually turned out the great
bulk of those that Sir John had loved so well. Though, it
is said, he did not evict any man directly, he is alleged
to have made their positions so hot for them that they had
to leave. Sir John could have raised hundreds of Volunteers on his estates—men who would have died for the
gallant old soldier. But how many could be now raised by
his son? Not a dozen men; though he goes about in-
specting Volunteers, and praising the movement officially
throughout the length and breadth of Scotland.

The author of the *New Statistical Account*, writing of the
Parish of Fortingall, of which the district referred to by our
correspondent forms a part, says : " At present [1838] no
part of the parish is more populous than it was in 1790;
whereas in several districts, the population has since decreased one half; and the same will be found to have taken
place, though not perhaps in so great a proportion, in most
or all of the pastoral districts of the County ".

According to the Census of 1801 the population was	. 3875.
,, ,, ,, ,, 1811 ,, ,, ,,	. 3236.
,, ,, ,, ,, 1821 ,, ,, ,,	. 3189.
,, ,, ,, ,, 1831 ,, ,, ,,	. 3067.
In 1881 it was reduced to	. 1690.

Upwards of 120 families, the same writer says, " crossed
the Atlantic from this parish, since the previous Account
was drawn up [in 1791], besides many individuals of both
sexes ; while many others have sought a livelihood in the
Low Country, especially in the great towns of Edinburgh,
Glasgow, Dundee, Perth, Crieff, and others. The system
of uniting several farms together, and letting them to one

individual has more than any other circumstance" produced this result.

———

BREADALBANE.

Mr. R. Alister, author of *Barriers to the National Prosperity of Scotland*, had a controversy with the Marquis of Breadalbane in 1853 about the eviction of his tenantry. In a letter dated July, of that year, Mr. Alister made a charge against his Lordship which, for obvious reasons, he never attempted to answer, as follows:—" Your Lordship states that in reality there has been no depopulation of the district. This, and other parts of your Lordship's letter, would certainly lead any who know nothing of the facts to suppose that there had been no clearings on the Breadalbane estates; whereas it is generally believed that your Lordship removed, since 1834, no less than 500 families! Some may think this a small matter; but I do not. I think it is a great calamity for a family to be thrown out, destitute of the means of life, without a roof over their heads, and cast upon the wide sea of an unfeeling world. In Glenqueich, near Amulree, some sixty families formerly lived, where there are now only four or five; and in America, there is a glen inhabited by its ousted tenants, and called Glenqueich still. Yet, forsooth, it is maintained there has been no depopulation here! The desolations here look like the ruins of Irish cabins, although the population of Glenqueich were always characterized as being remarkably thrifty, economical, and wealthy. On the Braes of Taymouth, at the back of Drummond Hill, and at Tullochyoule, some forty or fifty families formerly resided where there is not one now!

Glenorchy, by the returns of 1831, showed a population of 1806; in 1841, 831;—is there no depopulation there? Is it true that in Glenetive there were sixteen tenants a year or two ago, where there is not a single one now? Is it true, my Lord, that you purchased an island on the west coast, called Ling, where some twenty-five families lived at the beginning *of this year*, but who are now cleared off to make room for one tenant, for whom an extensive steading is now being erected! If my information be correct, I shall allow the public to draw their own conclusions; but, from every thing that I have heard, I believe that your Lordship has done more to exterminate the Scottish peasantry than any man now living; and perhaps you ought to be ranked next to the Marquis of Stafford in the uneviable clearing cele-brities.   If I have over-estimated the clearances at 500 families, please to correct me." As we have already said, his Lordship thought it prudent, and by far the best policy, not to make the attempt.

In another letter the same writer says:—" You must be aware that your late father raised 2300 men during the last war, and that 1600 of that number were from the Breadalbane estates.   My statement is, that 150 could not *now* be raised. Your Lordship has most carefully evaded all allusion to this,—perhaps the worst charge of the whole.   From your Lordship's silence I am surely justified in concluding that you may endeavour to evade the question, but you dare not attempt an open contradiction.   I have often made inquiries of Highlanders on this point, and the number above stated was the *highest* estimate.   Many who should know, state to me that your Lordship would not get *fifty* followers from the whole estates; and another says:—" Why, he would not get half-a-dozen, and not one of them unless they could not possibly do otherwise ".   This, then, is the position of the question ; in 1793-4, there was such a numerous, hardy, and industrious population on the Breadalbane estates, that there could be spared of valorous defenders of their country in her hour of danger . 1600

Highest estimate now 150

„ Banished 1450

" *Per Contra*—Game of all sorts increased a hundred-fold."

In 1831, Glenorchy, of which his Lordship of Breadalbane was proprietor, the population, was 1806 ; in 1841 it was reduced to 831. Those best acquainted with the Breadalbane estates, assert that on the whole property, no less than 500 families, or about 2,500 souls, were driven into exile by the hard-hearted Marquis of that day.

It is, however, gratifying to know that the present Lord Breadalbane, who is descended from a different and remote branch of the family, is an excellent landlord, and takes an entirely different view of his duties and relationship to the tenants on his vast property.

COUNTY OF ARGYLL.

In many parts of Argyllshire the people have been weeded out none the less effectively, that the process generally was of a milder nature than that adopted in some of the places already described. By some means or other, however, the ancient tenantry have largely disappeared to make room for the sheep-farmer and the sportsman. Mr. Somerville, Lochgilphead, writing on this subject, says, "The watchword of all is exterminate, exterminate the native race. Through this monomania of landlords the cottier population is all but extinct ; and the substantial yeoman is undergoing the same process of dissolution." He then proceeds :— " About nine miles of country on the west side of Loch Awe, in Argyllshire, that formerly maintained 45 families, are now rented by one person as a sheep-farm ; and in the island of Luing, same county, which formerly contained about 50 substantial farmers, besides cottiers, this number is now reduced to about six. The work of eviction commenced by giving, in many cases, to the ejected population, facilities and pecuniary aid for emigration ; but now the people are turned adrift, penniless and shelterless, to seek a precarious subsistence on the sea-board, in the nearest hamlet or village, and in the cities, many of whom sink down helpless paupers on our poor-roll ; and others, festering in our villages, form a formidable Arab population, who drink our money contributed as parochial relief. This wholesale depopulation is perpetrated, too, in a spirit of invidiousness, harshness, cruelty, and injustice, and must eventuate in permanent injury to the moral, political, and social interests of the kingdom. . . . . The immediate effects of this new system are the dis-association of the people from the land, who are virtually denied the right to labour on God's creation. In L——, for instance, garden ground and small allotments of land are in great demand by families, and especially by the aged, whose labouring days are done, for the purpose of keeping cows, and by which they might be able to earn an honest, independent maintainence for their families, and whereby their children might be brought up to labour, instead of growing up vagabonds and thieves. But such, even in our centres of population, cannot be got ; the whole is let in large farms and turned into grazing. The few patches of bare pasture, formed by the delta of rivers, the detritus of rocks, and tidal deposits, are let for grazing at the exorbitant rent of £3 10s. each for a small Highland cow ; and the small space to be had for garden ground is equally extravagant. The consequence of these exorbitant rents and the want of agricultural facilities is a depressed, degraded, and pauperised population." These remarks are only too true, and applicable not only in Argyllshire, but throughout the Highlands generally.

A deputation from the Glasgow Highland Relief Board, consisting of Dr. Robert Macgregor, and Mr. Charles R. Baird, their Secretary, visited Mull, Ulva, Iona, Tiree, Coll, and part of Morvern in 1849, and they immediately afterwards issued a printed report, on the state of these places, from which a few extracts will prove instructive. They inform us that the population of

The Island of Mull,

according to the Government Census in 1821, was 10,612 ; in 1841, 10,064. In 1871, we find it reduced to 6441, and by the Census of 1881, now before us, it is stated at 5624, or a fraction more than half the number that inhabited the Island in 1821.

Tobermory, we are told, "has been for some time the resort of the greater part of the small crofters and cottars, *ejected* from their holdings and houses on the surrounding estates, and thus there has been a great accumulation of distress"; and then we are told that "severe as the destitution has been in the rural districts, we think it has been still more so in Tobermory and other villages"—a telling comment on, and reply to, those who would now have us believe that the evictors of those days and of our own were acting the character of wise benefactors when they ejected the people from the inland and rural districts of the various counties to wretched villages, and rocky hamlets on the sea-shore.

Ulva.—The population of the Island of Ulva in 1849, was 360 souls. The reporters state that "a large portion" of it "has lately been converted into a sheep farm, and consequently a number of small crofters and cottars have been warned away" by Mr. Clark. "Some of these will find great difficulty in settling themselves anywhere, and all of them have little prospect of employment. . . . . Whatever may be the ultimate effect, to the landowners, of the conversion of a number of small crofts into large farms, we need scarcely say that this process is causing much poverty and misery among the crofters." How Mr. Clark carried out his intention of evicting the tenantry of Ulva may be seen from the fact that the population of 360 souls, in 1849, was reduced to 51 in 1881.

KILFINICHEN.—In this district we are told that, "The crofters and cottars having been warned off, 26 individuals emigrated to America at their own expense, and one at that of the Parochial Board; a good many removed to Kinloch, where they are now in great poverty, and those who remained were not allowed to cultivate any ground for crop or even garden stuffs. The stock and other effects of a number of crofters on Kinloch, last year (1848), and whose rents averaged from £5 to £15 per annum, having been sequestrated and sold, these parties are now reduced to a state of pauperism, having no employment or means of subsistence whatever." As to the cottars it is said that "the great mass of them are now in a very deplorable state". On the estate of

GRIBUN, Colonel Macdonald, of Inchkenneth, the proprietor, gave the people plenty of work, by which they were quite independent of relief from any quarter, and the character which he gives to the deputation of the people generally is most refreshing, when we compare it with the baseless charges usually made against them by the majority of his class. The reporters state that "Colonel Macdonald spoke in high terms of the honesty of the people and of their great patience and forbearance under their severe privations". It is gratifying to be able to record this simple act of justice, not only as the people's due, but specially to the credit of Colonel Macdonald's memory and goodness of heart.

BUNESSAN.—Respecting this district, belonging to the Duke of Argyll, our authority says :—" It will be recollected that the [Relief] Committee, some time ago, advanced £128 to assist in procuring provisions for a number of emigrants from the Duke of Argyll's estate, in the Ross of Mull and

Iona, in all 243 persons—125 adults and 118 children. When there, we made inquiry into the matter, and were informed [by those as it proved, quite ignorant of the facts] that the emigration had been productive of much good, as the parties who emigrated could not find the means of subsistence in this country, and had every *prospect* of doing so in Canada, where all of them had relations; and also because the land occupied by some of these emigrants had been given to increase the crofts of others. Since our return home, however, we have received the very melancholy and distressing intelligence, that many of these emigrants had been seized with cholera on their arrival in Canada; that not a few of them had fallen victims to it; and that the survivors had suffered great privations." Compare the "prospect," of much good, predicted for these poor creatures, with the sad reality of having been forced away to die a terrible death immediately on their arrival on a foreign shore !

IONA, at this time, contained a population of 500, reduced in 1881 to 243. It also is the property of the Duke of Argyll, as well as

The ISLAND OF TIREE, the population of which is given in the report as follows:—In 1755 it was 1509, increasing in 1777, to 1681; in 1801, to 2416; in 1821, to 4181; and in 1841, to 4687. In 1849, "after considerable emigrations," it was 3903; while in 1881, it is reduced to 2733. The deputation recommended emigration from Tiree, as imperatively necessary, but they "call especial attention to the necessity of emigration being conducted on proper principles, or, 'on a system calculated to promote the permanent benefit of those who emigrate, and of those who remain,' because we have reason to fear that not a few parties in these districts are anxious to get rid of the small crofters and cottars at all hazard, and without making sufficient provision for their future comfort and settlement elsewhere ; and because we have seen the very distressing account of the privations and sufferings of the poor people who emigrated from Tiree and the Ross of Mull to Canada this year (1849), and would spare no pains to prevent a recurrence of such deplorable circumstances. As we were informed that the Duke of Argyll had expended nearly £1200 on account of the emigrants (in all 247 souls) from Tiree ; as the Committee advanced £131 15s. to purchase provisions for them ; and as funds were remitted to Montreal to carry them up the country, we sincerely trust that the account we have seen of their sufferings in Canada is somewhat over-charged, and that it is not at all events to be ascribed to want of due provision being made for them, ere they left this country, to carry them to their destination. Be this as it may, however, we trust that no emigration will in future be promoted by proprietors or others, which will not secure, as far as human effort can, *the benefit of those who emigrate*, as well as of those who are left at home. . . . Being aware of the poverty of the great majority of the inhabitants of this Island, and of the many difficulties with which they have to contend, we were agreeably surprised to find their dwellings remarkably neat and clean—very superior indeed, both externally and internally, to those of the other Islands ; nay, more, such as would bear comparison with cottages in any part of the kingdom. The inhabitants too, we believe, are active and enterprising, and, if once put in a fair way of doing so, would soon raise themselves to comfort and independence." Very good indeed, Tiree !

THE ISLAND OF COLL, which is separated from Tiree by

a channel only two miles in width, had a population, in 1755, of 1193; in 1771, of 1200; in 1801, of 1162; in 1821, of 1264. In 1841, it reached 1409. At the time of the visit of the Deputation, from whose report we quote, the population of the Island was down to 1235; while in 1881, it had fallen to 643. The deputation report that during the destitution the work done by the Coll people " approximates, if it does exceed, the supplies given;" they are " hard working and industrious. . . . . . We saw considerable tracts of ground which we were assured might be reclaimed and cultivated with profit, and are satisfied that fishing is a resource capable of great improvement, and at which therefore, many of the people might be employed to advantage ; we are disposed to think that, by a little attention and prudent outlay of capital, the condition of the people here might ere long be greatly improved. The grand difficulty in the way, however, is the want of capital. Mr. Maclean, the principal proprietor, always acted most liberally when he had it in his power to do so, but, unfortunately he has no longer the ability, aud the other two proprietors are also under trust." Notwithstanding these possibilities the population has now been reduced to less than one half what it was only forty years ago.

WE shall now return to the mainland portion of County, and take a glance at the parish of

MORVERN.

THE population of this extensive Parish in 1755, was 1223; in 1795 it increased to 1764; in 1801 to 2000; in 1821 it was 1995; in 1831 it rose to 2137; and in 1841 it came down to 1781; in 1871 it was only 973; while in the Census Returns for 1881 we find it stated at 714, or less than one third of what it was fifty years ago.

The late Dr. Norman Macleod, after describing the happy state of things which existed in this parish before the clearances, says :—" But all this was changed when those tacksmen were swept away to make room for the large sheep farms, and when the remnants of the people flocked from their empty glens to occupy houses in wretched villages near the sea-shore, by way of becoming fishers—often where no fish could be caught. The result has been that 'the Parish' for example, which once had a population of 2,200 souls, and received only £11 per annum from public (Church) funds for the support of the poor, expends now [1863] under the poor law upwards of £600 annually, with a population diminished by one-half, [since diminished to one third] and with poverty increased in a greater ratio. . . . . . Below these gentlemen tacksmen were those who paid a much lower rent, and who lived very comfortably, and shared hospitality with others, the gifts which God gave them. I remember a group of men, tenants in a large glen, which now has not a smoke in it, as the Highlanders say, throughout its length of twenty miles. They had the custom of entertaining in rotation every traveller who cast himself on their hospitality. The host on the occasion was bound to summon his neighbours to the homely feast. It was my good fortune to be a guest when they received the present minister of 'the Parish' while *en route* to visit some of his flock. We had a most sumptuous feast—oat-cakes, crisp and fresh from the fire ; cream, rich and thick, and more beautiful than nectar,—whatever that may be ; blue Highland cheese, finer than Stilton; fat hens, slowly cooked on the fire in a pot of potatoes, without their skins, and with fresh butter—'stored hens', as the superb dish was called; and though last, not least, tender kid, roasted as nicely as Charles Lamb's cracklin' pig. All was served up with the utmost propriety, on a table covered with a fine white cloth, and with all the requisites for a comfortable dinner, including the champagne of elastic, buoyant, and exciting mountain air. The manners and conversations of those men would have pleased the best-bred gentleman. Every thing was so simple, modest, unassuming, unaffected, yet so frank and cordial. The conversation was such as might be heard at the table of any intelligent man. Alas! there is not a vestige remaining of their homes. I know not whither they are gone, but they have left no representatives behind. The land in the glen is divided between sheep, shepherds, and the shadows of the clouds."*

The Rev. Donald Macleod, editor of *Good Words*—describing the death of the late Dr. John Macleod, the "minister of the Parish" referred to by Dr. Norman in the above quotation, and for fifty years minister of Morvern—says, of the noble patriarch:—" His later years were spent in pathetic loneliness. He had seen his parish almost emptied of its people. Glen after glen had been turned into sheep-walks, and the cottages in which generations of gallant Highlanders had lived and died were unroofed, their torn walls and gables left standing like mourners beside the grave, and the little plots of garden or of cultivated enclosure allowed to merge into the moorland pasture. He had seen every property in the parish change hands, and though, on the whole, kindly and pleasant proprietors came, in place of the old families, yet they were strangers to the people, neither understanding their language nor their ways. The consequence was that

*Reminiscences of a Highland Parish—Good Words, 1863.

they perhaps scarcely realised the havoc produced by the
changes they inaugurated. 'At one stroke of the pen,' he
said to me, with a look of sadness and indignation, 'two
hundred of the people were ordered off.—There was not
one of these whom I did not know, and their fathers before
them ; and finer men and women never left the Highlands.'
He thus found himself the sole remaining link between the
past and present—the one man above the rank of a peasant
who remembered the old days and the traditions of the
people. The sense of change was intensely saddened as he
went through his parish and passed ruined houses here,
there, and everywhere. 'There is not a smoke there now,'
he used to say with pathos, of the glens which he had
known tenanted by a manly and loyal peasantry, among
whom lived song and story and the elevating influences of
brave traditions. All are gone, and the place that once
knew them, knows them no more ! The hill-side, which
had once borne a happy people, and echoed the voices of
joyous children, is now a silent sheep-walk. The supposed
necessities of Political Economy have effected the exchange,
but the day may come when the country may feel the loss
of the loyal and brave race which has been driven away,
and find a new meaning perhaps in the old question, ' Is
not a man better than a sheep ? ' They who ' would have
shed their blood like water ' for Queen and country, are in
other lands, Highland still, but expatriated for ever.—

> From the dim shieling on the misty island,
>   Mountains divide us and a world of seas,
> But still our hearts are true, our hearts are Highland,
>   And in our dreams we behold the Hebrides.
> Tall are these mountains, and these woods are grand,
>   But we are exiled from our father's land."*

Farewell to Fiunary, by Donald Macleod, D.D., in *Good Words* for
August, 1882.

GLENORCHY.

GLENORCHY, of which the Marquis of Breadalbane is sole proprietor, was, like many other places, ruthlessly cleared of its whole native population. The writer of the New Statistical Account of the Parish, in 1843, the Rev. Duncan Maclean, " Fior Ghaël " of the *Teachdaire*, informs us that the census taken by Dr. Webster in 1755, and by Dr. MacIntyre forty years later, in 1795, " differ exceedingly little," only to the number of sixty. The Marquis of the day, it is well known, was a good friend of his Reverence ; the feeling was naturally reciprocated, and one of the apparent results is that the reverend author abstained from giving, in his Account of the Parish, the population statistics of the Glenorchy district. It was, however, impossible to pass over that important portion of his duty altogether, and, apparently with reluctance, he makes the following sad admission :—" A great and rapid decrease has, however, taken place since [referring to the population in 1795]. This decrease is mainly attributable to the introduction of sheep, and the absorption of small into large tenements. The aboriginal population of the parish of Glenorchy (not of Inishail) has been nearly supplanted by adventurers from the neighbouring district of Breadalbane, who now occupy the far largest share of the parish. There are a few, and only a few, shoots from the stems that supplied the ancient population. Some clans, who were rather numerous and powerful, have disappeared altogether ; others, viz., the Downies, Macnabs, MacNicols, and Fletchers, have nearly ceased to exist. The Macgregors, at one time lords of the soil, have totally disappeared ; not one of the name is to be found among the population. The MacIntyres, at one time extremely numerous, are likewise greatly reduced."

By this nobleman's mania for evictions, the population of Glenorchy was reduced from 1806 in 1831, to 831 in 1841, or by nearly a thousand souls in the short space of ten years ! It is, however, gratifying to find that it has since, under wiser management, very largely increased.

In spite of all this we have been seriously told that there has been no

DEPOPULATION OF THE COUNTY

In the rural districts. In this connection some very extra-ordinary public utterances were recently made by two gentlemen closely connected with the County of Argyll, questioning or attempting to explain away statements, made in the House of Commons by Mr. D. H. Macfarlane, M.P., to the effect that the rural population was, from various causes, fast disappearing from the Highlands. These utterances were —one by a no less distinguished person than the Duke of Argyll, who published his remarkable propositions in the *Times ;* the other by Mr. John Ramsay, M.P., the Islay distiller, who imposed his baseless statements on his brother members in the House of Commons. These oracles should have known better. They must clearly have taken no trouble whatever to ascertain the facts for themselves, or, having ascertained them, kept them back that the public might be misled on a question with which, it is obvious to all, the personal interests of both are largely mixed up.

Let us see how the assertions of these authorities agree with the actual facts. In 1831 the population of the County of Argyll was 100,973 ; in 1841 it was 97,371 ; in 1851 it was reduced to 88,567 ; and in 1881 it was down to 76,468. Of the latter number the Registrar-General classifies 30,387 as urban, or the population of " towns and villages," leaving

us only 46,081 as the total rural population of the county of
Argyll at the date of the last Census, in 1881.

It will be necessary to keep in mind that in 1831 the
county could not be said to have had many " town and
village " inhabitants—not more than from 12,000 to 15,000
at most. These resided chiefly in Campbelton, Inveraray,
and Oban ; and if we deduct from the total population for
that year, numbering 100,973, even the larger estimate,
15,000, of an urban or town population, we have still left,
in 1831, an actual rural population of 85,973, or within a
fraction of double the whole rural population of the county
in 1881. In other words, the rural population of Argyllshire is reduced in fifty years from 85,973 to 46,081, or
nearly one-half.

The increase of the urban or town population is going on
at a fairly rapid rate ; Campbeltown, Dunoon, Oban, Balla-
chulish, Blairmore and Strone, Innellan, Lochgilphead,
Tarbet, and Tighnabruaich, combined, having added no less
than some 5,500 to the population of the county in the ten
years from 1871 to 1881. These populous places will be
found respectively in the parishes of Campbeltown, Lismore,
and Appin, Dunnoon and Kilmun, Glassary, Kilcalmonell
and Kilbery, and in Kilfinan ; and this will at once account
for the comparatively good figure which these parishes make
in the tabulated statement in the Appendix. That table
will show exactly in which parishes and at what rate
depopulation progressed during the last fifty years. In
many instances the population was larger prior to 1831 than
at that date, but the years given will generally give the best
idea of how the matter stood throughout that whole period.
The state of the population given in 1831 was before the
famine which occurred in 1836; while 1841 comes in
between that of 1836 and 1846-47, during which period

large numbers were sent away, or left for the Colonies. There was no famine between 1851 and 1881, a time during which the population was reduced from 88,567 to 76,468, notwithstanding the great increase which took place simultaneously in the " town and village " section of the people in the county, as well as throughout the country generally.

The Table in the appendix will be found, like its companions, of considerable interest and value, in the face of such absurd and groundless statements as those to which we have referred, coming as they do from such high authorities ! We venture to think that these Tables will not only prove interesting, but valuable, at a time like this, in helping to remove the dust thrown for so many years past in the eyes of the public on this question of Highland depopulation by individuals personally interested in concealing the actual facts from those who have it in their power to put an effective check on the few unpatriotic proprietors in the North who are mainly responsible for clearing the country, by one means or another, for their own selfish ends.

THE TESTIMONY OF A LIVING WITNESS.

THE Rev. Dr. Maclauchlan, Edinburgh, wrote a series of articles in the *Witness*, during its palmy days under the editorship of Hugh Miller. These were afterwards published, in 1849, under the title of "The Depopulation System of the Highlands," in pamphlet form, by Johnston and Hunter. The rev. author visited all the places to which he refers, and all Highlanders are glad that he is still among us—perfectly able to maintain the accuracy of the following extracts from his pages. He says:—

A complete history of Highland clearances would, we doubt not, both interest and surprise the British public. Men talk of the Sutherland clearings as if they stood alone amidst the atrocities of the system; but those who know fully the facts of the case can speak with as much truth of the Ross-shire clearings, the Inverness-shire clearings, the Perthshire clearings, and, to some extent, the Argyllshire clearings. The earliest of these was the great clearing on the Glengarry estate, towards, we believe, the latter end of the last century. The tradition among the Highlanders is (and some Gaelic poems composed at the time would go to confirm it), that the chief's lady had taken umbrage at the clan. Whatever the cause might have been, the offence was deep, and could only be expiated by the extirpation of the race. Summonses of ejection were served over the whole property, even on families the most closely connected with the chief; and if we now seek for the Highlanders of Glengarry, we must search on the banks of the St. Lawrence. To the westward of Glengarry lies the estate of Lochiel—a name to which the imperishable poetry of Campbell has attached much interest. It is the country of the brave clan Cameron, to whom, were there nothing to speak of but their conduct at Waterloo, Britain owes a debt. Many of our readers have passed along Loch Lochy, and they have likely had the mansion of Auchnacarry pointed out to them, and they have been told of the dark mile, surpassing, as some say, the Trossachs in romantic beauty ; but perhaps they were not aware that beyond lies the wide expanse of Loch Arkaig, whose banks have been the scene of a most extensive clearing. There was a day when three hundred able, active men could have been collected from the shores of this extensive inland loch ; but eviction has long ago rooted them out, and nothing is now to be seen but the ruins of their huts, with the occasional bothy of a shepherd, while their lands are held by one or two farmers from the borders. Crossing to the south of the great glen, we may begin with Glencoe. How much of its romantic interest does this glen owe to its desolation ? Let us remember, however, that the desolation, in a large part of it, is the result of the extrusion of the inhabitants. Travel eastward, and the foot-prints of the destroyer cannot be lost sight of. Large tracks along the Spean and its tributaries are a wide waste. The southern bank of Loch Lochy is almost without inhabitants, though the symptoms of former occupancy are frequent. When we enter the country of the Frasers, the same spectacle presents itself—a desolate land. With the exception of the miserable village of Fort-Augustus the native population is almost extinguished, while those who do remain are left as if, by their squalid misery, to make darkness the more visible. Across the hills, in Stratherrick, the property of Lord Lovat, with the exception of a few large sheep farmers, and a very few tenants, is one wide waste. To the north of Loch Ness, the territory of the Grants, both Glenmoriston and the Earl of Seafield, presents a pleasing feature amidst the sea of desolation. But beyond this, again, let us trace the large rivers of the east coast to their sources. Trace the Beauly through all its upper reaches, and how many thousands upon thousands of acres, once peopled, are, as respects human beings, a wide wilderness ! The lands of the Chisholm have been stripped of their population down to a mere fragment ; the possessors of those of Lovat have not been behind with their share of the same sad doings. Let us cross to the Conon and its branches, and we will find that the chieftains of the Mackenzies have not been less active in extermination. Breadalbane and Rannoch, in Perthshire, have a similar tale to tell, vast masses of the population having been forcibly expelled. The upper portions of Athole have also suffered, while many of the valleys along the Spey and its tributaries are without an inhabitant, if we except a few shepherds. Sutherland, with all its atrocities, affords but a fraction of the atrocities that have been perpetrated in following out the ejectment system of the Highlands. In truth, of the habitable portion of the whole country but a small part is now really inhabited. We are unwilling to weary our readers by carrying them along the west coast from the Linnhe Loch, northwards; but if they inquire, they will find that the same system has been, in the case of most of the estates, relentlessly pursued. These are facts of which, we believe, the British public know little, but they are facts on which the changes should be rung until they have listened to them and seriously considered them. May it not be that part of the guilt is theirs, who might, yet did not, step forward to stop such cruel and unwise proceedings?

Let us leave the past, however (he continues), and consider the present. And it is a melancholy reflection that the year 1849 has added its long list to the roll of Highland ejectments. While the law is banishing its tens for terms of seven or fourteen years, as the penalty of deep-dyed crimes, irresponsible and infatuated power is banishing its thousands for life for no crime whatever. This year brings forward, as leader in the work of expatriation, the Duke of Argyll. Is it possible that his vast possessions are over-densely peopled? " *Credat Judæus appelles.*" And the Highland Destitution Committee co-operate. We had understood that the large sums of money at their disposal had been given them for the purpose of relieving, and not of banishing, the destitute. Next we have Mr. Baillie of Glenelg, professedly at their own request, sending five hundred souls off to America. Their native glen must have been made not a little uncomfortable for these poor people, ere they could have petitioned for so sore a favour. Then we have Colonel Gordon expelling upwards of eighteen hundred souls from South Uist ; Lord Macdonald follows with a sentence of banishment against six or seven hundred of the people of North Uist, with a threat, as we learn, that three thousand are to driven from Skye next season; and Mr. Lillingston of Lochalsh, Maclean of Ardgour, and Lochiel, bring up the rear of the black catalogue, a large body of people having left the estates of the two latter, who, after a heart-rending scene of parting with their native land, are now on the wide sea on their way to Australia. Thus, within the last three or four months considerably upwards of three thousand of the most moral and loyal of our people—people who, even in the most trying circumstances, never required a soldier, seldom a policeman, among them, to maintain the peace—are driven forcibly away to seek subsistence on a foreign soil.

Writing in 1850, on more "Recent Highland Evictions," the same author says :—The moral responsibility for these transactions lies in a measure with the nation, and not merely with the individuals immediately concerned in them. Some years ago the fearful scenes that attended the slave trade were depicted in colours that finally roused the national conscience, and the nation gave its loud, indignant, and effective testimony against them. The tearing of human beings, with hearts as warm, and affections as strong as dwell in the bosom of the white man, from their beloved homes and families—the packing them into the holds of over-crowded vessels, in the burning heat of the tropics—the stifling atmosphere, the clanking chain, the pestilence, the bodies of the dead corrupting in the midst of the living—presented a picture which deeply moved the national mind ; and there was felt to be guilt, deep-dyed guilt, and the nation relieved itself by abolishing the traffic. And is the nation free of guilt in this kind of white-slave traffic that is now going on—this tearing of men whether they will or not, from their country and kindred—this crowding them into often foul and unwholesome vessels with the accompanying deaths of hundreds whose eyes never rest on the land to which they are driven. Men may say that they have rights in the one case that they have not in the other. Then we say that they are rights into whose nature and fruits we would do well to enquire, lest it be found that the rude and lawless barbarism of Africa, and the high and boasted civilisation of Britain, land us in the same final results. . . . . It is to British legislation that the people of the Highlands owe the relative position in which they stand to their chiefs. There was a time when they were strangers to the feudal system which prevailed in the rest of the kingdom. Every man among them sat as free as his chief. But by degrees the power of the latter, assisted by Saxon legislation, encroached upon the liberty of the former. Highland chiefs became feudal lords—the people were robbed to increase their power—and now we are reaping the fruits of this in recent evictions.

At a meeting of the Inverness, Ross, and Nairn Club, in Edinburgh, in 1877, the venerable Doctor referred to the same sad subject amid applause and expressions of regret. We extract the following from a report of the meeting which appeared at the time in the *Inverness Courier* :—The current that ran against their language seemed to be rising against the people themselves. The cry seemed to be, " Do away with the people : this is the shorthand way of doing away with the language ". He reminded them of the saying of a Queen, that she would turn Scotland into a hunting field, and of the reply of a Duke of Argyll—" It is time for me to make my hounds ready," and said he did not know whether there was now an Argyll who would make the same reply, but there were other folks—less folks than Queens—who had gone pretty deep in the direction in- dicated by this Queen. He would not say it was not a desirable thing to see Highlanders scattered over the earth —they were greatly indebted to them in their cities and the colonies ; but he wished to preserve their Highland homes, from which the colonies and large cities derived their very best blood. Drive off the Highlander and destroy his home, and you destroy that which had produced some of the best and noblest men who filled important positions throughout the Empire. In the interests of great cities—as a citizen of Edinburgh—he desired to keep the Highlanders in their own country, and to make them as comfortable as they could. He only wished that some of the Highland proprietors could see their way to offer sections of the land for improvement by the people, who were quite as able to improve the land in their own country as to improve the great forests of Canada. He himself would rather to-morrow begin to cultivate an acre in any habitable part of the Highlands of Scotland than to begin to cultivate land such as that on which he had seen thousands of them working in the forests of Canada. What had all this to do with Celtic Literature ? Dr. Maclauchlan replied that the whole interest which Celtic Literature had to him was connected with the Celtic people, and if they destroyed the Celtic people, his entire interest in their literature perished. They had been told the other day that this was sentiment, and that there were cases in which senti- ment was not desirable. He agreed with this so far ; but he believed that when sentiment was driven out of a Highlander the best part of him was driven out, for it ever had a strong place among mountain people. He himself had a warm patriotic feeling, and he grieved whenever he saw a ruined house in any of their mountain glens. And ruined homes and ruined villages he, alas! had seen—villages on fire—the hills red with burning homes. He never wished to see this sorry sight again. It was a sad, a lamentable sight, for he was convinced the country had not a nobler class of people than the Highland people, or a set of people better worth preserving.

Mr. ROBERT BROWN,

Sheriff-Substitute of the Western District of Inverness-shire, in 1806, wrote a pamphlet of 120 pp., now very scarce, entitled, "Strictures and Remarks on the Earl of Selkirk's 'Observations on the Present State of the Highlands of Scotland'". Sheriff Brown was a man of keen observation, and his work is a powerful argument against the forced depopulation of the country. Summing up the number who left from 1801 to 1803, he says:—"In the year 1801, a Mr. George Dennon, from Pictou, carried out two cargoes of emigrants from Fort-William to Pictou, consisting of about seven hundred souls. A vessel sailed the same season from Isle Martin with about one hundred passengers, it is believed, for the same place. No more vessels sailed that year; but, in 1802, eleven large ships sailed with emigrants to America. Of these, four were from Fort-William, one from Knoydart, one from Isle Martin, one from Uist, one from Greenock. Five of these were bound for Canada, four for Pictou, and one for Cape Breton. The only remaining vessel, which took in a cargo of people in Skye, sailed for Wilmington, in the United States. In the year 1803, exclusive of Lord Selkirk's transports, eleven cargoes of emigrants went from the North Highlands. Of these, four were from the Moray Firth, two from Ullapool, three from Stornoway, and two from Fort-William. The whole of these cargoes were bound for the British settlements, and most of them were discharged at Pictou."

Soon after, several other vessels sailed from the North-West Highlands with emigrants, the whole of whom were for the British Colonies. In addition to these, Lord Selkirk took out 250 from South Uist in 1802, and in 1803 he sent out to Prince Edward Island about 800 souls, in three different vessels, most of whom were from the Island of Skye, and the remainder from Ross-shire, North Argyll, the interior of the County of Inverness, and the Island of Uist. In 1804, 1805, and 1806, several cargoes of Highlanders left Mull, Skye, and other Western Islands, for Prince Edward Island and other North American Colonies. Altogether, not less than 10,000 souls left the West Highlands and Isles during the first six years of the present century, a fact which will now appear incredible.

SIR WALTER SCOTT

Writes :—" In too many instances the Highlands have been drained, not of their superfluity of population, but of the whole mass of the inhabitants, dispossessed by an unrelenting avarice, which will be one day, found to have been as short-sighted as it is unjust and selfish. Meantime, the Highlands may become the fairy ground for romance and poetry, or the subject of experiment for the professors of speculation, political and economical. But if the hour of need should come—and it may not, perhaps, be far distant —the pibroch may sound through the deserted region, but the summons will remain unanswered."

M. MICHELET,

The great Continental historian, writes :—" The Scottish Highlanders will ere long disappear from the face of the earth ; the mountains are daily depopulating ; the great estates have ruined the land of the Gael, as they did ancient Italy. The Highlander will ere long exist only in the romances of Walter Scott. The tartan and the claymore excite surprise in the streets of Edinburgh ; the Highlanders disappear—they emigrate—their national airs will ere long be lost, as the music of the Eolian harp when the winds are hushed."

Mr. ALFRED RUSSEL WALLACE.

In his recent work on the Nationalisation of Land, Mr. Alfred Russel Wallace, in the chapter on " Landlordism in

Scotland," says to the English people:—The facts stated in this chapter will possess, I feel sure, for many Englishmen, an almost startling novelty; the tale of oppression and cruelty they reveal reads like one of those hideous stories peculiar to the dark ages, rather than a simple record of events happening upon our own land and within the memory of the present generation. For a parallel to this monstrous power of the landowner, under which life and property are entirely at his mercy, we must go back to mediæval, or to the days when serfdom not having been abolished, the Russian noble was armed with despotic authority; while the more pitiful results of this landlord tyranny, the wide devastation of cultivated lands, the heart-less burning of houses, the reckless creation of pauperism and misery, out of well-being and contentment, could only be expected under the rule of Turkish Sultans or greedy and cruel Pashas. Yet these cruel deeds have been perpetrated in one of the most beautiful portions of our native land. They are not the work of uncultured barbarians or of fanatic Moslems, but of so-called civilised and christian men; and—worst feature of all—they are not due to any high-handed exercise of power beyond the law, but are strictly legal, are in many cases the acts of members of the Legislature itself, and, notwithstanding that they have been repeatedly made known for at least sixty years past, no steps have been taken, or are even proposed to be taken, by the Legislature to prevent them for the future! Surely it is time that the people of England should declare that such things shall no longer exist—that the rich shall no longer have such legal power to oppress the poor—that the land shall be free for all who are willing to pay a fair value for its use—and, as this is not possible under landlordism, that landlordism shall be abolished. . . . . The general results of the system of modern landlordism in Scotland are not less painful than the hardship and misery brought upon individual sufferers. The earlier improvers, who drove the peasants from their sheltered valleys to the exposed sea-coast, in order to make room for sheep and sheep-farmers, pleaded erroneously the public benefit as the justification of their conduct. They maintained that more food and clothing would be produced by the new system, and that the people themselves would have the advantage of the produce of the sea as well as that of the land for their support. The result, however, proved them to be mistaken, for thenceforth the cry of Highland destitution began to be heard, culminating at intervals into actual famines, like that of 1836-37, when £70,000 were distributed to keep the Highlanders from death by starvation, ... just as in Ireland, there was abundance of land capable of cultivation, but the people were driven to the coast and to the towns to make way for sheep, and cattle, and lowland farmers; and when the barren and inhospitable tracts allotted to them became overcrowded, they were told to emigrate. As the Rev. J. Macleod says :—" By the clearances one part is depopulated and the other overpopulated; the people are gathered into villages where there is no steady employment for them, where idleness has its baneful influence and lands them in penury and want ".

The actual effect of this system of eviction and emigration —of banishing the native of the soil and giving it to the stranger—is shown in the steady increase of poverty indicated by the amount spent for the relief of the poor having increased from less than £300,000 in 1846 to more than £900,000 now ; while in the same period the population has only increased from 2,770,000 to 3,627,000, so that pauperism has grown about nine times faster than population ! . . . . The fact that a whole population could be driven from their homes like cattle at the will of a landlord, and that the Government which taxed them, and for whom they freely shed their blood on the battle-field, neither would nor could protect them from cruel interference with their personal liberty, is surely the most convincing and most absolute demonstration of the incompatibility of landlordism with the elementary rights of a free people.

As if, however, to prove this still more clearly, and to show how absolutely incompatible with the well-being of the Community is modern landlordism, the great lords of the soil in Scotland have for the last twenty years or more, been systematically laying waste enormous areas of land for purposes of sport, just as the Norman Conqueror laid waste the area of the New Forest for similar purposes. At the present time, more than two million acres of Scottish soil are devoted to the preservation of deer alone—an area larger than the entire Counties of Kent and Surrey combined. Glen Tilt Forest includes 100,000 acres ; the Black Mount is sixty miles in circumference ; and Ben Aulder Forest is fifteen miles long by seven broad. On many of these forests there is the finest pasture in Scotland, while the valleys would support a considerable population of small farmers, yet all this land is devoted to the sport of the wealthy, farms being destroyed, houses pulled down, and men, sheep, and cattle all banished to create a wilderness for the deer-stalkers ! At the same time the whole people of England are shut out from many of the grandest and most interesting scenes of their native land, gamekeepers and watchers forbidding the tourist or naturalist to trespass on some of the wildest Scotch mountains.

Now, when we remember that the right to a property in these unenclosed mountains was most unjustly given to the representatives of the Highland chiefs little more than a century ago, and that they and their successors have grossly abused their power ever since, it is surely time to assert those fundamental maxims of jurisprudence which state that—"No man can have a vested right in the misfortunes and woes of his country," and that "the Sovereign ought not to allow either communities or private individuals to acquire large tracts of land in order to leave it uncultivated". If the oft-repeated maxim that "property has its duties as well as its rights" is not altogether a mockery, then we maintain that in this case the *total* neglect of all the duties devolving on the owners of these vast tracts of land affords ample reason why the State should take possession of them for the public benefit. A landlord government will, of course, never do this till the people declare unmistakably that it must be done. To such a government the rights of property are *sacred*, while those of their fellow citizens are of comparatively little moment; but we feel sure that when the people fully know and understand the doings of the land-lords of Scotland, the reckless destruction of homesteads, and the silent sufferings of the brave Highlanders, they will make their will known, and, when they do so, that *will* must soon be embodied into law.

After quoting the opinion of the Rev. Dr. John Kennedy of Dingwall, given at length at pp. 336-337, Mr. Wallace next quotes from an article in the *Westminster Review*, in 1868. "The Gaels," this writer says, "rooted from the dawn of history on the slopes of the northern mountains, have been thinned out and thrown away like young turnips too thickly planted. Noble gentlemen and noble ladies have shown a flintiness of heart and a meanness of detail in carrying out their clearings upon which it is revolting to dwell; and after all, are the evils of over-population cured? Does not the desease still spring up under the very torture of the knife ? Are not the crofts slowly and silently taken at every opportunity out of the hands of the peasantry ? When a Highlander has to leave his hut there is now no resting place for him save the cellars or attics of the closes of Glasgow, or some other large centre of employment; it has been noticed that the poor Gael is even more liable than the Irishman to sink under the debasement in which he is then immersed." The same writer holds :—" No error could be grosser than that of reviewing the chiefs as unlimited proprietors, not only of the land, but of the whole territory of the mountain, lake, river, and sea-shore, held and won during hundreds of years by the broad swords of the clansmen. Could any Maclean admit, even in a dream, that his chief could clear Mull of all the Macleans and replace them with Campbells; or the Mackintosh people his lands with Macdonalds, and drive away his own race, any more than Louis Napoleon could evict all the population of France and supply their place with English and German colonists?" Yet this very power and right the English Government, in its aristocratic selfishness, bestowed upon the chiefs, when, after the great rebellion of 1745, it took away their privileges of war and criminal jurisdiction, and endeavoured to assimilate them to the nobles and great landowners of England. The rights of the clansmen were left entirely out of consideration.*

* *Land Nationalisation, its Necessities and Aims ; being a comparison of the System of Landlord and Tenant with that of occupying Ownership, in their influence on the well-being of the people,* by Alfred Russel Wallace, author of " The Malay Archipelago," " Island Life,".&c. London : Trübner & Co., 1882.

MR. SAMUEL SMITH, M.P.

AT the Annual Meeting of the Federation of Celtic Societies, held in Liverpool, on the 2nd of January, 1883, a
Resolution dealing with Depopulation and Eviction in the
Highlands, was moved by Mr. D. H. Macfarlane, M.P.,
seconded by Mr. John Mackay, C.E., Hereford, and supported in a telling speech by Mr. Samuel Smith, M.P.,
recently returned as a supporter of the Gladstone Government for the City of Liverpool. Such a statement from so
influential a quarter is, in present circumstances, of great
importance, and deserves all the permanency and circulation
which this work can give it. The resolution, carried by
acclamation, by an audience largely composed of Englishmen, was as follows :—

*In view of the serious aspect recently assumed by events in
the Highlands of Scotland, and of the alarming decrease of the
rural population, as disclosed by the census returns of 1881,
the Federation of Celtic Societies is of opinion that such steps
ought to be immediately taken, as will deliver the Highland
crofters from the bondage in which they are at present held, increase the size of their holdings, relieve them from the fear of
arbitrary eviction, and define their rights to the soil upon
which they and their forefathers have lived from time immemorial.*

Mr. Smith, on rising to support this resolution, was received
with great enthusiasm, the audience rising to their feet, and
cheering lustily—as indeed they did throughout the delivery
of his able, eloquent, statesman-like, and sympathetic speech.
In the course of his remarks, he said :—

I am extremely happy to be with you to-night. I have

come here more to be a learner than a teacher. I have so large a sympathy with the Highland population, and such a general knowledge of the wrongs they have suffered, that I felt I was in my right place amongst you to-night. I have been deeply interested in listening to the speeches that have been made. In the main, I can testify from a general knowledge of the history of Scotland, that what has been stated to-night is quite correct, and I am very glad that these facts are coming to be known throughout the country, and are forming the basis of a tide of popular opinion which I am sure will, sooner or later, rectify many of those wrongs in the Highlands. The fact is, the Highlanders may be said in some sense, to have suffered from the remarkable loyalty and peaceableness of their character. There is no part of the British Islands in which there is so little crime as in the Highlands of Scotland. There is no part of the British Islands where the people are naturally more loyal, more orderly, and more religious. From many points of view the Highlanders are one of the most valuable portions of the British population, and certainly it ought to be the policy of any government to preserve and develop such a population, instead of suffering them to be driven from our shores. The point that strikes me most in connection with the wrongs of the Highlands, is the turning of large tracts of country into deer forests. I have long felt that this was a use of the rights of proprietors which can only be called the greatest abuse. It is a use which the law has sanctioned, I think, very wrongfully, and the time has come when we must reconsider the whole basis of our law, and admit new principles into it, which will put an end to the depopulation of huge tracts of country for the purposes of deer. I largely agree with what several speakers have said about the very arbitrary and extreme rights our law has conceded to pro-

prietors, and it ought to be well known to the English
public, that these principles of law which have been pushed
to such an unwarrantable degree in the Highlands, are
modern principles unknown to the ancient Gaelic law. The
ancient Gaelic law was identical with the ancient Irish
law. It was of the tribal order, in which the clan was full
proprietor with the chieftain. The Highlands were occupied
from time immemorial by clans, bodies of men bound together by common ties of kindred, having the same name,
presided over by an hereditary chief, and occupying a
certain portion of soil in common. That existed until the
battle of Culloden. After that the principles of English
law was introduced. The old rights of the clansmen were
confiscated, and superseded by a state of law totally unknown to them. In fact a very gross injustice was done,
which has been going on these 130 years, and has led to the
depopulation of large tracts of the Highlands, and to the loss
by this country of a most valuable element of the population.
Now, it has been strongly impressed upon my mind that
those principles which we have conceded to Ireland—and I
think justly conceded, for I believe Mr. Gladstone's Land
Act was based on great and broad principles of justice—I
think that the time has come when the same principles, perhaps modified by local circumstances, ought to be applied
to the crofter population of the Highlands. I only regret,
and I do so very deeply, that it is so very late in the day
that we have begun to repair the errors of our forefathers.
We have already lost a great portion of that loyal and brave
population, and it seems very difficult indeed to recall
them. Large tracts of the Highlands have been turned into
wildernesses, and it seems at this time of day almost too
late to bring back the native population. Were it possible
to restore them, were there means to re-people the country

with those hardy and loyal men who have been in the front
of every British battle for the last 150 years, I for one should
be very glad to consider them in order to see whether it was
practicable or not. But there are many wrongs which,
when once done, it is difficult to undo. Many of the people
have sunk into the purlieus of the large towns, descended
in the social scale, and lost the associations of their youth,
and it would be difficult to replant them ; but we ought to
do the best we can to retain what remains of that peasantry,
and root them to the soil of their birth by wise and just
laws. I do not suppose that any town population can
fully understand the intense love of home that belongs
to people among the mountains. All mountainous countries are patriotic in the highest possible degree. Whether it be Switzerland, the Tyrol, the Highlands of
Scotland, or any other mountainous country, there is an
intense love of country which exists nowhere else. That
intense love of country is a great force in the State, a great
power that ought not to be lightly thrown away. There is,
as it were, an immense reserve which a Government can
draw upon in a time of national crisis. There is no such
intense love of country in town populations. I attribute, in
some degree, that also to the strong tribal feeling, to the
wonderful loyalty that the Highland soldiers have always
shown to their leaders. There is also another point to be
considered. A great portion of this Highland population
has drifted away to our large towns. It has not always
emigrated. Those who have emigrated have done the best,
I think; they have improved their condition by going to
foreign countries—America and Canada. The Canadian
settlements have been on the whole prosperous. I do not
say, in the least degree, I object to a healthy emigration. I
hold for this densely-populated country a continuous stream

of healthy emigration is necessary to keep us in a proper
state, and whether in Ireland or in the Highlands of Scotland the population is congested—wherever there is an
immense number of small cottiers dwelling together—a
healthy emigration is not to be deplored.   But I object to
clear whole districts of a country to make room for deer.
And, as it has been well said by one of the speakers, these
wholesale clearances have in no way improved the condition of the people they leave behind.   If they had improved
the condition of those behind, one could have looked
upon them in a somewhat different light.   I think we
may even take broader grounds in looking at this question.
The whole tendency of English law for many years past
has been to deplete the rural districts.   It is a fact that
we have to look in the face, and a fact that we have to
deplore, that the rural population of the British Islands
has been steadily decreasing for many years past.   Now,
I think it is a matter of national policy to keep up the
rural population of the country.   The rural population,
I venture to say, is the backbone of any country.   The
rural populations are much hardier; they live in a much
simpler way; they are capable of undergoing greater fatigue
and toil than town populations.   A rural population which
drifts into a town often falls into a much lower state than
they occupied in their country homes.   They are not fitted
to contend with the temptations of large towns, and often-
times fall victims to the vices and habits of the low quarters
of our towns.   If a Gaelic population were drifted into
Edinburgh or Glasgow, it would be found, as in the case of
the Irish population who have come into our large English
towns, that a considerable part would fall into habits they
would not have contracted if they had remained in their
native place.   The associations of youth and the public

opinion of our native home is one of the most powerful
means of supporting people in the paths of virtue and rectitude. Break up these associations, separate people from
the friends of their youth, let them become mere units
amongst the masses, with poor and degraded people about
them, and you will find that, for the most part, they will
sink morally as well as socially. I think that it ought to be
the policy of any government to do whatever it can by wise
legislation to maintain the rural population, to encourage its
growth—at all events, to do what it can to prevent its
gradual extinction. I hold that the proprietorship of land
ought to be made subject to just laws, and that land ought
not to be treated as goods and chattels. I object to the
principle which our law at present recognises that, if a man
by the accident of birth happens to own a county in Scotland, he may drive out every human being in it, and put in
deer. I hold that no principles of justice can sanction such
rights as these. I look upon it as a gross abuse that a man
who owns a large track of country should drain it of the last
sixpence he can get, and then spend it perhaps at the gaming
tables of Paris, Baden-Baden, and such places. I hold very
strongly that property has its duties as well as its rights—
that proprietors should live during the greater part of the
year amongst their tenantry, that they should identify themselves with the people and cultivate a family feeling amongst
them, and be the friends of the weak and helpless. Where
proprietors perform these duties, and recognise the position
in which they stand, there are no men who are more popular,
or to whom is accorded more freely the first position in the
county in which they live ; but where, as I am sorry to say
it is so in too many cases, they entirely neglect those duties,
live for pure selfishness, and totally ignore the interests of
the tenants, they gradually lose all hold upon their attach-

ment; and I am afraid that has taken place already in too many cases in the Highlands. It is a very difficult thing, as we have found in Ireland, to define rights which existed some 200 years ago—rights which have no existence in the statute book, and which are only traditional; to restore such rights now by means of law, you must all admit, is an extremely difficult thing. But in the case of the small crofters it may be necessary. I don't think that with regard to the sheep farms it is necessary. In such cases the relations between landlord and tenant are purely commercial, and the large farmer can protect himself as well as the landlord. It is with regard to the small tenantry that I am speaking. I only desire to keep the rural population fixed upon the soil, and, in order to do so, to concede to them something like fixity of tenure. There are no people more valuable to the country than the Highlanders, and it is to the interest of the State to maintain that people. I hope that this agitation will be conducted constitutionally, and that all Highlanders will use their influence to prevent anything being done that will stain the character of that people with a dark blot. I think it is only a question of time, when these rights will be conceded. The county franchise must be soon extended, and when it is we will have a different class of representatives, not only in Scotland, but in England, who will be very much more alive to the interests of the labouring classes. This cannot be deferred for more than two or three years, and in the meantime your object should be to enlighten the people upon the subject, and to call upon the Government to appoint a Royal Commission to thoroughly and exhaustively analyse the subject, and prepare the way for a parliamentary measure which would do a great deal to satisfy our Highland brethren.*

* From the *Liverpool Mercury* of 3rd January, 1883.

M. DE LAVALEYE.

THE following remarks by the celebrated French economist, M. de Lavaleye, will prove interesting. There is no
greater living authority on land tenure than this writer,
and being a foreigner, his opinions are not open—as the
opinions of our own countrymen may be—to the suspicion
of political bias or partizanship on a question which is of
universal interest all over the world. Referring to land
tenure in this country, he says :—

The dispossession of the old proprietors, transformed
by time into new tenants, was effected on a larger scale by
the " clearing of estates ". When a lord of the manor, for
his own profit, wanted to turn the small holdings into large
farms, or into pasturage, the small cultivators were of no
use. The proprietors adopted a simple means of getting rid
of them ; and, by destroying their dwellings, forced them
into exile. The classical land of this system is Ireland, or
more particularly the Highlands of Scotland.

It is now clearly established that in Scotland, just as in
Ireland, the soil was once the property of the clan or sept.
The chiefs of the clan had certain rights over the communal
domain ; but they were even further from being proprietors
than was Louis XIV. from being proprietor of the territory
of France. By successive encroachments, however, they
transformed their authority of suzerain into a right of private
ownership, without even recognising in their old co-proprie-
tors a right of hereditary possession. In a similar way the
Zemindars and Talugdars in India were, by the Act of the
British Government, transformed into absolute proprietors.
Until modern days the chiefs of the clan were interested in
retaining a large number of vassals, as their power, and often
their security, were only guaranteed by their arms. But

when order was established, and the chiefs—or lords, as they now were—began to reside in the towns, and required large revenues rather than numerous retainers, they endeavoured to introduce large farms and pasturage.

We may follow the first phases of this revolution, which commences after the last rising under the Pretender, in the works of James Anderson and James Stuart. The latter tells us that in his time—in the last third of the 18th century —the Highlands of Scotland still presented a miniature picture of the Europe of four hundred years ago. "The rent" (so he misnames the tribute paid to the chief of the clan) "of these lands is very little in comparison with their extent, but if it is regarded relatively to the number of mouths which the farm supports, it will be seen that land in the Scotch Highlands supports perhaps twice as many persons as land of the same value in a fertile province." When, in the last 30 years of the 18th century, they began to expel the Gaels, they at the same time forbade them to emigrate to a foreign country, so as to compel them by these means to congregate in Glasgow and other manufacturing towns. In his observations on Smith's *Wealth of Nations*, published in 1814, David Buchanan gives us an idea of the progress made by the clearing of estates. "In the Highlands," he says, "the landed proprietor, without regard to the hereditary tenants" (he wrongly applies this term to the clansmen who were joint proprietors of the soil), "offers the land to the highest bidder, who, if he wishes to improve the cultivation, is anxious for nothing but the introduction of a new system. The soil, dotted with small peasant proprietors, was formerly well populated in proportion to its natural fertility. The new system of improved agriculture and increased rents demands the greatest net profit with the least possible outlay, and with this object the cultivators are got rid of as being of no further use. Thus cast from their native soil, they go to seek their living in the manufacturing towns." George Ensor, in a work published in 1818, says :—"They (the landed proprietors of Scotland) dispossessed families as they would grub up coppice-wood, and they treated the villages and their people as Indians harassed with wild beasts do in their vengeance a jungle with tigers. . . . Is it credible, that in the 19th century, in this missionary age, in this Christian era, man shall be bartered for a fleece or a carcase of mutton—nay, held cheaper ? . . . Why, how much worse is it than the intention of the Moguls, who, when they had broken into the northern provinces of China, proposed in Council to exterminate the inhabitants, and convert the land into pasture ! This proposal many Highland proprietors have effected in their own country against their own countrymen."

M. de Sismondi has rendered celebrated on the Continent the famous clearing executed between 1814 and 1820 by the Duchess of Sutherland. More than three thousand families were driven out ; and 800,000 acres of land, which formerly belonged to the clan, were transformed into seignorial domain. Men were driven out to make room for sheep. The sheep are now replaced by deer, and the pastures converted into deer forests, which are treeless solitudes. The *Economist* of June 2, 1866, said on this subject :—" Feudal instincts have as full career now as in the times when the Conquerer destroyed thirty-six villages to make the New Forest. Two millions of acres, comprising most fertile land, have been changed into desert. The natural herbage in Glen Tilt was known as the most succulent in Perth ; the deer forest of Ben Aulder was the best natural meadow of Badenoch ; the forest of Black Mount was the best pasturage in Scotland for black-woolled sheep. The soil thus sacrificed for the pleasures of the chase extends over an area larger than the county of Perth. The land in the new Ben Aulder forest supported 15,000 sheep; and this is but the thirtieth part of the territory sacrificed, and thus rendered as unproductive as if it were buried in the depths of the sea."

The destruction of small property is still going on, no longer, however, by encroachment, but by purchase. Whenever land comes into the market it is bought by some rich capitalist, because the expenses of legal inquiry are too great for a small investment. Thus, large properties are consolidated, and fall, so to speak, into mortmain, in consequence of the law of primogeniture and entails. In the 15th century, according to Chancellor Fortescue, England was quoted throughout Europe for its number of proprietors and the comfort of its inhabitants. In 1688, Gregory King estimates that there were 180,000 proprietors, exclusive of 16,560 proprietors of noble rank. In 1786, there were 250,000 proprietors of England. According to the "Domesday Book" of 1876 there were 170,000 rural proprietors in England owning above an acre, 21,000 in Ireland, and 8000 in Scotland. A fifth of the entire country is in the hands of 523 persons. "Are you aware," said Mr. Bright, in a speech delivered at Birmingham, August 27, 1866, "that one-half of the soil of Scotland belongs to ten or twelve persons? Are you aware of the fact that the monopoly of landed property is continually increasing and becoming more and more exclusive?"

In England, then, as at Rome, large property has swallowed up small property, in consequence of a continuous evolution unchecked from the beginning to the end of the nation's history; and the social order seems to be threatened just as in the Roman Empire.

An ardent desire for a more equal division of the produce of labour inflames the labouring classes, and passes
from land to land. In England, it arouses agitation among
the industrial classes, and is beginning to invade the rural
districts. It obviously menaces landed property, as constituted in this country. The labourers who till the soil will
claim their share in it; and, if they fail to obtain it here, will
cross the sea in search of it. To retain a hold on them they
must be given a vote; and there is fresh danger in increasing
the number of electors while that of proprietors diminishes,
and maintaining laws which render inequality greater and
more striking, while ideas of equality are assuming more
formidable sway. To make the possession of the soil a
closed monopoly and to augment the political powers of the
class who are rigidly excluded, is at once to provoke
levelling measures and to facilitate them. Accordingly we
find that England is the country where the scheme of the
nationalisation of the land finds most adherents, and is most
widely proclaimed. The country which is furthest from the
primitive organisations of property, is likewise the one where
the social order seems most menaced.

HARDSHIPS ENDURED BY THE FIRST HIGH-
LAND EMIGRANTS TO NOVA SCOTIA.

THE reader is already acquainted with the misery endured
by those evicted from Barra and South Uist by Colonel
Gordon, after their arrival in Canada. This was no isolated
case. We shall here give a few instances of the unspeakable
suffering of those pioneers who left so early as 1773, in the

ship *Hector*, for Pictou, Nova Scotia, gathered from trustworthy sources during the author's late visit to that country.
The *Hector* was owned by two men, Pagan and Witherspoon,
who bought three shares of land in Pictou, and they engaged
a Mr. John Ross as their agent, to accompany the vessel to
Scotland, to bring out as many colonists as they could
induce, by misrepresentation and falsehoods, to leave their
homes.   They offered a free passage, a farm, and a year's free
provisions to their dupes.   On his arrival in Scotland, Ross
drew a glowing picture of the land and other manifold
advantages of the country to which he was enticing the
people. The Highlanders knew nothing of the difficulties
awaiting them in a land covered over with a dense unbroken
forest; and, tempted by the prospect of owning splendid
farms of their own, they were imposed upon by his promise,
and many of them agreed to accompany him across the
Atlantic and embraced his proposals.   Calling first at
Greenock, three families and five single young men joined
the vessel at that port.   She then sailed to Lochbroom, in
Ross-shire, where she received 33 families and 25 single
men, the whole of her passengers numbering about 200
souls.   This band, in the beginning of July, 1773, bade a
final farewell to their native land, not a soul on board having
ever crossed the Atlantic except a single sailor and John
Ross, the agent.   As they were leaving, a piper came on
board who had not paid his passage; the captain ordered
him ashore, but the strains of the national instrument
affected those on board so much that they pleaded to have
him allowed to accompany them, and offered to share their
own rations with him in exchange for his music during the
passage.   Their request was granted, and his performances
aided in no small degree to cheer the noble band of pioneers
in their long voyage of eleven weeks, in a miserable hulk,

across the Atlantic. The pilgrim band kept up their spirits
as best they could by song, pipe-music, dancing, wrestling,
and other amusements, through the long and painful voyage.
The ship was so rotten that the passengers could pick the
wood out of her sides with their fingers. They met with a
severe gale off the Newfoundland coast, and were driven
back by it so far that it took them about fourteen days to
get back to the point at which the storm met them. The
accommodation was wretched, small-pox and dysentery broke
out among the passengers. Eighteen of the children died,
and were committed to the deep amidst such anguish and
heart-rending agony as only a Highlander can understand.
Their stock of provisions became almost exhausted, the water
became scarce and bad ; the remnant of provisions left consisted mainly of salt meat, which, from the scarcity of water,
added greatly to their sufferings. The oatcake carried by
them became mouldy, so that much of it had been thrown
away before they dreamt of having such a long passage; but,
fortunately for them, one of the passengers, Hugh MacLeod,
more prudent than the others, gathered up the despised
scraps into a bag, and during the last few days of the voyage
his fellows were too glad to join him in devouring this refuse
to keep souls and bodies together.

At last the *Hector* dropped anchor in the harbour,
opposite where the town of Pictou now stands. Though
the Highland dress was then proscribed at home, this
emigrant band carried theirs along with them, and, in
celebration of their arrival, many of the younger men
donned their national dress—to which a few of them were
able to add the *Sgian Dubh* and the claymore—while the
piper blew up his pipes with might and main, its thrilling
tones, for the first time, startling the denizens of the endless
forest, and its echoes resounding through the wild solitude.

Scottish immigrants are admitted upon all hands to have given its backbone of moral and religious strength to the Province, and to those brought over from the Highlands in this vessel is due the honour of being in the forefront—the pioneers and vanguard.

But how different was the reality to the expectations of these poor creatures, led by the plausibility of the emigration agent, to expect free estates on their arrival. The whole scene, as far as the eye could see, was a dense forest. They crowded on the deck to take stock of their future home, and their hearts sank within them. They were landed without the provisions promised, without shelter of any kind, and were only able by the aid of those few before them, to erect camps of the rudest and most primitive description, to shelter their wives and their children from the elements. Their feelings of disappointment were most bitter, when they compared the actual facts with the free farms and the comfort promised them by the lying emigration agent. Many of them sat down in the forest and wept bitterly; hardly any provisions were possessed by the few who were before them, and what there was among them was soon devoured; making all—old and new comers—almost destitute. It was now too late to raise any crops that year. To make matters worse they were sent some three miles into the forest, so that they could not even take advantage with the same ease of any fish that might be caught in the harbour. The whole thing appeared an utter mockery. To unskilled men the work of clearing seemed hopeless; they were naturally afraid of the Red Indian and of the wild beasts of the forest; without roads or paths, they were frightened to move for fear of getting lost in the unbroken forest. Can we wonder that, in such circumstances, they refused to settle on the company's lands? though, in consequence, when provisions arrived, the agents refused to give them any. Ross and the company quarrelled, and he ultimately left the new comers to their fate. The few of them who had a little money bought what provisions they could from the agents, while others, less fortunate, exchanged their clothes for food ; but the greater number had neither money nor clothes to spend or exchange, and they were all soon left quite destitute. Thus driven to extremity, they determined to have the provisions retained by the agents, right or wrong, and two of them went to claim them. They were positively refused, but they determined to take what they could by force. They seized the agents, tied them, tooks their guns from them, which they hid at a distance ; told them that they must have the food for their families, but that they were quite willing and determined to pay for them if ever they were able to do so. They then carefully weighed or measured the various articles, took account of what each man received and left, except one, the latter, a powerful and determined fellow, who was left behind to release the two agents. This he did, after allowing sufficient time for his friends to get to a safe distance, when he informed the prisoners where they could find their guns. Intelligence was sent to Halifax that the Highlanders were in rebellion, from whence orders were sent to a Captain Archibald in Truro, to march his company of militia to suppress and pacify them ; but to his honour be it said, he, point blank, refused, and sent word that he would do no such thing. " I know the Highlanders," he said, "and if they are fairly treated there will be no trouble with them." Finally, orders were given to supply them with provisions, and Mr. Paterson, one of the agents, used afterwards to say that the Highlanders who arrived in poverty, and who had been so badly treated, had paid him every farthing with which he had trusted them.

It would be tedious to describe the sufferings which they afterwards endured. Many of them left. Others, fathers, mothers, and children, bound themselves away, as virtual slaves, in other settlements, for mere subsistence. Those who remained lived in small huts, covered only with the bark or branches of trees to shelter them from the bitter winter cold, of the severity of which they had no previous conception. They had to walk some eighty miles, through a trackless forest, in deep snow to Truro, to obtain a few bushels of potatoes, or a little flour in exchange for their labour, dragging these back all the way again on their backs, and endless cases of great suffering from actual want occurred. The remembrance of these terrible days sank deep into the minds of that generation, and long after, even to this day, the narration of the scenes and cruel hardships through which they had to pass beguiled, and now beguiles many a winter's night as they sit by their now comfortable firesides.

In the following spring they set to work. They cleared some of the forest, and planted a larger crop. They learned to hunt the moose, a kind of large deer. They began to cut timber, and sent a cargo of it from Pictou—the first of a trade very profitably and extensively carried on ever since. The population had, however, grown less than it was before their arrival; for in this year it amounted only to 78 persons. One of the modes of laying up a supply of food for the winter was to dig up a large quantity of clams or large oysters, pile them in large heaps on the sea shore, and then cover them over with sand, though they were often, in winter, obliged to cut through ice more than a foot thick to get at them. This will give a fair idea of the hardships experienced by the earlier emigrants to these Colonies.

In Prince Edward Island, however, a colony from Lockerbie, in Dumfrieshire, who came out in 1774, seemed to have fared even worse. They commenced operations on the Island with fair prospects of success, when a plague of locusts, or field mice, broke out, and consumed everything, even the potatoes in the ground; and for eighteen months the settlers experienced all the miseries of a famine, having for several months only what lobsters or shell-fish they could gather from the sea-shore. The winter brought them to such a state of weakness that they were unable to convey food a reasonable distance even when they had means to buy it.

In this pitiful position they heard that the Pictou people were making progress that year, and that they had even some provisions to spare. They sent one of their number to make enquiry. An American settler, when he came to Pictou, brought a few slaves with him, and at this time he had just been to Truro to sell one of them, and brought home some provisions with the proceeds of the sale of his negro. The messenger from Prince Edward Island was putting up at this man's house. He was a bit of a humorist, and continued cheerful in spite of all his troubles. On his return to the Island, the people congregated to hear the news. "What kind of place is Pictou?" enquired one. "Oh, an awful place. Why, I was staying with a man who was just eating the last of his nigger"; and the poor creatures were reduced to such a point themselves that they actually believed the people of Pictou to be in such a condition as to oblige them to live on the flesh of their coloured servants. They were told, however, that matters were not quite so bad as that, and fifteen families left for the earlier settlement, where, for a time, they fared but very little better, but afterwards became prosperous and happy. A few of their children, and thousands of their grandchildren, are now living in comfort and plenty.

But who can think of these early hardships and cruel existences without condemning—even hating—the memories of the harsh and heartless Highland and Scottish lairds, who made existence at home even almost as miserable for those noble fellows, and who then drove them in thousands out of their native land, not caring one iota whether they sank in the Atlantic, or were starved to death on a strange and uncongenial soil? Retributive justice demands that posterity should execrate the memories of the authors of such misery and horrid cruelty. It may seem uncharitable to write thus of the dead; but it is impossible to forget their inhuman conduct, though, no thanks to them—cruel tigers in human form—it has turned out for the better, for the descendants of those who were banished to what was then infinitely worse than transportation for the worst crimes. Such criminals were looked after and cared for; but those poor fellows, driven out of their homes by the Highland lairds, and sent across there, were left to starve, helpless, and uncared for. Their descendants are now a prosperous and thriving people, and retribution is at hand. The descendants of the evicted from Sutherland, Ross, Inverness-shires, and elsewhere, to Canada, are producing enormous quantities of food, and millions of cattle, to pour them into this country. What will be the consequence? The sheep-farmer—the primary and original cause of the evictions—will be the first to suffer. The price of stock in Scotland must inevitably fall. Rents must follow, and the joint authors of the original iniquity will, as a class, then suffer the natural and just penalty of their past misconduct.

AN IRISH COMPANION PICTURE.

WE have read with warm sympathy and interest Mr. A. M. Sullivan's Chapter, entitled "Lochaber no more," in his brilliant and intensely interesting work, *New Ireland.* Mr. Sullivan has always exhibited a friendly side to the Highlanders of Scotland, and we desire to acknowledge this kindly sympathy in the only way which has yet presented itself, by calling attention on this side, among Highlanders especially, to this remarkable work, and, at the same time, quote from it, to give the reader an idea of the brutality meted out by Irish landlords to their countrymen in the past, in connection with this infamous mania for driving the people away from their native soil. Mr. Sullivan introduces his chapter on Irish evictions thus :—A Highland friend whose people were swept away by the great Sutherland clearances, describing to me some of the scenes in that great dispersion, often dwelt with emotion on the spectacle of the evicted clansmen marching through the glens on their way to exile, their pipes playing as a last farewell, "Lochaber no more "!

> Lochaber no more ! Lochaber no more !
> We'll maybe return to Lochaber no more !

I sympathised with his story ; I shared all his feelings. I had seen my own countrymen march in like sorrowful procession on their way to an emigrant ship. Not alone in one district, however, but all over the island, were such scenes to be witnessed in Ireland, from 1847 to 1857. Within that decade of years nearly one million of people were cleared off the island by eviction, or emigration.

The picture which Mr. Sullivan presents as to the attachment of his countrymen to their native soil, and the unspeakable cruelties involved in a simple eviction are equally true in the case of the Highlanders. He says:—As a rule, his farm has been to him and his forefathers for generations a fixed and cherished home. Every bush and brake, every shrub and tree, every meadow-path or grassy knoll, has some association for him which is, as it were, a part of his existence. Whatever there is on or above the surface of the earth in the shape of house or office, or steading, of fence or road, of gate or stiles, has been created by the tenant's hand. Under this humble thatch roof he first drew breath, and has grown to manhood. Hither he brought the fair young girl he won as a wife. Here have his little children been born. This farm-plot is his whole dominion, his world, his all; he is verily a part of it, like the ash or the oak, that has sprung from its soil. Removal in his case is a tearing up by the roots, where transplantation is death. The attachment of the Irish peasant to his farm is something almost impossible to be comprehended by those who have not spent their lives amongst the class, and seen from day to day the depth and force and intensity of these home feelings.

An Irish eviction, therefore, it may well be supposed, is a scene to try the sternest nature. I know sheriffs and sub-sheriffs who have protested to me that, odious and distressing as were the duties they had to perform at an execution on the public scaffold, far more painful to their feelings were those which fell to their lot in carrying out an eviction, where, as in the case of these "clearances," the houses had to be levelled. The anger of the elements affords no warrant for respite or reprieve. In hail or thunder, rain or snow, out the inmate must go. The bed-ridden grandsire, the infant in the cradle, the sick, the aged, and the dying, must alike be thrust forth, though other roof or home the world has naught for them, and the stormy sky must be

their canopy during the night at hand. This is no fancy
picture. It is but a brief and simple outline sketch of
realities witnessed all over Ireland in the ten years that
followed the famine. I recall the words of an eye-witness,
describing one of these scenes: "Seven hundred human
beings," says the Most Rev. Dr. Nulty, Catholic Bishop of
Meath, "were driven from their homes on this one day.
There was not a shilling of rent due on the estate at the
time, except by one man. The sheriffs' assistants employed
on the occasion to extinguish the hearths and demolish the
homes of those honest, industrious men, worked away with
a will at their awful calling until evening fell. At length an
incident occurred that varied the monotony of the grim and
ghastly ruin which they were spreading all around. They
stopped suddenly and recoiled, panic-stricken with terror,
from two dwellings which they were directed to destroy with
the rest. They had just learned that typhus fever held
these houses in its grasp, and had already brought death to
some of their inmates. They therefore supplicated the
agent to spare these houses a little longer; but he was inexorable, and insisted that they should come down. He
ordered a large winnowing sheet to be secured over the beds
in which the fever-victims lay—fortunately, they happened
to be delirious at the time—aud then directed the houses to
be unroofed cautiously and slowly. I administered the last
Sacrament of the Church to four of these fever-victims next
day, and save the above-mentioned winnowing sheet, there
was not then a roof nearer to me than the canopy of heaven.
The scene of that eviction day I must remember all my life
long. The wailing of women, the screams, the terror, the
consternation of children, the speechless agony of men,
wrung tears of grief from all who saw them. I saw the
officers and men of a large police force who were obliged to

attend on the occasion cry like children. The heavy rains that usually attend the autumnal equinoxes descended in cold copious torrents throughout the night, and at once revealed to the houseless sufferers the awful realities of their condition. I visited them next morning, and rode from place to place administering to them all the comfort and consolation I could. The landed proprietors in a circle all round, and for many miles in every direction, warned their tenantry against admitting them to even a single night's shelter. Many of these poor people were unable to emigrate. After battling in vain with privation and pestilence, they at last graduated from the workhouse to the tomb, and in little more than three years nearly a fourth of them lay quietly in their grave."

The picture is most painful, but the evicted must be followed yet a little further to complete it. The author, after giving a vivid description of the *mode* of eviction which had almost become a science in his native land, continues:—
The Irish exodus had one awful concomitant, which in the Irish memory of that time, fills nearly as large a space as the famine itself. The people, flying from fever-tainted hovel and workhouse, carried the plague with them on board. Each vessel became a floating charnel-house. Day by day the American public was thrilled by the ghastly tale of ships arriving off the harbours reeking with typhus and cholera; the track they had followed across the ocean strewn with the corpses flung overboard on the way. Speaking in the House of Commons on the 11th of February, 1848, [the late] Mr. Labouchere referred to one year's havoc on board the ships sailing to Canada and New Brunswick alone in the following words :—

Out of 106,000 emigrants who during the last twelve months crossed the Atlantic for Canada and New Brunswick, 6100 perished on the voyage, 4100 on their arrival, 5200 in the hospitals, and 1900 in the towns to which they repaired. The total mortality was not less than 17 per cent. of the total number emigrating to those places ; the number of deaths being 17,300.

In all the great ports of America and Canada, huge quarantine hospitals had to be hastily erected. Into these every day newly arriving plague-ships poured what survived of their human freight, for whom room was as rapidly made in those wards by the havoc of death. Whole families disappeared between land and land, as sailors say. Frequently the adults were swept away, the children alone surviving. It was impossible in every case to ascertain the names of the sufferers, and often all clue to identification was lost. The public authorities, or the nobly humane organisations that had established those lazar-houses, found themselves towards the close of their labours in charge of hundreds of orphan children, of whom name and parentage alike were now impossible to be traced. About eight years ago I was waited upon in Dublin by one of these waifs, now a man of considerable wealth and honourable position. He had come across the Atlantic in pursuit of a purpose to which he is devoting years of his life—an endeavour to obtain some clue to his family, who perished in one of the great shore hospitals in 1849. Piously he treasures a few pieces of a red-painted emigrant box, which he believes belonged to his father. Eagerly he travels from place to place in Clare, and Kerry, and Galway, to see if he may dig from the tomb of that terrible past the secret lost to him, I fear, for ever !

"From Grosse Island, the great charnel-house of victimised humanity," says the Official Report of the Montreal Emigrant Society for 1847, "up to Port Sarnia, and along the borders of our magnificent river ; upon the shores of Lakes Ontario and Erie—wherever the tide of emigration has extended, are to be found the final resting places of the sons and daughters of Erin; one unbroken chain of graves, where repose fathers and mothers, sisters and brothers, in one commingled heap, without a tear bedewing the soil or a stone marking the spot. Twenty thousand and upwards have thus gone down to their graves."*

LAND LEGISLATION IN THE FIFTEENTH CENTURY.

A REMARKABLE CONTRAST: 1482 v. 1882.

The following passage will be found in Bacon's History of Henry VII :—

" Inclosures at that time began to be more frequent, whereby arable land, which could not be manured without people and families, was turned into pasture, which was easily rid by a few herdsmen; and tenancies for years, lives, and at will, whereupon much of the yeomanry lived, were turned into demesnes. This bred a decay of people, and by consequence a decay of towns, churches, by this, and the like. The King likewise knew full well and in nowise forgot, that there ensued withal upon this a decay and diminution of subsidies and taxes; for the more gentlemen even the lower books of subsidies. In remedying of this inconvenience, the King's wisdom was admirable, and the parliament's at that time. Inclosures they would not forbid, for that had been to forbid the improvement of the patrimony

* *New Ireland: Political Sketches and Personal Reminiscences of Thirty Years of Irish Public Life*, by A. M. Sullivan.

of the Kingdom; nor tillage they would not compel, for that was to strive with nature and utility; but they took a course to take away depopulating inclosures and depopulating pasturage, and yet not by that name, or by any imperious express prohibition, but by consequence. The ordinance was, 'That all houses of husbandry that were used with twenty acres of ground or upwards, should be maintained and kept for ever'."

In the preambles to several acts of parliament about that date, references are found which are singularly appropriate to the present state of things in the Highlands of Scotland. In 4th Henry VII. c. 16, it is laid down that:—

"Forasmuch as it is to the King our Sovereign lord's great surety and also to the surety of this realm of England, that the Isle of Wight, in the county of Southampton, be well inhabited with English people for the defence as well of his antient enemies of the realm of France as of other parties, the which isle is lately decayed of people by reason that many towns and villages have been beaten down, and the fields ditched and made pastures for beasts and cattles ; and also many dwelling places, ferms and fermholds, have of late times been used to be taken in one man's hold and hands, that of old time were wont to be in many persons holds and hands, and many several households kept in them, and thereby much people multiplied, and the same isle well inhabited, the which now by the occasion aforesaid is desolate and not inhabited, but occupied with beasts and cattles. The enactment is, that none shall take more ferms than one in the Isle of Wight exceeding ten merks rent."

Another preamble not less remarkable is that of 25 Henry VIII. chap. 13. It is as follows:—

"Forasmuch as divers and sundry persons of the King's subjects of this realm, to whom God of His goodness hath disposed great plenty and abundance of moveable substance, now of late within few years have daily studied, practised, and invented ways and means how they might accumulate and gather together into few hands, as well great multitude of farms as great plenty of cattle, and in especial sheep, putting such lands as they can get, to pasture, and not to tillage, whereby they have not only pulled down churches and towns, and enchanced the old rates of the rents of the possessions of this realm, or else brought it to such excessive fines that no poor man is able to meddle with it, but also have raised and enchanced the prices of all manner of corn, cattle, wool, pigs, geese, hens, chickens, eggs, and such other, almost double above the prices which have been accustomed ; by reason whereof a marvellous multitude and number of the people of this realm be not able to provide meat, drink, and clothes, necessary for themselves, their wives, and children, but be so discouraged with misery and poverty that they fall daily to theft, robbery, and other in-conveniences, or pitifully die for hunger and cold ; and as it is thought by the King's most humble and loving subjects, that one of the greatest occasions that moveth and pro-voketh those greedy and covetous people so to accumulate and keep in their hands such great portions and parts of the grounds and lands of this realm from the occupying of the poor husbandmen, and so to use it in pasture and not in tillage, is only the great profit that cometh of sheep, which now be come to a few persons hands of this realm, in res-pect of the whole number of the King's subjects, that some have four-and-twenty thousand, some twenty thousand, some ten thousand, some six thousand, some five thousand, and some more, and some less ; by the which a good sheep for victual that was accustomed to be sold for two shillings fourpence, or three shillings at the most, is now sold for six shillings or five shillings, or four shillings at the least; and a stone of clothing wool, that in some shires in this realm was accustomed to be sold for eighteen-pence or twenty-pence, is now sold for four shillings, or three shillings fourpence at the least; and in some countries where it hath been sold for two shillings fourpence or two shillings eight-pence, or three shillings at the most, it is now sold for five shillings, or four shillings eightpence at least, and so raised in every part of this realm; which things, thus used, be princi-pally to the high displeasure of Almighty God, to the decay of the hospitality of this realm, to the diminishing of the King's people, and to the let of the cloth making, whereby many poor people have been accustomed to be set on work; and in conclusion, if remedy be not found, it may turn to the utter destruction and desolation of this realm, which God defend."

Hume, in his History of England, remarks that "during a century and a half after this period, there was a continual renewal of laws against depopulation, whence we may infer that none of them were ever executed. The natural course of improvement at last provided a remedy."—*Vol. III., p. 425, ed. 1763.*

Of the popular clamours on the subject, a curious speci-men occurs in some lines preserved in Lewis's *History of the English Translations of the Bible* :—

> " Before that sheepe so much dyd rayne,
>   Where is one plough there was then twayne ;
>   Of corne and victual right greate plentye,
>   And for one pennve egges twentye.
> I truste to God it will be redressed,
>   That men by sheepe be not subpressed.
>   Sheepe have eaten men full many a yere,
>   Now let men eate sheepe and make good cheere.

> Those that have many sheepe in store
> They may repente it more and more ;
> Seynge the greate extreme necessitee,
> And yet they shewe no more charitee."

Is this not, in many respects, curiously appropriate to our own day ?

THE ISLE OF SKYE IN 1882.

THE BRAES CROFTERS AND LORD MACDONALD.

No evictions have yet taken place in consequence of the social revolution which has, during this year, directed the attention of the world to the position of landlord and tenant in the Isle of Skye. Matters have, however, reached such a pass, that in a work like this considerable space must be devoted to what has already occurred. The writer went over the ground, and he has carefully considered the whole question. The following statement was published by him, on his return from the Island, in the *Celtic Magazine* for May last, and he has not hitherto found it necessary to modify a single sentence of what he then wrote, though he has watched all the proceedings which have since occurred— including the evidence given at the trial of the Braes crofters—with great care. Indeed, it has been admitted by those more immediately concerned on the landlords' side, that his account was exceedingly moderate in tone, carefully couched in temperate language, and accurately stated in all its details. It is as follows:—

That we were, and still are, on the verge of a social revo- lution in Skye is beyond question, and those who have any influence with the people as well as those lairds and factors who have the interests of the population virtually in their keeping, will incur a very grave responsibility at a critical time like this, unless the utmost care is taken to keep the action of the aggrieved tenants within the law, and on the other hand grant to the people, in a friendly and judicious spirit, material concessions in response to grievances regarding any hardships which can be proved to exist.

It is quite true that, though innumerable grievances unquestionably do exist, no single one by itself is of sufficient magnitude to make a deep impression on the public mind, or upon any mere superficial enquirer. It is the constant accumulation of numberless petty annoyances, all in the same direction, that exasperate the people. The whole tendency, and, it is feared, the real object of the general treatment of the crofter is to crush his spirit, and keep him enslaved within the grasp of his landlord and factor. Indeed, one of the latter freely admitted to us that his object in sometimes serving large numbers of notices of removal, which he had not the slightest intention of carrying into effect, was that he might " have the whip-hand over them ". This practice can only be intended to keep the people in a constant state of terror and insecurity, and it has hitherto succeeded only too well.

The most material grievance, however, as well as the most exasperating, is the gradual but certain encroachment made on the present holdings. The pasture is taken from the crofters piecemeal; their crofts are in many cases subdivided to make room for those gradually evicted from other places—in a way to avoid public attention—to make room for sheep or deer, or both. The people see that they are being gradually but surely driven to the sea, and that if they do not resist in time they will ultimately, and at no distant date, be driven into it, or altogether expelled from their native land. A little more pressure in this direction, and no amount of argument or advice will keep the people from taking the law into their own hands and resisting it by force. The time for argument has already gone. The powers that be has hitherto refused to listen to the voice of reason, and the consequence is that scarcely any one can now be found on either side who will wait to argue whether or not a change is necessary. It is admitted on all hands that a change, and a very material change, must take place at no distant date, and the only question at present being considered in the West at least, is, What is to be the nature of the change? This is what we have now been brought face to face to, and, however difficult the problem may be —and it is surrounded with endless difficulties on all sides —the change must come; and it is admitted all round that the day when it shall take place has been brought much nearer by the inconsiderate action and unbending spirit of those at present in power in the Isle of Skye. This is now seen and admitted by themselves. In short, a great blunder has been committed. This opinion is almost universal in the Island, and it will be a crime against owners of land, against the interests of society, and against common sense, if the blunder is not at once rectified by the good sense of those who have it in their power to do so. The error will soon be forgotten if rectified with as little delay as possible; and the class of men who are willing to sacrifice their own ideas of self-importance to confer a great boon upon society is so limited, that we appeal with no slight confidence to Lord Macdonald's factor to retrace his steps, and arrange a settlement with his people in the Braes; and thus assuredly raise himself to a higher position in public estimation than he has ever yet occupied, with all his power; and at the same time become an example for good to others. He can do all this with the less difficulty, seeing that not a single one of the grievances of the Braes tenants were originated since he became factor on the Macdonald estates, and that

the only thing with which he can fairly be charged in connection with them was a too imperious disinclination to
listen to the people's claims, and that he had not fully and
sufficiently early enquired into the justice of them. On his
prudence very much depends at present the amicable settlement of a great question, or at least the shape which the
present agitation for the settlement of the relations of landlord and tenant in the Highlands will ultimately take.

We believe that the sad consequences of the recent proceedings against the Braes tenants is deplored by himself as
much as by any in the Isle of Skye, where the feeling of
regret and shame is universal among the people, from the
highest to the lowest, irrespective of position or party.

There is a very strong feeling that the law must be maintained; but the opinion is very generally expressed that the
people ought not on this occasion, and in the present state
of the public mind, to have been brought into contact with
the criminal authorities; and that by a little judicious rea-
soning this could have been very easily avoided. We quite
agree that the law must not only be respected, but firmly
vindicated, when occasion demands it; but at the same
time the owners of land who press hard upon their poor
tenants are living in a fool's paradise if they expect that
harsh laws, harshly administered, will be allowed to stand
much longer on the statute-book if such as the recent proceedings at the Braes are to be repeated elsewhere throughout
the country. Just now the facts of history deserve careful
study, and we trust that the lessons they teach will not be
thrown away on those more immediately concerned in maintaining their present position in connection with the land.

An attempt has been made to show that the Braes tenants
have no real grievances; and our own opinion before we
went to examine them on the spot was, and it is so still,

that they are, from a legal standpoint, in a far worse position to assert their claims than the tenants of Glendale, Dr. Nicol Martin's, and other proprietors on the Island. We are now satisfied, however, that they have very considerable grievances from a moral standpoint, and no one will dispute that grievances of that kind are generally as important, and often more substantial and exasperating than those which can be enforced in a court of law.

The Braes tenants maintain that in two instances considerable portions of their lands have been taken from them without any reduction of rent, and their contentions are capable of legal proof.

I. There is no doubt at all that they had the grazings of Benlee—the original cause of the present dispute—down to 1865, when it was taken from them and let to a sheep farmer as a separate holding. It can be proved that Lord Macdonald paid them rent for a small portion of it, which he took into his own hands for the site of a forester's house and garden. It can also be proved that it was not a "common" in the ordinary acceptation of that term, though it is called so in a map made by a surveyor, named Blackadder, who, in 1810, divided the crofts from the run-rig system into ordinary lots, while the grazings of Benlee continued to be held *in common* as before. The Uist people, and others from the West, paid a rent for the use of it to the Braes tenants when resting their droves on their way to the Southern markets.

II. The townships are, or were, divided into seven crofts, occupied by as many tenants, and an eighth, called the shepherd's croft, which that necessary adjunct to a common or club farm received in return for his services. The shepherd's croft has been since withdrawn, and let direct by the factor to an eighth tenant, and that without any reduction of rent to the other seven crofters in each township, while they have now to bear the burden of paying their shepherd from their own resources.   This is a virtual raising of the rents, without any equivalent, by more than 13½ per cent., altogether apart from the appropriation of Benlee.

These grievances took shape long before the present factor came into power, and he himself has stated that it was only since the present agitation began that he became even acquainted with the complaint regarding the shepherds' crofts.   For townships to have such a croft is quite common in the Island, and the practice is well known and understood.

It has been stated that the rents are now not higher than they were in 1810, but, apart from the fact that Benlee and the eighth croft have since been taken away, why compare the present with 1810, a time at which, in consequence of the wars of the period, and the high price obtained for kelp, rents and produce of every kind were very high.   The rental of Lord Macdonald's Skye property, we understand, was £8000, while in 1830, it fell to £5000, but no corresponding reduction was made in the Braes.   The tenants maintain that they have repeatedly claimed Benlee, and that the late factor told them if they had been firm when the previous lease expired, they would have got it, though whether with or without rent was not stated.   This is admitted, though different views were held by each as to the payment of rent —the tenants expecting they were to get it in terms of their request, without any payment, while the factor says that he meant them to get it on payment of the then rent.   In any case it is impossible that they can now obtain a decent livelihood without additional pasture for their stock, for they have been obliged to allow a great portion of their arable land to run into waste, to graze their cattle upon it.   They are willing to pay some rent for Benlee, and it is to be hoped, in all the circumstances, that the factor will meet them in a liberal spirit (as he can, without difficulty, get the lands from the present tenant at Whitsunday next),* and thus avoid further heart-burnings and estrangements between the landlord and his tenants. That they have moral claims of a very substantial character cannot be disputed, and the mere fact that the lands have been taken from them so long back as 1865, can scarcely be pleaded as a reason why this state of matters should be continued. It has indeed been suggested, with some amount of apparent justice, whether in all the circumstances the people have not a moral claim to a return of the value of Benlee for the period during which it has been out of their possession, seeing that they still have the arable portions and part of the grazings of their original holdings.

GLENDALE.

We visited this property, some 30 to 35 miles from Portree, and 7 to 12 miles from Dunvegan, accompanied by the special commissioners for the *Aberdeen Daily Free Press*, the *Dundee Advertiser*, and the *Glasgow Citizen*. The whole surroundings of Glendale at once indicate a more than average comfortable tenantry, indeed, the most prosperous, to outward appearance, that we have seen in the North-West Highlands. The estate is owned by the Trustees of the late Sir John Macpherson Macleod. The people are remarkably intelligent and well informed, and their grievances place those of the Braes men entirely in the shade. The following account of them and their position generally, largely from Mr. William Mackenzie's account in

* This was written in April, 1882.

the *Free Press*, and taken down in the presence of the writer, may be accepted as a true statement of their case :—

While the people are thoroughly firm in their demands, it would be a mistake to call their attitude and actions a "no rent" agitation. They are all alive to their obligation to pay rent to the landlord, and where rent is witheld that is done, not in defiance of the landlord's rights, but as the best, and perhaps the only, means they can devise to induce the landlord to consider the claims and grievances of the people. The estate managed by the trustees of the late John Macpherson Macleod consists of about a dozen townships. According to the current valuation roll, lands, etc., of the annual value of £400 9s. are in the occupancy of the trustees. Dr. Martin pays £133 for Waterstein, and the shooting tenant pays £140. The ground officer pays some £30 for lands at Colbost, while the rest of the estate is occupied by crofters, who among them pay a rent of about £700. The extent of the estate is about 35,000 acres. Ten years ago the rent was £1257, while now it is £1397 odds, shewing a net increase on the decade of £139 16s. 1d. or slightly over 11 per cent.

The tenants complain that the different townships were deprived of rights anciently possessed by them ; that some townships were by degrees cleared of the crofters to enable the laird or the factor to increase his stock of sheep, and that such of these people as did not leave the estate were crowded into other townships, individual tenants in these townships being required to give a portion of their holdings to make room for these new comers. They also complain of the arrogant and dictatorial manner in which the factor deals with them. So the Glendale crofters, wearied for years with what they have regarded as oppression, have now risen as one man, resolved to unfold before the public gaze those matters of which they complain, and to demand of their territorial superiors to restore to them lands which at one time were occupied by themselves and their ancestors, to lessen, if not to remove, what they regard as the severity of the factor's yoke, and generally to place them in that position of independence and security to which they consider they are fairly and justly entitled. The functions performed by the factor of Glendale are exceedingly varied in their character. He is, they say, as a rule, sole judge of any little dispute that may arise between the crofters. He decides these disputes according to his own notions of right or wrong, and if anyone is dissatisfied—a not uncommon occurrence even among litigants before the Supreme Courts —the dissatisfied one dare not carry the matter to the regularly constituted tribunals of the land. To impugn the judgment of the factor by such conduct might entail more serious consequences than any one would be disposed to incur, and, further, the extraordinary and mistaken notion appears to have prevailed that if any one brought a case before the Sheriff Court the factor's letter would be there before him to nonsuit him. This factorial mode of administrating the law is probably a vestige that still lingers in isolated districts of the ancient heritable jurisdiction of Scotland; and it is only right to state that Glendale is not the only place in the Highlands where the laird or the factor have been wont to administer the law. Among the privileges which the Glendale people formerly possessed was the right to collect and get the salvage for timber drifted from wrecks to the shore. Of this privilege it was resolved to deprive them, as may be seen from the following written notice which was posted up at the local post-office, the most public part of the district :—

Notice.—Whereas parties are in the habit of trespassing on the lands of Glendale, Lowergill, Ramasaig, and Waterstein, in searching and carrying away drift timber, notice is hereby given that the shepherds and herds on these lands have instructions to give up the names of any persons found hereafter on any part of said lands, as also anyone found carrying away timber from the shore by boats or otherwise, that they may be dealt with according to law.—Factor's Office, Tormore, 4th January, 1882.

The lands over which they were thus forbidden to walk, consist mainly of sheep grazing, in the occupation of the trustees, and managed for them by the factor. The people were also forbidden to keep dogs.

These notices, it is stated, had the desired effect; trespassing ceased, and the crofter, with a sad heart, destroyed his canine friend. Grievances multiplying in this way, it was resolved by some leader in the district to convene a public meeting of the crofters to consider the situation. The notice calling the meeting together, was in these terms :—

We, the tenants on the estate of Glendale, do hereby warn each other to meet at Glendale Church on the 7th day of February, on or about one P.M., of 1882, for the purpose of stating our respective grievances publicly, in order to communicate the same to our superiors, when the ground-officer is requested to attend.

Such a revolutionary movement as this, the people actually daring to meet together to consider their relations with the laird, and make demands, was not to be lightly entered upon, and it need not be wondered at if some of them at first wanted the moral courage to come up to the occasion. If any one showed symptoms of weakness in this way he was encouraged, and on the appointed day the clansmen met and deliberated on the situation. At that meeting their grievances received full expression. It was in particular pointed out that the township of Ramasaig, which fifteen years ago was occupied by 22 separate crofters, is now reduced to two, the land taken from or given up by the other twenty families having been put under sheep by the factor. The people, who presumably were less valuable than the sheep, in some cases left the country altogether, while those that remained were provided with half crofts on another part of the estate.

For instance, a crofter who perhaps had a ten pound croft, say, at Milivaig was requested to give up the one-half of it to a crofter removed from Ramasaig, a corresponding reduction being made in the rent. In this way, while the sheep stocks under the charge of the factor were increasing, the status of the crofters was gradually diminishing, and the necessity for their depending more and more on other industries than the cultivation of their croft was increasing. To illustrate this all the more forcibly, we may state that the crofters at Ramasaig had eight milk cows and their followers, and about forty sheep on each whole croft—altogether over a hundred head of cattle and from 300 to 400 sheep. Lowerkell was similarly cleared. At the meeting of the crofters, to which I have alluded, it was resolved that, as a body, they should adopt a united course of action. They were all similarly situated. Each man and each township had a grievance, and no individual was to be called upon to make a separate claim. Each township or combination of townships was to make one demand, and if any punishment should follow on such an act of temerity, it should not be allowed to fall on any one person, but on the united body as a whole. To guard against any backsliding, and to prevent any weakling or chicken-hearted leaguer (if any should exist) from falling out of the ranks, they, one and all, subscribed their names in a book, pledging themselves as a matter of honour to adhere in a body to the resolution thus arrived at. The scheme having thus been formulated, each township or combination proceeded to get up petitions embodying their respective cases, and sending them to the trustees, Professor Macpherson, of Edinburgh, and his brother.

The tenants of Skinidin claim two islands, opposite their crofts, in Loch Dunvegan. Apart from this, they complain that they do not get the quantity of seaweed to which they were entitled. This may appear to some a small matter, but to the cultivator of a croft it is a matter of great import- ance, for seaware is the only manure which he can conveni- ently get, excepting, of course, the manure produced by his cows. The quantity of ware promised to the Skinidin crofters was one ton each, but the one-half of it, they say, was taken from them some time ago, and given to the " wealthy men " and favourites of the place. The result is that they have to cross to the opposite side of Loch Dun- vegan and buy sea-ware there at 31s. 6d. per ton. This is not only an outlay of money, which the poor crofters can ill afford to incur, but it also entails great labour, which is attended with no inconsiderable danger to life. The crofters accordingly demand the quantity of ware to which, they say, they are entitled.

The Colbost tenants, to the number of twenty-five, also sent in a petition, in which they complained of high rents, and stated that owing to incessant tilling the land is becom- ing exhausted, and ceasing to yield that crop which they might fairly expect. In 1848, they say they got Colbost with its old rights at its old rent with the sanction of the proprietor. The local factor, Norman Macraild, subse- quently deprived them of these privileges, while the rents were being constantly increased. They accordingly demand that their old privileges should be restored, and the rents reduced to the old standard, otherwise they will not be able to meet their engagements.

We shall next take the petition of the Harmaravirein crofters. The place is occupied by John Campbell, who pays £9 15s. 4d.; John Maclean, £5 3s. 4d.; John Mackay, £6 2s. 8d.; and Donald Nicolson, £4 12s. The petition, which was in the following terms, deserves record :—

We, the crofters of Harmaravirein, do humbly show by this petition that we agree with our fellow-petitioners in Glendale as to their requests. We do, by the same petition, respectfully ask redress for grievances laid upon us by a despotic factor, Donald Macdonald, Tormore, who thirteen years ago for the first time took from us part of our land, against our will, and gave it to others, whom he drove from another quarter of the estate of Glendale, to extend his own boundaries, and acted similarly two years ago, when he dispersed the Ramasaig tenantry. We, your humble petitioners, believe that none of the grievances mentioned were known to our late good and famous proprietor, being an absentee, in whom we might place our confidence had he been present to hear and grant our request. As an instance of his goodwill to his subjects, the benefits he bestowed on the people of St. Kilda are manifest to the kingdom of Great Britain. We, your petitioners, pray our new proprietors to consider our case, and grant that the tenantry be reinstated in the places which have been cleared of their inhabitants by him in Tormore.

The petition of the Upper and Lower Milivaig and Borrodale crofters set forth that, notwithstanding their going north and south all over the country to earn their bread, they are still declining into poverty. The crofts too are getting exhausted through constant tilling. Before 1845 they say there were only 16 families in the two Milivaigs and one in Borrodale. There are now 5 in Borrodale, 19 in Upper Milivaig, and 20 in Lower Milivaig, averaging six souls in each family. The rent before 1845 for the two Milivaigs was £40. At the date mentioned, Macleod of Macleod, who was then proprietor, divided each of the two Milivaigs into 16 crofts.

They prayed that they might get the lands of Waterstein now tenanted by Dr. Martin. The petition concluded:—

Further, we would beg, along with our fellow-petitioners in Glendale, that the tenantry who have been turned out of Lowerkell, Ramasaig, and Hamara by our ill-ruling factor be reinstated.

The tenants of Holmesdale and Liepbein, 29 in number, stated in their petition, that 48 years ago the place was let to ten tenants at about £60, and afterwards re-let to 25 tenants at about £85, besides a sum of £3 2s. 6d. for providing peats for the proprietor. The rents, they say, have nearly doubled since then, and the inhabitants increased, the present number being nearly 200, occupying 33 dwellings. There was much overcrowding, there being as many as 15 persons upon crofts of four acres. The petition contained the following estimate of factors:—"Unless poor crofters are to be protected by the proprietor of the estate, we need not expect anything better than suppression from factors who are constantly watching and causing the downfall of their fellow-beings, in order to turn their small portion of the soil into sheep-walks." These tenants prayed that the evicted townships of Lowerkell, Ramasaig, and Hamara, should be restored to the tenants, and thus to afford relief to the overcrowded townships. The crofters of Glasvein said they had no hill pasture for sheep, and no peat moss to get their fuel from. When some of the present crofters, they say, came into possession of their crofts, the township of Glasvein was allotted to seven tenants, each paying an average rent of £5, whereas now the township is in the possession of 12 crofters, paying each an average rent of £4 or so. They accordingly sought to have this matter remedied.

It may be stated that most of the tenants of Glendale

appear to be all hard-working, industrious men, and their houses are better, on the whole, than any crofter district that that we have yet visited in Skye. The soil is more fertile, well drained, and comparatively well cultivated. The men seem to be thoroughly intelligent, and some of them not only read newspapers, but have very decided opinions in regard to some of them. One of these, the *Scotsman*, we heard them designating as "The United Liar". But newspaper reading—that is Liberal newspaper reading—is not encouraged in Glendale. One man whom we met informed us that a crofter in Glendale was accused of reading too many newspapers, a circumstance which the factor strongly suspected accounted for the heinous crime of the crofter being a Liberal. At one time there were some small shops in Glendale, but these would appear to have practically vanished. Some years ago the factor set up a meal store himself, and the crofters, we are informed, were given to understand that shopkeepers would have to pay a rent of £2 each for these so-called shops, in addition to their rents. No one, however, appears to have ever been asked to pay this, but the shops ceased to exist !

Perhaps the most indefensible custom of all was to compel the incoming tenant to pay up the arrears, however large a sum, of his predecessor. This appeared so incredible that no one present felt justified in publishing it ; but on our consulting the factor personally, he not only admitted but actually defended the practice as a kind of fair enough premium or "goodwill" for the concern, and said it was quite a common practice in the Isle of Skye. We would describe it in very different terms, but that is unnecessary. It only wants to be stated to be condemned by all honest men as an outrage on public morality.

As we left the district the crofters were in great glee at the

prospect of a visit from the trustees to arrange matters with
them.   They are hopeful that important concessions may be
made to them, and if these hopes should not be realised,
they appear to be animated with an unflinching determination
to stand by one another, and, shoulder to shoulder, agitate
for the redress of what they firmly maintain to be great and
serious grievances.

Dr. Martin's Estate.

We have left ourselves but little space to speak of the
condition of affairs on the estate of Dr. Martin.   This
estate is one which is of great interest to Highlanders.
Borreraig, one of the townships in revolt, was anciently
held rent free by the MacCrimmons, the hereditary pipers
of Macleod of Dunvegan.   The principal grievance complained of by the crofters may be briefly stated.   The
crofters are required to sell to the laird all the fish they
catch at a uniform rate of sixpence for ling and fourpence
for cod, and we have actually been informed of a case
where some one was accused at a semi-public meeting of
interfering in a sort of clandestine way with the doctor's
privileges by buying the fish at higher prices.   The
crofters were also required to sell their cattle to the doctor's
bailiff at his own price.   A man spoke of his having some
time ago sold a stirk to a foreign drover, and was after all required to break his bargain with the outsider and hand over
the animal to the bailiff.   This bailiff was, however, dismissed last Whitsunday, a fact stated in defence by Dr.
Martin's friends.   Tenants are also required to give eight
days' free labour each year to the laird, failing which to pay
a penalty of 2s. 6d. per day ; and while thus working, we
were informed that if any one by accident broke any of the

tools he used, he was required to pay for the damage. The breaking of a shearing-hook subjected the man who did it to pay 2s. 6d. for it. We are aware that the friends of the laird maintain that the labour thus contributed by the people is in reality not for labour, but an equivalent for a portion of the rent. This is a very plausible excuse, but it will not bear examination. If it is regarded as a part of the rent, rates should be paid upon it, and the "annual value" or rent returned to the county valuator each year should be the amount actually paid in money plus the value of the eight days' labour. Thus, either the labour is free, or there is an unjust and inequitable burden thrown on the other crofters in the parish who do not perform such labour, as, of course, the labour given by Dr. Martin's tenants is not rated. The tenants have now struck against performing this work, and Dr. Martin's work was done this year on ordinary day labour.

The people also complain that the hill land was taken from the tenants of Galtrigill, and the hill grounds of Borreraig, the neighbouring township, thrown open to them. This was a very material curtailment of the subjects let, but further, sums of from 10s. to 30s. were added to the rent of each holding. No crofter on the estate has a sheep or a horse, and they are obliged to buy wool for their clothing from a distance, as Dr. Martin, they say, will not sell them any. The tenants paid their rents at Martinmas last, but they have given notice that unless their demands are conceded they will not pay the rent due at Martinmas next. The leading points of their petition are that the rents be reduced, the old land-marks restored, and the hill grounds as of old given to them. This petition the tenants sent to Dr. Martin some time ago, but he has not made any reply. The tenants do not appear to be very hopeful that

he will make any concession, but they are evidently determined to walk in the same paths as their neighbours on the
estate of Sir John Macpherson Macleod, and they are in
great hopes that the friends of the Gael in the large towns
of the south will manfully aid them in their battle against
landlordism.   This statement will enable the reader to form
his own opinion on the question which has produced such a
feeling of insecurity and terror in the minds of both crofter
and proprietor for the last two years in the Isle of Skye,
indeed throughout the whole Highlands.

BURNING THE SUMMONSES IN THE BRAES.

We shall next give a short account of what followed upon
the refusal of these proprietors to give favourable consideration to the claims of their crofting tenantry.   A correspondent of the *Free Press*, early in April last, described what
had occurred—after the tenants had refused to pay any rent
until their grievances were considered—in the following
terms :—

The quarrel between Lord Macdonald and his tenants of
Balmeanach, Peinichorrain, and Gedintaillear, in the Braes
of Portree, is developing into portentous importance.   His
lordship, it appears, has made up his mind to put the law in
force against them, and not on any account to yield to their
demands ; and on Friday a sheriff-officer and assistant,
accompanied by his lordship's ground-officer from Portree,
proceeded to serve summonses of removing, and small debt
summonses for rent upon about a score of the refractory
ones.   The tenants, however, for some time past, since they
took up their present attitude, have been posting regular
sentinels on watch to give warning of any stranger's approach,
and when the officer and his party were at the Bealach near

the schoolhouse, two youngsters who were on duty there-
about gave the signal, and, immediately, it was transmitted
far and near with the result of bringing together from all
quarters from their spring work a gathering of about 150 or
200 men, women, and children, who rushed to meet the
officer before he had got near the intended scene of his
operation, viz., the townships of Peinichorrain, Balmeanach,
and Gedintaillear, and, surrounding him, demanded his
business.   Upon understanding it, and being shown the
summonses, the documents were immediately taken from
him and burnt before his eyes, and thereupon he was coolly
requested to go to his master for more of them.   The officer,
who is well known among them, with good tact, humoured
them, and so escaped with a sound skin, so that no violence
was used ; but it appears the temper of the people was such
that had he been less conciliatory, or had he attempted to
resist the people, the consequence would have been inevitably very serious for him.   When they were gathering from
the sea-shore, where many of them were cutting sea-ware
with reaping-hooks, their leaders judiciously shouted out to
leave their hooks behind, which was done, so that the risk
of using such ugly arms in the event of a *melée* was avoided.
The officer spoke lightly before proceeding to the place of
the resistance he was likely to meet, and thought there
would really be none, as he knew the people so well and
they knew him, many of them being his relations, but his
impressions now of the real state of the people's minds is
said to be very different, and he believes there would be
no use attempting any legal steps again by the employment
of the officers of civil law.   The same paper in a later issue
says :—

We have received the following narrative of the manner
in which the summonses were burned on Friday last :—The

people met the officer on the road, about a mile from the scene of his intended labours. They were clamorous and angry, of course. He told them his mission, and that he would give them the summonses on the spot if they liked. They said, " Thoir dhuinn iad," (Give them to us) and he did so. The officer was then asked to light a fire. He did so; and a fish liver being placed upon it, that oily material was soon in a blaze. The officer was then peremptorily ordered to consign the summonses to the flames, which he did! The summonses were of course straightway consumed to ashes. The interchange of compliments between the officers of the law and the people were, as might be expected, of a fiery character. The chief officer was graciously and considerately informed that his conduct—as he had only acted in the performance of a public official duty—was excusable; but with his assistant, or concurrent, it was different. He was there for pay, and he would not go home without it. Certain domestic utensils, fully charged, were suddenly brought on the scene, and their contents were showered on the unlucky assistant, who immediately disappeared, followed by a howling crowd of boys.

MARCH OF THE DISMAL BRIGADE.

The summonses were never served, and the County Authorities after full consideration determined to arrest and punish the ringleaders for deforcing the officers of the law. Sheriff Ivory obtained a body of police from Glasgow, and with these, twelve from the mainland of the County of Inverness, and the Skye portion of the force, he, with the leading county officials invaded the Isle of Skye during the night of the 17th of April. After consulting with the local authorities in Portree, an early start was made for the Braes to surprise and arrest the ringleaders. The secret was well kept, but two newspaper correspondents were fortunate enough to get an inkling of the proceedings, namely, Mr. Mackinnon Ramsay, of the *Citizen*, who followed the invading force from Glasgow, and Mr. Alexander Gow, a special correspondent of the *Dundee Advertiser*, who had gone to Portree a few days before the Battle of the Braes. These gentlemen accompanied the county officials, saw the whole proceedings, and sent a full description of the desperate and humiliating scrimmage to their respective papers. We give below Mr. Gow's graphic account, every particular of which we found corroborated by the leading county officials on our arrival in Portree the same evening. After describing the state of feeling, and the acts on the part of the crofters which led up to direct contact with the criminal authorities, Mr. Gow proceeds :—

Here we were, then—two Sheriffs, two Fiscals, a Captain of police, forty-seven members of the Glasgow police force, and a number of the county constabulary, as well as a couple of newspaper representatives from Dundee and Glasgow, and a gentleman representing a well-known Glasgow drapery house—fairly started on an eight-mile tramp to the Land League camp at Braes, in weather that for sheer brutal ferocity had not been experienced in Skye for a very long time. In the cold grey dawn the procession wore a sombre aspect. It looked for all the world like a Highland funeral. It was quite on the cards, indeed, that the return journey might partake of the nature of a funeral procession. There could be no doubt that every one was fully impressed with the gravity of the mission on which we were proceeding. It is literal truth to say that no member of the company expected to return without receiving knocks, if not some-

thing more serious. We were perfectly aware that the
crofters had made preparations for giving us a warm reception. In front, some distance ahead of the main body,
walked the sheriff-officer, a policeman, and another person
occupying for the time being some official position. Then
came the police detachment, and the Sheriffs and the Fiscals
brought up the rear—the three unofficial persons already
mentioned forming what may be termed the rearguard. In
this manner we proceeded without incident for four miles,
when the Sheriff and his friends left the vehicle and sent it
back. About half-past six o'clock we reached the boundary
of the disaffected district nearest Portree. Hitherto scarcely
a single soul was observed along the route, and some surprise was expressed by those in charge. At the schoolhouse,
however, it was expected that a portion of the colony would
be encountered, but the place was untenanted. On another
mile, and signs of life appeared among the hillocks. Presently our ears were saluted with whistling and cheering,
and this was interpreted as a sign that it was time to close
the ranks. Gedentailler township was passed without any
demonstrations of hostility. At the south end of this township there is an ugly looking pass, which seemed to cause
some anxiety to the officers in charge. No wonder, as there
could not be a finer position for an attack on a hostile body
of men. On the west, a steep rocky brae rises sheer from
the road to the height of about 400 or 500 feet. On the
other side, a terrific precipice descends to the sea. We
passed through it in safety, however, but Inspector Cameron,
of the Skye police, had reason to believe that the return
passage would be disputed.

Arrived at the boundary of Balmeanach, we found a collection of men, women, and children, numbering well on to
100. They cheered as we mounted the knoll, and the

women saluted the policemen with volleys of sarcasms about
their voyage from Glasgow. A halt was then called, and a
parley ensued between the local inspector and what appeared to be the leader of the townships. What is passing
between the two it is difficult for an outsider to understand,
and while the conversation is in progress it is worth while
to look about. At the base of the steep cliff on which we
stood, and extending to the seashore, lay the hamlet of
Balmeanach. There might be about a score of houses
dotted over this plain. From each of these the owners were
running hillward with all speed. It was evident they
had been taken by surprise. Men, women, and children
rushed forward, in all stages of attire, most of the females
with their hair down and streaming loosely in the breeze.
Every soul carried a weapon of some kind or another, but
in most cases these were laid down when the detachment
was approached. While we were watching the crowds
scrambling up the declivity, scores of persons had gathered
from other districts, and they now completely surrounded the
procession. The confusion that prevailed baffles description.
The women, with infuriated looks and bedraggled dress—for
it was still raining heavily—were shouting at the pitch of
their voices, uttering the most fearful imprecations, hurling
forth the most terrible vows of vengeance against the enemy.
Martin was of course the object of greatest abuse. He was
cursed in his own person and in that of his children, if he
should have any, one female shrieking curses with especial
vehemence. The authorities proceeded at once to perform
their disagreeable task, and in the course of twenty minutes
the five suspected persons were apprehended. A scene utterly
indescribable followed. The women, with the most violent
gestures and imprecations, declared that the police should be
attacked. Stones began to be thrown, and so serious an aspect

did matters assume that the police drew their batons and charged. This was the signal for a general attack. Huge boulders darkened the horizon as they sped from the hands of infuriated men and women. Large sticks and flails were brandished and brought down with crushing force upon the police—the poor prisoners coming in for their share of the blows. One difficult point had to be captured, and as the expedition approached this dangerous position, it was seen to be strongly occupied with men and women, armed with stones and boulders. A halt was called and the situation discussed. Finally it was agreed to attempt to force a way through a narrow gully. By this time a crowd had gathered in the rear of the party. A rush was made for the pass, and from the heights a fearful fusilade of stones descended. The advance was checked. The party could neither advance nor recede. For two minutes the expedition stood exposed to the merciless shower of missiles. Many were struck, and a number more or less injured. The situation was highly dangerous. Raising a yell that might have been heard at a distance of two miles, the crofters, maddened by the apprehension of some of the oldest men in the township, rushed on the police, each person armed with huge stones, which, on approaching near enough, they discharged with a vigour that nothing could resist. The women were by far the most troublesome assailants. Thinking apparently that the constables would offer them no resistance, they approached to within a few yards' distance, and poured a fearful volley into the compact mass. The police charged, but the crowd gave way scarcely a yard. Returning again, Captain Donald gave orders to drive back the howling mob, at the same time advising the Sheriffs and the constables in charge of the prisoners to move rapidly forward. This second charge was more effective, as the attacking force was

driven back about a hundred yards. The isolated constables now, however, found their position very dangerous.
The crofters rallied and hemmed them in, and a rush had
to be made to catch up the main body in safety. At this
point several members of the constabulary received serious
buffetings, and had they not regained their comrades, some
of their number would in all probability have been mortally
wounded. Meanwhile the crowd increased in strength.

The time within which summonses of ejectment could
be legally served having expired, the crofters had for a
day or two relaxed their vigilance, and not expecting the
constables so early in the morning, they had no time
to gather their full strength. But the " Fiery Cross " had
in five minutes passed through the whole township from
every point. Hundreds of determined looking persons
could be observed converging on the procession, and
matters began to assume a serious aspect. With great
oaths, the men demanded where were the Peinichorrain men.
This township was the most distant, and the men had not
yet had time to come up. But they were coming. Cheers
and yells were raised. "The rock ! the rock !" suddenly
shouted some one. "The rock ! the rock !" was taken
up, and roared out from a hundred throats. The strength
of the position was realised by the crofters ; so also it
was by the constables. The latter were ordered to run at
the double. The people saw the move, and the screaming
and yelling became fiercer than ever. The detachment
reached the opening of the gulley. Would they manage
to run through ? Yes ! No ! On went the blue coats, but
their progress was soon checked. It was simply insane to
attempt the passage. Stones were coming down like hail,
while huge boulders where hurled down before which
nothing could stand. These bounded over the road and

descended the precipice with a noise like thunder. An order was given to dislodge a number of the most determined assailants, but the attempt proved futile. They could not be dislodged. Here and there a constable might be seen actually bending under the pressure of a well-directed rounder, losing his footing, and rolling down the hill, followed by scores of missiles. This state of matters could not continue. The chief officials were securing their share of attention. Captain Donald is hit in the knee with a stone as large as a matured turnip. A rush must be made for the pass, or there seems a possibility that Sheriff Ivory himself will be deforced. Once more the order was given to double. On, on, the procession went—Sheriffs and Fiscals forgetting their dignity, and taking to their heels. The scene was the most exciting that either the spectators or those who passed through the fire ever experienced, or are likely ever to see again. By keeping up the rush, the party got through the defile, and emerged triumphantly on the Portree side, not however, without severe injuries. If the south end township had turned out, the pass would, I believe, never have been forced, and some would in all probability have lost their lives.

The crofters seemed to have become more infuriated by the loss of their position, and rushing along the shoulder of the hill prepared to attack once more. This was the final struggle. In other attacks the police used truncheons freely. But at this point they retaliated with both truncheons and stones. The consequences were very serious indeed. Scores of bloody faces could be seen on the slope of the hill. One woman, named Mary Nicolson, was fearfully cut in the head, and fainted on the road. When she was found, blood was pouring down her neck and ears. Another woman, Mrs. Finlayson, was badly gashed on the cheek with some missile. Mrs. Nicolson, whose husband, James Nicolson, was one of the prisoners, had her head badly laid open, but whether with a truncheon or stone is not known. Another woman, well advanced in years, was hustled in the scrimmage on the hill, and, losing her balance, rolled down a considerable distance, her example being followed by a stout policeman, the two ultimately coming into violent collision. The poor old person was badly bruised, and turned sick and faint. Of the men a considerable number sustained severe bruises, but so far as I could ascertain none of them were disabled. About a dozen of the police were injured more or less seriously. One of the Glasgow men had his nose almost cut through with a stone, and was terribly gashed about the brow. Captain Donald, as already stated, was struck on the knee, and his leg swelled up badly after the return to Portree. Neither the Sheriffs nor the Fiscals were injured, but it is understood that they all received hits in the encounter on the hill.

After the serious scrimmage at Gedintailler, no further demonstrations of hostility were made, and the procession went on, without further adventure, to Portree. Rain fell without intermission during the entire journey out and home, and all arrived at their destination completely exhausted. On arrival in town the police were loudly hooted and hissed as they passed through the square to the jail, and subsequently when they marched from the Court-house to the Royal Hotel. The prisoners were lodged in the prison. There names are :—Alexander Finlayson, aged between 60 and 70 years ; Malcolm Finlayson, a son of the above, and living in the same house (the latter is married) ; Peter Macdonald has a wife and eight of a family ; Donald Nicolson, 66 years of age, and is married ; and James Nicolson, whose wife was one of the women seriously injured.

Unless appearances are totally misleading, the work which they were obliged to accomplish was most repugnant to Sheriff Ivory, Sheriff Spiers, Mr. James Anderson, Procurator-Fiscal for the County, and Mr. MacLennan; and the hope may be expressed that they will never again be called upon to undertake similar duties.

The "Battle of the Braes" has been capitally hit off in the following parody, published in the *Daily Mail* of the 26th of April last:—

CHARGE OF THE SKYE BRIGADE.

Half a league, half a league !
  Four a-breast—onward !
All in the valley of Braes
  Marched the half-hundred.
"Forward, Police Brigade !
In front of me," bold Ivory said ;
Into the valley of Braes
  Charged the half-hundred.

"Forward, Police Brigade !
Charge each auld wife and maid !"
E'en though the Bobbies knew
  Some one had blundered !
Their's not to make reply ;
Their's not to reason why ;
Their's but to do or die ;
Into the valley of Braes
  Charged the half-hundred.

"Chuckies" to right of them,
"Divots " to left of them,
Women in front of them,
  Volleyed and thundered !
Stormed at with stone and shell,
Boldly they charged, they tell,
Down on the Island Host !
Into the mouth of—well !
  Charged the half-hundred.

Flourished their batons bare,
Not in the empty air—
Clubbing the lasses there,
Charging the Cailleachs, while
    All Scotland wondered !
Plunged in the mist and smoke,
Right thro' the line they broke ;—
Cailleach and maiden
Reeled from the baton stroke,
    Shattered and sundered ;
Then they marched back—intact—
    All the half-hundred.

Missiles to right of them,
Brickbats to left of them,
Old wives behind them
    Volleyed and floundered.
Stormed at with stone and shell—
Whilst only Ivory fell—
They that had fought so well
Broke thro' the Island Host,
Back from the mouth of—well !
All that was left of them—
    All the half-hundred !

When can their glory fade ?
O, the wild charge they made !
    All Scotland wondered !
Honour the charge they made !
Honour the Skye Brigade !
    Donald's half-hundred !

                    ALFRED TENNYSON, JUNIOR.

TRIAL OF THE BRAES CROFTERS.

WHEN the " Battle of the Braes " had been fought and won,
and the gallant Sheriff with his brave contingent of blue-
coats covered with the mud of the Braes and the glory of

their masterly retreat before the old men and women of
Gedintailler had retired to their quarters in Portree, the
friends of the prisoners began to think of their defence when
they came before the Law Courts for trial.

A few hours after the Police Brigade returned to Portree,
Dean of Guild Mackenzie, Inverness, editor of the *Celtic
Magazine*, who had gone, as representative of the Highland
Land Law Reform Association, to report upon the alleged
grievances of the crofters in Skye, arrived ln Portree. Him
the friends of the prisoners consulted, with the result that
he dispatched a telegram to Mr. Kenneth Macdonald,
Town Clerk of Inverness, asking him to undertake the
defence. Curiously enough a number of sympathisers in
Glasgow, who had formed themselves into a defence committee, met about the same time, and they also, through
their secretary, Mr. Hugh Macleod, Writer, Glasgow, telegraphed to know if Mr. Macdonald would defend the
prisoners. Both telegrams were delivered about the same
time and to each an affirmative reply was immediately
sent.

At this time nothing definite was known of the charge
preferred against the prisoners, and it was not until the 26th
of April, 1882, a week after the arrest, and when they could
no longer be legally detained without having a copy of the
charge delivered to them, that the prisoners were committed
for trial and allowed to see an adviser. Such is the
humanity of the Criminal Law of Scotland. During the
week which a prisoner can thus be legally kept in close
confinement, he will not be permitted to see friend or
adviser of any kind, but he may be brought day after day
before the Sheriff and subjected to examination by a
skilful lawyer whose main if not sole object is to get from
him admissions which will tend to prove his guilt, and every

word he utters during this time is taken down for the purpose of being used against him at his trial.

After the prisoners were committed for trial, they were visited by their agent, with the editor of the *Celtic Magazine* as interpreter, and in course of conversation, and in reply to questions, the prisoners expressed a desire to get home to proceed with the spring work on their crofts. By this time the sympathy with the prisoners among the outside public, not merely in the Highlands but in the large cities of the south, had extended through all classes of society. Many who were in entire sympathy with them in their personal grievances thought that they saw in the proceedings taken against them, and in the outrages perpetrated in Skye in the name of law, a means of creating a public opinion which would compel the Legislature to take up the question of land tenure in the Highlands. It was the desire of this party that the accused should be allowed to remain in prison until their trial came on, in order that the public sympathy which their apprehension and imprisonment evoked should have time to take definite form. If the calculations of these sympathisers should turn out accurate, the infliction of a slight hardship upon these men would result in permanent good to themselves and the whole class to which they belonged. The desires of the men themselves, however, of their friends in Inverness, and the interest of their families, naturally guided Mr. Macdonald's proceedings, and he presented a petition to the Sheriff to fix bail. The bail was fixed by Sheriff Blair at £20 sterling for each prisoner —£100 in all—and immediately it became known that persons were wanted, to sign the bond, gentlemen offered themselves, the required subscriptions were obtained, and the five prisoners were liberated that night. The gentlemen who signed the bond were : Mr. John Macdonald, merchant, Exchange; Dean of Guild Mackenzie; Councillor Duncan Macdonald; Councillor W. G. Stuart; Mr. Wm. Gunn, Castle Street; Mr. T. B. Snowie, gunmaker; Mr. Donald Campbell, draper; and Mr. Duncan MacBeath, Duncraig Street—all of Inverness. On the following day the accused left Inverness for Skye by the 9 A.M. train, accompanied to the station by several of their friends, including the Reverend and venerable Dr. George Mackay.

The following account of the reception of the liberated men on their return to Portree is taken from the *Aberdeen Daily Free Press*, whose special correspondent, Mr. William Mackenzie, was on the spot:—

The five men from the prison of Inverness arrived at Portree this evening, and were received with unbounded enthusiasm. Early in the day a telegram was received intimating that they had left Inverness in the morning, and that the venerable pastor of the North Church, the Rev. Dr. Mackay, gave them there a friendly farewell. Mairi Nighean Iain Bhain, to whose poetic effusions on the men of the Braes and Benlee, I have formerly alluded, went by the steamer from Portree in the morning to meet them at Strome Ferry. She was accompanied by Colin the piper, and on the homeward journey the men were inspired with the songs of the poetess, the music of the Highland war-pipe, and a scarcely less potent stimulant, the famous Talisker. It was known far and wide that the men were to come to-night, and their fellow-crofters in the Braes resolved to give them a hearty reception. The Braes men accordingly began to straggle into the town in the afternoon, and groups of them might be seen along the street eagerly discussing the situation. Endeavours were made to induce the "suspects" to leave the steamer at Raasay and row afterwards to the Braes. This would, of course, deprive their friends of any chance to give them an ovation at Portree, and lead outsiders to suppose that the Portree people regarded the matter with indifference. The liberated men were, however, warned against being caught in the snare which was laid for them, and they came straight on to Portree. The steamer did not arrive till about eight o'clock, but whenever she reached the quay the assembled multitude raised a deafening cheer, again and again renewed, which completely drowned Colin's pipes. As soon as the steamer was brought alongside the quay, Colin stepped out, playing "Gabhaidh sinn an rathad mor ". He was followed by the poetess, and after her the five liberated men. Each man, as he stepped on the quay, was embraced by the males, and hugged and kissed by the females, amid volumes of queries as to their condition since they left, and congratulations on their return. These friendly greetings were not allowed to be of any duration, for each man was hoisted and carried shoulder-high in triumph through the streets of Portree. The Braes men themselves mustered in full force, and in the procession they were joined by numerous sympathisers in the district and the village of Portree. The crowd, headed by the piper and the poetess, proceeded along the principal thoroughfare to the Portree Hotel. Bonnets were carried on the tops of walking sticks, and held up above the heads of the people, amid cries of "Still higher yet my bonnet," while the women of Portree waved their white hand-kerchiefs and shouted Gaelic exclamations of joy as the "lads wi' the bonnets o' blue" were carried along in triumph. On reaching the Portree Hotel a number of them, including the "suspects," went in, and Mr. MacInnes, the popular tenant of that excellent and well-conducted establishment, treated the "suspects" to refreshments. Who should happen to turn up unexpectedly at the hotel but the factor, accompanied by some of his friends, and when that individual emerged from the door of the hotel, he was received with a volume of groans. The Braes men left the hotel without any delay and marched to their homes in a body, shouting and cheering as they proceeded on their way. A carriage was sent after them to convey the five men from Inverness to their respective places of abode.

In the meantime an intimation had been conveyed to the Prisoners' Agent by Mr. James Anderson, Procurator-Fiscal of Inverness, that he had been ordered by the Crown Agent to have the prisoners tried summarily before the Sheriff for the crimes of deforcement and assault. This was, so far as known, the first time in Scottish Legal History that so serious a crime, so seriously treated by the authorities at the outset, had been ordered for summary trial. There was something suspicious in the order, and although the letter of it was adhered to, it is probable that but for the protests made on behalf of the prisoners, both in and out of Parlia-ment, the true meaning of the order would have been made evident at the trial. On receiving intimation of the order, Mr. Macdonald wrote to the Lord-Advocate for Scotland, requesting that he should instruct the trial to proceed before a jury. To that letter the following reply was received :—

WHITEHALL, April 29, 1882.

SIR,

I am directed by the Lord-Advocate to acknowledge receipt of your letter of 27th current, and to say in reply that he sees no reason for re-calling the order for trial of the Skye crofters charged with assault and deforcement before the Sheriff summarily, and that the order will there-fore be carried out.

I am,

Sir,

Your obedient servant,

D. CRAWFORD.

KENNETH MACDONALD, Esq.

Mr. Macdonald, immediately on receiving the reply, addressed the following letter to the Lord-Advocate :—

INVERNESS, 1st May, 1882.

MY LORD,

I have received from your Secretary a letter stating that you "see no reason for recalling the order for trial of the Skye crofters charged with assault and deforcement before the Sheriff summarily, and that the order will therefore be carried out". I thought when I first wrote you that the request for a jury trial was so fair and reasonable that I did not require to adduce any reason in support of it, and that it lay with you, if you refused it, to give a reason for the refusal. Since, however, you do not seem to take this view of the matter, you will permit me to state some of the reasons which I think ought to induce you to grant the request of the prisoners.

The crime with which the men are charged is said to have been com-mitted in the Skye district of this county. In that district there is a Court which has hitherto, so far as I can ascertain, tried *all* summary cases arising in the district. And yet without any reason assigned, the present case has been ordered for trial at Inverness. Had the case been sent for a jury trial it would have been the usual, and indeed, necessary, course to try the case here, but it is a thing hitherto unheard of that a summary trial from one of the outlying districts of the county should be taken here. With a complete machinery for conducting summary trials in the District Court, the prisoners are entitled to some explanation of the reason why they are put to the expense of bringing their witnesses and themselves from Skye to Inverness, when, in the ordinary course of things, they ought to go no further from home than Portree. It may be answered that as the resident Sheriff at Portree was engaged in the apprehension of the prisoners, he ought not to try the case. That is perfectly true. The prisoners quite agree that it would be improper to have the case tried by Mr. Spiers, but they are not responsible for what he has done, and ought not to suffer for it. If Sheriff Spiers has disqualified himself from trying the case, that affords no reason for punishing the persons to be tried. All that would be required to be done would be to have the trial conducted in Portree by Sheriff Blair, who would, according to your order, conduct it in Inverness.

What I have said is sufficient to show that your order is an exceptional one, and the prisoners, and, I believe, the public also, will expect you to justify it. Had these prisoners stood alone, their poverty would have prevented them bringing a single witness from Skye to establish their innocence, and your order would have meant a simple denial of justice.

But, further, the crime with which these men are charged is that of deforcement of an officer of the Sheriff of Inverness, and your order is that the Sheriff, whose servant is said to have been deforced, shall be the sole judge of whether the crime was committed or not. It is not my wish to draw historical parallels, but the circumstances will, no doubt, suggest to your lordship a series of trials which took place in Scotland nearly ninety years ago, when Muir and his fellow-reformers were convicted of sedition. It is not for me to suggest, and I do not suggest, that any of our local judges would deal unfairly with the prisoners, but I ask what is your reason for refusing them a trial by jury. It is to *you* they look in the first instance, and it is *your* reasons for pursuing an exceptional course with men who have already been harshly dealt with that the public will canvass.

I presume the object of the proceedings which have already been adopted with regard to these men, and of the trial which is to follow, is to inspire them and their fellows with a proper respect for the law. If this is so, let them have no excuse for saying they have not got fair play. If their crime was so important as to call for the exceptional measures taken for their apprehension, it is surely too important to be

disposed of by a Court whose duties are usually confined to mere
matters of police.   The belief of the prisoners is that the object of
your order is to secure their conviction at all hazards irrespective of
their guilt or innocence, and this belief is shared by a growing number
of the outside public.   It is for you to dispel this misapprehension if it
is one.

In such circumstances as I have described a summary trial would be
little else than a farce ; and you will never inspire the Highland crofters
or their friends with respect for the law if you persist in enacting such
a farce in its name.   I trust, therefore, you will reconsider your resolution, and yet order the trial of the prisoners in a manner which will
inspire them with confidence in the administration of the law of their
country.

> I am,
>
> Your obedient servant,
>
> KENNETH MACDONALD.

The Honourable the LORD-ADVOCATE for Scotland,
    Home Office, Whitehall, London, S.W.

On the same evening that the letter was written Mr.
Fraser-Mackintosh (M.P. for the Inverness Burghs), in the
House of Commons, asked the Lord-Advocate whether he
would order that the Skye crofters now committed for trial
should, instead of being tried summarily, have the privilege
of being tried by a jury of their countrymen, and that the
presiding judge should be one disconnected with the
exceptional proceedings attendant on their recent apprehension ?

Mr. Dick Peddie had also the following question to ask
the Lord-Advocate—Whether it is the case that instructions
have been given that the five crofters recently arrested in
Skye, and now released on bail, be tried summarily; whether
they have applied through their agent to be tried by jury :
and whether he intended to comply with their application ?

The Lord-Advocate, in reply, said he saw no reason for
recalling the order for the trial before a summary magistrate.

After due consideration with his learned friend, the Solicitor-General for Scotland, this decision had been arrived at when the case was before them during the Easter recess. The people of Skye were generally peaceful, and having reason to believe that they were misled by bad advice, or they would not have resisted officers of the law in the execution of a legal warrant, he, with his learned colleague, thought that the offence would not be repeated if it was made clear to the people as rapidly as possible that the law will be vindicated. The charges preferred were of the least grave class that could be preferred on behalf of the Crown, and summary trial proceedings afforded little delay. The maximum sentence that could be inflicted was sixty days, and of course a lighter sentence would be passed if in the discretion of the magistrate it met the justice of the case. As to the last part of the question, it was intended that the trial should proceed before the Sheriff of Inverness who had not hitherto taken part in measures which unfortunately became necessary to vindicate the authority of the law in Skye.

The refusal of a Jury trial was final so far as the Crown was concerned. Curious as it may seem, an accused person in Scotland has no right to demand a trial by his peers. Our forefathers were not so careful of their liberties in this respect, or not so powerful to enforce them as our neighbours over the border. They took care centuries ago to secure this right; we have not secured it yet.

What might have occurred in this particular case but for the fear of public indignation it is hard to say. Tyranny has a peculiar fascination for weak men. Lord-Advocate Balfour, a good lawyer, but a weak politician, the holder of an office which was long since stripped of most of its power, and which immediately before his accession to it was so emasculated that his predecessor declined to sacrifice his

self-respect by continuing to hold it,—desired to do one
official act which had an appearance of strength about it
without the reality. He had brought contempt upon the
administration of the law by sanctioning or suggesting the
sending of a large body of police from Glasgow to Skye to
arrest a few old men of peaceful habits and general good
character, whose worst weapon, it has been proved, was a
lump of wet turf, and when the whole country was indulging
in a roar of laughter over the ignominious retreat of the invading army of policemen before the women of the Braes,
and the ridiculous ending of a performance which was intended to represent the dignity of the Law, he, the person
primarily responsible for the mistake which had been committed, would naturally desire to cover his blunder by
securing a conviction against the few harmless cottars whom
the policemen in their blind panic had first laid hands
on.

If ever there was a case which ought to be tried by a
Jury this was one. At no time is the right of Jury trial
more valuable than when the opinions of the public, and the
acts of the Crown, as represented by its officials, run counter
to each other, and when these acts are in any way connected
with the offence to be tried. At no time ought the right to
be more readily conceded. Here, however, it was deter-
minedly denied. To Mr. Macdonald's second letter no
answer was ever given. We believe none was expected.
Except in the answer given to the questions of Mr. Fraser-
Mackintosh and Mr. Dick Peddie in the House of
Commons, at least twenty-four hours before Mr. Macdonald's letter reached him, the Lord-Advocate did not
attempt either to explain or defend his conduct. In point
of fact, complete explanation or defence was impossible.
All that time the Crown officers must have known what was

not known to the prisoners' advisers at the time, that there was no evidence against the prisoners upon which any sane Jury would convict. But the Lord-Advocate seems never to have forgotten that the officialism of the County of Inverness had involved itself in the mess, and in a summary trial officialism might be left to vindicate its own dignity. This would also vindicate the dignity of the law, and the wisdom of its administrators—at least so they thought. This theory was universally accepted outside official circles as the reason for the resolution to try summarily, and but for the protests made by outsiders, and particularly a number of Scottish Members of Parliament to secure a fair trial for the prisoners, most people believed that the trial would have been even a greater farce than it turned out to be, but with a far different ending.

The efforts of the Scottish Members to obtain a Jury trial did not end with the questions in the House of Commons. Efforts were made privately by some of these gentlemen to save the Administration of Justice in Scotland from being sullied, but without result, and when all their efforts failed, the members who had taken most interest in the matter, published the following protest in the *Times* of 10th May, 1882, from which it was quoted by almost every newspaper in the Kingdom :—

The circumstances of the arrest, by a large body of police brought from Glasgow, of half-a-dozen Skye crofters, accused of deforcing a sheriff's officer who went among them to serve writs, and the attempt at a rescue which attended it, must be fresh in the minds of your readers. We need not say that the case has excited great public interest in Scotland. It is most important, therefore, in order to secure any moral effect, that the trial should be conducted under such circumstances as will place the verdict above all suspicion. This, we regret to say, is not to be done, and already many persons who sympathise with the men, and desire that their case shall be fairly heard, openly accuse the Executive of resorting to unworthy means to obtain a conviction. For ourselves, we may at once state our perfect belief in the sincerity of the Lord Advocate in his profession of a desire, while vindicating the law, to provide for the accused that form of trial which will protect them from an unnecessarily heavy punishment. But punishment pre-supposes guilt, while what the accused contend is that they are not guilty. What they claim is that they shall first have their guilt established in the ordinary way, and if found guilty they are willing to take their chance of that punishment their conduct may seem to deserve.

Now, persons accused of crimes committed in Skye have !hitherto been invariably tried in one of two ways. If the cases are considered so trivial as to be dealt with summarily, they are tried by a sheriff-substitute sitting at Portree. This course secures to the accused the important advantage that evidence for his defence is procurable at a *minimum* of expense and inconvenience. If the case is of a grave character, it is tried by a jury at Inverness. This, of course, involves much more inconvenience and expense to the defence, but it secures the services of a jury, a tribunal which, for the purpose of deciding on matters of fact, is admittedly superior to a Judge, however impartial, sitting alone. But in the case of the Skye crofters the trial is to be at Inverness, without a jury. The defence thus incurs all the inconvenience and expense usually attendant on a jury trial, and obtains none of the advantages in the way of a tribunal the best qualified to pronounce on the question of the guilt or innocence of the accused. It is stated that Portree is in such an excited state that it is unadvisable that the trial should take place there, and that, therefore, it has to be removed to Inverness. There is not the smallest reason, however, why, being held at Inverness, it should not be held in the usual manner. The accused dispute the facts alleged by the prosecution. Their agent has asked for a jury to decide on the question of fact. A jury trial is the invariable mode of disposing of Skye cases tried at Inverness ; but a jury trial, though in this case specially demanded, has been refused. The reason given for its refusal is that the Crown authorities having originally intended that the trial should be a summary one at Portree, though it has now been deemed advisable to remove it to Inverness, they see no reason to change the form of trial on that account. The reply is that at Portree there would have been nothing unusual in a summary trial, and trial at Portree would have secured material advantages to the accused. At Inverness the summary trial of a Skye case is unprecedented, and the expense to the accused as heavy as would be that of a jury trial.

But the Lord Advocate has explained that if the cases had been tried by jury the sentences might have been much heavier than those to which they would be exposed on summary conviction. That is true, but it is equally true that the judge might have awarded sentences as light as he deemed proper. In the interests of justice it is desirable that the punishment should be commensurate with the offence. There is no reason why a judge sitting with a jury on circuit or in the Sheriff Court should not award the slightest possible sentence. That is what the agent for accused thinks, and, knowing their case, he is willing to take his chance of the heavier sentence if they are found guilty and are thought to deserve it.

On the point of guilt or innocence, however, he prefers the verdict of a jury to the decision of a judge, and that has been refused. In criminal cases in Scotland a bare majority of the jury convicts, and if the case is not strong enough to convince eight men out of fifteen, the prisoners are surely entitled to the benefit of the doubt. That is all that has been asked, and that, despite the strongest representations, has been refused. To us its refusal in this particular case, on grounds of public policy, seems particularly regretable, and we beg through your columns publicly to protest against it.

CHARLES CAMERON.
C. FRASER-MACKINTOSH.
P. STEWART MACLIVER.
JAMES COWAN.
FRANK HENDERSON.
J. DICK PEDDIE.
JAMES W. BARCLAY.

House of Commons, May 9, 1882.

Commenting on this protest the *Pall Mall Gazette* of 10th May, said :—

It is hard to see what answer there can be to the protest on behalf of the Skye crofters raised in the *Times* this morning by seven Scotch members. Skye cases have hitherto always been disposed of either summarily at Portree or by trial before a jury at Inverness. If the accused had not the satisfaction of submitting his case to a jury, he was, at least, relieved from the expense of being tried at a distance from home. But in the present instance it is proposed to try the crofters at Inverness, but without a jury. Why should the crofters be subjected to the disadvantage of both methods of trial without the benefit of either ?

Whether if published earlier this Protest would have had any effect it is hard to say. Probably not. As it was, it only appeared in the *Times* the day before that fixed for the trial. By that time the arrangements were complete. Some days before then Mr. Macdonald, the accused's agent, finding that the trial was to proceed summarily, had gone to Skye and precognosced a large number of witnesses, several of whom were cited for the defence. On the morning the Protest appeared in the *Times* the accused and the witnesses for the prosecution and defence left Portree for Inverness, the trial having been fixed for the 11th of May, 1882.

On that day the accused took their place at the Bar of the Sheriff Court in the Castle of Inverness. The hour of commencement was noon, and by that time the Court-house was crowded. Sheriff Blair, the presiding judge, was accompanied on the bench by Sheriff Shaw, late of Lochmaddy. Besides numerous members of the Faculty, there were around the bar—Mr. Alex. Macdonald, factor, Portree; Mr. Macleod, secretary of the Skye Vigilance Committee, Glasgow; Dean of Guild Mackenzie; Bailie Smith; Mr. Alex. Macdonald Maclellan; Mr. MacHugh; Mr. Cameron of the *Standard*, and several others.

The indictment set forth that Alexander Finlayson, tenant or crofter ; Donald Nicolson, tenant or crofter ; James Nicolson, now or lately residing with the said Donald Nicolson; Malcolm Finlayson, son of, and now or lately residing with, the said Alexander Finlayson ; and Peter Macdonald, son of, and now or lately residing with, Donald Macdonald, tenant or crofter, all residing at Balmeanach, had all and each, or one or more of them, been guilty of the crime of *deforcing an officer of the law in the execution of his duty ; or of the crime of violently resisting and obstructing an officer of the law in the execution of his duty, or persons employed by and assisting an officer of the law in the execution of his duty ; and also of the crime of* assault, or of one or other of these crimes, actor or actors or art and part, in so far as Angus Martin, now or lately residing at Lisigarry, near Portree, in the parish

Portree aforesaid, having been as a sheriff-officer of the County of Inverness, on or about the 7th day of April, 1882, instructed by Alexander Macdonald, solicitor in Portree aforesaid, as agent for the Right Honourable Ronald Archibald Macdonald, Lord Macdonald, of Armadale Castle, Skye, to go to Balmeanach, Penachorain, and Gedentailor, three of the townships in the district of Braes, in the parish of Portree aforesaid, to serve actions of removing, which, with the warrants thereon, he delivered to the said Angus Martin for that purpose, raised in the Sheriff Court of Inverness, Elgin, and Nairn at Portree, at the instance of the said Right Honourable Ronald Archibald Macdonald, Lord Macdonald, upon the tenants in the said townships . . . and also to serve small debt summonses for debt . . . and the said Angus Martin having upon the said 7th day of April, 1882, or about that time, proceeded towards, or in the direction of the said three townships of Balmeanach, Penachorain, and Gedentailor, in order to serve the said actions and small debt summonses, accompanied by Ewen Robertson, now or lately residing at Lisigary aforesaid, as his concurrent and assistant, and by Norman Beaton, ground-officer on the estates of the said Lord Macdonald, and now or lately residing at Shullisheddar, in the parish of Portree aforesaid, the said Alex. Finlayson, Donald Nicolson, James Nicolson, Malcolm Finlayson, and Peter Macdonald, did all and each, or one or more of them, assisted by a crowd of people to the number of 150 or thereby, whose names are to the complainer unknown, actors or actor, or art and part, at or near Gedentailor aforesaid [and at a part thereof three hundred yards or thereby on the south of the schoolhouse, known by the name of MacDermid's Institution, on the lands of Olach in the parish of Portree aforesaid, and now or lately occupied by Kenneth MacLean, teacher there], wickedly and feloniously attack and assault the said Angus Martin, *well knowing him to be an officer of the law, and in the execution of his duty as such, and that he held the said actions and small debt summonses and warrants for service,* and the said Ewen Robertson, *well knowing him to be the assistant and concurrent and witness of the said Angus Martin* and the said Norman Beaton, and did knock them, or one or more of them to the ground, and did by force at or near Gedentailor aforesaid, forcibly seize hold of, and destroy the service copies of the actions and small debt summonses before mentioned, and did also upon the lands of Upper Olach, being another township in the said district of Braes, and in the parish of Portree aforesaid [and at a part of said lands occupied by Donald Macpherson, crofter, there, forty yards or thereby on the south of the said schoolhouse], forcibly seize hold of and burn, or cause, or procure to be

burned, the principal copies of the said actions and small debt summonses and warrants thereon, and did further upon the said township of
Gedentailor, and upon the said township of Upper Olach, and upon
the high road leading from these townships to Portree aforesaid [and on
that part of said road lying between Gedentailor aforesaid and the said
Schoolhouse], throw stones and clods of earth and peat at the said
Angus Martin, Ewen Robertson, and Norman Beaton, by which they,
or one or more of them were struck to the hurt and injury of their persons ; *and by all which or part thereof the said Angus Martin, and the
said Ewen Robertson were deforced and by force, prevented from executing
and discharging their duty and from serving the said actions and small
debt summonses.*

Mr. James Anderson, Procurator-Fiscal for the county,
conducted the prosecution, and Mr. Kenneth Macdonald,
solicitor, and Town Clerk of Inverness, appeared for the
prisoners.

The Procurator-Fiscal asked that certain amendments
should be made on the complaint with the object of more
specifically defining the places at which the acts charged
against the prisoners were alleged to have been committed.
The amendments were not objected to and were allowed.
The lines introduced are those within [   ] in the preceding
copy of the libel.

Immediately after the amendments had been made, Mr.
Macdonald said that, before the complaint was gone into,
he had to state objections to the relevancy of the indictment and also to the competency of the Court to try the
case. He objected to the competency of the Court on the
ground that the crime charged was of such a serious nature
that it ought to be tried by a jury ; and he objected to the
competency of the complaint on the ground that the punishment attached by law to the crime charged in the indictment
is beyond that which could be imposed in that court. The
charge in this case was that of deforcing an officer of the
law in the execution of his duty, and that was said to have

been done by the prisoners in concert with a crowd of 150 people; so that the deforcement ran into the other serious charge of mobbing and rioting, the most serious kind of deforcement known to the law. This was the first time, he believed, in the legal history of Scotland that a charge of such a serious nature had been tried in a Summary Court. The accused had been brought to that Court; they objected to being brought there. The public prosecutor had no right to dictate what was the competent Court for the trial of a case; it was for his lordship to say whether the Court was competent or incompetent. The public prosecutor had refused to go to a higher Court; he had refused to give these men the benefit of trial by jury; and it was now for his lordship to say whether these men were to have that bene- fit. It had been said that the reason for bringing the trial in the Summary Court was the fact that the maximum sentence was so small, but his lordship had the same power in the Jury Court as he had in the Summary Court.

The Sheriff said there was no question whatever in regard to the power of a judge sitting in the Jury Court to inflict the minimum punishment in a case of deforcement; and he instanced a case of that kind, tried by Lord Young at the Inverness Circuit Court, in which the sentence was a fine of 40s., with the alternative of one month's imprison- ment.

Mr. Macdonald quoted the acts of the Scottish Parlia- ment of 1581 (C. 118), 1587, (C. 85), and 1591 (C. 152), which regulated the punishment which by statute followed on conviction, to show the serious nature of the charge against the prisoners, and argued that as the libel concluded generally for "the pains of law" and these pains were statutory and such as were beyond the power of a Court of summary jurisdiction to inflict, the Court was incompetent to dispose of the cause. He also quoted from Hume and Alison to show that the High Court had frequently suspended sentences pronounced in a Summary Court when the crime charged was too serious for such a mode of trial. He maintained that before 1864 there never was a case of such magnitude tried before a Summary Court, and if not before 1864 there was nothing in the Act of that date which would entitle them to try it.

The Sheriff said that this was an offence at common law as well as under the statute. They were proceeding at common law, and the pains and penalties which the prosecutor asked should be inflicted, were the pains and penalties applicable under the Summary Procedure Acts.

Mr. Macdonald held that the punishment was statutory, even though the offence was charged at common law.

The Sheriff said the punishment was statutory if the prosecution was under the statute ; but if the prosecution was at common law, it was not necessary for the Court to take the statutory penalty.

Mr. Macdonald contended that when his lordship was asked generally, as in this complaint, to inflict the pains of law upon defenders, that carried them back to the statute law.

The Sheriff—That carries you back to the statute under which you are proceeding; and the statute under which you are proceeding is the Summary Procedure Acts.

Mr. Macdonald—If that is your lordship's view, there is no use in any further pressing my contention.

The Sheriff said that was the view he was inclined to take. He might mention that he had been aware that some objection of this sort might be taken, and he had given the point careful consideration. Personally he should have preferred that the case had been tried by jury, on the ground that it would have relieved him of a considerable deal of personal responsibility; but it was not what he desired, but what was really the law on the point. It was quite true, and it had been the opinion of most distinguished lawyers in this country, that there was no point less fixed than as to when a trial was to be by jury or not. In the present case, even should he have been of opinion—which he was not—that the nature of the offence as detailed in the complaint before him was unfit for summary trial, he did not think he could interfere with the discretion of the public prosecutor in trying under the Summary Procedure Acts, as the penalty craved did not extend beyond the limits set forth in these Acts.

Mr. Macdonald then stated that he objected to the relevancy of the indictment. The libel amounted to this—that Angus Martin, who lived at Portree, proceeded on a certain day towards, or in the direction of, certain townships; and that on the way there, at a certain place, he was met by certain people, and had his warrants taken from him. The question for his lordship was whether that amounted to deforcement. The act charged in the indictment, Mr. Macdonald contended, might be theft, or mobbing and rioting, or assault, but it was not deforcement. To be deforced, an officer must be assaulted, and be in bodily fear while in the execution of his duty; but in the libel it was not mentioned that Martin ever made an attempt to execute the warrants he carried. There was nothing to show that the officers had got near to the residences of any of the persons upon whom they meant to serve the summonses—nothing even to show that even on the road they were near to any of the men against whom they held summonses. He quoted from Hume, Alison, and Macdonald's works on Criminal Law to show that an officer could only be deforced while he was actually in the execution of his duty as an officer, or *in actu proximo* to its execution. There was nothing in the libel to show that the officers in this case were in the execution of their duty, or on the point of executing it, or even near any of the places where their duty fell to be executed, indeed, the presumption was, from the terms of the libel—and this presumption was strengthened by the amendments just made by the Public Prosecutor—that they had not reached the place when they were met by the people.

As to the alternative charge of violently resisting and obstructing an officer of the law in the execution of his duty, that was simply an unsuccessful attempt at deforcement, and would only be committed in circumstances which, had the resistance been successful, would have amounted to deforcement. In short, here also the officer must be executing, or on the point of executing, his duty, otherwise the crime would not be committed. If, therefore, the libel was irrelevant as regarded the charge of deforcement it was necessarily so as regards the less serious charge of obstructing also.

The Procurator-Fiscal, in reply, quoted from Alison and Macdonald to show that it was unquestionably deforcement if when a messenger had come near to the debtor's house he was met by a host of people who drove him off on notice or suspicion of his purpose. In this case the officer was in the immediate neighbourhood of the place where he intended to serve his warrants, as stated in the libel ; and therefore the act charged amounted to deforcement.

The Sheriff, after full consideration, said—The objection taken to the complaint is one of very great importance, and if sustained detracts very materially from the gravity of the offence with which they are charged. The offence of deforcement, as Mr. Hume says, is not to the individual, but to the officer and the law, which is violated in his person; and it lies in the hindrance of these formal and solemn proceedings, which took place under regular written authority, which it belongs only to an officer of the law to perform. It therefore appears to me to be indispensable that the complaint should bear that the officer said to be deforced was at or near the premises of the parties against whom the writs were issued; or that the officer had assumed that official character and entered on his commission, being in the near and immediate preparation with proceeding to the first formalities in the execution of that commission. This complaint does not, in my opinion, contain those essentials; and therefore, to the extent that I have now stated, the objection must be sustained.

The Procurator-Fiscal—In these circumstances, there is no case of deforcement, and I propose now to proceed with the case as one of assault.

The Sheriff—Of course the offence, though not deforcement, may be assault and battery, aggravated certainly by the station of the officer.

Mr. Macdonald—All that there is in the complaint regarding assault is the phrase, "as also of the crime of assault". There is not a single word about aggravation. I hope there will be no attempt to prove aggravation when there is no aggravation libelled.

The Sheriff—The offence now to be tried is that of assault. Assault, as we know, may be of various degrees. It may be of such a character as would be met by the minimum sentence, and it may be a serious assault. I used the word "aggravated" in the popular rather than the technical sense. The case to be tried was not an assault with an aggravation, but an assault which might or might not be of a serious character.

The effect of this judgment was that the charge of deforcement was struck out of the libel and the words printed in italics were held as deleted.

The prisoners were then asked to plead to the charge of assault, and Mr. Macdonald stated that their plea was "Not Guilty".

THE SHERIFF-OFFICER AT THE BRAES.

Angus Martin, sheriff-officer, Portree, was the first witness called. Examined by Mr. Anderson, he said—A few days before the 7th April last I received instructions to go to the Braes for the purpose of serving summonses. I went on the 7th April to the Braes, which is about eight miles from Portree. It is on the estate of Lord Macdonald. The summonses I had were for removal, and I had also some small debt summonses for arrears of rent. I left Portree about twelve o'clock, accompanied by Ewen Robertson, and Norman Beaton. As we were going towards the Braes, my attention was directed to two little boys, who came out on the road and looked at us. They ran away, but returned a second time with small flags in their hands. Then they ran towards the townships of Balmeanach, Peinachorrain, and Gedintailler. When I went to Gedintailler I saw two young men with flags. They were bawling out and waving the flags, the boys were also waving their flags. When I got to Gedintailler a great number of persons came out.

The Sheriff—Were there two flags? Witness—Yes.

The Sheriff—After the waving a great many people came? Witness —Yes. A crowd came from the townships.

The Sheriff—How many would there be? Witness—I should say there would be from 150 to 200, including women and children. (Laughter.)

Mr. Anderson—When you say women and children do you also include men? Yes.

Did they surround you? Yes, sir, they did.

The Sheriff—They came towards you and surrounded you? Yes, my lord. I had not then gone off the public road.

Mr. Anderson—Did they ask you anything?—They called out to me to return. I had the summonses in my pocket, and I took them out and told them my name was Angus Martin, and that I was a sheriff-officer from the Sheriff. When I took out the summonses they rushed forward and snatched the summonses out of my hand. This was done by Donald Nicolson.

Mr. Macdonald—I think we might stop this line of examination now.

Mr. Anderson—On what principle?

Mr. Macdonald—The charge is one of assault merely, and the evidence with which it was intended to support the charge of deforcement is now being led for the purpose as I take it of proving an aggravation which is not libelled.

The Sheriff overruled the objection.

Mr. Anderson—Were the crowd quiet at that time?—No. They were very excited.

What was done with the summonses?—They tried to tear them up and threw them on the ground.

Did any person come up to you then?—Yes, Alex. Finlayson, who had a staff in his hand. He told us that unless we turned back we would lose our lives, meaning myself and the ground-officer.

Did he dare you to proceed further?—Yes. He was also brandishing the stick. Stones were thrown by the crowd, and the whole five prisoners were amongst the crowd. I cannot say who threw the stones. My concurrent was taken hold of by Donald Nicolson, who said, "Get away you b——". He had a hold of Robertson about the back, and Robertson was afterwards thrown to the ground. Nicolson said (evidently referring to the summonses), "Lift them now, and take them away, you——". I do not know who it was among the crowd who threw Robertson on the ground. The women were very busy at that time. (Laughter.) I saw James Nicolson when my concurrent was on the ground. He rushed forward with his two hands closed, and asked who was that? On being told, he said, "Kill the b——". I can't say what Robertson did then, as I did not like to turn my back. I wished to keep my front to them. (Laughter.) I think he ran towards Portree. He was followed by a large crowd. The crowd continued to threaten me. I spoke to them, and tried to pacify them as best I could, though I was very shaky. (Laughter.) I proceeded towards Portree, but the crowd followed, and continued to threaten me. Stones were thrown by the crowd from Gedintailler until I reached the schoolhouse at Olach, when I got rid of them.

Mr. Anderson—Did they say anything about you not coming back there again?—Yes. They told me not to come back, because I might be killed, and said if it had been any other officer he would have been killed.

Mr. Anderson—Did Malcolm Finlayson do anything?—He came to me in a great hurry and said the people wished to speak to me; and I said I would be very glad. He asked me, If I had any summonses, and I told him I had the principals and copies. He snatched them out of my hand, and after trying to tear them threw them on the ground. The crowd were about me at this time, and one of the prisoners, Peter Macdonald, said something about burning the summonses. He said, addressing me, "unless you burn these you will not go home alive". There were murmurs among the crowd and I was asked to burn the summonses. They tried to burn the summonses themselves first, and tried to light them at a burning peat, but were unsuccessful. When I was threatened with my life, I asked for a piece of paper, and one of the crowd handed me a bit of the torn summons. I blew the burning peat as hard as I could to make it burn and I lighted the piece paper at the burning peat, and handed it to some one in the crowd, crying "go ahead". I was induced to do this, because I was afraid of my life, as I had been told before I went up that I would be killed. Nothing else induced me to burn the summonses.

Mr. Anderson—You were afraid of your life?—Yes; I was, and I was very glad to get away. (Laughter.)

Between the place where the summonses were torn and where they were destroyed was there much stone-throwing?—Yes, stones and clods, but I was not struck with them.

Did you see your assistants struck?—Well, I did not like to look back—(Laughter)—but I think they must have been getting some of them.

When you got home you reported the matter to the Fiscal?—Yes.

Cross-examined by Mr. Kenneth Macdonald—What do you do?—I am a sheriff-officer and auctioneer.

Are you also a clerk in the office of Lord Macdonald's factor?—I am.

Mr. Macdonald—Anything else?—I am sanitary inspector, clerk to the Local Authority, and clerk to the Road Trustees.

Do you hold many other offices?—I am a crofter. (Laughter.)

In which capacity did you go to the Braes?—I went in my capacity as sheriff-officer. I called in to Mr. Macdonald, the factor's office, that morning to tell that I was going away for a time. I did not get the summonses against these people signed as the Factor's clerk. They were handed to me by the Sheriff-Clerk. I was instructed to get them from him by Mr. Macdonald, and I proceeded to the Braes to serve them. I was quite sober then, as sober as I am now, and I think I am sober. Donald Nicolson snatched the summonses from me.

Mr. Macdonald—Will you swear to that ?—Yes.

Who saw him ?—Lots of people, besides my concurrent and the ground-officer. He tore some of them and did not hand them back to me. I turned my back shortly afterwards, but by that time the papers were lying on the ground.

Did Nicolson ask you for the summonses ?—No.

How did he come to get them from you?—I did not give them to him.

How did he come to have them then?—I took them out of my pocket and said I would give the summonses to them as I saw some of the persons for whom they were in the crowd.

Was the bundle tied up ?—There was an elastic band about it.

Did you hand the summonses to anyone?—They were snatched out of my hand by Nicolson.

Do you swear that he did not hand them back ?—No. I swear that, so far as I can remember.

You must remember that ?

The Sheriff—Have you any doubt about it ?—No, my lord.

Mr. Macdonald—What became of the summonses ?—I don't know. They were lying on the road.

You were not struck by a stone ?—No.

Or by anything else ?—One of the women, I think, struck me with some soft stuff on the head.

One of the women ?—I think so.

Was that Mrs. Flora Nicolson ? Witness—Which Mrs. Nicolson ?

Mr. Macdonald—You know Mrs. Nicolson ?—There are so many Mrs. Nicolsons.

Do you know Widow Nicolson, to whom you made the statement about the widows of Gedintailler ?—I know two widows of that name.

Do you remember a widow you made remarks about before that ?—There are so many of them I can't remember.

Do you know Widow Nicolson of Gedintailler to whom you made a statement about the widows of Gedintailler ?—I know more than one Widow Nicolson in Gedintailler, but I don't know their first names.

The Sheriff—Did you see any of these widows ?—Yes, I saw Widow Nicolson, Balmeanach.

By Mr. Macdonald—Did she strike you ?—No, Sir.

Did she call upon the widows of Gedintailler to come round Martin to get their character ?—No, I am not sure.

Did you make a statement about the widows of Gedintailler in Portree before that?—I do not think it. I would always be speaking to them about rents.

Did you make a statement about the character of the widows?—No, no.

Were you rebuked by Norman Beaton about the filthiness of your language about these women?—Filthy language! I do not remember. I was not checked by Norman Beaton or any other.

The Sheriff objected to this, but Mr. Macdonald said he wished to show that the whole of the disturbance arose out of an attack made by Martin a short time before, on the character of the ladies who formed the major part of the crowd.

Mr. Macdonald—Did Widow Nicolson strike you?—No.

Did any one strike you?—No, but it was a narrow shave.

Did any one threaten to strike you?—Yes, Donald Finlayson with a stick.

And you did not attempt to proceed further?—No, not I.

Did you make any attempt to regain the doubles of your summonses? I just let them go.

I suppose you were glad to get rid of them?—Oh no, not in that way.

How far had you gone back towards Portree before you were again overtaken by the crowd?—Well, I think it would be about three-quarters of a mile. Malcolm Finlayson came up to me then, and I took the summonses out of my pocket. He snatched them from me, although I had a good hold of them. He did not return them, and I heard nobody tell him to return them to me.

You said some one tried to burn the summonses and failed?—Yes.

And then you said "I have a good breath," did you not?—I was hearing murmurs in the crowd that they would make me burn them, so I took a piece of paper and set fire to a bit of one of the summonses.

What did you say then?—I handed it to some one in the crowd, and immediately there was a great clapping of hands.

Now, did you not set fire to the summonses?—No, I set fire to a bit of one of them with a piece of paper which I lighted at a burning peat.

Did you not bend down and set fire to them?—No, I am quite certain I did not.

Did you not, Martin, in setting fire to these summonses say, "Now, keep back, boys, and give it air?"—I did not set fire to the summonses, but after they set fire to them there was a great cheering.

Did you call on the crowd to keep back and give it (the fire) air ?— I may have said stand back, but not to give it air.

Now, why did you say that ?—In order to please them.

Did you make a speech after that ?—Yes, for their kindness. I thanked them because they had not struck me, and as I wanted to get rid of their company.

Did anbody say—"Angus, boy, you need not fear?"—Yes. That was at the first stage of the proceedings, when I said don't kill me.

Did you say you were not afraid of anything ?—I said I was there independent of factor or anybody else.

Did you say you were not afraid of anybody ?—Well, I might have said so.

Was that true ?—No, it was not. (Laughter).

Did you say that all the people of the Braes would not hurt you ?— Very likely.

And that was not true ?—Well, I saw it was not true at that stage. (Laughter).

Did you tell any more lies that day ?—Well, I do not remember. It is not my profession to tell lies.

You seem to practice it occasionally. (Laughter).

You asked for a smoke ?—Yes.

Why did you ask for that ?—I was not a smoker, but I asked for it to please them.

How long did you smoke ?—For five or six minutes.

In answer to further questions, witness said that when leaving he shook hands with a number of the men in the crowd. He denied having advised the crowd, in his speech, to be smart and hard about Ben-Lee, and that they would get it. He had no whisky that day, and denied emphatically that he had lately been dismissed for drunkenness. He reported the case to the Fiscal when he went home.

Mr. Macdonald—Is this the first criminal charge against the Braes tenants ?—No.

There was a charge of intimidation, but it broke down ?—Yes.

Did you go to the Braes with the intention of serving these summonses ?—Yes, and I thought I was safe in serving summonses in any part of Skye up to that time,

Is it not the case that you were sent to the Braes with the view of getting up a charge of deforcement against these people ?—It was not, sir.

EVIDENCE OF EWEN ROBERTSON, PORTREE.

Ewen Robertson, who spoke through Mr. Whyte as interpreter,

said—I am a labourer, residing at Portree. On the 7th April last, I went as witness with Angus Martin to the Braes with summonses. The ground officer, Norman Beaton, was also with us. When we came to Gedintailler we saw two boys, and they had flags in their hands on the point of a stick. They ran ahead of us. They were waving the flags, and ran away to a knoll on the low side of Gedin-tailler. When we went on we saw a man, and he came down where we were. A number of people collected, but I do not know how many. The crowd surrounded us. I knew the people, but did not see but Donald and James Nicolson. The crowd knocked me down three times. I was pushed down on the road. The crowd was much excited. I was hurt every time they knocked me down. I went off when I got on my feet. I heard them saying to us that they would kill us. I heard James Nicolson saying so. I did not hear Donald. After throwing the summonses down, Donald seized me by the back of the neck. Donald plucked the summonses from Martin and tore them, and then seized me. He did not throw me down, but caught me by the back of the neck and told me to lift the pieces, and I said there was no use of them. He told me where the summonses were. I was frightened at that stage, "and it was not little". The crowd were excited, and I took myself away, and was followed by about a dozen youths throwing mud at me. I do not know who knocked me down, but I was thrown down three times. They also threw a pail of water at me, but I don't know who did. When I ran away a great deal of stones and earth were thrown at me. Some of them struck me, but I was avoiding them as well as I could. It was only a few youths who followed me. The youths were among the crowd first.

You did not go back again?—Oh, indeed, I would not go. I did not see the summonses burned, and was frightened for my life.

By Mr. Macdonald—What is your occupation?—Anything I can do if I get payment for it.

Are you in the habit of accompanying Martin?—Yes, and his father before him for forty years, and others of the same kind before him, and nothing ever happened to me.

This profession I take it is not very highly respected in the Island of Skye?—I never heard anything about it. Before that time everything went on quietly, and we did our message and got the best in the house before we went away.

Did you see anything happen to Martin?—No ; I did not. I went away.

When you were asked in Portree to submit to precognition on behalf of the Prisoners, what was your reply the first time ?—I said who asked that of me.

Did you refuse to answer any question when I asked you ?—I said I had been already examined, and until I would go before the judge I would not answer more questions.

You came the following day and gave information. What led to the change in your opinion ?—Yes ; I did that when I heard who it was.

Did I not tell you the first night who it was ?—Oh, yes, you did. (Laughter).

What brought about the change ?—I did not wish to be examined.

Did Martin tell you not to answer any questions ?—He did not.

Did you see Martin that night ?—Yes.

Where ?—On the street at Portree.

At the hotel door ?—Yes.

Waiting for you ?—I do not know whether he was or not.

Did he tell you to refuse to answer questions ?—No ! he did not indeed.

How did Donald Nicolson come to get hold of the summonses ?—He just came over from where he was and took them from him.

How long had Martin the summonses in his hand before Nicolson got them ?—No time ; and he said he had come to deliver the summonses with the Sheriff's warrant.

Did he take them out of his pocket ?—Yes.

How long was that before Nicolson got them ?—I cannot say what time. I had no watch.

Did Martin offer the men the summonses ?—I did not hear him. The people would not take them from him.

Then he did offer them ?—He did not offer them at that time.

Why had he the summonses in his hand ?—There were some there for whom the summonses were.

My question was, why had Martin the summonses in his hand ?—Oh, God ! How could I know what they were in his hand for.

Did he offer them ?—He did not require to offer them.

How long were you beside Martin at this time ?—I was not long when I was thrust away by the people.

Did you know all the people ?—I did not know them all.

Had they anything on their heads ?—The women had handkerchiefs on their heads, but I do not know was it to protect them from the sun or hide them.

Why did you not lift up the summonses ?—Why should I lift them when they were in pieces.

Who tore them ?—Nicolson did.

Did you see him ?—I will swear that.

Did you see the destruction of the other summonses ?

Witness (before interpretation)—No.

Mr. Macdonald—This witness had good English a week ago. (Laughter).

Did you see any person touch Martin ?—No, I did not see them.

Or Beaton?—No, I do not, but they might have killed him for all I know.

You ran home?—I ran back as fast as I could.

Did any of them touch you?—I am not aware of any of them touching me.

EVIDENCE OF NORMAN BEATON.

Norman Beaton, ground-officer, said—I reside at Shullisheddar. I accompanied the sheriff-officer on 17th April last. I went to point out the places. He had summonses to serve at Penachorrain, Balmeanach, and Gedintailler. On coming near Gedintailler we saw two boys, and they ran away. We afterwards saw a man with a flag waving it. They came and asked where we were going, and Martin said he was going to serve summons on them. He took the summonses out of his pocket. Alexander Finlayson said he would not allow them to go on. He said lifting his staff, "You won't go any further". He said, "Surely you all know me, I came here by order of the Sheriff". Donald Nicolson took the summonses out of Martin's hands and threw them on the road, but I could not say who tore them. I saw them in bits on the road. The people were gathering. There was about 150 altogether—men, women, and children and girls. I saw them all in the crowd. Martin I and returned back towards Portree. Robertson turned first, and after he left I saw him knocked down in the road. The crowd followed us when we turned back to Portree, and some of them were throwing stones and clods at us, near Gedintailler on the road. Not many of them struck me. Near Murchison's schoolhouse, about three-quarters of a mile from the place where the summonses were destroyed, the crowd followed us, and amongst them were James Nicolson, Peter Macdonald, and Malcolm Finlayson. They were very much excited, and using threats. They ran after us, and asked if we had any more summonses. Martin said he had the principal summonses to bring them back to Portree. He took them out of his pocket and showed them, and Malcolm Finlayson snatched them out of his hand

and threw them in the road. They were not torn, and I could not say if they were afterwards torn. I saw peat lying beside them; it was alive. Martin stood on the road, and I stood nearer Portree. I saw smoke, but could not say if the summonses were burning. I was alarmed but not hurt, and afraid to go on.

Cross-examined by Mr. Macdonald—In what capacity did you go with Martin to the Braes ?—I think I went as ground-officer—as Lord Macdonald's servant.

You did not go as Martin's concurrent ?—I was sent there by Lord Macdonald's factor, by whom I was employed. Martin was not to pay me.

Were the crowd principally women and children ?—Yes, and men.

Were they principally women and children ?—No answer. Were there more women and children than there were men ? I believe there were more men. To make three shares of them, I believe there were more men. More than one third were men.

You said that Robertson was knocked down by some women and men ?—Yes.

He had gone away from the crowd at that time ?—Yes.

When Martin came up first with the summonses, how was it he happened to take them out of his pocket ?—They asked him where he was going, and what brought him there, and he took the summonses out of his pocket. He told them it was for that purpose he came. He kept the summonses in his hand.

Close to his body ?—He held them out a little. He said, " Here they are". Donald Nicolson then took them. He was not very close to them, just past him a yard or two.

Was not this what took place ? Did not Nicolson put out his hand and take them ?—He was not so close as that.—Was Martin offering them at the time ?

The Procurator-Fiscal—Martin did'nt say that. You are putting words in the witness's mouth he never used.

Mr. Macdonald—If I put a question, it is not the part of the Procurator-Fiscal to instruct his own witness what to say in answer to it.

Cross-examination continued—What were Martin's words ?—He said, "Here they are". I swear he did not say, " Here they are to you". I will swear to that.

Were they pointed in the direction of Nicolson ?—They were pointed in the way of the crowd as well as Nicolson. He was along with the crowd.

And he took the summonses ?—Yes.

Did he offer them back to Martin?—I did not see that. I was close to Martin all the time and I did not see that. I was very close behind.

Might they have been offered to Martin without you seeing it?—They could not, and I did not see them offered. He tore the summonses. I could not see Nicolson put them on the ground.

Were they torn then?—No, they were not torn when he put them on the ground.

How long after you first saw them on the ground did you see them torn?—I could not say. It was some little time.

Did you see them in anybody's hand between the time you saw them on the ground untorn and when you saw them torn?—No.

The whole crowd was walking over them. I cannot say if that would account for the tearing of them. The band which bound the summonses was off when I saw them on the road. It was torn off about the time they were dropped upon the road. Nicolson took the band off and threw it upon the road. By the time I went down to the school-house, I was struck with stones and clods by some women—not by men—in the crowd.

Did you hear anything said by Mrs. Nicolson there as to the character of the women of Gedintailler?—I did not.

Did not you hear her say, "Now, come, women of Gedintailler, and hear your character from Angus Martin?"—I did. I heard her also say that he should burn the summonses. I heard her say that he was saying some words to her in Portree about the character of the women of Gedintailler. She told words to me herself at that time.

At what time?—At Olach. Not in the presence of Martin. It was said to me near Murchison's school-house. Martin was not there at the time.

She complained of the language Martin had used?—I cannot remember what words he had used. It occurred after the meeting of the Disaster Committee in Portree. I did not hear anything about the language till she told me there that day.

Is it not a fact that you and Lachlan Ross checked him for the language in Portree?—I can't remember of it. Was it filthy language? —Yes, very filthy.

And she referred to it this day at Gedintailler?—Yes.

After you got down to near Murchison's school-house the principal summonses were produced by Martin?—Yes. He was asked if he had any more of them, and he took them out of his pocket. He caught them in his hand and told me to bring them back to Portree. He did not offer them to Malcolm Finlayson. He said, "I have them here, and I have to take them back to Portree ". I did not hear him ask for a match. I heard some one in the crowd ask for a match to burn them. I did not see any weapons in their hands.

No sticks or anything of that sort ?—No.

I heard Martin asking for a smoke from some of the crowd who were about. I think he got a smoke. I believe Martin was afraid.

And yet he asked for a smoke ?—Yes.

How long did he stand smoking?—I could not say. I saw him on the road and some of the crowd speaking to him. It was about that time Mrs. Nicolson came, and there were some women with her.

She wanted Martin to repeat what he had said at Portree ?—I could not say.

Did you hear Martin make a speech ?—No, sir.

Did you observe her speaking to the crowd—can you tell us what was said ?—No. I could not say how many he shook hands with. There was not many about that time. I was struck in Gedintailler with stones and clods by the women. They did not hurt me. I was struck at Olach with stones and clods again, but they did not hurt me. Some women were throwing them.

Did one of the men wipe off the mark of a clod on Martin's clothes with the sleeve of his coat ?—I saw that done to Martin. A woman before that had taken a handful of turf and rubbed it on his jacket.

Did one of the men come and wipe it off with his sleeve ?—One of the men of the crowd came and wiped off the mark with his coat.

Mr. Macdonald here turned to consult his notes, and witness, who was apparently getting rather uneasy, hurriedly left the box. Mr. Macdonald, without turning fully round, put the question, "Did Martin make a speech," but getting no answer he found to his surprise that the box was empty, and the witness escaping rapidly by the door of the Court-room. He was recalled amidst much laughter, and, having answered a few questions, was allowed to go.

ESTATE MANAGEMENT IN SKYE.

EVIDENCE OF MR. MACDONALD, FACTOR FOR LORD MACDONALD.

Alexander Macdonald, factor, examined—I am a solicitor at Portree, and act as factor for Lord Macdonald. In the middle of April, I instructed summonses against Donald Nicolson, Balmeanach; Alex. Finlayson, do.; Samuel Nicolson, do.; John Nicolson, do.; James Matheson, Widow C. Matheson, Widow C. Nicolson, Widow Mac-

kinnon, John Stuart, and Donald Macwilliam. I instructed Martin to
go and serve the summonses, and he proceeded to do so.

Cross-examined by Mr. Macdonald—Is Martin your clerk ?—Yes,
and has been so for a long time.

How long has he been so ?—I think he entered my office first, at the
very beginning, and then he went to Glasgow, and came back, and has
been with me for the last eight or ten years.

From the beginning of what ?—Of his career.

How many years will that be ?—I cannot tell you, Mr. Macdonald.

He was in your office before he became sheriff-officer ?—Yes.

Is he your clerk still ?—Yes.

Was he absent for a time recently ?—Well, I think he was.

What was that for ?—I cannot tell you. I was away (a pause). Let
me see (another pause). I think I was away in the south somewhere,
and when I came home (a pause)——

Mr. K. Macdonald—Oh, don't be afraid—(laughter).

Witness—I am not afraid at all. I beg to assure you——

Mr. Macdonald—Well, go on then.

Witness—I was absent from the office lately, and, during my absence
from home, I understand he was absent.

The Sheriff—What was the cause of the absence ?

Witness—I don't know. He was absent when I returned. I think
he was absent for a fortnight, or nine or ten days.

Did you enquire what was the cause of his absence ?—No, I did not
enquire particularly.

The Sheriff—Did you not enquire at all ?—Yes.

By Mr. Macdonald—And what was the result of your enquiries ?—
I heard a suspicion cast on him by some people that he was rather un-
steady, but I do not think it is true at all.

Did you dismiss him ?—No, certainly not.

You took him back whenever he came ?—I forget the circumstances.
I was not prepared to speak to this. I took him back.

And made little enquiry ?—I asked of his mother and wife, but I
don't remember much about it,

Martin is your clerk and a sheriff-officer. Does he hold other offices ?
—He is clerk to the Road Trustees and collector of rates for the parish
of Snizort, about five miles from Portree, and collector of poor rates for
Bracadale, nine miles away. I do not recollect if he is collector for any
other parish.

How many proprietors are you factor for besides Lord Macdonald ?

—Macleod of Macleod, Mr. Macallister of Strathaird, Mr. Macdonald of Skaebost, and Major Fraser of Kilmuir.

I suppose that is the greater part of Skye ?—Yes, decidedly.

And in addition to this you are also a landed proprietor yourself?—Well, I believe I am. (Laughter).

You are also a solicitor and bank-agent ?—Yes.

And I believe you are agent for Captain Macdonald of Waternish ?—Oh, I have a number of appointments besides these, and lots of clients.

And your influence extends all over the Isle of Skye?—I do not know about my influence, but I hold the positions mentioned.

You are distributor of stamps ?—Yes.

And Clerk of the Peace for the Skye district ?—Yes, Depute under Mr. Andrew Macdonald. (Laughter).

Any other offices ?—I may have some, but I do not remember any more. I do not see what right you have to ask these questions. Do you mean to assess my income ? I will tell the Assessor of Taxes when he asks me, but you have no right to inquire.

You are also a coal-merchant ?—I am not aware, Mr. Macdonald. (Laughter).

And how many School Boards and Parochial Boards are you a member of ?—Several.

The Sheriff—I don't want to interrupt you, but what has this to do with the case ?

Mr. K. Macdonald—To show that this gentleman is the King of Skye —the uncrowned King of the Island—(laughter)—an absolute monarch who punishes a murmur by transportation to the mainland. There are some other offices which you hold in Skye ? Witness—Yes.

Mr. Macdonald—In point of fact, you and Martin hold between you pretty much all the valuable offices in Skye except that of parish minister ?—(great laughter). Witness (warmly)—Not all, sir ; not at all—(laughter).

Did the people of the Braes petition you about Benlee ?—They lodged a document, but I do not call it a petition. I call it a demand or ultimatum. The witness read the document, which was to the effect that the petitioners "demand" the grazings of Benlee, otherwise they would not pay their rents.

Mr. K. Macdonald—These people of the Braes are not very well educated ? Witness—Some of them are.

What did you do with that petition when you got it ?—I kept it.

Did you send it to Lord Macdonald ?—No, but I wrote to Lord Macdonald about it.

Did you make any inquiry on the spot as to the grievances of these people?—I understood what they meant by the petition itself.

Did you make any inquiry to ascertain if their grievances could be substantiated?—Yes, I made inquiries of a number of people.

Did you go to the place to make the inquiries?—No, I do not require to do that, as I know the place perfectly well.

Is the statement which they made true or not?—I believe that the demand for the exclusive possession of Benlee is not a well founded claim.

The Sheriff—That is irrelevant; we need not go into that matter.

Mr. Anderson was of the same opinion, but would not object.

Mr. K. Macdonald—If your lordship wishes me to stop, I will do so. I am probably outside of the immediate issue now, but I am led on by the hope that if an explanation is now made of the position taken up by Lord Macdonald and his factor in relation to the demands of the prisoners and their neighbours in Skye, an arrangement may be come to which will prevent a recurrence of the events which have led to the present trial.

The Sheriff—If any opposition was taken by the prosecution, I would stop this course of examination at once.

Mr. Anderson—I do not object, my lord.

The Sheriff—I do not see what bearing it has on the case.

Mr. K. Macdonald—Did these people refuse to pay their rents until the grievances complained of were inquired into and redressed?—Until they got Benlee. I sent them circulars and letters, copies of which are produced.

You state in the printed letter that they have each 6½ acres arable land, with a right to keep 5 cows, 20 sheep, and 1 horse?—Yes.

Did you ascertain the accuracy of that statement before you made it?—I have only acted as factor for two and a-half years, and that statement regarding the townships was given to me shortly after I entered, and I think it is quite correct.

Are you not aware now that, if these tenants would put all these cattle and sheep on the ground, they would die from starvation?—I am not aware of anything of the sort, sir, but we are quite prepared to look into that. The request was never civilly made.

Did a deputation of these people come to you in November last?—There was a deputation of their sons, but there were no tenants except one.

An old man of 85?—I do not think he was 85. I told them the tenants must come themselves, and not their sons. I saw this man

Nicolson, but I do not think Nicolson came into my office, though I met him on the street.

Was there a man Angus Stewart there ?—Well, I don't remember.

Was not Angus Stewart, a tenant of Lord Macdonald for the last 65 years, their principal speaker ?—You refer to a different occasion.

When was that ?—When they came arm-in-arm and shoulder-to-shoulder with a piper at their head. (Laughter).

Is it not the case that they were met by this piper, who plays for money in Portree ?—On the first occasion there was no piper, but on the second occasion they came with this piper, and would scarcely listen to me. They never came quietly to me. (Laughter). The time they came with a piper they entered the rent collection room and would scarcely listen to me. I called over their names to see I had nobody but tenants to deal with.

What was the object of this, Mr. Macdonald ?—I told you before that it was to ascertain that I had nobody but tenants to deal with.

No intimidation in it ?—I do not believe the men were ever afraid of me, nor that they are so yet. (Laughter). I do not see why they should be so unless they were doing wrong.

Did you prefer a criminal charge against some of these men before this charge was made ?—Two widows——

Mr. Kenneth Macdonald—Never mind the widows.

Witness (excitedly)—You have asked me a question, and I must answer it.

The Sheriff—Did you make a criminal charge against these people? Witness—I cannot answer no or yes, but two widows came to me weeping, saying they had been intimidated by a number of men in the Braes for paying their rents, and I went with these two widows to the Fiscal.

Mr. K. Macdonald—Was there a charge of intimidation made to the Fiscal?

The Sheriff—He says the two old ladies——

Mr. K. Macdonald—They are widows, my lord, but not old. (Laughter.)

The Sheriff—The question is a simple one. Did you or did you not? Witness—They made a charge of intimidation.

Mr. K. Macdonald—But the charge fell through?—Not so far as I know.

When did you hear the last of it ?—I do not know if I have heard the last of it yet. (Laughter.)

Did you hear that Crown Counsel had órdered no further proceedings to be taken on that charge ?—Yes.

Was it after that you caused the summonses of removing to be prepared ?—Yes, but the one thing has no connection with the other. There may have been a coincidence of time, but there was no relation between the two cases. The summonses were for ejectment for non-payment of rent.

Was it not the fact that Martin arranged to be deforced before he left Portree ?—Certainly not ; he did not expect it. (Laughter.)

The Sheriff—Is Martin a native of the Braes ?—No ; he is a native of Portree. His people belong to Kilmuir.

Mr. K. Macdonald—Is it your practice to issue summonses of removing that you have no intention to enforce ?—No, of course I do not enforce them if the cause for which they were issued has been removed.

Question repeated ?—No, but they may not be followed out, because if the rent be paid there is nothing more about it.

Then you intend to evict these people ?—Certainly, if they do not pay their rent, or show good reason why they should not.

Had you Lord Macdonald's authority for evicting these people ?—I did not want to evict them, nor do I intend to evict them if they pay their rent.

Mr. Macdonald—Kindly answer my question. Had you Lord Macdonald's authority for what you did ?—I cannot give you a more direct answer. 1 believe I said something to Lord Macdonald that it would be necessary to do something to the ringleaders. I did not ask for any instructions to evict, but said it would be necessary to warn them out for not paying their rents.

Had you Lord Macdonald's authority for evicting these people ?—I did not require his authority for that.

The Sheriff—Were your instructions special or general ?—I had no special instructions, as I did not ask for them.

Mr. Anderson—When you got the petition, Mr. Macdonald, did you write to say that they would get the hill according to the value of the present day, and expressed your wish to have it valued by an experienced person, and sent to Lord Macdonald for his consideration ?

Witness—Yes, but I got no answer from them.

Did you also offer them Benlee ?—I offered them Benlee if they would pay for it, and would give a lease of it to any tacksman who would come forward.

The Sheriff—That will do.

Witness—(sharply)—Are you done, Mr. Macdonald ? (Laughter.)

Mr. K. Macdonald—Oh, yes.

PRISONERS' DECLARATIONS.

The prisoners' declarations were then read. They are as follows :—

Donald Nicolson, Balmeanach, sixty-six 'years of age, declared—I know Angus Martin, Portree, and I know that he is a sheriff-officer. I also know, but only by sight, Ewen Robertson, residing at Lisigarry, Portree. I also know Norman Beaton, ground-officer, Portree. I saw the three of them at Braes about a fortnight ago. They were on the township of Gedintailler, and there was a crowd about them. We were hearing that they were going up with summonses of removing. I was in the crowd, and I saw papers in Martin's hand. I could not tell what they were.

Did you take the papers out of his hands ?—He knows himself. There were plenty of witnesses if they saw me do so. I did not catch hold of Ewen Robertson or touch any one there ; neither did I throw anything, nor was I swearing. I asked Robertson to lift up the papers which were at the time scattered on the road.

James Nicolson, son-in-law, residing with the above Donald Nicolson, is 30 years of age. He knew Martin to be a sheriff-officer, and he also knew Robertson and Beaton. He saw the three of them at Gedintailler on the occasion in question. The Declaration continued— There was a crowd about them when I saw them. I joined the crowd. I knew that it was with summonses of removing they had come. When I joined the crowd I did not cry out to kill Martin. I have no recollection of saying, or hearing said, that even with the support of the Volunteers no one would dare to come to Braes to put us out. I saw Martin having papers. I did not know what the papers were, but I thought they were the summonses. I saw Martin handing out the papers, and some one taking them out of his hand, and I afterwards saw them on the road torn. I did not see Ewen Robertson down on the ground. I saw a crowd of boys and girls after him along the road. They were saying that I was cursing and swearing, but I was not, and I did not put a hand on any one that day or on the papers which the sheriff-officer had. I did not think there was any harm in anything I saw done.

Peter Macdonald, Balmeanach, aged 48, and married, said he heard that Martin was a sheriff-officer. He saw Martin and Beaton at the Braes, but not Robertson. He was not present when Martin arrived. The Declaration continued—We were thinking it was with the summonses of removing he (Martin) came. There was a crowd gathered about him when he arrived of about 150 women and children. I did not see papers with him until I saw them on the road at Olach. I saw them before they were burnt. The crowd called out—that is, the women called out—that Martin and his assistants would require to burn them themselves. I did not say to Martin that he would be made to burn them himself. It was at Olach that I joined the crowd. I have nothing further to say but that Martin burned the papers himself. The place Olach above alluded to is about half a-mile from Gedentailler, in the direction of Portree.

Alexander Finlayson, Balmeanach, 70 years of age, declared that he did not know until Martin arrived that he had come to the Braes to serve the summonses. He was not present when Martin arrived, and he saw him first among a number of men, women, and children at Gedentailler. He did not know that Robertson was helping Martin. The Declaration continued—I told him to return and burn them. At this time there was some torn papers scattered about the road, and it was to these papers I referred. The papers were torn and on the ground before I joined the crowd. I did not know that these papers were summonses of removing, but some of the people were saying that they were. I did not know that Martin was going with summonses to us that day, but we were hearing a rumour that we were to be warned. I did not dare Martin to proceed further with his summonses that day. I had a staff in my hand. I was not flourishing it. I did not hear Martin say that he had the Sheriff's warrant for serving the summonses that day. I thought we ought to get justice concerning the matter in dispute, which was the hill pasture of Benlee, which we ever had. When had you the pasture ?—We had it ever in connection with our town-ships. It was taken from us about sixteen years ago by bad rulers. We have not possessed it for the last seventeen years. It was let to another tenant. I and my father before me, and my grandfather, great-grandfather, and great-great-grandfather, have been living in the township of Balmeanach, and the hill of Ben-lee was all that time connected with our township.

Alex. Finlayson, son of and residing with the said Alex. Finlayson, Balmeanach, is married, and about thirty years of age. He saw Martin at the Braes on the day in question. The Declaration continued—I did not know then that Martin was a sheriff-officer. I only knew that he was the factor's clerk when I saw him at the Braes on that occasion. Martin had a bunch of papers. I did not know what the papers were, but he told us they were summonses, some of removing and some of rent. I did not take these papers out of Martin's hands, but after seeing them in his hands, I saw them torn and scattered on the road. I saw some of the papers which Martin had burnt at Olach that day, but these were different papers from those I saw scattered on the road at Gedentailler. It was I who took the papers which were burnt at Olach out of Martin's hand. He stretched out his hand holding these papers, and I took them out of his hands. Somebody said I should not take them, and I offered them back to him, but he would not take them, and I let them fall on the road. At this time there were a good many people about Martin, and some of them cried out to burn the papers, but I am not sure whether I said this or not. Martin then asked for a match, but there was no match to be found. A lighted peat, however, was produced, and Martin set fire to one of the summonses, and then the whole caught fire and were burned. The crowd did not very much force Martin to burn the summonses. They told him to burn them, and he did so. The crowd did not call bad names to Martin, but he told the people he would be put out of his situation by the factor if he had not come to give them the summonses that day. They did not say anything worse than his name to him. I told him to move on, as I was afraid the scholars and women would come and hurt him. He then asked us to see him safe over the burn, and we did so.

THE EVIDENCE FOR THE DEFENCE.

Mr. Donald Macdonald, Tormore, examined by Mr. K. Macdonald —You were factor for Lord Macdonald until about two years and a-half ago ?—Some time about that.

You know the Braes ?—I do.

When you were factor did the tenants of the Braes townships complain to you about the want of the hill of Ben-Lee ?—They may have done. I have no distinct recollection about their making any specific charge.

You know the story about the shepherd's house being built, about which some of the crofters complained ?—Yes.

What did you do ?—Well, the complaint was that the tenant of Benlee was building a house on a portion of what they considered their land.

The Sheriff—All this occurred two or three years ago, Mr. Macdonald ?—Yes.

The Sheriff asked Mr. K. Macdonald if he meant to justify the action of the prisoners by this evidence ? He did not see that it had any relevancy.

Mr. K. Macdonald—It has a bearing on what followed.

Mr. K. Macdonald (to witness)—There was a lease of Benlee which expires at Whitsunday 1882. Is not that so ?—I believe it does.

And the people wished to get the land back at that term ?—There was some indication that way.

Did you make them any promise ?—I made no promise.

Did you hold out any hope ?—No ; certainly no distinct hope.

Then, was it from you they got their information ?—I don't remember, but it is quite possible.

Did you renew the lease during your factorship ? I believe I did.

For a further period ?—Yes. And without informing them ? I don't remember, but it is quite possible.

In answer to Mr. Anderson, Mr. Macdonald said Benlee had not been in the possession of the crofters for the past 16 or 17 years.

The Sheriff.—Benlee is advertised to let now.

Mr. K. Macdonald—Yes, in the *Courier* of to-day.

Mr. A. Macdonald, factor—And the tenants may have it if they like to pay rent for it.

EVIDENCE OF CROFTERS.

John Finlayson, a tenant of the Braes, said, in reply to Mr. Macdonald—I was at the Braes when Martin arrived, and saw him with the papers in his hands. He handed them over to Donald Nicolson, who took them and threw them back to Martin, who turned his back, and I think refused to take them back. Some one in the crowd said to Nicolson that he had no right to the papers, and he then dropped them on the ground, and the children trod upon them. No one struck Martin, or even threatened to strike him. I heard some one saying to Martin, "Be not afraid, no one will touch you". Robertson at this time had gone homewards, the children following him. Martin also followed, but after he had gone some distance he stopped, and asked for a light. He got an ember of a peat, with which he set a paper (a paper about the size of a summons) on fire, and put some more with it. He said, "Stand back and don't smother it," and added, "There it is for you, boys". He appeared to be laughing, and did not seem to be afraid. He afterwards had a smoke and chatted with the people. He made a speech before leaving, in which he said, "Be hardy and active ; you will not see me again, and you will get Benlee". He also said he did not blame them for what they had done, and said if he had been in their place he would have done the same thing. He shook hands with a number of people before leaving. I did not see any person strike Martin.

By Mr. Anderson—I joined the crowd when they began. I went there just because I followed the rest.

You saw some boys with flags on the watch?—There were.

And what were these boys to do?—They were to give us notice.

Of what?—About the force that was being sent to us.

Was that a sheriff-officer you expected?—We did not know that it was a sheriff-officer.

Did you expect Martin?—No.

Did you expect summonses?—Yes, I expected a summons.

Now, was it for persons coming with summonses that you placed the boys on the watch?—Yes.

And it was arranged that as soon as a boy saw them he was to give warning?—Yes.

And you were to collect then?—Yes.

Mr. Macdonald objected to this line of examination, as being really an attempt to prove the charge of Deforcement which the Prosecutor had not been able to libel relevantly. The Sheriff however allowed it.

Was it said that he would not be allowed to serve a summons?—I did not hear that.

What were you going to do when you met the persons coming with the summonses?—To return them.

That is to return him to Portree?—I do not know where. (Laughter.)

I suppose you know that you were to turn him off the Braes?—Yes, we were going to turn him off the Braes.

Are you any relation of Finlaysons in the box?—I am a brother of Malcolm's and a son of Alexander Finlayson.

Did you see any stones thrown?—No.

Nor clods of earth?—No.

Nor peats?—No.

Did you see Robertson on the ground?—Yes.

Did you see him lying on the ground?—No.

Did you see anybody touch him?—No.

What became of him?—I saw him going away, and the children were cheering him home. (Laughter.)

Were they throwing anything after him?—I did not see, I was far from him. Witness saw only two of the prisoners, Malcolm Finlayson and Patrick Macdonald following Martin to the second crowd, near Murchison's schoolhouse.

Alexander Finlayson, Peinachorrain, was at Gedentailler on the day when Martin came with the papers. He knew that Martin was the factor's clerk, but did not know that he was a sheriff-officer. The papers were lying on the road when he saw them first, and Martin was laughing and talking, and did not appear to be frightened. He generally corroborated the previous witness regarding the burning of the papers, and said he did not see any stones thrown at Martin. In answer to Mr. Anderson, he said he was a son of Alexander Finlayson, one of the prisoners, and brother of Malcolm Finlayson, another of the prisoners. Martin did not seem to be in the least afraid.

James Mathieson, on being asked to take the oath in English, declined. He said—Oh no. All the speaking in this case has been done in Gaelic, and I am not going to interpret Gaelic into English. (Laughter.) The oath having been administered in Gaelic, he said he resided at Balmeanach, and was at Gedentailler on the 17th April when Martin came to serve the summonses. When the people came up Martin held out some papers in his hands. He held them out in the direction of Donald Nicolson, and said, "There they are, take them". I don't know whether he said this to Nicolson or to the rest of the people. Nicolson, however, took them. He did not snatch them from Martin, and Martin did not endeavour to keep them from him. In answer to other questions, witness said Martin did not appear to be frightened, and had no occasion to be so.

What occurred near Murchison's schoolhouse?—I saw him with more papers there. When I arrived he had them in his hand as at first. He was offering them to anyone who would receive them. I don't know where Robertson was. He went along before them. I don't know if they were following him at that time, but they were before that, and some children.

Was Martin quite sober at that time?—Well, I don't know. I would think him like a man that would have a little.

Did you hear Martin ask for a match?—Yes. He said, Was there no one there had a match? They replied that they had a burning ember for lighting his pipe. After this Martin asked where it was. They said, It was here. I was standing at the side of the road, and I saw him go over by the papers. I saw him point to them and say, "Lads, there is a fire, stand back and don't choke it". I saw the papers on fire after that. I saw him drink at the well. He was inclined to bend at the well, but they told him there was a pail. He asked, Have any of you a pipe till I smoke? Alexander Nicolson went to give him his pipe, but it was broken. Nicolson then went to get another man's, and after cleaning it so (here the witness made a movement as if wiping a pipe clean) he handed it to Martin, and Martin smoked it. He (Martin) was in the very middle of the crowd smoking it.

Was he talking to them and smoking?—Yes, smoking and talking. I did not see any appearance of fright about him. There was no occasion for his being frightened.

Did you hear Murdo Nicolson say anything to him ?—I heard some one say, I am not very certain if it was Angus Nicolson, but I heard some one say, " No one here will do anything to him ".

What did he say to that ?—He said, " Oh, I had no fear. I know that the Braes people will not do anything to me." He was shaking hands with the people before he went away. He was shaking hands and thanking them for dealing so gently with him. He told them to be active after this, as it was now they had it to do. I don't know what he meant by that. I did not hear him say he was a sheriff-officer, or that he came from the Sheriff. I know he is the factor's clerk in Portree. I thought the "bailie" sent him there that day. I saw the widows standing up as if they were speaking to him. One of them, Widow Nicolson, seemed to be angry. I did not hear Martin say anything to her at the time. She was done speaking to him before I came. I don't know what they were talking about, but people were telling me afterwards. I did not see anyone touching Martin other than to shake him by the hand.

John Nicolson, Gedintailler, gave corroborative evidence. He saw no one putting a hand on Martin, and said Martin seemed quite pleased, and put the papers on the top of the fire.

John Nicolson, Peinachorrain, also gave evidence regarding the proceedings at Martin's visit. He saw no stones thrown. In cross-examination by Mr. Anderson, he admitted that clods had been thrown by the school children, but if Martin was frightened it was only at seeing so many women. (Laughter.)

John Maclean, Balmeanach, described the scene at the schoolhouse where the papers were burnt. He said Martin stepped into the centre of the crowd, and getting a fire-brand blew it until he had lighted the papers. He then set them on the ground, and said, "Men of the Braes, I am obliged to you for your kindness". He appeared quite hearty, and shook hands with the people. There was no reason for Martin fearing anything. He added, I was in the factor's office in November last as one of the deputation. Our names were taken down at that time, and we were charged with impertinence. The factor was sending us letters after that threatening us.

This brought the evidence to a close.

Mr. Anderson did not address the court, but simply asked a conviction for assault.

Mr. Macdonald began by showing the effect upon the indictment, of the judgment sustaining his objection to the relevancy of the charge of deforcement, and the minor charge of obstructing an officer of the law in the performance of his duty; and he read what was left of the indictment, to show that all that remained was a charge of simple assault against the prisoners. He went on to say:—When I first addressed your Lordship to-day, I attempted to show that the case as it then stood was too important for trial in this court. It has now been reduced to such slender proportions that the wonder is it was ever brought into any court. It has been attempted, by leading irrelevant evidence, to give the case a fictitious importance, but the prosecutor has been flogging a dead horse. A common assault such as is now charged would never have justified the measures taken to apprehend the men now in the dock. Would the public have looked on in silent wonder if they had been told that the army of policemen sent to Skye had been sent there to apprehend a few men—most of them old men—whose only crime was that they looked on while a few respectable women threw dirt at a man who had slandered them. I rather think they would then do what those of them who have not to pay for it will do now—they would laugh outright. I really feel some difficulty in discussing seriously the very small mouse which this mountain in labour has brought forth. The charge is assault. What is the evidence in support of it? It is certainly not the sort of evidence usually led in cases of assault. We heard of a sheriff-officer being sent from Portree to serve writs at a place nine or ten miles away, of his seeing boys with flags and afterwards being met by a crowd of people, of his papers being burnt by himself, and of his making a speech thanking the people for their kindness to him, and encouraging them to persevere in their demands; but very little, and that unreliable, of an assault by anybody, nothing of an assault by the men at the bar. In fact the public prosecutor never anticipated having to prove a charge of assault, and had no evidence to support it. The turn the case took when the Court held his main charges irrelevantly stated had taken him by surprise, and he ought then to have thrown up the whole case. He had not done that. He had led evidence which showed that the prisoners had done certain things which might or might not be criminal, but which certainly did not constitute the crime with which they now stood charged, nor, for that matter, any of the crimes with which the indictment, as it originally stood, sought to charge them. The prosecutor had not stated the grounds upon which he asked for a conviction on the charge of assault,—there were none to state. The only hope he could have was that the Court would convict them of a crime of which they were not guilty, because the evidence showed that they came near committing another and a totally different offence with which they could not be charged. If this was the hope of the prosecutor, he hoped it would be disappointed, and that these men would not be convicted of a crime of which they were not guilty simply because some victims were required to shield officials from the charge of playing a huge practical joke at the expense of the public. I shall now, with your Lordship's permission, go over the evidence shortly, and I think I shall be able to show that there is no evidence—no reliable evidence—that any one of the accused committed an assault, while there is a considerable amount of reliable evidence to show that not only was no assault committed, but that Martin and the ground-officer were on the best of terms with the prisoners while they were together—terms so friendly that the idea of an assault having been committed during the interview is utterly precluded. As to Robertson, he was clearly not a popular favourite, and he retreated towards Portree at an early stage, followed by some children. If he was assaulted at that time, the prisoners were no parties to it. Robertson was, however, the only person who was said in evidence to have been touched by one of the accused; but the evidence on that point came from so suspicious a source, and was, as would be shown immediately, so strongly contradicted, that I have no hesitation in asking your Lordship to disbelieve it. Mr. Macdonald then proceeded to review the evidence for the purpose of showing that Martin, Robertson, and Beaton had contradicted each other in important particulars in their account of what had taken place, and that the story told by the witnesses for the defence was consistent throughout, and entirely inconsistent with those of Martin and his associates. Martin, he said, had to account to his master, the factor, for his failure to serve the summonses, if, indeed, it was not intended before he went that he should fail; and this was the story he told on his return. The enlightened management of Lord Macdonald's estates in Skye by his omnipotent and unapproachable factor had brought about a state of matters which the usual machinery of the factor's office—summonses of removing and occasional evictions, supplemented by threats of undefined pains and penalties—was unable to deal with. An attempt even to get up a criminal prosecution had failed. What more natural, then, than to get up a sensational charge which would bring a large force to the rescue of the powerless factor without expense to his employer. I do not say this is the explanation of what took place, but it is a possible interpretation of the evidence, and it would go a long way to account for the peculiar "coincidence," as Mr. Macdonald calls it, that while the criminal authorities intimated the abandonment of the first criminal charge on 1st April, the attempt to serve the summons of removing was made on the 7th of the same month. Be that, however, as it may, the evidence which, by the forbearance of the Court, I was permitted to lead, showed that the present unhappy state of matters among Lord Macdonald's tenants was entirely attributable to mismanagement on the part of successive factors. Before 1865 those people were comfortable and contented. They had their patches of arable land near the sea and the hill grazings beyond. The grazings were on Benlee, of which so much has been heard. The rent for both lands was paid in one sum, and was fixed on the basis of the number of cattle, sheep, and horses each tenant was able to keep. In 1865, however, a factor deprived them of the hill while their rents remained the same. They were pushed down towards the sea-shore, and there, under the shadow of their mountain, and a few inches above highwater mark, on what was at no very distant date a sea-beach, they eked out a precarious living from their patches of mixed rock and sand, dignified with the name of arable land. For years these people went on uncomplainingly, while year by year they became poorer. Their horses first went,—in 1865 every man had a horse—most of them several; now there is not a horse for every three tenants. Then the little stocks of sheep and cattle gradually dwindled down, while all the time their owners were paying rents for the grazing of three or four times the number of sheep and cattle the grazings left to them would feed. At last the inevitable came—the people saw starvation or pauperism staring them in the face, and they made a humble appeal for redress. To whom ? To Lord Macdonald ? No ! To his factor, and the factor made fair promises—at least so say the people. He told them, they say, that the hill was let on lease, but the lease would expire in 1882, when they would get it. How does he keep his promise ? Several years before 1882, he, without saying anything to the crofters who were patiently enduring poverty and hardship waiting for the fulfilment of his promise, let the hill on a new lease, and then leaving this little complication for his successor to settle, he resigned his factorship. The successor was Mr. Alexander Macdonald. It was Mr. Macdonald's misfortune that in his time the crofters found out how they had been deceived, and that, not taking the trouble to understand their grievances, he threatened them when he ought to exhihit at least the appearance of sympathy, and to attempt to conciliate them. To the crofters Martin was simply the factor's clerk, Beaton the factor's underling, and with the factor and all his belongings they resolved to have nothing to do. To Lord Macdonald they must appeal. They believed that he had never authorised the harsh measures adopted towards them, and the evidence led to-day shows that their belief was well founded. Lord Macdonald, in whose name these proceedings were carried on, never authorised them, was never even consulted about them. Proceedings which had for their ostensible object the eviction of the inhabitants of three townships,— several hundred people in all,—were not important enough forsooth to lead the factor to consult his master. The people knew well that less than thirty years before similar proceedings had been carried out to their bitter end in the name of their landlord's father without his authority, and they knew that to the day of his death that Lord Macdonald bitterly regretted these proceedings. Well might they believe that this Lord Macdonald would not lightly consent to their wholesale eviction and expatriation. They knew, and he knew, that the strong arm of *their* ancestors was the only title deed by which *his* ancestors held their land, and that but for the sturdy clansmen of the Isles, Lord Macdonald would not now hold an acre of land in Skye. It was not, therefore, the

law in the person of its officers, it was not even their landlord, these men resisted, it was the factor—the man who was
in their eyes the impersonation of all the injustice and hardship to which they had been subjected, and I ask was there
not some justification for their resistance? This being the
position taken up by the accused and their neighbours, was
it probable that they would degrade themselves and their
cause by assaulting a person in Martin's position? I think
not. Further, was Martin's own story consistent with the
theory of an assault? Would a man who had just been
assaulted, and who was in mortal terror, as Martin says he
was, find himself so sound in wind as Martin admits he was.
When a lighted peat was procured to burn the summonses,
some of the men in the crowd tried to blow it into a flame
but failed. Martin, however, notwithstanding his terror
found himself, as he admits, "in better breath" than his
alleged assailants, and succeeded in blowing the peat into a
flame when they had failed to do so. (Laughter.) Though
terror-stricken and in mortal fear he managed somehow to
enjoy a smoke quietly. When he wanted a drink of water
he was not afraid to go off the road to a well, and to go on
his knees and dip his head into it. It never occurred to him
that this dangerous crowd finding his head in the water might
keep it there. He gauged the crowd correctly enough as his
conduct showed. He stood among them, chatted with them,
drunk out of their pails, borrowed and smoked one of their
pipes, and on parting made them a speech. · That was the
evidence of the prosecution, as well as of the defence. The
Prosecutor did not make an attempt, after hearing the
evidence, to argue that Martin had been assaulted. To do
so in the face of such evidence would be an outrage on
common sense. Mr. Macdonald concluded by asking for a
verdict of not guilty. (Applause.)

THE PRISONERS FOUND GUILTY—THE SENTENCE.

The Sheriff said—The charge now is one of assault against these men combinedly or against one or other of them, "actor or art and part," so that if the prosecution has proved that one of them assaulted one or other of the men said to be assaulted, and that the other prisoners aided and abetted them in that assault, that, I take it, would be sufficient to enable me to find the whole of them guilty as libelled. Throwing aside all that is really unnecessary, the simple question for me to determine is this—Did these men "or one or other of them" do something to one or other of the three men, Martin, Beaton, and Robertson, which in the eye of the law is assault? Now, it is quite true that there are certain discrepancies in the evidence which has been adduced. There is no doubt whatever that the witnesses for the defence do not support the evidence for the prosecution; but the evidence for the defence confirms to a very great extent the statements that are made by the principal witnesses for the prosecution. And part of the evidence of the defence is really of a mere negative character. Certain of the witnesses —the first three—say that they were not present at the beginning of this disturbance. They came to the ground after the papers were taken out of Martin's pocket. Now, Martin says that when he came to the place he had the papers in his pocket, and they were only taken out of it when he was asked for them. I may mention, before proceeding further, that I see no reason whatever to doubt Martin's statement. Martin gave his evidence fairly, and in a way which convinced me at least that he really was telling the truth, and I do not think there was anything in his cross-examination which tended to render Martin's evidence untrustworthy. Now Martin says that Donald Nicolson took a leading part in this affair, and he stated that Donald Nicolson caught hold of Ewen Robertson by the back of the neck "and called out to me in language which was not very polite," but it had reference to things which had taken place before then. Robertson tells us more particularly how Donald acted after the summonses had been plucked from Martin. He laid hold of him by the neck and so on. Now, I take it that this is an assault within the four corners of this complaint. It will not do for any one to say that because five or six witnesses did not see this that the affair did not take place. There is the direct evidence of two witnesses which is a great deal better than the indirect evidence or negative testimony of a score. Therefore, if Robertson's and Martin's evidence were true, Donald Nicolson was guilty of an assault. Now, if Donald Nicolson was guilty of an assault, the question will then come to be, what part did the others take in regard to this? Donald Nicolson, according to Martin, came forward and took the papers from him. The next person who comes on the scene is Alex. Finlayson, and the proceedings that he adopts are certainly of a most threatening character. There is no doubt whatever that he had a stick in his hand, and the testimony given by Robertson and others is that he comes forward and threatens them, flourishing his stick and daring them to proceed further. And then he proceeds to tell us of the throwing of stones, in which Finlayson took an active part, and in this way he became "art and part" with Nicolson in the assault upon these men. I therefore take it that when you have Nicolson behaving as he had done, and Finlayson being there with him, and taking the part he did, that Finlayson is guilty of the assault as a party—as one acting art and part with Nicolson. Then the next persons who come before us are James Nicolson and the other two.

These three men are not said to have done anything except to be accessories along with these people. Peter Macdonald, indeed, after a time, comes to make himself conspicuous by telling Martin that unless he burns his papers, Martin would not get home alive; but there is no evidence of Macdonald doing anything in particular beyond threatening Martin and the others. Malcolm Finlayson appears afterwards near the schoolhouse, and all three form part of the threatening crowd. It appears to me, however, that Peter Macdonald, Malcolm Finlayson, and James Nicolson did not take that conspicuous part which Donald Nicolson and Alexander Finlayson took. And, therefore, although the case against each and all of these prisoners has been proved, I think there is a distinction between the conduct of Donald Nicolson, and Alexander Finlayson, and the others. These two are really the persons who committed the assault, and a distinction must be made between them and the others. The judgment of the Court is that Donald Nicolson and Alexander Finlayson be each fined £2 10s., or, failing payment, one month's imprisonment; and the other three prisoners, Peter Macdonald, Malcolm Finlayson, and James Nicolson, be each fined 20s., or fourteen days' imprisonment.

LIBERATION OF THE PRISONERS.

The result was received with some surprise, though not with dissatisfaction. As the Sheriff summed up strongly against two of the prisoners it was anticipated that the full penalty in their case, at least, would be inflicted, and that on the other three prisoners the sentence would have been more severe than that pronounced. The leniency of the judgment, therefore, was satisfactory to the audience. Dean of Guild Mackenzie at once passed a cheque for the full amount of the fines to Mr. Anderson, but the agent for the prisoners (Mr. Macdonald) intimated that it was paid under protest in order to enable him to lodge an appeal if this should afterwards be resolved upon. *

The prisoners, who had been confined between two policemen throughout the day, were then liberated. As they emerged from the Castle, they were met by a large crowd, who greeted them with cheers and calls for a speech. They, however, were allowed to proceed to their hotel without any further demonstration.

The men and the witnesses were lodged, and provided with a liberal supply of all the creature comforts, in the Glenalbyn Hotel, where they were visited by many of those in Inverness who sympathised with their position. Next morning they left by train and steamer for Portree, their fares having been paid, and provision made for anything they might require on the journey. On their arrival the same evening in the Capital of Skye they were met by their friends and the people of Portree, who greeted them with great enthusiasm, and many of whom convoyed them the greater part of their way to the Braes.

THE AUTUMN CAMPAIGN.

NOTHING of importance occurred for months after the trial, until the crofters appear to have allowed their sheep to take possession of Benlee, and, it is alleged, refused to take them back to their own ground.

Early in October, Lord Macdonald's Edinburgh agents

* A cheque for the whole amount of the fines was shortly afterwards received from Mr. Norman Macleod, Bookseller, Bank Street, Edinburgh, on behalf of a few Highlanders in that city, who were quite willing to subscribe much more had it been found necessary. The whole of the other expenses of the Trial was paid by the Federation of Celtic Societies.

sent to the Braes crofters registered letters requesting them
to withdraw their stock from Benlee without delay. These
letters were, in the ordinary course, sent to the district post-
office. Delivery of two or three was accepted, but on their
contents becoming known the rest of the crofters resolved to
have nothing to do with them, and refused to take delivery.
A copy of one of these letters appeared at the time in the
Aberdeen Free Press. The burden of its contents was a
request to the crofters to pay up their arrears and remove their
stock from Benlee, otherwise proceedings would be taken
against them. The rents had not been paid, the stock was
still on Benlee, and the threat by Lord Macdonald's agents
was immediately followed up ; the Court of Session granted
notes of suspension and interdict against the crofters with
regard to the grazings of Benlee. Mr. Alexander Macdonald, Messenger-at-arms, Inverness, proceeded from
Inverness with the Court of Session writs in his possession.
On Saturday morning, the 2nd of September, he left Portree
for the Braes to serve the writs, accompanied by Lord
Macdonald's ground-officer. Gedentailler is the township
nearest to Portree, and on arriving there the officer of Court
proceeded to serve the documents on the different crofters.
He appears to have got on smoothly enough there, but word
seems to have been sent to Balmeanach, the largest of the
three townships, that the officer and his companions were
approaching. Thereupon the women and children of
Balmeanach gathered in large numbers, covering their heads
with handkerchiefs to disguise themselves as well as they
could. They proceeded towards Gedentailler, and met the
officers on the way. There the second Battle of the Braes
began. Stones and clods were flying freely, the officers
thought it expedient to beat a retreat, and the writs were not
served in the township of Balmeanach, or Peinachorrain.

Mr. William Mackenzie, the special correspondent of the *Aberdeen Free Press*, to whom we are indebted for the narrative of these proceedings, visited the Braes on the following Tuesday, while the sheriff-officers were still in Portree, waiting for further instructions from the authorities at Inverness. He writes on Tuesday evening :—

The serving of writs at Gedentailler was evidently managed with great rapidity, for the work was done before the people realised their position. The people of the other townships got hurried word of what was going on, and they mustered and drove the officers away before they reached Balmeanach. The whole of the people are now in a state of great anxiety, and every stranger visiting the district is watched. The children, indeed, run away weeping and crying " Tha iad a' tighinn, tha iad a' tighinn " (They are coming, they are coming), on the approach of any suspected person. An impression was abroad last night that the officers were again to proceed to the Braes to-day, and, accordingly, the women and children, in large numbers, gathered and formed themselves into two divisions—the one being detailed to watch and protect Peinachorrain—(the farthest south of the townships), in case of the officers coming on them from Sligachan, and the other to defend Balmeanach, the middle township, in case of their coming from Portree. They occupied their respective positions for a considerable time during the day, but ultimately as the " foe " did not appear, they retired to their homes, leaving sentries on duty, to warn them of the approach of danger. These sentinels soon saw me, and gave the alarm, and in a very short time I was surrounded by a large crowd of women and children, and a few men. Each Amazon as she came up looked anything but friendly ; but as I came to be known I received a cordial welcome. The old men who were present regarded the conduct of the proprietor towards them as harsh; but they thought that the Court of Session writs should be peaceably accepted. The Amazons, however, thought otherwise, and they expressed in no qualified terms their intention to resist.

Those who suffered in spring are looked upon as heroes and martyrs, and some feel themselves driven to such a state of desperation and exasperation that they are well nigh indifferent as to what may happen. " Whatever becomes of us," they say, " we cannot he worse off than we are." The application of force may crush them individually, but in the present frame of mind of these people, force will be no more a remedy in the Braes than in Ireland; and I am satisfied that any attempt at evicting them, or selling them out, without some attempt at an amicable settlement, will be attended with some rough work.

The officers were re-called to Inverness on the 11th of September, having remained in the Island for nine days without again attempting to serve the writs.

The same correspondent, in one of a series of able articles, writes, under date of 11th October, regarding a rumour which was then current in well-informed circles, to the following effect:—" During the week of the Argyle-shire gathering, when the gentry and nobility of the west were promoting social intercourse in Oban, an informal meeting of proprietors was there held in private, to consider the present position and future prospects of land ownership in the Highlands. The Skye question naturally formed a leading topic of discussion, and the opinion was expressed that Lord Macdonald, in the interests of his class, ought to have gone long ago to the Braes and to have endeavoured to settle the dispute between himself and the crofters; and it was felt that so long as the question remained in its present aspect it will naturally be kept before the country, and the popular mind will be imbibing doctrines with regard to the land which may probably end in restricting the liberties in dealing with landed estates now enjoyed by their owners." The Northern Meeting at Inverness took place on 21st and 22nd September (in the following week), and many of the gentlemen present at the Argyleshire Meeting attended the meeting in the Highland capital. Lord Macdonald was also present. Whether his lordship had any interview with those gentlemen I know not, but on Saturday, 23rd of September, he left Inverness, and on Monday, the 25th, he visited the Braes. The conference was fruitless. The tenants, who had hitherto demanded Benlee free of rent, now, in order to put an end to the present turmoil, offered to give about £40. Lord Macdonald, who receives £128 from the present tenant, agreed to accept £100. Possibly another interview might lead to a compromise between parties—the tenants offering more and the landlord agreeing to accept less. But whether there will be another interview or not is a matter that must lie with the proprietor, for in their present frame of mind the tenants are not likely to seek an interview at the stage which the case has now reached.

Now, with regard to the threatened military invasion. That it was the intention of the authorities at one time to send one or two companies of soldiers to Skye is not denied; aud that these companies were to go from Fort-George. This would undoubtedly be very distasteful work to Highland soldiers, but if *ordered* they would have no alternative but to obey. That they were warned to be in readiness for "active service" in the Braes is certain; but I have good reasons for stating that military opinion at the Fort was decidedly against any such task being assigned to Highland soldiers, and that such remonstrances as could be made consistent with military discipline were sent to the superior authorities. The reasons for this are obvious. The country is now divided into regimental districts, and Skye is one of the recruiting districts for the Highland regiments which have their depôts at Fort-George. The belief among Highland officers is that if a company of Highland soldiers were sent to Skye on such an errand there would be no more recruits from that island for at least half a century. That this opinion is a sound one will be readily admitted by any one acquainted with the Highland character.

It was ultimately resolved to make another attempt, with a larger force of police, to serve the writs on the tenants of Balmeanach and Peinachorrain, on Tuesday the 24th of October. The special correspondent of the *Inverness Courier*, who accompanied the expedition, describes the proceedings thus :—

At half-past eight this morning, in weather as pleasant as one could desire, there drove from Portree for the Braes two waggonettes containing Mr. A. Macdonald, messenger-at-arms, Inverness (who was to serve the writs); his concurrent; his guide, the ground-officer on Lord Macdonald's estates ; Mr. Aitchison, superintendent of the County Police ; Mr. Macdonald, inspector, Portree ; and a body of nine police constables. Some newspaper correspondents followed in a third conveyance. All along the route there was manifested the most intense interest—I may say excitement. Soon after leaving Portree we met two pleasant old men—crofters at Balmeanach—who had not heard that the officers were coming, but who, when asked as to what kind of reception they might expect, shook their heads, and indicated that their reception would be somewhat warm, but decidedly unpleasant. One of them told us that the officers had spoken to him as he came along, he having been pointed out as one of the crofters in question by Mr. Beaton. They asked him to accept the "paper," but he would have nothing to do with it ; he did not understand that it was anything else than a paper the reception of which would end in his being reduced to misery and want. Then, as we proceeded, we met people who told us that a reception was quite prepared at the Braes for the officers, and for the police. Here, and at several other points, information which we received in Portree last night was confirmed, information, namely, that the crofters had been advised that officers were approaching them, had been counselled to receive the papers, and that they had been on the watch all night. We passed on and on through a country which plainly had at one time been thickly peopled, but which is now a scene solitary to an extent that is painful to contemplate. At a little township near the Braes, women stopped their work at the peats to look at the passing carriages. A little further on the officers and policemen left their waggonettes, and walked to Gedintailler—a distance of over two miles—on foot. We adopted the same course.

The high green hill which, at the very entrance to the township of Gedintailler, rises right up from the roadside, was soon before us—a little over a mile ahead. We could see that there were groups of people on the height, and a couple of crofters belonging to a place immediately on the Portree side of Gedintailler, and who joined us here—going forward to see the fun—said that sixty people had been on the watch there ever since the dawn of day, and that they carried flags with which they were to wave to the whole community signals of approaching strangers. As soon as we approached the borders of Gedintailler, it was plainly seen that the officers, who were now a third of a mile ahead of us, were engaged in a task of a most delicate and

difficult nature.   A band of young men, and   stout
lads, and girls, occupied a height, from which, with
stones, they could command the passage by the road
underneath.   Here we learned that the people whose
writs were served successfully on the 2nd September last had
driven their cattle off, thinking that the officers had come to
seize them.   Further on, we could see that the officers and
the policemen were marching along a road, on each side of
which were gathered here and there small knots of men,
women, and children.   As the officers and police force
advanced, these knots of people retreated before them—all,
however, to concentrate at a point just within the march that
separates the township of Gedintailler from the township of
Balmeanach.   The people were angry and excited. Some
carried sticks.   Others doubtless were quite prepared to use
the stones that lay everywhere about.   Many wore an aspect
of determination which was ominous in the extreme.   It was
clear that a whole country-side was up in arms against the
messenger-at-arms, the police, and the writs.   One young
fellow, in answer to a question by myself, spoke in a tone and
with a look which were the opposite of encouraging ; and
only changed his behaviour when he heard that I had come
from a newspaper.   This much must be said of everyone
else ; they were kind and courteous to those who were not
connected with the officials who came to visit them ; they
seem well disposed too so long as you did not propose to
take Benlee from them ; in appearance and demeanour
altogether there was nothing when they were away from the
officers, but what is creditable.   They, however, hate the
writs, and all connected with them ; and they entertain a
bitter aversion to the very word " police "—an aversion
deeply rooted in the minds of the youngest—because presumably of the recollection of the visit which was made to

them in April last. But extreme excitement is perfectly compatible with this courtesy towards those who they know are not connected with the writs. If I were asked to describe the Braes to-day, I should say the whole community resembled a barrel of gunpowder that only required the lighted match to produce an explosion.

The officers and the police were stopped at the entrance to the township of Balmeanach—quite near the first house in the township—by a body of men, women, and children, variously estimated at from 140 to 160 individuals.

The scene, while officers and crowd were face to face with each other, was one both striking and picturesque. While officers and people discussed in Gaelic we wandered around to see what was to be seen, and hear what of English was to be heard. There they were, a great crowd engaged in loud and angry talk, varied now and again by strange cries and shouts from the women ; and the very gathering and the noise and the excitement lent additional interest to the more distant scenes, which were already striking in solitude and grandeur. The girls, who were attending to the cattle on the green hill-sides, gathered in little knots to hear what was going on. The children who played on the roadside, or watched on the green turf infants of tender years, whose mothers were confronting the officers, seemed to have a perfect idea of what was taking place. At the beach, far down below the roadway, there lay a little boat in which three fishermen were engaged in shaking out of the nets some herrings which the night before they had got in Loch-Eynart. They, too, had to be apprised of what was going on. Occasionally one of the crew would land, ascend the steep brae, and look on the crowd. But while he was in the boat a knot of young women far up above the beach, would report the movements.

The interview between the people and the officers continued near an hour and a-half. The conversation was carried on in Gaelic. It would appear that every advice given to the crofters to receive the writs was lost upon them ; they apparently did not know what the papers were, what they meant, or what the receiving of them would result in beyond the taking from them of Benlee. It is said they had been advised to receive the writs by two ministers and others ; and in the afternoon we were shown the following telegram which had been handed in at Inverness at 4.52 P.M., Monday, and which had been received in Portree at 5 P.M. :—

" *From Dean of Guild Mackenzie, Inverness.*

" *To Mr. Neil Buchanan, or any of the Braes Crofters, near Portree.*

"Sheriff-officers, with body of County Police, left to-day with writs for Braes crofters. Be wise. Receive summonses peaceably. Trust to support of public opinion afterwards."

But the unfortunate crofters declined the counsel thus given. They regard Benlee as belonging to their holdings, and Benlee, and nothing but Benlee they would have.

There were heads of families in the crowd, and these were pointed out to the messenger-at-arms by the ground-officer. The messenger-at-arms then endeavoured to effect the service of the writs, but his efforts were of no avail. The officer tried them over and over again, but in vain. At length, he said he would go to the houses, and lodge the papers there. He endeavoured to go, but women rushed to intercept him, carrying stones and sticks, and all indicating that the proposed action on the part of the officers would not be allowed. At this stage, Beaton, the ground-officer, declined to go further to point out the houses, the enterprise threatening to be accompanied with danger. Shortly thereafter Mr. Macdonald said, " Very well, good-bye, ladies and gentlemen ". Some women replied, " Good morning and a half to you, sir ". The officers and the police force—the " dismal brigade," as they were once happily termed—turned their backs on the Braes, marched to the spot where the waggonettes were awaiting them, and re-turned to Portree, bearing with them the undelivered writs of the Court of Session.

During the interview with the officers, some of the women were weeping, and even at a distance from the crowd could be heard exclamations in Gaelic about the number of help-less widows and orphans that were in the Braes. Some called out that the curses of the orphans and widows would follow all these things. One woman said she would not like to see any one suffer greatly, but if those over them continued these actions much longer she did not know what she might wish them. Once a man was heard to say that the officers seemed to have come in a friendly way; but he was replied to with a chorus of voices that they came in no friendly way, that they were come to ruin poor people, and that they would not be allowed to go further. The police came in for a considerable share of the angry ex-pressions of the women. One person reminded the police that there were people there who yet suffered from wounds they received in April. Actions and expressions were fre-quently greeted with cries on the part of the crowd, which were very far from encouraging to the officers. Occasion-ally, however, there were signs of good humour; but these were few, and disappeared as soon as the officers tried to go to the dwelling-houses. Altogether, as will have been clearly seen, the atmosphere was troubled in the extreme. A single injudicious act on the part of the messenger or police would unquestionably have produced an explosion of feeling which would have compelled the legal force to retreat with greater haste and with less dignity than that with which they did actually retire. At one point a row seemed imminent, but it was prevented by the officers and the police exercising prudence as the better virtue.

Judging from the appearance and the demeanour of the people to-day, my own opinion is that, if these writs are to be served by force, they must be served by men protected by the military. This, too, is the opinion of many people in Portree. The truth is, these frequent visits of officers and men in driblets to serve papers, which the crofters associate with impending misery, and possibly, eviction, are irritating and distressing the people. As it is, the people have become exasperated ; and it will be absolutely cruel, considering their ignorance of legal forms, their extreme poverty, and their attachment to the soil, to serve the writs by any other force than one which, by previously overawing them, will preclude the possibility of inflicting personal wounds on either man or woman. The appearance of the military may possibly overawe them, if they be sent in sufficient force ; but a police force will only still more exasperate them, and lead to a repetition of the painful scenes of April last.

The tone and spirit of this communication was altogether different to anything that had hitherto appeared in the *Courier*. It began to dawn upon the landlords that there must be something in the complaints of the people, after all, when this newspaper published such an account of the Braes and its unfortunate inhabitants. The change in its views produced a sensation, and pressure was immediately brought to bear upon Lord Macdonald by some of the Highland lairds to bring about a settlement with his people, if at all possible; but hitherto, so long as he expected a military force to crush them, without avail.

The urgent appeals made by the County authorities to the Home Office for a military force completely failed. It is well known in certain circles that Sir William Harcourt would not even listen to the proposal, and that he openly ridiculed the idea of sending Her Majesty's soldiers to settle a paltry dispute between a landlord and a few of his crofters, which, by the exercise of a little sound judgment and ordinary prudence, could be arranged by sensible men in a few minutes. In consequence of this attitude on the part of the Crown authorities further pressure was brought to bear upon Lord Macdonald to come to terms with the Braes crofters, and it is well known in well-informed circles that under this pressure he finally agreed to enter into negotiation, in the event of proposals to that effect emanating from the crofters themselves or from any of their friends. After a good deal of private correspondence in influential circles on both sides, negotiations were arranged, as we shall see hereafter, which ultimately ended in a settlement satisfactory in the circumstances to all concerned.

The special correspondence in the *Courier* had an effect also in other quarters than that of the landowners. Immediately on its perusal a patriotic Highland gentleman of means, who resides in the Channel Islands during the winter months, telegraphed on the 28th of October, as follows, to the writer of these pages :—

"*To Alexander Mackenzie, Esq., Dean of Guild of Inverness, from Malcolm Mackenzie, Vue du Lac, Guernsey.*

"Tender by telegraph to Lord Macdonald's agent all arrears of rent due by Braes crofters, and to stay proceedings. I write by post and send securities for one thousand pounds on Monday."

These instructions were carried out, and the following reply was received in due course :—

5 Thistle Street, Edinburgh, 30th Oct., 1882.

Sir,—We have received your telegram of to-day stating that you are authorised by a Mr. Malcolm Mackenzie, Guernsey, to tender payment of the last two years' arrears of rent due to Lord Macdonald by the Braes crofters, on condition that all proceedings against them are stopped, and that you will be prepared to deposit securities for one thousand pounds to-morrow.

Although we know nothing of the gentleman you mention, we will communicate your telegram to Lord Macdonald. At the same time, we must observe, that you seem to be labouring under a misapprehension as to the matter at issue between his lordship and the crofters, the proceedings against whom were raised for the purpose of preventing trespass, and not for recovering arrears of rent.—We are, &c.,

(Signed) JOHN C. BRODIE & SONS.

To Dean of Guild Mackenzie, *Celtic Magazine* Office, Inverness.

To the above letter the writer replied as follows :—

Celtic Magazine Office, Inverness, Nov. 1, 1882.

Sirs,—I am in receipt of your favour of Monday acknowledging my telegram on behalf of Malcolm Mackenzie, Esq., Guernsey, offering to pay arrears of Braes crofters on terms stated therein.

I was fully aware of the *nature* of the proceedings against the crofters, though possibly Mr. Mackenzie was not, and I simply carried out my instructions. I think, however, that, if Lord Macdonald desires to settle amicably with the people, this proposal, if it does nothing else, will give him an opportunity of doing so without any sacrifice of his position beyond showing a willingness to discuss the matter with a view to settle it in a way that will extricate all parties from a difficult position.

Mr. Mackenzie has now, through me, deposited securities amounting to over £1000 in bank here, and I shall be glad to hear from you when you shall have heard from his lordship.—I am, Sirs, your obedient servant,

A. MACKENZIE.

Messrs. John C. Brodie & Sons, W.S.

Lord Macdonald's agents having published their letter, as above, in the *Inverness Courier* of 2nd November, Dean of Guild Mackenzie wrote them another letter in the course of which he said :—

Referrring to the second paragraph of my letter of yesterday, permit me to express my opinion that a favourable opportunity has now arrived to compromise the question in dispute advantageously to both parties, and if I can in any way aid in that object, nothing will give me greater satisfaction. I have had no communication either direct or in-direct with the Braes people since the recent trial, except the telegram which has appeared in the papers ; but if a desire is expressed for an amicable arrangement, I shall be glad to visit them and do what I can to bring such about. I believe if a proposal were made to appoint an independent valuator connected with the West, and one in whom the people might fairly place confidence as to his knowledge of the country and the climate, the question might be settled in a few days. This valuator should value the crofts and Benlee together, and name one sum for the whole. Though I have no authority for making this pro-posal, I believe it could be carried out to the satisfaction of all concerned, and it would extricate the authorities and Lord Macdonald from a most unenviable position.

To these letters no reply was received.

Mr. Malcolm Mackenzie followed up his telegram of 28th October with a letter, of the same date, at once published in almost all the newspapers in Scotland, in the course of which he said :—

On reading in the *Inverness Courier* an account of the proceedings of Tuesday last against the Braes crofters, I thought that something might be done to take everybody out of a difficulty, and wired you the following message :—" Tender by telegraph to Lord Macdonald's agent all arrears of rent due by Braes crofters, and to stay proceedings. I write by post, and send securities for one thousand pounds on Monday."

I trust that Lord Macdonald will be advised to accept payment of arrears, and to leave the people of the Braes in peace until the Govern-ment of the country can overtake measures to judge between him and them. It will be a heavy responsibility and a disgrace to call soldiers to Skye at the present time. Her Majesty has more important work to do with her soldiers than to place them at the service of the Court of Session in vindication of an unconstitutional law which is not based on principles of justice, and which has, by the progress of events and the evolution of time, become inoperative. The Court of Session looks for precedents. Where are these precedents for the reign of Queen Victoria?

Our dual system is no longer possible. Lord Macdonald does not know what to do. Nobody knows what to do. There is an absence of law and justice. In Scotland the administrator of justice is the robber who deprives the people of their natural and indefeasible right to the soil and of the labour which they have incorporated with it. Is that not a terrible contingency for any country to be in? It is peculiarly disgraceful that it should be so in respect of the Highland race, who successfully defended their country, their lands, and liberties, against Romans and Normans. What have we come to? Are they going to send for the Highland Brigade from Egypt to slaughter the people of Skye?

We call for Mr. Gladstone. What can poor Mr. Gladstone do, with time against him, society in a state of revolt, a demoralised House of Commons, a recalcitrant House of Lords, and the Court of Session at its wit's ends? Let us pray that he may be able to act as a *governor* on this rickety steam-engine of society which, under high pressure, and by reason of great friction, is in danger of tearing itself to pieces. In the meantime, and until the machine is put in some sort of order, by Rules of Procedure and alteration of the law, it is every man's duty to keep her Majesty's peace and prevent bloodshed ; and as you appear to me, sir, to be doing yours, like a good Seaforth Highlander, or Ross-shire Buff, allow me to subscribe myself, very faithfully and loyally yours.

The following letters explain themselves :—

TO THE EDITOR OF THE INVERNESS COURIER.

Celtic Magazine Office, 2 Ness Bank, Inverness, 8th November, 1882.

Sir,—I have just received the enclosed letter from Mr. Malcolm Mackenzie, Guernsey. Please publish it in the *Courier*, as you have already published the reply to my telegram from Lord Macdonald's agents.

Permit me, at the same time, to state that the sum of £1000, in actual cash, has now been placed by Mr. Mackenzie at my disposal in the Caledonian Bank, and, in the event of his offer being entertained by

Lord Macdonald, that I shall be ready at any moment to implement Mr. Mackenzie's offer.—I am, &c.,

ALEXANDER MACKENZIE.

Guernsey, 4th November, 1882.

Alexander Mackenzie, Esq., Dean of Guild, Inverness.

Dear Sir,—I am in receipt of your letter of the 1st, enclosing the reply of Lord Macdonald's solicitors to your telegram tendering them payment of two years' rent due by the Braes crofters.

From Lord Macdonald's dignified position, he might be thought entitled to ask me for an introduction before accepting any assistance on behalf of his tenants ; but acting as I was, on the spur of the moment, to prevent bloodshed, and possibly to avert an act of civil war, I did not think that in these hard-money days his solicitors would raise any objections on the ground of my being unknown to them, especially as I made the Dean of Guild of Inverness the medium of my communication.

As the days of chivalry are gone, and as clan ties and feelings of patriotism and humanity are no longer of binding obligation, I could not imagine that a firm of solicitors would stand on so much ceremony.

Whatever misapprehension Lord Macdonald's advisers are labouring under, I can assure them that I am labouring under none as to the real issues between him and his crofters. It would, doubtless, suit them to have the case tried on a false issue of trespass before a Court which must be bound by former decisions and prevailing canons as to the rights of Highland landlords. The plea of the poor people is that Lord Macdonald is the trespasser, in depriving them of their mountain grazings, without consent or compensation, and thereby reducing them to abject poverty. What can they do ? It would raise the whole question of constitutional right, and, as I have said, the Court is bound by former decisions that the landlord has the right to resume possession, and to evict and *banish* the peasantry after having first reduced them to the last nettle of subsistence. A sentence of banishment used to be regarded as a punishment only next to death, but in the phraseology of landlords it is now an "improvement".

In the days of "bloody" George of our own ilk, the Court of Session knew better how to apply the "boot" and the thumb-screw than constitutional law. Even later, such ruffians as old Braxfield recognised no right in the people, and according to their dog Latin, they found that the landlord was the only person who had a *persona standi*. It might, indeed, be an interesting question for more enlightened and better men to discuss, whether the Crown of Scotland conferred on the chieftains by their charters the right of wholesale clearances and forcible banishment of the people from their native country ; and when their military service was commuted into rent charges, if it extended to the landlord the right to make it so oppressive that they could not live without appealing to the public bounty for charity. But I fear it is now too late to expect the High Court of Scotland to remedy the evil, and that we must look to some other Court for redress.

It is in the hope that such a Court of equity may be established for Scotland as regards land and the well-being of the people, that I ventured to offer my assistance, and I thought that Lord Macdonald and his advisers would be glad to make it the means of getting out of a difficulty, and quashing a case that has become a public scandal, instead of standing on ceremony.—I am, sir, faithfully yours,

(Signed)   MAL. MACKENZIE.

No further reply was received from Lord Macdonald or his agents to Mr. Mackenzie's munificent offer, the accepting of it being understood by them as equivalent to giving up the grazings in question to the people, without any rent whatever, the only proceedings then current against them being the Note of Suspension and Interdict to remove and keep their stock off Benlee. They quite understood that, if these proceedings were withdrawn, as conditioned in Mr. Mackenzie's offer, the Braes Crofters would have the grazings in dispute on their own terms, until some settlement was arrived at between them and Lord Macdonald; and rather than agree to this, his Lordship, if the crown authorities had been pliant enough, would have chosen to see them slaughtered by a military force. Better counsels have fortunately prevailed, and his Lordship was saved by others from making his name for ever infamous among the Highlanders, especially among his own clansmen, and this although it was only through the strong arms and trusty blades of their forbears that his ancestors were able to leave him an inch of his vast estates !

While strong efforts were being made in private to induce his Lordship to yield, the following letter, refusing the expected military force, was received from the Lord Advocate by the Sheriff of the County :—

Whitehall, 3rd November, 1882.

Sir,—I received on the 28th ulto. the Report of the Procurator-Fiscal at Portree, relative to the occurrences which took place at Braes on the 24th, and the precognitions referred to in the Report reached me on the 30th. These documents have been carefully considered, along with the previous papers, and I have now to communicate to you the view entertained by the Government on the subject to which they relate.

It is clear that Lord Macdonald is entitled to have adequate protection for the Messengers-at-Arms whom he may employ for the purpose of serving writs upon the crofters at Braes, and the question to be determined is, by whom should that protecting force be provided, and should it consist of police or soldiers ?

The duty of preserving the peace and executing the law within the County rests upon the County Authorities, who are by statute authorised to provide and maintain a police force for these purposes. The number of the force must necessarily depend upon the condition of the county, and the nature of the services which require to be performed in it. Recourse should not be had to military aid unless in cases of sudden riot or extraordinary emergency, to deal adequately with which police cannot be obtained, and soldiers should not be employed upon police duty which is likely to be of a continuing character. From the various reports which have been received, it appears that one or more places in the Island of Skye are in a disturbed condition, though actual riot or violence is not anticipated unless on the occasion of the service of writs, or the apprehension of offenders, and it further appears, that any force employed in protecting the officers performing such duties would probably be required not once only, but in connection with services falling to be made throughout the successive stages of the process of Suspension and Interdict, and of the Petition for Breach of Interdict, by which it would, in all likelihood, be followed. It further seems to be the view of the Authorities in Skye that the force would require to remain in the Island for a considerable time. These considerations have led the Government to the conclusion that they ought not to sanction the employment of a military force under existing circumstances, but that the County Authorities should provide or obtain the services of such a force of police as they may consider necessary for preserving the peace and executing the law within the county. It is not for the Government to prescribe or even to suggest the particular mode in which the County Authorities should fulfil this duty, whether by adding to their own police force, or by temporarily obtaining the services of police from other Counties or Burghs, but I am authorised by Sir William Harcourt to say, that if they should resolve to make an addition to the number of their own police, he will be ready to grant his consent, in terms of section 5 of the Police (Scotland) Act of 1857, to whatever addition they may consider requisite.—I am, Sir, Your obedient Servant,

(Signed)   J. B. BALFOUR.

To William Ivory, Esq., Sheriff of Inverness.

This letter was a bitter pill for the County Authorities, who naturally desired to escape the serious responsibility of serving the writs in Skye by the small police force at their disposal. The Police Committee held a meeting on the 13th of November to consider the document, and to decide what was necessary to be done in the altered circumstances. After serious deliberation Mackintosh of Mackintosh moved :

"That while protesting against the assumption that under existing circumstances the county was bound, without the special aid asked for from the Government, to execute the Supreme Court's warrants within the disturbed districts ; and while disclaiming all responsibility for any consequences which may result from the action which is now forced upon them, the Committee ageee to make a strenuous effort to execute the Court's warrants, and with that view they resolve that the police authorities of Scotland be immediately communicated with, asking them to furnish the largest number of constables they can possibly spare on a given date, and to place this force at the disposal of the executive of the county;" which motion was seconded by Mr. Davidson of Cantray, and unanimously agreed to.

Lord Lovat then moved "That the Committee recommend to the Commissioners of Supply to increase the present force by 50 constables;" which motion was seconded by Mr. Davidson, and unanimously agreed to.

It was also agreed to recommend that a meeting of Commissioners be held on Monday following to consider and dispose of this recommendation.

The meeting of Commissioners of Supply was duly held on the following Monday, when the subjoined interesting Report, dated Edinburgh, 18th November, was submitted by Sheriff Ivory :—

1. The second deforcement at the Braes took place on 2nd September, 1882. A full account of that and the previous deforcement is given in my report to the Home Secretary, and appending which is sent herewith.

2. On 6th September an order was issued by Crown Counsel, after consultation with the Lord Advocate, to serve on upwards of fifty crofters at Braes notes of suspension and interdict prohibiting them from trespassing on Benlee, which was then, and had been for seventeen years previous, occupied by another tenant, at a rent of £130.

3. That order was given to the Procurator-Fiscal of the Skye district, who was directed to judge of the amount of the police force that would be required, and to ask the police authorities to furnish it, the particular mode in which the writs were to be served being distinctly specified in Crown Counsel's order.

4. The above order was on the 7th September communicated by the Procurator-Fiscal (Skye District) to the Clerk of the Police Committee, the former intimating at the same time that he and Sheriff Spiers considered 100 police necessary, and that they should be supported by troops. The order was thereafter communicated to me as Chairman of the Police Committee, whereupon I at once put myself in communication with the Lord Advocate, and asked for instructions.

5. The Lord Advocate thereafter requested the Procurator-Fiscal of Inverness-shire and myself to go to Edinburgh, and consult with him there. We went, and on the 16th September, after a long and anxious consultation (in the course of which I strongly advocated an expedition with a Government steamer and marines), it was finally resolved that, as the calling in of strange police had caused a serious riot on a previous occasion, and would be likely on the next occasion to cause much more disturbance and bloodshed than a military force, it was the best course to prevent a serious riot and perhaps loss of life, to call in the aid of the military, and I was requested by the Lord Advocate to make the necessary requisition to the military authorities.

6. On 21st September I intimated to the Home Secretary that, after consultation with the Lord Advocate, I intended to make a requisition for troops, and sent him at the same time, through the Lord Advocate,

a full report in regard to the disturbed state of Skye, and the previous deforcements and assault on 50 Glasgow police and myself at Braes.

7. The requisition for troops was made by me on 23rd September, and on my informing the Lord Advocate of the fact, his lordship wrote me on 25th September that he did not see that the county authorities had then any alternative but to request military aid.

8. On 30th September the Home Secretary wrote me deprecating the use of military, unless it was absolutely necessary, and suggesting that if the expedition had not started I should again consult with the Lord Advocate on the subject.

9. On 30th September, and again on 1st October, I pressed on the Lord Advocate my decided opinion that (failing the Government furnishes a steamer and marines) it was absolutely necessary to make use of the military.

10. Shortly after this Lord Macdonald visited the Braes, and in consequence the Lord Advocate directed me to suspend the requisition for the military; and on 12th October, I intimated this order to Colonel Preston.

11. On 17th October, the Lord Advocate wrote me that the Braes arrangement was at an end; that the position of matters had altered since the requisition for the military was made; and that, in his lordship's opinion, a further attempt should be made to ascertain, by the test of experience, whether a military force was absolutely essential.

12. That further attempt was made on 23rd October and failed. A full report of the expedition was afterwards communicated to the Lord Advocate.

13. Considerable misapprehension exists in regard to this expedition. The Lord Advocate was of opinion that, from what passed during the negotiations between Lord Macdonald and his crofters, the latter had indicated a more peaceable frame of mind, and that there was no ground for assuming that they would forcibly resist a well-conducted service. The Police Sub-committee and I entertained doubts as to the propriety of sending such a small force of police to the Braes, as in the present excited state of the people they might suffer severe injury. These doubts were intimated to the Lord Advocate and Home Secretary, but at the same time, in deference to the views of the former, the expedition was carried out. In giving their consent to this expedition, the Sub-committee stated that they 'were decidedly of opinion that if the messenger should be deforced on this occasion it will be absolutely necessary that a military or naval force should immediately thereafter be sent with the messenger to insure service and the vindication of the law. The com-

mittee were strongly of opinion that a gun-boat and naval force would be preferable, and that the boat should remain for some time in the district.

Sheriff Ivory here relates, in paragraphs 14, 15, and 16, the resolution of the Police Committee to apply to counties and burghs in Scotland for a special police force, and to permanently increase the force of the county by 50 men (see excerpt from their minute already given). He proceeds—

17. These resolutions on the part of the Police Committee are in my opinion highly creditable to them, and I sincerely trust that they will be unanimously approved of and adopted by the Commissioners of Supply. For, while the latter have no doubt great reason to complain of the great delay that has already occurred in consequence of the manner in which the Government has acted, and of the delay that in all probability must still take place, if the Government adhere to their resolution to refuse military aid, and while I think the Commissioners ought to protest against the present attempt of the Government to throw on the county authorities the whole responsibility of serving writs, apprehending offenders, executing the law, and preserving the peace of the county, without naval or military aid, in the present disturbed state of Skye, and to disclaim all responsibility for the consequences, should serious bloodshed or loss of life ensue—I am of opinion that the conduct of the Government in the matter renders it all the more necessary for the county authorities to do their utmost in the meantime to preserve the peace, and vindicate the authority of the law in Skye.

18. For my own part I regret exceedingly the delay that has already occurred, and that will in all probability still occur, before the law is duly vindicated in Skye. Such delay will be most prejudicial, in my opinion, to the best interests of the island. Had I foreseen the course which matters have unfortunately taken, I should at once have recommended the county authorities—when application was made to them for a sufficient force to serve the writs—to do then what they propose to do now—viz., to apply to Glasgow and other police authorities for a larger force of police to ensure the due service of the writs. But this course appeared to me objectionable in many respects. In particular, nothing gave such great offence to the crofters and their friends as the sending on the last occasion a large force of strange police to Skye, and I am credibly informed, and believe that if such a force was sent again, a serious riot, and probably bloodshed would ensue. Further, it appeared to me far from a judicious course to apply to Glasgow and other burgh and county authorities for police, thereby necessitating innumer-

able discussions regarding the rights of crofters before the Police Com-
mittees of Scotland, while at the same time it was very doubtful
whether these authorities could or would supply the necessary force.
On the other hand, I was assured by many persons who were much
interested in Skye, and who knew the people well, that if a force was
sent by Government—whether naval or marine—the people would see
that the Government were determined to vindicate the law in Skye—
that in that case in all probability no resistance would be offered, and
the writs would not only be served in peace and quietness, but in all
likelihood the people would in future refrain from trespassing on ground
to which they had no right or committing breaches of interdict, or
otherwise setting the law at defiance.   On these grounds when I failed
to get the use of a Government steamer and marines, I willingly accepted the other alternative of making a requisition for military aid.
It must be kept in view, however, that the suggestion for military aid
came neither from the county authorities nor from myself. It was
originally insisted on by the Procurator-Fiscal of Skye (acting as the
hand of the Lord Advocate in the matter) as necessary to enable him
to fulfil the order of the Crown Counsel to serve the writs at Braes ; it
was afterwards adopted by the Lord Advocate, after long and anxious
consultation with the parties on whose judgment his lordship thought
proper to rely—as the best course to be followed in all the circumstances;
and while the formal requisition was made—as it could only formally
be made by me as Sheriff of the county—in point of fact the requisition for military aid, which has now after two months' delay been
refused by her Majesty's Government, was truly made at the request,
and for the purpose of carrying out the views of the Lord Advocate,
who at the time represented her Majesty's Government in Scotland.

                              (Signed)   W. IVORY.

The following excerpt from the Minutes of the Police
Committee Meeting, held on the 18th of September was
also read :—

The Committee, having reference to the Procurator-Fiscal's letter, as
to the nature and extent of the force necessary to be employed, and to
the reports made to them at the time of the previous disturbances at the
Braes, were of opinion that no force of police at their disposal will be
adequate to the duty the county authorities are now called upon to perform, and that with the view not only of securing the service of the
writs, and the apprehension of the accused parties, but of duly impressing

the people of Skye with the resolution of the authorities to maintain the law, a military or naval force should accompany the authorities in their endeavour to enforce the law, to be employed as a protection and aid to the civil officers, in the event of their being overpowered; and the Sheriff was requested to make requisition to that effect in the proper quarter.

It was agreed that the county police force should be placed at the Sheriff's disposal, but they do not think it advisable again to apply for police from Glasgow. Especially, seeing that a strong feeling of irritation was excited in Skye against them on the former occasion, the moral effect would be less than were the military employed, and also because difficulties may be anticipated with the Glasgow Town Council in procuring the necessary force.

After considerable discussion and some opposition, it was resolved to increase the police force of the county from 44 to 94 men ; at an estimated cost of over £3000 per annum. It was also agreed

"To make a strenuous effort to execute the Court's warrants, and with that view they resolve that the police authorities of Scotland be immediately communicated with, asking them to furnish the largest number of constables they can possibly spare on a given date, and to place this force at the disposal of the executive of the county."

The police authorities of Scotland had been applied to, and the response was of so discouraging a character that the proposed police force has not yet been sent to Skye, and it is most unlikely that it ever shall be. A few counties agreed to send small detachments, which resolution some of them afterwards rescinded. All the burghs point blank refused to send any. This indicated an ominous state of adverse feeling throughout the country regarding the proposed action of the Inverness County Authorities, and they became paralyzed in consequence. The Commissioners of Police for the Burgh of Inverness, on the motion of the present writer, refused the application of the County Authorities (on the evening of the day on which the Commissioners of Supply resolved to ask for it), by a majority of 14 to 5, the minority, it has been pointed out, consisting of three factors—Culloden's, Sir Alexander Mathieson's, and Flichity's, with Lord Lovat's Law Agent, and the local architect of Mackintosh and Sir John Ramsden.

What was to be done next? Neither military nor police could be had to serve Lord Macdonald's writs ; the county authorities were virtually powerless, and various efforts were made to secure a settlement. They had in fact to fall back on the friends of the crofters, one of whom, a gentleman in Skye, was communicated with by his Lordship's agents, urging him to use his good offices to get the crofters to let his Lordship drop easy, by getting proposals of settlement to emanate from them. The result was a visit by the factor, Mr. Alexander Macdonald, to the Braes, on the 27th of November last ; a long conference with the tenants, and a final settlement, the people agreeing to pay a rent of £74 15s. a year for the now celebrated Benlee, for which the late tenant, Mr. John Mackay, had been paying £128 per annum, and he, who was joint-petitioner with Lord Macdonald, in the Note of Suspension and Interdict, in the Court of Session, having given his consent, the case was withdrawn in the month of December, and peace, which, with a little prudence, and the exercise of the smallest modicum of common-sense, need never to have been broken, now reigns supreme in the Braes.

It should be mentioned that the Braes crofters told their friends from the beginning that, although they considered themselves entitled to Benlee without any rent, still they were willing to pay a fair sum for it, if Lord Macdonald or his factor would only listen to their grievances or condescend to discuss with them, with the view of arriving at any reasonable compromise, such as that which has now been agreed upon, apparently to the satisfaction of all concerned.

THE GLENDALE CROFTERS IN THE COURT OF SESSION.

It appears that the Glendale crofters have permitted their stock to remain on the farm of Waterstein, notwithstanding an interdict procured against them, in absence, in the Court of Session, and they are now further charged with an assault on one of the shepherds. Unlike the Braes tenants, they are apparently not only quite willing to receive any number of writs, but they are at the same time most courteous to the officers of the law, who have had occasion to visit them repeatedly in the performance of their official duties. On the last occasion they, with the greatest consideration, ferried Mr. MacTavish, the sheriff officer, across the loch from one district to another with the unserved portion of the writs, for those on the opposite side, in his possession.

The following report of what took place in the Court of Session will explain how the matter stands with them, as we go to press —

PETITION AND COMPLAINT.—MACLEOD'S TRUSTEES v. MACKINNON AND OTHERS,—GLENDALE CROFTERS.

This petition and complaint was presented by the Trustees of the late Sir John Macpherson MacLeod, of Duirinish, K.C.S.I., and the petitioners complain of various breaches of interdict against five of the crofters on the estate of Duirinish and Glendale, in the island of Skye, which estate is in the hands of the petitioners as trustees. The case was before the Court on the 11th of January, when

Mr. Murray, for the petitioners, appeared and said—In this case no answers have been lodged, and I have to ask your lordships to pronounce an order ordaining the respondents to appear at the bar. In the special circumstances of this case I shall ask your lordships to allow us to send the order by registered letter.

The Lord-President—What is the order you ask for?

Mr. Murray—The order I ask for is to ordain the respondents to appear at the bar.

Lord Mure—How many respondents are there?

Mr. Murray—There are five of them.

The Lord-President—Have you any precedent for that mode of sending an order, Mr. Murray?

Mr. Murray—No, my lord : there is no authority.   I think the matter is entirely in your lordships' hands.   The matter is not regulated by any express enactment.   The Act of Sederunt that deals with it is 28, which simply says that the procedure shall be, so far as possible, the same as the procedure in a petition and complaint against the freeholders. Your lordships see that this is really simply intimating an order of Court, and one great reason for this, without directing your attention to any other special circumstances, is the very large expense that is incurred by service in such a remote part.   The service in this case practically costs £40.   Now, there have already been three services.   There was first the original service of interdict; and then there was the service of interim interdict ; and then, lastly, there was the service of the petition and complaint.

The Lord-President—Is there any messenger-at-arms?

Mr. Murray—There is nobody nearer than Glasgow or Inverness.

Lord Mure—What do you say the expense was?

Mr. Murray—£40 on each occasion.   £30 of fee, and £10 of expenses.

The Lord-President—Is there a Sheriff Court officer in Skye?

Lord Mure—There is a Sheriff-Substitute at Skye if there is not a sheriff officer.

After a consultation the Lord-President stated that their

lordships would dispose of the matter in the course of the day.

When the case again came up in the afternoon, the Lord-President said their lordships did not see their way to grant the request to serve the order by registered letter, and they would just have to serve it in the ordinary way. They would make an order for the respondents to appear personally at the bar, but he thought probably they had better make it so many days after service. He supposed it was a matter of no consequence whether they authorised it to be done by a sheriff officer rather than a messenger-at-arms.

Mr. Murray said it would be better if they had the option of employing either the one or the other. He would not like to be tied down to a sheriff officer.

The Court, therefore, in respect of no answer and no appearance for the respondents, made an order for them to appear personally at the bar on the 1st day of February next, provided this order was served on them ten days before that date, and authorised either a sheriff officer or messenger-at-arms to serve the order.

The Sheriff-Officer, in due course, proceeded to Skye, to serve the Order of the Court, but on arriving in Glendale he was met by a large crowd of men, women, and children, who refused to receive the writs. As we go to press with these lines, a warrant has been granted for the apprehension of four of the men on the charge of deforcement, but what the result may be it is difficult to predict. Application has again been made to the Crown authorities for a military force for the apprehension of the accused, without which it is admitted on all hands, no apprehensions can possibly be made.

Alluding to our present Land Laws, St. Michael, ad-

dressing the Preacher, in a recently published extreme, but,
in many respects, true and powerful poem, says :—

> Can Law be Law when based on Wrong ?
> Can Law be Law when for the strong ?
> Can Law be Law when landlords stand
> Rack-renting mankind off the land ?
> By ' Law ' a landlord can become
> The ghost of every Crofter's home ;
> By ' Law ' their little cots can be
> Dark dens of dirt and misery ;
> By ' Law ' the tax upon their toil
> Is squandered on an alien soil ;
> By ' Law ' their daughters, sons, and wives,
> Are doomed to slavish drudgery's lives ;
> By ' Law ' Eviction's dreadful crimes
> Are possible in Christian times ;
> By ' Law ' a spendthrift lord's intents
> Are met by drawing higher rents ;
> By ' Law ' all food-producing glens
> Are changed from farms to cattle pens :
> This is your ' Law ' whereby a few
> Are shielded in the deeds they do.*

---

* *St. Michael and the Preacher, a Tale of Skye.*   By the Rev. Donald
MacSiller, Minister of the [New] Gospel, Portree.   Inverness: Law, Justice,
and Co.

APPENDIX.

———

THE figures given in the following tables will show at what rate the population increased or decreased in the different Parishes, in whole or in part, within the counties named, during the periods between 1831, 1841, 1851, and 1881, and, in the case of the County of Sutherland, during each decennial period since 1801. The total population of each County for each decade is as follows :—

PERTH.—This County had a total population, in 1801, of 126,366; in 1811, of 135,093; in 1821, of 139,050; in 1831, of 142,166; in 1841, of 137,457; in 1851, of 138,660; in 1861, of 133,500; in 1871, of 127,768; and in 1881, of 129,007. The present total population will thus be found more than 6,000 less than it was 70 years ago; 10,000 less than it was 60 years ago ; and more than 13,000 less than it was 50 years ago. The town and village population increased in the last decade—from 1871 to 1881— by 14,420. The total rural population in 1881 was 57,016, against 78,364 in 1831, making a decrease in the rural inhabitants of the County in 50 years of 21,348 souls, or considerably more than one-third of the present rural population of the County. A few parishes, in the more Southern, non-Highland, portions of this County are not given in the Table applicable to it in this Appendix.

ARGYLL.—This County had a population in 1801, of of 71,859; in 1811, of 85,859; in 1821, of 97,316; in 1831, of 100,973; in 1841, of 97,371; in 1851, of 89,298; in 1861, of 79,724; in 1871, of 75,679; and in 1881, of 76,468. The present total population will thus be found 9,117 less than it was 70 years ago; 20,848 less than it was 60 years ago; and 24,505 less than it was 50 years ago. The town and village population increased, between 1871 and 1881, from 25,713 to 30,387; while during the same decennial period, the rural population decreased from 49,966 to 46,081, or by nearly 4,000 souls. The rural population of the County in 1881 was 46,081. Thus, while the town population more than doubled since 1831, the rural population decreased by more than one-half. There could not have been 15,000 of a town population in 1831, as suggested at page 362, and therefore the decrease in the rural population is necessarily greater than is there stated.

INVERNESS.—This County had a population in 1801, of 74,292; in 1811, of 78,336; in 1821, of 90,157; in 1831, of 94,797; in 1841, of 97,799; in 1851, of 96,500; in 1861, of 88,261; in 1871, of 88,015; and in 1881, of 90,454. The present total population of the County will thus be found only 297 more than it was 00 years ago; 4,343 less than it was 50 years ago; and 7,345 less than it was 40 years ago, notwithstanding that the population of the Town of Inverness alone increased during the last 50 years, from 9,663, in 1831, to 17,385, in 1881, or 7,922 souls. The village population also increased considerably during the same period. From 4,624 in 1871, it increased to 5,714 in 1881, while, during the same decade, the rural population shows a decrease from 68,881, in 1871, to 67,355, in 1881, or 1,526 souls. The town and village population of the County in 1881, was 23,099. Of this number there could not have been more than 12,000 in 1841, making the rural population at that date nearly 86,000, as against 67,355, in 1881, or a reduction of considerably more than one-fourth, of the present rural population of the County, in forty years.

Ross and Cromarty.—The population of these Counties, combined, in 1801, was 55,343. In 1811, they had a population of 60,853; in 1821, of 68,828; in 1831, of 74,820; in 1841, of 78,685; in 1851, of 82,707; in 1861, of 81,406; in 1871, of 80,955; and in 1881, of 78,547. These figures show an increase of 3,727 on the population of 1831, or of fifty years ago, while they show a decrease of 238 on that of 1841, and a reduction of 4,160 on that of 1851. The population of the towns and villages appear to have remained stationary, except in the villages of Alness and Invergordon, on the mainland. The latter accounts for the increase which appears in the Table, in the population of the parishes of Roskeen and Fearn. The same remarks hold true of the town and parish of Stornoway, in the Lews. The rural population of Ross and Cromarty decreased from 53,223 in 1871, to 49,882 in 1881; or 3,341 during the last ten years.

Sutherland.—This County had a population in 1801, of 23,117; in 1811, of 23,629; in 1821, of 23,840; in 1831, of 25,518; in 1841, of 24,782; in 1851, of 25,793; in 1861, of 25,246; in 1871, of 24,317; and in 1881, of 23,370. It will be seen that the population of the whole County was, in 1881, only 253 souls more than it was in 1801, and that it was decreasing at the rate of nearly 1000 each decade since 1851. The County may be said to be entirely rural, if we except the wretched villages of Bonar, Dornoch, Helmsdale, Embo, and Portskerra, with those of Golspie, and Brora, which are in a slightly less wretched condition from their contiguity to Dunrobin Castle. These, among them, had a village population of 4,674, in 1881, as against 4,779, in 1871. Most of these villages have arisen since the Clearances, which took place in the beginning of the century, and the result of which, in the parishes more particularly affected, may be traced in the tabulated statement for the County, which is carried back to 1801, for this purpose.

CAITHNESS.—This County had a population, in 1801, of 22,609; in 1811, of 23,419; in 1821, of 30,238; in 1831, of 34,529; in 1841, of 36,343; in 1851, of 38,709; in 1861, of 41,111; in 1871, of 39,992; and in 1881, of 38,865. In 1811, the population of the town of Wick was only 994; in 1881, it was 1,860. The population of Pultneytown, Louisburgh, and Bankhead, in 1811, was only 755; in 1881, it numbered 6,193; total in 1811—1749; total in 1881—8,053. The fishing villages of Broadhaven, Staxigoe, Papigoe, and others, have also added considerably to the population of the Parish. The same remarks also hold true of the parish of Olrig, which includes the modern village of Castletown, containing a population of 932, mainly slate quarriers, in 1881. The town of Thurso had a population of only 2,429, in 1831; in 1881, it increased to 4,055. From these figures it is clear that the rural population of the County, which, in 1881, only numbered 24,309, is rapidly decreasing. Since 1871, it fell from 25,763 to 24,309, or 1,454 in one decade.

Population in 1831, 1841, 1851, *and* 1881, *of all the Parishes in whole or in part in the* COUNTY OF PERTHSHIRE.

	1831.	1841.	1851.	1881.
Aberdalgie	434	360	343	297
Aberfoyle	660	543	514	465
Abernethy	1915	1920	2026	1714
Abernyte	254	280	275	275
Arngask	712	750	685	547
Auchterarder	3182	3434	4160	3648
Auchtergeven	3417	3366	3232	2195
Balquhidder	1049	871	874	627
Bendochy	780	783	773	715
Blackford	1897	1782	2012	1595
Blair-Athol	2495	2231	2084	1742
Blairgowrie	2644	3471	2497	5162
Callander	1909	1665	1716	2167
Caputh	2303	2317	2037	2096
Cargill	1628	1642	1629	1348
Cluny	944	763	723	582
Collace	730	702	581	409
Culross	1484	1444	1487	1130
Comrie	2622	2471	2463	1858
Dron	464	441	394	335
Dull	4590	3811	3342	2565
Dunbarney	1162	1104	1066	756
Dunkeld	2032	1752	1662	791
Dunning	2045	2128	2206	1639
Errol	2992	2832	2796	2421
Findo-Gask	428	436	405	364
Forgandenny	913	796	828	617
Forteviot	624	638	638	618
Fortingall	3067	2740	2486	1690
Fossoway and Tulliebole	1576	1724	1621	1267
Fowlis-Wester	1681	1609	1483	412
Glendevon	620	157	128	147
Inchture	878	769	745	650
Kenmore	3126	2539	2257	1508
Killin	2002	1702	1608	1277

	1831.	1841.	1851.	1881.
Kilmadock	3752	4055	3659	3012
Kilspindie	760	709	684	693
Kincardine	2455	2232	1993	1351
Kinclaven	890	880	881	588
Kinfauns	732	720	650	583
Kinnaird	461	458	370	260
Kinnoull	2957	2879	3134	3461
Kirkmichael	1568	1412	1280	849
Lethendy and Kinloch	708	662	556	404
Little Dunkeld	2867	2718	2155	2175
Logierait	3138	2959	2875	2323
Longforgan	1638	1660	1787	1854
Madderty	713	634	593	527
Meigle	873	728	686	696
Methven	2714	2446	2454	1910
Moneydie	300	315	321	233
Monzie	1195	1261	1199	753
Monievaird and Strowan	926	853	790	700
Moulin	2022	2019	2022	2066
Muckhart	617	706	685	601
Muthill	3297	3067	2972	1702
Redgorton	1866	1929	2047	1452
Rhynd	400	402	338	297
St. Madoes	327	327	288	316
St. Martins	1135	1071	983	741
Scone	2268	2422	2381	2402
Tibbermore	1223	1661	1495	1883
Trinity-Gask	620	620	597	396
Tulliallan	3550	3196	3043	2207
Weem	1209	890	740	474

Population in 1831, 1841, 1851, *and* 1881, *of all the Parishes in whole or in part in the* COUNTY OF ARGYLL.

	1831.	1841.	1851.	1881
Ardchattan and Muckairn..............	2420	2264	2313	2005
Ardnamurchan..........................	5669	5581	5446	4105
Campbelton.............................	9472	9539	9381	9755
Craignish...............................	892	970	873	451
Dunoon and Kilmun....................	2416	2853	4518	8002
Gigha and Cara.........................	534	550	547	382
Glassary.................................	4054	5369	4711	4348
Glenorchy and Inishail.................	1806	831	1450	1705
Inveraray................................	2233	2277	2229	946
Inverchaolain...........................	596	699	474	407
Jura and Colonsay......................	2205	2291	1901	1343
Kilbrandon and Kilchattan............	2833	2602	2375	1767
Kilcalmonell and Kilberry.............	3488	2460	2859	2304
Kilchoman..............................	4822	4505	4142	2547
Kilchrenan and Dalavich..............	1096	894	776	504
Kildalton...............................	3065	3315	3310	2271
Kilfinan.................................	2004	1816	1695	2153
Kilfinichen and Kilviceuen............	3819	4102	3054	1982
Killarrow and Kilmeny.................	7105	7341	4882	2756
Killean and Kilchenzie.................	2866	2401	2219	1368
Kilmallie................................	4210	5397	5235	4157
Kilmartin...............................	1475	1213	1144	811
Kilmodan...............................	648	578	500	323
Kilmore and Kilbride..................	2836	4327	3131	5142
Kilninian and Kilmore.................	4830	4322	3954	2540
Kilninver and Kilmelford..............	1072	970	714	405
Knapdale, North.......................	2583	2170	1666	927
Knapdale, South	2137	1537	2178	2536
Lismore and Appin.....................	4365	4193	4097	3433
Lochgoilhead and Kilmorich..........	1196	1100	834	870
Morvern.................................	2036	1781	1547	828
Saddell and Skipness	2152	1798	1504	1163
Small Isles..............................	1015	993	916	550
Southend...............................	2120	1598	1406	955
Strachur and Stralachan...............	1083	1086	915	932
Tiree and Coll...........................	5769	6096	4818	3376
Torosay.................................	1889	1616	1361	1102

Population in 1831, 1841, 1851, *and* 1881, *of all the Parishes in whole or in part in the* COUNTY OF INVERNESS.

	1831.	1841.	1851.	1881.
Abernethy	2092	1920	1871	1530
Alvie	1092	972	914	707
Ardersier	1268	1475	1241	*2086
Ardnamurchan	5669	5581	5446	4105
Boleskine and Abertarff	1829	1876	2006	1448
Cawdor	1187	1150	1202	1070
Cromdale	3234	3561	3990	3642
Croy	1664	1684	1770	1709
Daviot and Dunlichity	1641	1681	1857	1252
Dores	1736	1745	1650	1148
Duthil	1920	1759	1788	1664
Glenelg	2874	2729	2470	1601
Inverness	14324	15418	16496	21725
Kilmallie	4210	5397	5235	4157
Kilmonivaig	2869	2791	2583	1928
Kilmorack (including Beauly)	2709	2694	3007	2618
Kiltarlity	2715	2896	2965	2134
Kingussie and Insh	2080	2047	2201	1987
Kirkhill	1715	1829	1730	1480
Laggan	1196	1201	1223	917
Moy and Dalarossie	1098	967	1018	822
Petty	1836	1749	1784	1531
Urquhart and Glenmoriston	2942	3104	3280	2438
Urray	2768	2716	2621	2478
Insular—				
Barra	2097	2363	1873	2161
Bracadale	1769	1824	1597	929
Duirinish	4765	4983	5330	4319
Harris	3900	4429	4250	4814
Kilmuir	3415	3629	3177	2562
North Uist	4603	4428	3918	4264
Portree	3441	3574	3557	3191
Sleat	2756	2706	2531	2060
Small Isles	1015	993	916	550
Snizort	3487	3220	3101	2120
South Uist	6890	7333	6173	6078
Strath	2962	3150	3243	2616

* Including 948 military and militia in Fort-George in 1881.

Population in 1831, 1841, 1851, *and* 1881, *of all the Parishes in whole or in part in the* COUNTIES OF ROSS AND CROMARTY.

	1831.	1841.	1851.	1881.
Alness	1437	1269	1240	1033
Applecross	2892	2861	2709	2239
Avoch	1956	1931	2029	1691
Contin	2023	1770	1562	1422
Cromarty	2900	2662	2727	2009
Dingwall	1159	2100	2364	2220
Edderton	1023	975	890	431
Fearn	1695	1914	2122	2135
Fodderty	2232	2437	2342	2047
Gairloch	4445	4880	5186	4594
Glenshiel	715	745	573	424
Killearnan	1479	1643	1794	1059
Kilmuir-Easter	1556	1486	1437	1146
Kiltearn	1605	1436	1538	1182
Kincardine	1887	2108	1896	1472
Kintail	1240	1186	1009	688
Knockbain	2139	2565	3005	1866
Lochalsh	2433	2597	2299	2050
Lochbroom	4615	4799	4813	4191
Lochcarron	2136	1960	1612	1456
Logie-Easter	934	1015	965	827
Nigg	1404	1426	1457	1000
Resolis or Kirkmichael	1470	1549	1551	1424
Rosemarkie	1799	1719	1776	1357
Rosskeen	2916	3222	3699	3773
Tain	3078	3128	3754	3009
Tarbat	1809	1826	2151	1878
Urquhart and Logie-Wester	2864	2997	3153	2525
Urray	2768	2716	2621	2474
Insular—				
Barvas	3011	3850	4189	5325
Lochs	3067	3653	4256	6284
Stornoway	5491	6218	8057	10389
Uig	3041	3316	3209	3489

Population in 1801, 1811, 1821, 1831, 1841, 1851, 1871, *and* 1881, *of all the Parishes in whole or in part in the* COUNTY OF SUTH-ERLAND.

	1801.	1811.	1821.	1831.	1841.	1851.	1871.	1881.
Assynt	2419	2479	2803	3161	3178	2989	3006	2781
Clyne	1643	1639	1874	1711	1765	1933	1733	1812
Creich	1974	1969	2354	2562	2852	2714	2524	2223
Dornoch	2362	2681	3100	3380	2714	2981	2764	2525
Durness	1208	1155	1004	1153	1109	1152	1049	987
Eddrachillis	1253	1147	1229	1965	1699	1576	1530	1525
Farr	2408	2408	1994	2073	2217	2403	2019	1930
Golspie	1616	1391	1049	1149	1214	1529	1804	1556
Kildonan	1440	1574	565	257	256	*2288	1916	1942
Lairg	1209	1354	1094	1045	913	1162	978	1355
Loth	1374	1330	2008	2234	2526	*640	583	584
Reay	2406	2317	2758	2881	2811	2506	2331	2191
Rogart	2022	2148	1986	1805	1501	1535	1341	1227
Tongue	1348	1493	1736	2030	2041	2018	2051	1929

* The lands of Helmsdale and others previously in the Parish of Loth were, about this time, added to Kildonan, which accounts for this large increase. It also accounts for the decrease in Loth.

Population in 1831, 1841, 1851, *and* 1881, *of all the Parishes in whole or in part in the* COUNTY OF CAITHNESS.

	1831.	1841.	1851.	1881.
Bower	1615	1689	1658	1608
Canisbay	2364	2306	2437	2626
Dunnet	1906	1880	1868	1607
Halkirk	2847	2963	2918	2705
Latheron	7030	7637	8224	6675
Olrig	1146	1584	1873	2002
Reay	2881	2811	2506	2191
Thurso	4679	4881	5096	6217
Watten	1234	1966	1351	1406
Wick	9850	10393	11851	12822

SPLICING SYSTEMS
1000 B05

SPLICING SYSTEMS
1000 B05